Literature-Based History Activities for Children, Grades 4–8

Patricia L. Roberts

California State University–Sacramento

Allyn and Bacon

Boston ▪ London ▪ Toronto ▪ Sydney ▪ Tokyo ▪ Singapore

Dedicated to James E. Roberts,
who has a wonderful sense of history

Copyright © 1997 by Allyn & Bacon
A Viacom Company
Needham Heights, MA 02194

Library of Congress Cataloging-in-Publication Data

Roberts, Patricia
    Literature-based history activities for children,
grades 4–8 / Patricia L. Roberts.
       p. cm.
    Includes bibliographical references (p.   ) and indexes.
    ISBN 0-205-14737-2
     1. History--Study and teaching (Elementary)--United States.
2. Education, Elementary--Activity programs--United States.
I. Title.
LB1582.U6R63   1996
372.89'044--dc20   95-48955
                                         CIP

Printed in the United States of America
10 9 8 7 6 5 4 3 2 1   00 99 98 97 96

Contents

List of History Masters

Preface

You will certainly not be able to take the lead in all things yourself, for to one man a god has given deeds of war, and to another the dance, to another the lyre and song, and in another wide-sounding Zeus puts a good mind.

—Homer

Get your students together for a literature-based focus on history—it can be a period of intense history storytelling and studying in which the students hear, read, and dramatize stories, interpret poetry selections about historical figures, participate in choral reading, and present brief reports with their ideas in written compositions about their reflections of places and faces from prehistory to the present. By gathering data together, your students can participate in activities and acquire history literacy as they gain an understanding of the *ideas* and the *usefulness* of history. The concept of *idea* is explained by Katherine Paterson in *The Spying Heart* (Dutton, 1989) when she asks, "What exactly is an idea?" She responds, "In Japanese, the word is made up of two characters—the character for *sound* and the character for *heart*—so an idea is something that makes a sound in the heart." Various ideas of history in children's literature may make "a sound in the heart" of students and add an affective touch to history's usefulness when it enlarges their experiences and extends their feelings and emotions about what has happened in the past. The *usefulness* of history has been explained by Henry Steele Commanger in "Why History" in *American Education*. Commanger states, "History is useful in the sense that art is useful—or music or poetry or flowers.... The first and perhaps the richest pleasure of history is that it adds new dimensions to life itself by enormously extending our perspective and in enlarging our experience."

To assist you as you present history's ideas and usefulness and add new dimensions to your students' lives related to history, this book offers historical views through quality children's books with perspectives that may make "a sound in the heart" for many readers. Using this book will enable preservice and inservice teachers, classroom aides, resource teachers, principals, curriculum directors, parents, and others to locate children's books that will enrich students' knowledge of the people, places, and events in the past.

How to Use This Book

The purpose of this book is to provide you with some background and practical ideas for a history program related to children's literature in which students actively think and communicate. The emphasis is on teaching views of history through selected children's books for grades 4 through 8. In this book, a strong focus is placed on children's literature, related activities, and multicultural charts for each time period, as well as on ways to extend students' experiences with the books that reflect topics in history. Though group size is suggested for the activities, you will decide when the activities are best suited for the whole group, small group, partnerships, and individual inquiry according to your teaching needs. Specifically, the features in this book include:

- *Multicultural Perspectives.* Each time period begins with a multicultural chart that focuses on several perspectives reflected in children's literature and their actions in the time period. The books are perspectives of the heritage related to African Americans,[1] Asian Americans, Latino and Hispanic Americans,[2] Original Native Americans,[3] European Americans, as well as the differently abled, women and girls, and religious minority groups. The perspectives are included so students can listen to the heritage of each other's voices and recognize that as soci-

---

1. The term *African American* refers to individuals of African origin now American citizens regardless of their most recent country of residence. The term is not considered correct by everyone.
2. The term *Latino/Hispanic* refers to individuals of Spanish origin regardless of their most recent country of residence. The term is not considered correct by everyone.
3. The term *Original Native American* refers to people referred to as American Indian and Indian. None of these terms is considered correct by everyone.

ety becomes larger, individuals seem to require not only the larger identity of being American but also the smaller identities of their heritages. The books are suggested so students can share their heritages with one another and foster an understanding of a healthy diversity that acknowledges the varied sources of the American people.

Each multicultural chart can be used as a reference to views about a particular period through children's literature. With the chart as a resource, an interested student can read about an overall view of the heritages of different people in the time period. A reader also can follow a selected perspective (e.g., developmentally different, women and their rights, religious minorities) from the chart in one time period to the chart in another time period to gather information about the similarities, differences, conflicts, or changes related to a perspective over time. Tracking a perspective through time periods can develop the students' insights into the idea that some feelings, emotions, and problems are universal, even though the specifics of a time period are different.

• *Black Line History Masters.* The children's books and History Masters (Black Line Reproducibles) in this resource will complement many topics of history and will assist you as you work to enrich the curriculum that is described in your district and state history curriculum materials. To assist you, the books in the main body of this book have been indexed according to author, illustrator, and title.

• *Book Lists and Activities.* Beginning with prehistory, this book offers fiction and nonfiction with settings from sequential centuries that are mentioned along with selected literature. If students become aware of historical events in a particular time period related to a heritage, then they will begin to see the ways that the historical fiction on the lists relates to the places, faces, and times of the period in which the fiction was written. They will begin to see how historical circumstances elaborate on the fiction they read and can add to their understanding and enjoyment of fiction and history. They will discover, further, that the writings of authors who wrote at approximately the same time often have something in common with one another.

This book will assist you as you gain more first-hand experience with children's literature related to history—an opportunity that will be both a reading adventure and a creative project you will long remember. This is an opportunity that, as you suspect, will have no end.

Approximately 30 percent of the books cited on these pages have been published in the last five years. Thus, many are books of the 1990s. It is important to note that the research that accompanied the writing of this book indicated a need for additional children's books in all of the historical time periods related to the heritages of minorities—in particular, Asian Americans and Latino and Hispanic Americans. In some cases, several of the books listed may be out of print by the time this book is published but they are too good to miss and they should be readily available in a large library near you. Some of the books that are cited can be found in a library's Caldecott or Newbery Medal collection. Wherever you find the books, you can experience adventure through history yourself by prereading children's literature that will promote views of history during a study in your classroom. Such a study can be an experience that makes a "sound in the heart."

CHAPTER ONE

Prehistory–4 Million B.C.

What was going on in prehistory?

Multicultural Perspectives

A unit of prehistory[1] study has creative teaching potential—it can be concerned with the early ancestors of today's people, their actions, and what their habitats and events of prehistory were like in their early time period. Such a unit can offer possibilities to learn about African people, Arctic-dwelling Eskimos, and resilient Ice Age inhabitants in Europe and Asia, as well as what lives were like for the differently abled, women and girls, and others who were the ancestors of many of us in the United States today—these were the people who once lived in areas now known as the Americas, Africa, Asia, Australia, the Middle East, and Europe. The classroom's colorful bulletin boards can be designed, made, and captioned by the students and can feature sketches of various people and the different geographical environments they faced, as well as some colorful maps that show the migratory routes to the people's seasonal destinations. Individual or group inquiry can begin.

Regardless of the topic of study, the class environment and lessons can be carefully planned to help the students develop concepts and generalizations as they learn about others through the vehicle of a thought-provoking prehistory unit. Some of the perspectives of people's lives in parallel cultures in this period are shown in Figure 1–1.

---

1. If you are interested in teaching a *prehistory unit about Where Did We Find Out about the Dinosaur's?*, turn to the teaching resource guide, *A Green Dinosaur Day: A Guide to Developing Thematic Units for Literature-Based Instruction, K–6* (Allyn and Bacon, 1992) by Patricia L. Roberts. The guide has step-by-step information for developing thematic units plus a complete chapter on resources for a dinosaur unit.

Activity #1: "Now You're Here"

Relate the reading about early encounters of people in parallel cultures (see Figure 1–1) to the present by engaging students in a monthly Friendship Day where they become a Friend-for-a-Day in a partnership with a nonacquaintance. They can eat unfamiliar foods together at a Friendship breakfast at school, assist one another in lessons, and listen to their classmates' parents and community role models who have achieved career goals. They can interview one another, hear testimonials of partners who describe one another with 10 or more positive words, and display collages showing the positive characteristics of their new acquaintances. They can make gifts for their partners pertaining to their cultures, perform dances, learn new games, and engage in singing songs from parallel cultures.

Encounter with Others

"I wonder/ If on some far hillside/ There is a boy who sits alone," are the thoughts of a boy in prehistory who keeps his responsibilities in Baylor's *One Small Blue Bead*. Read aloud to your students some excerpts from the story about the people who think *they* are the only humans. Discuss the boy's first encounter with another boy—a stranger from another group who offers a turquoise bead, a sign of gift giving, friendship, and material exchanges among people. With an emphasis on developing awareness of cultural diversity long ago, encourage the students to team up in pairs and play the roles of the young boy and the stranger who gives him a bead. Ask students what questions could be asked by the two boys and what each boy would feel, say, and do in the situation when the bead is offered and

FIGURE 1–1   Children's Books about Prehistory–4 Million B.C.

PERSPECTIVES FOR PREHISTORY–4 MILLION B.C.

African Heritage

Anderson, D. A. *The Origin of Life on Earth: An African Creation Myth.* Sights Productions, 1993. Tells of humankind's respect for determination, effort, generosity, and the sacredness of life. Folk literature. Grade 4 and up.

Asian Heritage

Fagan, B. M. *The Great Journey: The Peopling of Ancient America.* Thames and Hudson, 1987. Discusses the arrival of ancient travelers to North America and their history. Nonfiction. Grades 5–7.

Sattler, H. R. *The Earliest Americans.* Ill. by J. D. Zallinger. Clarion, 1992. Recounts the arrival of humans to North America who drifted across an early land bridge between Siberia and Alaska. By following an early coastline, more people moved onto the continents of the Americas and adapted to the climate and the geography. Maps, index, and time line included. Nonfiction. Grades 5–8.

European Heritage

Turner, A. *Time of the Bison.* Ill. by B. Peck. Macmillan, 1987. In this story of family life in prehistoric times, Scar Boy wants to earn a new "true" name and is surprised when he is honored for sculpting a horse's image from clay. Fiction. Grades 4–5.

Latino/Hispanic Heritage

Baumann, H. *Las Cuevas de los Grandes Cazadores.* Barcelona, Juventud, n.d. A Spanish language text that discusses the life of early cave dwellers. Nonfiction. Grade 6 and up.

Jimenez, C. M. *The Mexican American Heritage.* COSMEP, 1993. Portrays history from prehistoric times to present day. Nonfiction. Grade 5 and up.

Original Native American Heritage

Lopez, B. *Crow and Weasel.* North Point Press, 1990. A fictionalized account of the first meeting of homo sapiens. Fiction. Grade 4 and up.

Differently Abled Heritage

De Armond, D. *The Seal Oil Lamp.* Sierra/Little, 1988. The sensitivity of some early people to the differently abled is shown in this ancient Eskimo tale about Allugua, a longed-for child who was born blind. He was allowed to live until he was age 7, a time when his community determined that he should be abandoned and left behind. Mouse Woman, however, intervened to save him. Folk literature. Grades 4–5.

Female Image Heritage

Tumbull, A. *Maroo of the Winter Caves.* Clarion, 1984. Tells the heroic actions of Maroo, a young girl during the Ice Age, who saved her family in the area that is now southern France. Fiction. Grade 6 and up.

Religious Minority Heritage

Finkelstein, N. H. *Remember Not to Forget.* Ill. by L. & L. Hokanson. Mulberry Books, 1992. Discusses the history and origins of anti-Semitism. Nonfiction. Grades 4–6.

accepted. Have students reverse their roles and then replay the situation. Ask the students to transform one of the role-play situations into an artistic format and draw, paint, or sketch how the encounter might have happened. Make overhead transparencies of the sketches to use for background scenery for additional role-playing. To connect an awareness of cultural diversity of long ago with today's society, ask the students to play the roles of two boys or girls who meet for the first time in a modern context and discuss what each would say, do, and feel in the situation.

Activity #2: "Contrast, Compare, Share"

Focus student interest on the first encounters of early humans and the development of human societies by reading aloud excerpts from Baylor's *One Small Blue Bead* and *Crow and Weasel* by Lopez. Ask students to meet with partners and compare and contrast the first meeting of the two young boys with the first encounter of Crow and Weasel with other humans.

First Meeting

One Small Blue Bead	*Crow and Weasel*
1. Friendly	1. Fearful

In his book, Lopez describes Crow and Weasel on horseback on a river bank, frightened as they faced some flat-faced strangers in boats. The two friends believed the strangers would use their "teeth" (ivory knives as long as a man's arm) to kill them. Strong with the courage of their friendship, Crow brandishes his lance and Weasel waves his knife, and the strangers lower their "teeth." From the back of the first boat, an older stranger says, "We have killed some fine caribou. You young men are full of courage. The world is full of strange things impossible to understand. Let us land there where you are and we will eat."

To choose new partners to discuss the conversations of the encounters further, establish a different social context in the classroom for a discussion of "first encounters of a different kind," and ask each student to put up either a thumb or a little finger to indicate a choice between the stories—a thumb for *Crow and Weasel* and a little finger for *One Small Blue Bead*.

1. Direct the students on the right side of the room who have their thumbs up to move "way over" to the left side of the room and find another student who also has a thumb up to be a partner. Ask partners to talk about the encounters in the two books

and participate in a "first encounter discussion." They can talk about what was alike and what was different in the encounters.

2. Direct the students on the left side of the room who have their little fingers up to move "way over" to the right side and find another student who has a little finger up to be a partner for this activity.

3. Ask the students to make further suggestions for similarities and contrasts and record them.

4. Ask the partners to join the whole group and elicit from the group their suggestions for additional similarities and contrasts from the stories and write the information on the board. Show students the way you would categorize their suggestions in an overlapping Venn Diagram of two circles, as seen in Figure 1–2.

5. Demonstrate how you would use the information in the circles to write a brief paragraph about the books on the board or on an overhead transparency. Show the students the way you select the main idea and sentences that provide the supporting details about similarities/differences from their suggestions.

6. Engage the students in writing a class paragraph about the similarities, then the differences. When completed as a group, partners can work together and take turns telling/reading/writing their own original descriptive paragraphs.

7. Back in the whole group, ask two students to be scribes for the class and write any additional similarities and differences from the reports of the partners in columns on the board under the headings "Similarities" and "Differences." After discussing this information, ask the students to illustrate a similarity or a difference for a class display about a first encounter with early people.

8. Suggest a question census to find out what the students would like to find out further about prehistoric people. Accept all of the students' questions and write them on an overhead transparency or chart. Use the questions as topics for future inquiries into this time period. After discussion, post the results of the question census for all to see.

9. Ask students in small groups to brainstorm more about what an anthropologist does and then elicit the investigative steps of questioning, hypothesizing, predicting, investigating, analyzing, evaluating data, and drawing conclusions from the discussion. Write these steps on the board. Show students a small blue bead and say, "Suppose you were going to study this

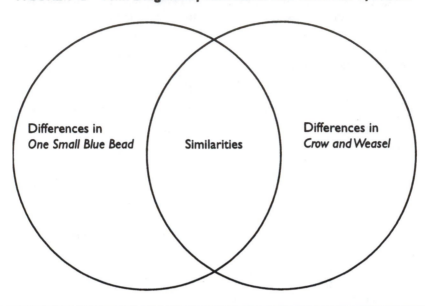

FIGURE 1–2   Venn Diagram of Similarities and Contrasts of Stories

Differences in
One Small Blue Bead

Similarities

Differences in
Crow and Weasel

blue bead and what it could be used for, and I told you that you would be working in the manner of an anthropologist. What will you be doing? What are the steps we wrote on the chart that an anthropologist does? How would you do each step?" Review the investigative steps with the students and then give each small group a blue bead and a task such as:

a. "Suppose you were an anthropologist and had never seen a blue bead like this before. What would you do to investigate it?"
b. "What questions would you ask about it?"

"Discuss these questions in your group and be prepared to tell the whole group what you would do—such as, ways you would investigate the object, how you would do it, and why you would do it. You can refer to the steps on the chart if you need to do so." Have a student from each group report back to the whole class.

Governments of Early People

"Three ideas are basic to the understanding of the organization of human societies," explain Jarolimek and Parker (1993), authors of *Social Studies in Elementary Education*. "One is that all societies have developed ways of establishing and maintaining social order; the second is that the central order-maintaining instrument has great power over the lives of individuals subjected to it; the third is that

all such systems demand and expect a loyalty to them when they are threatened by hostile opposing forces." These three basic idea's about societies have been verified by children's literature, and are sometimes found in the talking animal tales where animals act like humans. Read aloud *Why Mosquitoes Buzz in People's Ears* (Dial, 1975, all ages) retold by Verna Aardema. This talking animal tale can build the students' awareness about an early world that had a type of government:

1. The idea that all societies have developed ways of establishing and maintaining social order and the idea that this was a part of early societies is shown in *Why Mosquitoes Buzz in People's Ears*. In the story, a sequence of events prevents the owl from waking the sun and bringing in a new day. The social order of the animals is revealed by the way the people value a council when King Lion calls a meeting of the animal council to uncover the reason for the long night. After hearing of all the events, the king discovers the culprit—the mosquito.

2. The idea that the central order-maintaining instrument in a society has great power over the lives of individuals subjected to it is also shown in Aardema's story when the mosquito attempts to hide from the king and the other animals by taking cover. To this day, the insect buzzes in people's ears to say, "Zeee! Is everyone still angry at me?"

3. The idea that all systems demand and expect a loyalty whenever threatened by hostile opposing forces is also shown in this cumulative retelling about a community concern expressed by the animals. The animals' interaction demonstrates their protective group loyalty when they suspect a hostile act has happened in their community.

Focusing further on this topic, write the word *government* on the board and ask the students what meaning(s) the word has for them. Record their ideas on the board and discuss them with the students. Show the students how they can transform information to poetry. Demonstrate this by reading an encyclopedic definition of *government* and then by changing a line or two into an example of free verse:

> In a democratic county
> like the United States,
>   government is the means
>   the people use
>   to promote
>   the welfare of the nation.

Next, ask the students to write their ideas about government and then transform their ideas into free verse so that their words look like a poem. Ask the students to exchange their written ideas with another. Let the receiving student transform the written ideas into another free verse. Have students return the papers and read what has been created.

After further discussion, record the students' examples of ways early people were governed. Ask students to contrast the early governments for differences and then compare them for similarities and tell what they learned to the whole group. Record what the students discover on the board to be used as a reference as you demonstrate a way to write an original brief paragraph about the differences and

similarities of selected governments. Encourage the students to use the information when they write their own brief paragraphs telling what they learned about the governments of early people. If appropriate, ask the students to transform sentences from their informational paragraphs into a form of free verse about early governments and display the verses in the room.

Activity #3: "Early Governments"

Read aloud excerpts about the different styles of leadership in governments of early people from *Mother's Blessing* (Atheneum, 1992, grades 6–8) by P. K. Spinka, or another literature source. Introduce students to the usefulness of writing information on a data-retrieval chart (such as Figure 1–3) and add their examples of governments on the left-hand side and questions of interest across the top.

Ask the students to add to the chart any facts about early government they find after reading, browsing, and scanning data sources. Have them write the facts on adhesive-backed notepaper and affix them to the chart. After verifying with the group that information has been gathered and written on adhesive-backed notepaper and put on the chart, ask students to talk about the differences in the governments they found. With the overhead, demonstrate to students a way to write a brief summary using the information they found that focuses on: "There are ways of governing people who have *differences* that include _____." Additionally, talk about the similarities in the governments the students have noticed and again demonstrate a way to write another brief summary that focuses on: "There are ways of governing people who have *similarities* that include _____." Next, ask students to suggest ways of combining the two summaries; write their suggestions on the board as models. Ask them to write their own summary combinations and to

---

FIGURE 1–3   Data-Retrieval Chart for Governments of Early People

GOVERNMENTS OF EARLY PEOPLE

Government of People	Majority rule?	Minority protection?	Laws
1. (book title)			
2.			

include their thoughts about what government means to them. If appropriate, extend the study further by:

1. ***Inventing a Word.*** Ask interested students to create and invent words such as *paleo-groups, leader-ocracy, ruler-ocracy, prehist-oracy, paleo-ocracy ethnic group-ocracy*, or *demo-groups* and use them to describe the governments of early people in the summaries.

2. ***Matching Attributes of Governments.*** Ask the students to list on the board the attributes (characteristics) of one early government they know about and then locate further examples of governments anywhere that seem to match the attributes. Compare one of the early government to some of the features in America's democratic republic today (e.g., in what way did the early government have majority rule, minority protection, and a way to maintain their "laws"?).

3. ***Observing.*** Engage students in closely observing illustrations in books to see if they find an artist's interpretation of any of the attributes of early governments they listed.

4. ***Finding Examples That Don't Match Students' Ideas of "Early Government."*** Elicit information from the students about any cases, illustrations, instances, attributes, and characteristics of early government that don't "fit" or "match" features of America's democratic government. When an example of "it doesn't fit" is found, ask the students to describe some of the changes that would have to be made in the early government to "match" the features of majority rule, minority protection, and maintenance of laws that are part of America's government today.

CHAPTER TWO

4 Million–19,000 B.C.

What was going on in ancient times?

Multicultural Perspectives

A study of this time period can present busy Native Americans in ancient North America making shelters, clothing, and tools to culltivate corn in areas known today as New Mexico and the Ohio River Valley, traveling across the beautiful environment, fishing in streams and rivers, hunting large and small animals, gathering plants, exploring caves, and painting the cave walls. Student-designed paintings can re-create the pictographs their artists left. Examples of the people's shelters can be drawn on posters (e.g., longhouses, hogans, earth lodges, tipis, kivas, and plank shelters) and the students' sketches of the people's animal traps, baskets, clothing, implements, pottery, tools, weapons, and other possessions can be displayed in oversize book formats. Several questions can be developed as captions and lead the students to inquiries about ways people adjusted to their environment and to other humans in this period. To assist students further in their inquiries, Figure 2–1 has perspectives of selected people for this time period.

FIGURE 2–1   *Children's Books about 4 Million–19,000 B.C.*

PERSPECTIVES FOR 4 MILLION–19,000 B.C.

African Heritage

Aardema, V., reteller. Misoso: *Once Upon a Time Tales from Africa.* Ill. by R. Ruffins. Knopf, 1994. Tales include a cumulative Swahili story, "Gogo the Teacher," and a "Why" tale, "Leelee Goro," from Sierra Leone about how crying and other phenomena came into being. Folk literature. Grades 4–6.

Asian Heritage

Yue, C., & Yue, D. *The Igloo.* Houghton Mifflin, 1988. Portrays the life and survival of the ancestors of the Eskimos, the Thule People, who journeyed to early Alaska across the Bering Strait. Nonfiction. Grade 4 and up.

European Heritage

Barringer, D. M. *And The Waters Prevailed.* Ill. by P. Hutchinson. Dutton, 1956. After his rite of manhood, Andor journeys to a special place (now called the Strait of Gibraltar) on the shores of a great water (now called the Atlantic Ocean). Andor notices the waves, how they pound against the rocks, and sees that the water may break though and flood his people's land. Fiction. Grades 4–6.

continued

FIGURE 2–1   Children's Books about 4 Million–19,000 B.C.

Craig, R. *Malu's Wolf.* Orchard Books, 1995. Malu defies the taboos of her Cro-Magnon tribe in southern Europe and teaches herself to hunt and raises an orphaned wolf pup. Fiction. Grades 5–8.

Latino/Hispanic Heritage

Bendick, J. *Tombs of the Ancient Americas.* Watts, 1993. Has factual text supported by photographs showing people's ornaments, the city of Cuzco of the Incas, and the fortress of Sacsaythuaman. Nonfiction. Grades 4–6.

Original Native American Heritage

Ayeer, E. J. *The Anasazi.* Walker, 1993. Discusses the prehistoric basket makers and the historic Pueblo People as features of the Anasazi civilization. Describes methods that archaeologists use to find evidence which leads to theories about the lifestyle of the past Anasazi population. Nonfiction. Grades 6–8.

Bruchac J. *Gluskabe and the Four Wishes.* Ill. by C. Nyburg Shrader. Cobblehill, 1995. In this Abenaki tale, four men are given their wishes in pouches by Gluskabe on the condition they not look into their pouches until they are home. The three who look in the pouches are given their wishes in unwanted ways, and the fourth, who wished to be a better hunter to provide food for his people, is able to learn all of the secrets of the animals. Folk literature. Grades 4–6.

Monroe, J. G., & Williamson, R. A. *First Houses: Native American Homes and Sacred Structures.* Houghton Mifflin, 1993. Portrays the connection between Native people's myths and the design and construction of their traditional Native American dwellings. Discusses the Iroquois longhouse, Mohave house, a Navajo hogan, Northwest Coast dwelling, Pawnee earth lodge, Plains tipi, and Pueblo kiva. Includes glossary and notes with references. Nonfiction. Grade 6 and up.

Differently Abled Heritage

Dyer, T. A. *A Way of His Own.* Houghton Mifflin, 1981. Living in a band of hunters and gatherers, young Shutok was abandoned because they believed his crippled back had an evil spirit that was responsible for their bad luck and misfortunes. Fiction. Grade 6 and up.

Female Image Heritage

Green, R. *Women in American Indian Society.* Chelsea House, 1992. Depicts Native American women from the pre-explorers' contact to the present when over 10 percent of the communities have women leaders. Includes bibliography, glossary, and index. Nonfiction. Grade 7 and up.

Olsen, K. *Chronology of Women's History.* Greenwood, 1994. This chronology begins in 20,000 B.C. and records multicultural women's achievements in religion, government, military, law, arts, athletics, exploration, education, science, medicine, and business. Nonfiction. Grades 5–8.

Trager, J. *The Women's Chronology: A Year-by-Year Record from Prehistory to the Present.* Holt, Rinehart and Winston, 1994. The chronology begins in 3 million B.C. and is arranged in categories that range from education to politics. Easy-to-read entries place women's achievements in historical context. Nonfiction. Grades 7–8.

Religious Minority Heritage

Aroner, M. *The Kingdom of Singing Birds.* Kar-Ben, 1993. This is a classic Hasidic tale about making one's own choices, where Rabbi Zusya is called by the king to make his silent birds sing. Zusya tells the king that if he truly wants to hear the songs of the birds, he must set them free. Folk literature. Grades 4–5.

Conflicts of Early Societies

"Child readers learn that some problems are universal; they are present despite the outward details of the era," states John Warren Stewig (1988), author of *Children and Literature*. A teacher might, for instance, choose a problem such as greed; he or she can select several books, from differing time periods, in which a character exemplifies this problem. In groups, children can discuss various manifestations of this problem and how people react differently to it in different times. As Stewig suggests, you can introduce the lifestyles of early humans, their societies, and the conflicts–the universal problems they faced—by reading aloud a legend portraying a conflict from a particular culture.

Read aloud the conflict faced by Xiao Sheng and others in his village during a time of drought in J. Lawson's *The Dragon's Pearl* (Clarion, 1993, grades 4–5). When the land is ruined, Xiao Sheng discovers a shiny magic pearl that keeps his mothers food jars and money box "full" and she shares with others during this difficult time to repay their kindness to her. After hearing the story, ask students what they know about the hardships of drought (and some of the other conflicts they believe ancient families faced). Have them identify the hardships that they think people in today's time period endure that are similar to the hardships of people in ancient times. This will help them link the people of the past to the people of the present (see Figure 2–2).

Activity #4: "The Magic Amulet"

Ask the students to rephrase the extent to which the conflicts of early people in the stories in Figure 2–2

FIGURE 2–2   *Children's Books about Conflicts Faced by Early People*

Conflict with Basic Needs: Food, Clothing, and Shelter

Goble, P. *Crow Chief.* Orchard, 1992. When Crow Chief warns the buffalo of the Native American hunters, Falling Star, one of the hunters, captures Crow Chief and ties him where the tipi poles cross until his feathers turn black from the tipi's fire. When Crow Chief learns that everyone must share, he is released. Folk literature. Grade 4 and up.

Conflict with Clan Taboos and Customs

Denzel, J. *The Boy of the Painted Cave.* Philomel, 1988. A boy is banished from his clan for breaking a taboo. Fiction. Grade 5 and up.

Garcia, A. *Spirit on the Wall.* Holiday House, 1982. A grandmother defies a clan's customs and supports her granddaughters artistic skills. Fiction. Grade 5 and up.

Conflict with Climate, Natural Forces, and Elements

Aardema, V. *Bringing the Rain to Kapiti Plain: A Nandi-Tale.* Ill. by B. Vidal. Dial, 1981. Accumulating tale of drought from Kenya. Folk literature. Grades 4–6.

Anderson, M. *Light in the Mountain.* Knopf, 1982. Early Maori people overcame a cold and harsh climate. Folk literature. Grade 4.

Lasky, K. *Cloud Eyes.* Ill. by B. Moser. Harcourt, 1994. This tale is told in the style of a Native American legend and is about a young man, Cloud Eyes, who uses smoke from his peace pipe to quiet a treeful of bees and uses his music and dance to quiet the greedy bears that also are after the honey. His actions give his people their share of honey from the tree. Folk literature variant. Grades 4–5.

Conflict with Powerful Others

Young, E. reteller. *Little Plum.* Ill. by the author. Philomel, 1994. This is the Chinese tale of a tiny son who boasts "there is nothing I cannot do" and grows into a resourceful hero who defeats soldiers pillaging his village. Folk literature. Grades 4–5.

might be present in people's lives today, and invite them to begin literature or history journals—spiral-bound notebooks—by drawing pictures of the conflicts they have faced that they think are similar to the conflicts of early people. Discuss ways early people coped with the hardships brought about by droughts, famines, and harsh climates through stories, and ask students to point out the solutions in the tales that they think would work or not work today.

To develop another insight about conflict, ask students to compare the way people today interact with developmentally different individuals with the way prehistoric people acted toward them after listening to the treatment of a developmentally different boy in William Steele's *The Magic Amulet*. Discuss the decrees of abandonment, banishment, and other actions the disabled received from ancient people, and engage students in identifying the extent to which those behaviors would be acceptable today, and have them tell *why* they think so.

Rethinking Africa and Other Cultures

"Each year skits...are repeated in hundreds of classrooms throughout the country—Pilgrims celebrating the first Thanksgiving, a meeting of the Iroquois League, a wagon train family along the Oregon Trail, rancho life in early California, plantation life in antebellum days," state Jarolimek and Parker (1993), social studies specialists. They continue, "These activities have two important values. First, they are highly motivating for children.... Second, the use of a dramatic activity to recreate a situation under study gives children tangible purposes for doing their information gathering." As Jarolimek

and Parker have suggested, you can motivate the students to learn more about the history of a culture and its people as they enjoy a drama activity and become involved in research about it.

For example, in a study about Africa's cultures, students can visualize a play or skit as a brief chronicle of a time period and re-create a performance from a resource such as *Plays from African Tales: One-Act, Royalty-Free Dramatizations for Young People, from the Stories and Legends of Africa* (Plays, Inc., 1992, all grades) by Barbara Winther. The book introduces plays related to the stories of nations and cultures of Africa. Winther's material also includes a brief history of each tale and a description of the tale's cultural beginnings that can initiate additional cross-checking of facts by the students. Engage the students in photocopying a page from an encyclopedia, a dictionary, and an informational book, and make transparencies to explain how they cross-checked information in one of the plays. Related to this, the use of a play or skit from a selected country gives students a purpose for gathering information about a country and its people, and the students can insert some of what they learned from their cross-check into the drama.

Because Winther's plays are set in a country other than the United States, it will be valuable to determine what knowledge the students have about Africa and the people who live there. To do this, project a web format on the board as a guide for the students to record information. (Make an overhead transparency of History Master 1, "Information Web"; all History Masters are found near end of book). Ask a student to write the word *Africa* in the center of the web, and have others suggest categories such as housing, climate, and so on (see Web 2–1).

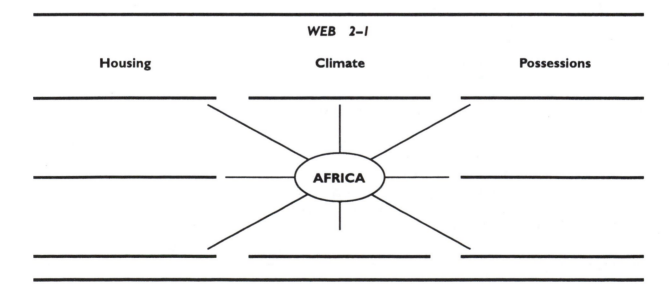

WEB   2–1

Housing   Climate   Possessions

AFRICA

Ask the students for any knowledge they have of the country and write their comments on the board. As the graphic is created, show them the way to group the information in categories to organize their thoughts and enable them to better understand Africa and the people.

With a selected play from Winther's book, talk with the students about the author's note, the production possibilities, and the characters in the play. Encourage them to suggest dance movements or music for the performance, For instance, they can add a musical background and choreograph some simple dance moves when they "stage" the production and invite another class to be the audience.

Activity #5: "Africa"

Before students select a play or skit to perform, have them reflect about the place of Africa in world history. Explain the concept of size and distance by comparing Africa with the size of the students' state and then the United States. Ask one volunteer to trace the state on one transparency and another to make an overlay transparency of the outline of Africa and the United States. Ask the students to compare the shapes on the overhead and discuss how large Africa is compared to the students' state and the United States. If appropriate, also show how maps can be distorted by asking students to trace the outline of Africa from a globe and a flat map and then comparing the two outlines.

Engage the students in gathering facts about some ancient African influences on Greek life, and later, on Western civilization. With students, record several examples of African influence and write the suggestions under headings on a word map similar to the one shown in Web 2–2.

Ask, "How can we be *sure* that the suggestions tell us something about Africa?" Have students locate evidence from children's historical fiction, biographies, information books, and references to show that the words on the board *really* represent information about Africa. If appropriate, ask the students to copy the word map or create their own and use it as a reference when researching further information on the topic. Make a list of the ways the students can incorporate the information they found into the play or skit they want to perform.

Folktales Tell Inner Feelings

"In recent years, as we have seen, anthropologists study folklore in order to understand the inherent values and beliefs of a culture," state Huck, Hepler, and Hickman (1987), authors of *Children's Literature in the Elementary School.* "Psychologists look at folktales and myths and discover something of the motivations and inner feelings of humans." Thus, folktales, like plays and skits, add an enriching dimension in historical study, and with students, a read-aloud folktale such as Gail E. Haley's book *A Story, A Story* (Atheneum, 1970, all grades) can introduce the topic of studying folktales to understand the values of a culture. The tale can help the students connect the past to the present through a story that is enjoyed by all who hear it.

Haley's story is a tale of how Anansi, the Spider man-trickster of Africa, receives the world's stories from Nyame, the Sky god, and brings them down to earth. In the story, the Spider man's character emphasizes that a small person's wit can overcome strength, verbal ability, and the achievement of others. Invite students to locate and read other African

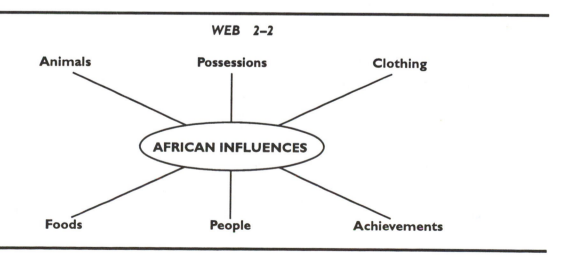

WEB 2–2

Animals — Possessions — Clothing — **AFRICAN INFLUENCES** — Foods — People — Achievements tales to identify some of the values and beliefs of the people who first told the stories. Additional folktales from parallel cultures, about which the students can discuss similarities, are in Figure 2–3.

Activity #6: "Be Amateur Psychologists"

After seeing the development of humankind in *Early Humans* (Knopf, 1989, grades 4–6) by N. Merriam, the students can read and work in small groups. The students can identify human feelings and read several examples of the different types of tales and record what they found on a data sheet similar to Figure 2–3. If appropriate, they can use History Master 2, "Traditional Folktales" and History Master 3, "Folk Literature from Different Cultures."

Ask each group to reread each of the tales they select to discover some of the motivations and inner feelings of humans—joy, fear, grief, awe—ex-

---

FIGURE 2–3   Traditional Folktales

African Heritage

Bryan, A. *The Ox of the Wonderful Horns: And Other African Folktales.* Macmillan, 1993. Five stories suitable for reading aloud. Folk literature. Grades 4–6.

Asian Heritage

Carpenter, F. *Tales of a Korean Grandmother.* C. E. Tuttle, 1972. Tales from various sources. Folk literature. Grade 4 and up.

Yep, L. *The Man Who Tricked a Ghost.* Bridgewater Books, 1993. When Sung meets a fierce warrior ghost, he says he is a novice ghost. Traveling with the ghost as a companion, Sung learns the warrior's secret, which Sung uses to defeat him, and in doing so, makes himself rich. Folk literature. Grade 4.

European Heritage

Gag, W. *Gone Is Gone.* Putnam, 1960. Tale of Fritzl who takes over Liesi's work. Folk literature. Grade 4.

Latino/Hispanic Heritage

Aardema, V. *The Riddle of the Drum: A Tale from Tizapin, Mexico.* Ill T. Chen. Four Wind 1979. To marry the king's daughter, a man must guess the kind of leather in a drum. Folk literature. Grade 4.

Dupré, J. *The Mouse Bride: A Mayan Folk Tale.* Knopf/Umbrella Books, 1993. This fable, told by the Choi Indians who are descendents from the Mayans, is about a pair of mice who want their daughter to marry the most powerful force in the universe and finally select a mouse for her husband. Folk literature. Grade 4.

Original Native American Heritage

Bierhorst, J. *The Naked Bear: Folktales of the Iroquois.* Ill. by D. Zimmer. Morrow, 1987. Explains ways the tales were collected and offers traditional characters. Folk literature. Grade 4 and up.

Rodanas, K. *Dance of the Sacred Circle: A Native American Tale.* Little, Brown, 1994. An orphaned scarfaced boy goes on a quest to the Great Chief. The boy hopes that buffalo will be sent to help his starving people and he receives the gift of the horse. Folk literature. Grades 4–5.

Stevens, J. *Coyote Steals the Blanket: A Ute Tale.* Holiday House, 1993. Whiskered Coyote takes and wears a beautiful blanket that isn't his and Hummingbird warns him of the consequences to come. But Coyote says, "I go where I want. I do what I want, and I take what I want." Coyote's consequence comes in the shape of a magic boulder that pursues him. Folk literature. Grade 4.

pressed in the tales. Have each group tell the whole class about the tales they located and add their information to the data sheet.

Economics Network in Class

"Economics is the study of the production, distribution, exchange, and consumption of goods and services that people need or want," state Jarolimek and Parker (1993). And when early traders encountered other early traders in North America, a type of economic network was developed. The students can gain insights into what early traders might have faced in their transactions by establishing an economic network at their school with the materials they are using each day.

To launch their students into just such a network, teacher Donald Love and his associates at Meadowbrook Intermediate School in Poway, California, initiated an economy situation so students could develop a deeper understanding of economics (Shirts, 1972). To begin, one class was given the scissors, brushes, and the use of the duplicating machine. Another class became the owners of paint, paste, and art paper. A third class received lined paper, duplicating paper, and masters. When any of the classes had a project that involved the materials they did not "own," they had to engage in an economic transaction. The transactions began with haggling, went on to annoyance about the amount of time needed to carry on the transactions, and then concluded with the development of a rate or exchange: 32 sheets of paper was equal to 18 masters. When this exchange became cumbersome, a class printed some "money" but found the other two classes would not accept it as payment. Finally, the classes decided there should be one currency for all three classes. It then became obvious that a government was needed to control the amount of currency to be printed and to decide to whom it would be distributed and other matters related to the currency. Through the project, the students quickly learned basic economic principles with the materials they used every day. These ideas can assist students as they consider the concept of trading used by early Native American economies and the concepts of money and currency used by a contemporary economy.

Activity #7: "From Trading to Money"

Have students give their definitions of *trading* and write their ideas on the board. Ask them to gather facts about several Native American tribes related to the trading that each tribe did. Use the facts to establish decision-making activities. As examples, see the following decision-making activities. They are based on Evelyn Wolfson's *Abenaki to Zuni: A Dictionary of Native American Tribes* (Walker, 1988, grade 5 and up):

1. Imagine that you are a member of the Mohawk tribe in the Northeast. Your tribe wants to trap furs and trade the furs to European traders for axes, knives, and sword blades (and later, guns). What arguments do you have for trapping or not trapping as the European traders want you to do? What suggestions would you make to your tribe for the trading exchange? (How many axes, knives, and sword blades should your tribe receive for one fur?) (p. 110). What reasons can you give for your decision(s)? Demonstrate your decisions in a role-play situation with other students as European traders and then, in a group, talk about what you did and write up a description of the role-play situation. Include trading considerations, if any, that your group should have included but did not. For example, how did your group consider the size and weight and quality of the fur versus the size and number and quality of the axes, knives, and sword blades?

2. Pretend that you are a member of the Tlingit tribe in the Northwest. Your tribe trades copper and sea otter skins for shells from other coastal tribes. What suggestions would you make to your tribe for the exchange? (How many shells should your tribe receive for one sea otter skin?) (p. 163). What did you consider in making your decision(s)? Demonstrate your decisions in a role-play situation with another student who plays the member of a coastal tribe.

3. Imagine that you are a member of the Tsimshian tribe in the Northwest. Your tribe catches candlefish in the Skeena River and you trade the fish oil (along with your tribe's special Chilkat blankets made of double-woven cedar bark) for tusk shells with the Tlingits who live north of you and to the Kwakiutl who live south of you. You also trade the oil with inland tribes for furs and with the Haida tribe for large canoes, totem poles, and sea otters. What suggestions would you make to your tribe for the exchange? (How much oil or number of blankets should your tribe give for tusk shells? for a fur? for a large canoe? for a totem pole? for a sea otter? for copper?) (pp. 167–168). What considerations helped you make your decision(s)? Demonstrate your decisions in a role-play situation with other students representing the other tribes.

CHAPTER THREE

19,000–1200 B.C.

What was going on in 19,000–1200 B.C.?

Multicultural Perspectives

Like being a newcomer in a strange land, a study of this period requires the students' adjustment to reading about strange places and different faces. Like becoming a friend of a newcomer, such a study can lead to new understandings about the similarities of people. Gathering facts about this time period asks that the students travel vicariously back through reading to a different time and place. To do so will put the students close to the land and people thousands of years before Columbus. There will be ancient artists, larger-than-life adventurers of Maya, Greek, and other grand civilizations, and rugged individualists in the Stone Age—all of whom can help students learn about the fishing, berry gathering, hunting, clothes making, trading, weapon making, and fighting that took place in the early villages and regions of this period. To support the students' independent reading, guide them to stories about their interests. To assist the students in following their interests, Figure 3–1 has more perspectives of people for this period.

Myths and Legends

"Every culture has a story about how the world began, how people were made, how the sun and the moon got in the sky," state Huck, Helpler, and Hickman (1987), specialists in children's literature. "These are called creation myths, or origin myths; they give an explanation of the beginning of things." As these authors point out, you can acquaint students with an expanded view of history by reading aloud culturally accurate myths and legends, which, in turn, can foster the students' understanding of the reasons behind differing attitudes and behaviors held by people in various regions. You also can discuss the distinction between myths and legends, *Myths* are stories from early times that try to explain why things happen as they do; *legends* are stories based some way on ancient *facts* that have been passed down by people over many years. Both legends and myths offer a way for students to discover some of the ideas early people valued. In addition, point out to older students that some of the stories may have metaphorical meanings and others may indicate there is another world view in which a scientific explanation of the universe is not the major objective of the story. Additionally, focusing on one of the cultures mentioned in the activities in this section may give students an opportunity to gain a deeper understanding of a culture they select to study, as well as gain understandings of parallel cultures.

Invite the students to listen to a legend and show them how to use the legend as a clue to the value system of the ancient people from whom the story originated. Ask students to use what they learned from the story and predict/decide what they think the ancient people valued in their lives. In support of this experience, Vugrenes(1981)says that telling a culturally accurate myth or legend can be one of those "teachable moments." Additionally, Nessel (1985) recommends telling a classic myth, gothic tale, or Indian legend to develop elementary students' schema for other literature they will eventually read. As an example of a legend to tell or read aloud while studying the literary heritage of the people of early Europe, select Kate Seredy's *The White Stag* (Viking, 1965, grades 5–8), one that describes the migration of the people into the region that becomes Hungary:

FIGURE 3–1 *Children's Books for 19,000–1200 B.C.*

PERSPECTIVES FOR 19,000–1200 B.C.

African Heritage

Macdonald. F. *Ancient Egyptians.* Barron's, 1993. Portrays the African civilization with photographs of Egyptian art, clothing, jewelry, monuments, pottery, textiles, and weapons. Includes maps, time charts, fold-out pages, glossary, and index. Nonfiction. Grade 4 and up.

Asian Heritage

Jiang, W. *La Heroina Hua Mulan/ The Legend of Mu Lan.* Ill. by author and Xing Gen. Monterey: Victory Press/ T. R. Books, 1992. Set in ancient China, Mu Lan disguises herself as a boy to fight for her country. Folk literature. Grade 4.

Maestro, B. *The Discovery of the Americas.* Lothrop, 1991. Supports view that people crossed the Bering Land bridge over 20,000 years ago to North America. Details travels of Stone Age people and visits by others from Phonecia, Eire, Japan, and Vinland. Maps included. Nonfiction. Grades 4–5.

European Heritage

Getz, D. *Frozen Man.* Ill. by P. McCarty. Holt, 1994. About 3, 000 B.C., a man died in a frozen site and in the 1990s, his body was discovered and studied by scientists. Full-color photographs. Grades 4–7.

Martell, H. M. *Over 6,000 Years Ago: In the Stone Age.* Macmillan, 1992. Portrays culture and development during the Stone Age based on archaeological evidence found mainly in Europe. Nonfiction. Grades 4–6.

Latino/Hispanic Heritage

Baquedano, E. *Aztec, Inca & Maya.* Knopf, 1993. Introduces three major civilizations of the Americas in a compare-and-contrast approach through photographs of the Mexican National Archeological Museum's re-creations of ancient activities such as trading, paying tribute, and healing. Nonfiction. Grades 4–5.

Caselli, G. *Las Primeras Civilizaciones.* Madrid: Generales Anaya, 1985. A Spanish language text that reviews early civilizations. Nonfiction. Grade 6 and up.

Original Native American Heritage

Arnold, C. *The Ancient Cliff Dwellers of Mesa Verde.* Ill. by R. Hewett. Clarion, 1992. Portrays Anasazi people in Mesa Verde, their cliff dwellings, artifacts, and contemporary archaeologists of today at work. Describes discovery and development of the area in late nineteenth century as a National Park. Nonfiction. Grades 4–6.

Martin, P. *Indians Before Columbus: Twenty Thousand Years of North American History Revealed by Archaeology.* University of Chicago Press, 1975. Illustrations provide a useful resource for students. Nonfiction. Grades 5–6.

Differently Abled Heritage

Pryor, B. *Seth of the Lion People.* Morrow, 1988. Abandoning his cave clan people, Seth, an orphan boy with a withered leg, searched for a new home with the Goat People. Fiction. Grade 6 and up.

continued

FIGURE 3–1 Continued

Female Image Heritage

Brennan, J. H. *Shiva's Challenge: An Adventure of the Ice Age*. HarperCollins, 1992. Set around 14,000 B.C., Shiva used her skills and finds her way home from the icebound frozen wasteland in which she finds herself. Fiction. Grades 5–8.

McGraw, E. J. *Mara, Daughter of the Nile*. Coward, 1953. During the rule of Hatshepsut, Mara, a slave, tries to escape and is bought by a man who offers her luxury if she will spy for the queen. Mara also sells her services as a spy for the king to a young nobleman, Lord Sheftu. Eventually, her love for Sheftu changes her from a spy into a selfless heroine who endures torture rather than betray her new loyalties. Fiction. Grade 7 and up.

Religious Minority Heritage

Behn, H. *The Faraway Lurs*. Putnam, 1982. In a forest, Heather, a young girl, meets Wolf Stone, son of the chieftain of the Sun People, as he searches for a mighty tree that her peaceful people worship. The two fall in love, an event which ends in a "Romeo and Juliet" resolution. The author writes that he was motivated to write this story after speculating on what might have caused the death of an 18-year-old girl who was found perfectly preserved for some 3,000 years in a "wet grave" on a Danish farm. Fiction. Grade 6 and up.

Chaikin, M. *Exodus*. Holiday House, 1987. Adaptation of the story of the departure of the 12 tribes of the Israelites from the bondage of the Egyptians. Nonfiction. Grade 6 and up.

En el tiemo de los Hebreos. Leon, Spain: Everest/Coleccion Saber mas, n. d. Spanish language text about the ancient Hebrews. Includes illustrations, maps, and photographs. Nonfiction. Grade 6 and up.

The Jews: A Treasury of Art and Literature. Museum of Fine Arts, Boston, 1990. Portrays over 5, 000 years of tradition through art selections from the Bible, art from the Middle Ages and a presentation of Anne Frank's true story. Nonfiction. Grade 8 and up.

Kuskin, K. *Jerusalem, Shining Still*. Harper and Row, 1987. A poetic telling of the 4,000-year-old history of Jerusalem, a city holy to many people and the capital of King David in 1000 B.C. Nonfiction. Grade 6 and up.

Pirotta, S. *Jerusalem*. Dillon/Macmillan, 1993. Discusses the city's special role as the center of three major religious faiths, its history and places of worship, as well as its influences on art, architecture, and culture. Nonfiction. Grades 4–6.

In the Hungarian legend, Nimrod, a respected leader in early Hungary, prophesies that his people will find a promised land between two great rivers far to the West, and so his two sons, Hunor and Magyar, follow a white stag west to a blue lake. The people follow and the sons marry moonmaidens. To Hunor and his wife is born a son, Beneguz, who was destined to be called White Eagle and become the father of Attila, the Red Eagle. When the people later divide into two groups, Magyar's followers remain on the land in the East of Europe and the followers of Hunor, the Huns, move to the West. When Attila's mother dies at his birth, Attila lacks tenderness and love and grows to be ruthless in battle. As the legend goes, the Huns, with Attila as their leader, finally reach their promised land by following another white stag in a fierce storm through a pass in the Carpathian Mountains.

Ask students to use what they learned from the legend and tell what they think the ancient people who first told the story *valued in* their lives. Since legends are based some way on ancient facts, what do the students want to select from the story that might be *facts*.

Activity #8: "What Do Myths and Legends Tell about Early People?"

With the whole group, discuss the students' ideas (guesses, hunches, predictions) about what the people of ancient Hungary valued and why there might be differing attitudes and behaviors toward each other by today's descendents of the followers of Magyar and Hunor. To further extend this activity for older students, Nessel (1985) recommends that legends from the Original Native Americans and the Greek myths be told, and suggests that students dramatize a scene from a myth or legend and then describe their favorite scene as an extension of the myth or legend. Indeed, acting out some of their favorite scenes can be a way for the students to develop different descriptions and elaborations about the people and places in myths and legends.

Exciting descriptive scenes can be found in several children's books and the students can be encouraged to add an interesting dimension to a dramatization (or to a description of a scene) by suggesting background music and body movements to show various actions of the main characters. Some books, such as the lyrical version of an Aztec myth in R. Lewis's *All of You Was Singing* (Atheneum, 1991, all grades) and the story of the interdependence of humans and animals in *Buffalo Dance: A Blackfoot Legend.* (Little, Brown, 1993, grade 4) by Nancy Van Laan, have scenes suitable for dramatization, just as those listed on History Master 4, "Multicultural Legends and Myths."

People of Prehistory

"Long before Columbus arrived, civilizations flourished" state Charlotte and David Yue in *The Pueblo* (Houghton Mifflin, 1986, grades 4–6), an overview of the lifestyle of the Pueblo people that has been handed down for generations. With older students (grades 4 and up), read aloud excerpts from the first chapter and discuss the idea that ancient societies of people in North and South America, including the ancestors of the Pueblo people, were in existence before Columbus and other explorers came to the Americas. As more recent examples of early humankind, early people had societies in the Ohio River area 19,000 years ago; in western Pennsylvania 14,000 years ago; in northern Alaska 11,000 years ago; in northeastern Colorado in the Arikaree River Valley 10,000 years ago; and in other parts of North and South America. All of these places have been documented by archaeological findings and can be located on a map or globe by the students. If desired, use the overhead to represent the sun with the globe to demonstrate day and night and seasonal change in the places the students locate.

Although it is of value for you to emphasize the rich cultural integration in contemporary United States that has taken place, it is also important for you to teach students awareness about their own cultures along with the parallel cultures of others. In support of this, you can provide information to help the students become more knowledgeable about

original Native Americans with an informative video such as *The Pueblo Peoples: First Contact* (PBS Video, 1320 Braddock Place, Alexandria, VA 22314, 1990, advanced grade 6 and up). This video recreates the Pueblo people's civilization and their first encounter with European explorers and settlers. Ask students to take notes about any new information they learn from the video and refer to their notes in a postvideo discussion about any changes that occurred in their thoughts about the Pueblo people as a result of seeing the video.

Activity #9: "Video History"

"Videos are as important as books in confirming, illuminating, or extending the life experiences of those who perceive them…. For many young people, videos are the literature of choice," state Kay E. Vandergrift and Jane Anne Hanigan (1993), specialists in children and their literature. "Videos are becoming increasingly important in library collections and in school curricula as more and more professionals learn to value films for what they can contribute."

As an example of the value of a video, mention that students will hear new information and ask them to listen for facts about the Native Americans of prehistory who lived in the Ohio area 19,000 years ago. To begin, you can assess the current knowledge that students have about the original Native Americans (in the area now Ohio) before they see the video. To do this, use tracing paper and a map that shows the Ohio River area. Trace around Ohio state and the states that border it from a map of the United States and make photocopies for the students. If appropriate, ask the students to trace their own maps and write the names of each state on their copies. Ask them to check their labels with the map of the United States and make needed corrections.

Before showing the video, have students dictate some items they think would be important to have in a "good" video about the Native Americans who lived long ago in the Ohio River area. Write their ideas on the board. After watching the video, determine:

1. The number of items the students mentioned that *were included* in the video
2. Other items in the video; items they mentioned that were *not* in the video
3. Any questions the students *now have* after seeing the video
4. Any ideas in the video that *conflicted* with the ideas the students had about early Native Americans

Additionally, introduce more information about this early culture group with other videos and invite the students to record what they know/learned about the culture with semantic word maps drawn on the back of their state maps both *before and after* seeing the video. For example, the students can map the locations of the Native People to show their highest population centers and determine the geographical features that could have influenced the selection of the site(s). The pre- and postword maps about the early people in the region now the Ohio River area might look like the ones in Figures 3–2 and 3–3.

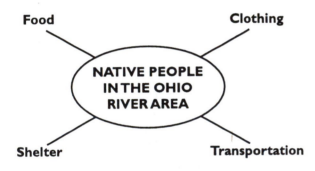

FIGURE 3–2   *Prevideo World Map*

BEFORE THE VIDEO

World Map #1:
What I Know about the Native People
in the Ohio River Area

Food   Clothing

NATIVE PEOPLE
IN THE OHIO
RIVER AREA

Shelter   Transportation

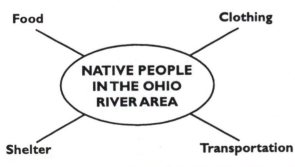

FIGURE 3–3   *Postvideo World Map*

AFTER THE VIDEO

World Map #2:
What I Know about the Native People
in the Ohio River Area

Food   Clothing

NATIVE PEOPLE
IN THE OHIO
RIVER AREA

Shelter   Transportation

Carefully selected videos to supplement the information in books will allow the students to make additional inferences about the people and their way of life. If needed, the following videos can provide views of early people and their lifestyles as well as become a forum for students to tell in what ways their ideas about Native Americans changed after viewing the material:

- *19,000 Years Ago in Ohio.* Found in Meadowcroft in a rock shelter above Cross Creek, a tributary of the Ohio River, several archeological findings revealed the Native People's hearths, stone tools, blades, and fire pits that are perhaps as old as 19,000 years. From the findings, it appeared the people hunted elk and caribou and collected nuts and berries.
  Videos: American's Indian Heritage: Rediscovering Columbus (Films for the Humanities & Sciences, 1991) reviews the lives of ancient Native Americans who lived in the area now Columbus, Ohio. Advanced grade 6 and up. *American Indians: A Brief History* (National Geographic, 1985) emphasizes the cultural traditions of the ancestors of the Adena people and other Native Americans in Ohio. Grades 3–6.

- *14,000 Years Ago in Western Pennsylvania and Colorado.* About 14,000 years ago, people had an ancient society in the area now western Pennsylvania, and about 1 0,000 years ago, paleo-people lived in shelters made of poles and bison hides in northeastern Colorado in the Arikaree River valley. Archeological findings indicate that the people wore clothes made from hide stitched with sinew with the fur turned inside; they made fires in the 40-below-zero cold and ate bison meat jerky or pemmican made with powdered jerky; using hammerstones, they broke up lumps of chert; with antler hammers, they made spearpoints from chert and wore deer-hide pads to protect their hands from sharp stone slivers; and they honed their spearpoints to the desired sharpness with antler flakers.
  Video: Mesa Verde (Finley-Holiday, 1989) portrays the ancient and early history of Mesa Verde, Colorado, and shows the cliff dwellings, ancient pottery, and other artifacts of the people who lived there. Grades 3–6.

- *13,000 Years Ago in Nevada.* Some paleo-people, perhaps predecessors of the Shoshone, lived in a rock shelter in Monitor Valley in Nevada, now called Gatecliff. At Gatecliff, the people lived on pinon nuts, rice grass seeds, fish, birds, rabbits, and other small game. Findings from the site indicated they used flint, made tools, fashioned rabbit nets from plant fibers, and roasted pinon nuts over fires. Their rock art emphasized hunting scenes. Do the students suppose the scenes were a summary of a hunt, a hunting story that was told, a hunting strategy discussed before a real hunt, or wishful thinking?

Videos: Ancient Indian Cultures of Northern Arizona (Finley-Holiday, 1985) portrays ancient civilizations of the Sinugua and the Anasazi as well as the national monuments of Montezuma Castle, Wupatki, Tuzigoot, Walnut Canyon, and Sunset Crater. Grades 3–6. *Emergence: A Navajo Myth* (Barbara Wolk Productions, 1981) explains the winter ceremony of the Emergence ritual from the past and includes scenes from the Navajo reservation in Arizona and other sites. Grade 5 and up.

• *12,000 Years Ago in Pacific Northwest.* Native people held similar beliefs about the connectedness of living things.

Videos: Landmarks of Westward Expansion: First Peoples (AIT, 1987) shows that Native people of the Pacific Northwest had different lifestyles but held similar beliefs about the value of living things. Grades 4–6. *Starlore: Ancient American Sky Myths* (Pyramid *Films/ Museum* of the American Indian, 1983) has legends of the Eskimos and others. Grades 4–6.

After viewing an informational video, ask the students to return to their state maps and write additional facts they learned about early Native Americans living in their state from the video they saw. For an option, distribute copies of maps of other areas inhabited by other paleo-people–such as a map of Colorado that shows Mesa Verde. Introduce the topic by reading about some of the discoveries made and artifacts that have been uncovered by archaeologists from *Native Americans and Mesa Verde* (Macmillan, 1993, grades 4–7) by Hazel Mary Martell, and *The Ancient Cliff Dwellers of Mesa Verde* (Clarion, 1993, grades 4–7) by Caroline Arnold. After you have introduced the topic, repeat the pre-post word map activity with an informational video about the early people of Mesa Verde.

Multicultural "How and Why" Tales

If students are interested in more "How and Why" stories, distribute History Master 5, "Multicultural

'How and Why' Tales." This thematic booklist identifies some related study topics in the tales from different cultures for individual and group inquiry. Students may work alone or in groups according to their interests in "How and Why" tales (e.g., animal characteristics, natural events, seasons, etc.). If students work in groups, they can read the tales and take notes on the explanations of the origins of animals characteristics, natural events, seasons, origins of the skies, and other topics from different cultures. Invite them to read or tell one of the tales to others in another group. With others in their group, the students can write a group story about the origins of a topic (skies, seasons) that the group selects. Encourage them to read it aloud to others. Here are some examples of selected interests:

> *Topic for Group #1: Animal Characteristics.* Read and study several folktale origins of animal characteristics through "How and Why" tales from different cultures.
>
> *Topic for Group #2: Natural Events.* Read and study several folktale origins of natural events through "How and Why" stories from different countries.
>
> *Topic for Group #3: Seasons.* Read and study several folktale origins of the seasons through "How and Why" tales from different countries.

Activity #10: "What Do 'How and Why' Stories Tell about Early People?"

Read aloud to students selections about what early life was like for humans in different environments. For example, *Kemi: An Indian Boy Before the White Man Came* (World Richie Pr., 1966, grades 5–7) by M. and C. Buff will give students a look at Native People who traded with others hundreds of years before Columbus arrived.

Discuss with students the idea that the early people's folk literature expresses and reveals what they valued and respected as well as what they did *not* value or respect. Before listening to a Cheyenne story, *Her Seven Brothers* (Bradbury, 1988), by P. Goble, write on the board the students' guesses or hunches about what they know about the respect of the Cheyenne people for certain values. After hearing the story, ask them to discuss which of their hunches (guesses, hypotheses, predictions) about the Cheyenne people were supported or refuted by Goble's story by reviewing their ideas on the board. After this analysis, ask the students to conclude what the story tells them about the early Cheyenne people and record the students' ideas on the board:

Example: Goble's **Her Seven Brothers**

What the Story Told Us

1. Herds of buffalo were close by. People knew the value of buffalo.
2. People lived near tall trees. People knew the value of trees.
3. People knew the value of ladders. They fashioned bows and arrows and were good "shots."
4. The "good people" were the Native Americans and the "villain" in the story was the buffalo leader.
5. Being brave and protecting a family member and using weapons and surroundings were actions that counted.

Conclusions: Based on this story, the early Cheyenne people valued and respected... (elicit the students' comments).

Superheroes and Heroines

"The worlds of folk heroes are set apart from our own world, but there is reassurance in these other worlds," state Sam Sebesta and William Iverson (1975), authors of *Literature for Thursday's Child*. "The heroes (especially epic heroes) are sorely tried. They may make grave mistakes and sometimes falter, but they struggle on, rising above human failings, and remaining to the end, 'bloody but unbowed.'" Indeed, the heroes and heroines in myths and folktales from different cultures allow students to learn about a culture in an historical time period through the hero's or heroine's struggles as well as through ways the people explain the times in which they lived.

Although you probably will want to emphasize the artistic reading and telling of the tales—especially folktales—several studies have confirmed additional psychological functions of the stories. For example, Blackway's (1986) study points out that conflicts found by children of today are not too different from problems faced by the main characters in folktales from centuries ago. This similarity becomes a way for students to link the past to the present. In her study, Blackway analyzed nine tales from the Grimms' tales for symbolism, theme, and type, and considered the question: What is in fairy tales to help children recognize problems or areas of conflict they might face? Areas of conflict from the tales that were identified as prevalent today were autonomy, initiation, maturity, rivalry with siblings, low self-esteem, separation or loss, and withdrawal. Blackway proposes the use of fairy tales in school and home is essential to a child's ability to meet

problems today and resolve inner conflicts in his or her surroundings.

Activity #11: "A Circle of History"

With students, use masking tape to make a circle on the floor—large enough to hold two chairs in which at least two students (knowledgeable about the same historical figures) can sit facing one another or sit side by side. Label the circle "A Circle of History" and mention that it is a circle of sharing knowledge. Elicit from students the idea that sometimes two classmates can share information that can help one another learn more about history. To do this, you want them to have a Circle of History. Elicit from the students the idea that they can be responsible for their own learning with others and talk about some of the benefits that can happen in the Circle of History. For example, students with information—such as knowledge about historical figures—ask for time in the Circle of History and go to the circle to talk about what they know. Some students can request to join the circle to add information in a cooperative manner. Other students may want to sit at the edge of the circle and be neutral fact-finders to help their classmates resolve any particularly "sticky" discussion. Still others can suggest additional ways to research information and briefly sit in on the discussion that goes on in the circle.

Ask any two students who request time in the circle to give you a report about what went on so you can guide them to further inquiry. If needed, see History Master 6, "Heroes and Heroines," for several tales about historical heroes from different countries.

Activity #12: "Conflicts in Folktales"

Relying on Blackway's research, you can help students identify areas of conflict in folktales that are also areas of conflict for children today. History Master 7, "Conflicts Faced by Early People in Folktales," lists some of the tales that show these conflicts. After reading aloud a selected folktale that includes a conflict, invite the students to participate further and make a children's theater with the overhead. They can stage their own brief productions of their favorite tales. Ask them to draw, color, and cut out any figures they need and paste them on tongue depressors. For the actions and events, ask the students to look at different illustrations of the characters in a variety of conflict situations and then act out the conflicts with the figures and theater or dictate/write/draw responses to one or more of the following:

1. The character got really angry when _____
   _____.

2. For the character, happiness/peace was _____
   _____.

3. A time when the character was sad was when
   _____.

4. The character felt good when _____.

5. The character showed the conflict about autonomy (initiation, maturity, rivalry with siblings or others, separation, loss, self-esteem, withdrawal) when_____.

Have students replay the scenes with cutout shapes of contemporary figures.

Motifs in Tales Say Something

"Themes in folktales, obvious, though not stated explicitly, express the values of the people who created them and, pieced together, reflect their philosophy of life," writes Bernice Cullinan (1981), author of *Literature and the Child*. "They have been called 'primers' of the picture language of the soul." To introduce a folktale as "picture language" and as an expression of the values of the early people who created it, ask students to listen to a tale to determine something about the people who told the tale. The students, for instance, can listen to different folktales from different countries as well as *the same tale* from different cultures to determine what similarities people in parallel cultures had in common.

Activity #13: "Early People Had Similar Problems"

Students can search for similarities and differences in tales from different cultures to support the idea that people everywhere had similar problems, thoughts, and aspirations. As a way to introduce students to some motifs—the similar patterns in tales—read excerpts aloud from *Flying with the Eagle, Racing the Great Bear: Stories from Native North America* (Bridgewater, 1993, grade 5 and up) retold by Joseph Bruchac. Though the tales come from different Native Peoples, they have many of the same motifs (i.e., symbols, journey-and-return plots, transformations, magical forces and objects, identities who are helpers or hinderers, and magical places). Before the students begin their searches for tales with similar motifs, review some of the motifs with the letters M O T I F S to represent the different features the students might find: the letter *M* stands for *magical places* found in folktales; the letter *O* stands for magical *objects;* the letter *T* stands for magical *transformations* (shape changes) in the tales; the letter *I* stands for *identities* that help or hinder a character; the letter *F* stands for a force (a power); and the letter *S* stands for *symbols*.

With guidance, the students can determine any similarities of the motifs in the stories they read. Ask them to meet in small groups and discuss the following study statements to prove/disprove as they review motif features in folktales from different countries. Examples of study statements for different groups are:

> *Research Guide for Study Group #1*. Folktales from different countries can include magical places visited by the main character.
>
> *Research Guide for Study Group #2*. Folktales from different countries can include magical objects that help/hinder the main character.
>
> *Research Guide for Study Group #3*. Folktales from different countries can include magical transformations.
>
> *Research Guide for Study Group #4*. Folktales from different countries can include identities that can hinder or help the main character.
>
> *Research Guide for Study Group #5*. Folktales from different countries can include a force (power) that can help or hinder the main character.
>
> *Research Guide for Study Group #6*. Folktales from different countries can include symbols.

If titles of books are needed, lead students to some of the stories found on History Master 8, "Motifs in Folk Literature from Different Cultures." Ask each group to report back to the whole group on the tales that supported or did not support their research statement.

Tales of Ancient India, Mesopotamia, and Sumer

"Why did the Gilgamesh story have enough stature to last more than 5,000 years?" ask Glazer and Williams (1979). "Two characteristics seem significant. First, the hero is close to the gods; the heavens watched his deeds, and sometimes, intervened. Gilgamesh is similar to the figures in tall tales in that his dimensions are bigger than life. Second, with his high standing as king and favored son of the heavens, Gilgamesh is vulnerable." You may want to review this information with older students (grades 4 and older) as you introduce a study of people in the early civilizations in the Near East and India with *Gilgamesh*. Engage the students in selecting portions of the *Gilgamesh* legend, the oldest legend known to our world, to verify that Gilgamesh is similar to a figure in a tall tale and yet vulnerable. Ask them to select a brief part to present as a choral reading or a reader's *theater presentation*. *As* an example, you can introduce *Gilgamesh* (Knopf, 1984, grade 4 and up) by John Gardener and John Maier. If needed as background for the students, mention that the legend was written 3,000 years before the birth of Christ. Ask the students who know the Greek myths about Hercules, Jason, and Theseus if they can recognize any similarities in the tale.

Activity #14: "*Gilgamesh* from Mesopotamia"

After discussing *The Beginning of Cities* (Coward, 1968, grade 6 and up) by L. Weisgard, introduce a story about Gilgamesh who rules over the city of Uruk with *Gilgamesh the King* (Tundra, 1993, grades 4–6) retold by Ludmila Zeman. Show features of the art work from the Sumerian, Assyrian, and Babylonian people that are incorporated into the illustrations. Discuss the scene where the people ask for relief from their oppression, which appears in the figure of Enkidu, a man from the wilderness. To divert Enkidu, Gilgamesh sends a temple woman, Shambat, to lure the man to the city. Enkidu returns with her and engages Gilgamesh in combat. After Enkidu saves the king's life, however, the two become best friends. Discuss with students the rivalry that turns into friendship in the story and have them relate the action to experiences in their own lives or to experiences of book characters.

Early Families, Circa 4000 B.C.

To help students understand that families in all time periods share customs and traditions, and to point out that the customs and traditions may vary from time period to time period and group to group and location to location, read excerpts from O. Dunrea's *Skara Brae: The Story of a Prehistoric Village* (Holiday House, 1986, grades 4–6). Dunrea presents information about the people living on the Orkney Islands around 4,000 B.C., and the way the families developed a social, political, cultural, and religious life in their Neolithic "village of hilly dunes." His

discussion is documented by the excavation of a 4,000-year-old archaeological site.

Read aloud other books that relate to key ideas about families as a basic part of society. Engage students in exploring a family theme in international settings and the interdependence of family members wherever they live and in whatever historical period they lived. For selections about intergenerational issues, see History Master 9, "Intergenerational Relationships."

Activity #15: "Diverse Families"

Initiate a study of families in communities in different parts of the world and write on the board the phrase, "What I Want to Know." Ask students to brainstorm questions they have about people who lived in other places in this time period and write them under the heading. Rearrange the list into a visual graphic similar to Figure 3–4.

Engage students in reading, reporting, charting, and recording their findings as they explore sources about people, their families, and places around the world. Their reports and findings can be collected into a volume entitled *A Look-It-Up Book of Families Around the World in Early Times*.

Early Communities, Circa 4000 B.C.

"Understanding people and their relationships to each other and to their environments should not be limited by time boundaries," writes Elliot Seif (1977), author of *Teaching Significant Social Studies in the Elementary School*. "It is possible to study events in history in order to better understand others and to put one's life in perspective. It is possible to study 'change' over time in order to have a better perspective on one's own life as well as the lives of others in the past, present, and future." To assist students as they study the idea of change overtime, you can read aloud excerpts from books that give the big picture about some of the earliest communities—for instance, the community of Mesopotamia located between the Tigris and Euphrates Rivers and *Sumer in* the pre-Babylonia area are discussed in *The Earliest Cities* (Silver Burdett, 1987, grade 4 and up) by Jean-Michel Coblence. To give a specific picture, talk about the currency used in these ancient civilizations with the in-depth information in Joe Cribb's *Eyewitness Books: Money* (Knopf, 1990, grade 6 and up) and have students learn more about the "change" in currency over time.

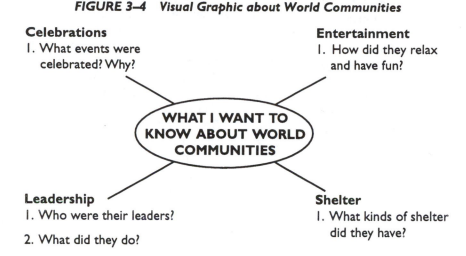

FIGURE 3–4   Visual Graphic about World Communities

Celebrations
1. What events were celebrated? Why?

Entertainment
1. How did they relax and have fun?

WHAT I WANT TO KNOW ABOUT WORLD COMMUNITIES

Leadership
1. Who were their leaders?
2. What did they do?

Shelter
1. What kinds of shelter did they have?

Activity #16: "Services in Early Communities"

With a world map, ask the students to identify the locations of Sumer and other early communities and tell what they know about them. Read aloud selected parts from *History Begins at Sumer: Thirty-Nine "Firsts" in Man's Recorded History* (University of Pennsylvania Press, 1982, grade 5 and up) by Samuel N. Kramer, and *Science in Ancient Mesopotamia* (Watts, 1988, grade 6 and up) by Carol Moss, to provide background information about the inventions and other interests in these early communities.

To evaluate life in Sumer, ask students to respond to such questions as: In spite of the "Thirty-Nine 'Firsts'" at Sumer, what's wrong with this early community from your point of view? What services for the people are missing? How could the Sumerians have made their community a better place to live? After discussion, engage the students in drawing pictures to show what a community service in Sumer could have been like if people had acted differently and provided improved services. For further extension of the topic, engage students in one or more of the following:

1. Display a book's illustrations and ask students to dictate/write the ideas shown in the drawings.
2. List the ideas on the board and ask the students to suggest conclusions about an ideal community in Sumer from the list.
3. Write the conclusions on the board and ask students to sketch additional ideas they now have.

Tell the students to make a double-collage that contrasts the early Sumer community (collage #1) with their ideas of an ideal community for Early Sumer (collage #2). Demonstrate how to make a simple double-collage by folding a large sheet of paper in half so the two collages are placed side by side.

4. Invite students to write and explain their art work on the back of the collages.
5. Later, with the whole group, ask students to display their double-collages and discuss the ideas shown in their drawings and written on the back.

Ancient Egypt: Time Travel

A historical time travel adventure is fanciful fiction and the author "creates another world for characters and readers, asking that readers believe this other world could and does exist within the framework of the book," states Rebecca J. Lukens, author of *A Critical Handbook of Children's Literature* (1982). An example of the "other world" as an historical world is found in *Cat in the Mirror* (Dell, 1978, grade 6 and up) by Mary Stolz, a story of a girl in ancient Egypt who becomes aware of another girl's existence in New York City 3,000 years later. To older students, read aloud selected parts from Stolz's story and elicit the names of places and people mentioned. Write the names on the board and invite the students to work with partners and search other references to determine if the items on the list are *real* places and people. Have the partners report back to the whole group to list real people's names on a chart and to locate any real places on a map or globe.

Activity #17: "Historical Time Travels"

To focus students' interest in historical time travel adventures, introduce *Cat in the Mirror* and a reading list of fanciful fiction books with historical settings such as those on the list on History Master 10, "Historical Time Travelers." As an option, the students can advance through time periods of history by reading several time-travel adventures in chronological sequence or reading one or two books to study a particular time period in depth. After reading a story about a time traveler with strong personal characteristics, invite each student to write reasons why he or she would (or would not) want the time traveler for a friend if the two of them had lived in the same time period.

Pyramid Tales

"The teacher and librarian should guide children to read not just the necessary reference and nonfiction titles but also other less-obvious literary genres," suggest Ammon and Weigard (1993). Additionally, Patricia Manning (1989), a children's librarian, recommends searching for books about history *everywhere* in the library book collection. So, before a trip to the library, suggest to students that they look for books about a particular topic in history on *any* shelf in the library's collection. As an example for the subject of Egypt, introduce the students to *You Can Be a Woman Egyptologist* (Cascade Press, 1993, grades 4–6) by Betsy M. Bryan and Judith L. Cohen. It is a discussion by an Egyptologist who tells students how she became interested in the profession, what work she does, and some of the discoveries she has made. Using a chart of the Dewey decimal numbers on a transparency to discuss the system of classification, you also can guide the students to poetry related to Egypt in Dewey's 800 classification; to books about art, music, and architecture of the times in the 700s; and to related technology in the 600s.

To foster more library research during a study about ancient Egypt, the students can be shown to the 300s section in the library and the books about mummies and burial customs in Egypt and other cultures. Examples of more useful books for older students in this section are *Mummy* (Knopf, 1991) by Jim Putnam, *Wrapped for Eternity: The Story of the Egyptian Mummy* (McGraw-Hill, 1974) by Mildred Mastin Pace, and *Tales of Ancient Egypt* (Penguin, 1972), a collection of Egyptian myths by Roger Lancelyn Green. In another section, the 400s, show the students the books about hieroglyphs—perhaps Joseph Scott's *Egyptian Hieroglyphs for Everyone* (Crowell, 1968). Then guide the students to the 700s section and to books about the pyramids with illustrations and text about how tons of stone were moved and shaped into the magnificent tombs that have stood for over 5,000 years.

Activity #18: "Life in Ancient Egypt"

To focus a discussion on life in ancient Egypt, elicit facts about what the students know about Egypt and record their ideas in a list on the board. For instance, *the students can offer* their ideas about pharaohs, pyramids, and the arts. Some may mention facts about jewelry, mummies, and picture writing, while others may talk about scientific achievements or the gods mentioned in Egyptian myths. Write the students' ideas on the board and demonstrate to them the way you can identify a topic from their ideas (e.g., words about wall paintings and statues can help you identify the topic of art). With the students, identify as many topics as their ideas will allow and list them. Use the overhead to show a transparency of an outline map of Egypt on butcher paper on the wall. Ask the students to write notes on the outline related to the topics as they do individual research. Then introduce a compare-contrast situation with a question such as: *Looking at the topics we listed, what are the differences and similarities between the topics in our country now and in Ancient Egypt?* If needed, distribute History Master 11, "Ancient Egypt." It has a list of related topics and references and can guide students in researching a topic.

CHAPTER FOUR

1200–500 B.C.

What was going on in 1200–500 B.C.?

Multicultural Perspectives

Philosophers in Athens, writers of tragedies, charioteers with their bronze helmets, and other people from all parts of the world can be combined in a unit about this time period. Students can investigate what life was like in Africa for kings, doctors, traders, and nomads as well as for those who lived in the port city of Carthage and in the ancient city of Meroe in the Kingdom of Kush. Some colorful related maps made by the students can show the early routes of the traders. The display boards can feature the people of ancient Asia, Australia, Europe, and Greece, and show such activities as Asian craftspeople making their wares, Greek athletes training for the Olympics and people trading in the different environments in Europe. Individual and small group inquiry can focus on:

- *China*. A student-created display can interest others in the subject of Chinese silk technology in 1000 B.C., when artisans began to raise silk worms, weave silk fabrics, and prohibit the export of silk, silkworms, and their knowledge about silk to other countries. Recently, a Vienna University team of chemists recently found a few strands of silk in the hair of an Egyptian female mummy (1069–945 B.C.), which raised a question and a history mystery students can ponder: If there was a prohibition on silk exports by China in this period, then how did silk threads reach Egypt in 945 B.C.? Gifts from royalty to royalty? Smugglers?
- *Greece*. The students can show some of the events that happened in Greece in the time period between the Trojan War and the Golden Age of Athens, and then gather data about what was going on in this same period among the Olmec people on Mexico's Gulf Coast.
- *Olmec People on the Gulf Coast*. The students can display some of the drawings from the *National Geographic Magazine* (Stuart, 1993) about the Olmec people (which means "rubber people" in Aztec), apparently Meso-America's first civilization in the rubber-producing area now Veracruz. It seems the Olmec people gradually progressed from a gathering of corn farmers who enjoyed shellfish, fish, turtles, and deer, to become important political and religious centers with carefully designed ritual centers, pyramids, plazas, platforms, tombs, ball courts, and pole-and-thatch houses. They had basalt and travertine workshops and craft areas where statues, jaguar masks, and special beads of ilmenite, a weighty lustrous ore, were made. Their hieroglyphs have been found on stones and some were early political posters about their leaders.

Drawings of families and their daily activities from various areas around the world and headings on the bulletin boards can guide the students to a study about systems and interactions of people who, like the Olmec, adjusted not only to their physical and social environment in this period but developed political and religious centers. To guide interested students to multicultural aspects of this time, Figure 4.1 includes perspectives of people of different heritages.

FIGURE 4–1 Children's Books about 1200–500 B.C

PERSPECTIVES FOR 1200–500 B.C.

African Heritage

Jupo, F. *Atu, The Silent One*. Holiday House, 1967. Depicts the life of Atu, an African boy, and the way his people, called the Bushmen, might have lived years ago. Fiction. Grade 4.

Metropolitan Museum of Art. *The Giant Book of the Mummy*. New York: Metropolitan Museum, 1991. This is two-foot-high book describes life in ancient Egypt circa 1000 B.C and the discovery of the tomb of Tutankhamen, the Boy King who ruled Egypt, and the treasure buried with him. Nonfiction. Grade 4.

Asian Heritage

Hoobler, D., & Hoobler, T. *Chinese Portraits*. Ill. by V. Bruck. Scholastic, 1990. Has brief portrayals of prominent Chinese individuals in chronological order beginning with the first emperor, Shi Huang Di, and other officials, artists, poets, and scientists. Biography. Grade 6 and up.

European Heritage

Humble, R. *The Travels of Marco Polo*. Ill. by R. Hook. Watts, 1990. Describes the world, its politics, and religions of Polo's time period and refers to the completion of his book, *Description of the World*, while a prisoner in Genoa. His book, also known as *Travels* (1299), became a source of knowledge about China and was based on his service to the great Khan, the Mongolian ruler (1167–1227). Includes time chart, glossary, and index. Nonfiction. Grades 4–6.

Lyttle, R. B. *Land Beyond the River: Europe in the Age of Migration*. Atheneum, 1986. Historical figures as Alfred the Great, Attila, Genghis Khan, and Mohammed are presented in this review from the second to the ninth centuries. Index. Nonfiction. Grade 4 and up.

Latino/Hispanic Heritage

Gemming, E. *Lost City in the Clouds: The Discovery of Machu Picchu*. Ill. by M. Eagle. Putnam, 1980. Tells about Hiram Bingham's archeological work at Machu Picchu. Nonfiction. Grade 7 and up.

Meyer, C., & Gallenkamp, C. *The Mystery of the Ancient Maya*. Atheneum, 1985. Portrays actions of early explorers and their discoveries. Nonfiction. Grade 7 and up.

Original Native American Heritage

Costable, E. D. *The Early People of Florida*. Ill. by author. Atheneum, 1992. Details the life of the indigenous people of the area now Florida from prehistoric times to 1845. Discusses arrival of the Spanish, French, and English, and the events that led to statehood. Nonfiction. Grades 4–5.

Female Image Heritage

Coolidge, O. *Men of Athens*. Houghton Mifflin, 1962. In contrast to the title, stories are included about women such as Aspasia, the gifted mistress of Pericles, Xanthippe, the complaining wife of Socrates, and others. Folk literature. Grade 6 and up.

Mediterranean Heritage

Sutcliff, R. *Black Ships Before Troy: The Story of the Iliad*. Ill. by A. Lee. Delacorte, 1993. This is a retelling of the violent Trojan War from its origin, with drawings of authentic uniforms, weapons, and ships. Grade 4 and up.

***FIGURE 4–1*   Continued**

Religious Minority Heritage

Eisler, C. *David's Songs: His Psalms and Their Story*. Ill. by J. Pinkney. Dial, 1992. Forty-two Psalms that have endured for over 2,000 years are from David, the young shepherd who became King of Israel. Nonfiction. All grades.

Kuskin, K. *Jerusalem, Shining Still*. Harper, 1987. Poetic telling of the 4,000-year-old tumultuous history of Jerusalem, a city holy to many people and the capital of King David in 1000 B.C. Later, in 586 B.C., Nebuchadnezzar besieges the city and takes slaves back to Babylonia. Jerusalem also is ruled by Alexander the Great (332 B.C.), by the Ptolemies, the Kings of Egypt, and Antiochus (168 B.C.). Still later, Jerusalem is ruled by the Greek rulers of Syria, the Romans (63 B.C.), and the Moslems (636 A.D.). In ensuing years, Jerusalem is conquered by the Tartars, Egyptians, and Turks, until 1917, when it is declared through the League of Nations (when Great Britain governs Palestine) that Palestine will become a Jewish country. Grade 4 and up.

Ancient Greece, Circa 1200 B.C.

"Myths represent societies' attempts to deal with the three most crucial mysteries of life: creation, the nature of life itself, and death," writes John Warren Stewig (1988), children's literature specialist. "Many myths provide accounts of the beginning of the world; others explain natural phenomena or prescribe desirable behaviors for members of a particular society; still others describe death and the afterlife." Indeed, it is the myths and their attempts to deal with the cycle of life that may make "a sound in the heart" for many of the students who study the western cultures of Ancient Greece and Rome. To students interested in myths related to the history of non-Western cultures, a familiar mythology may be found in *The Mythology of South America* (Morrow, 1988, grade 4 and up) by John Bierhorst, or *Many Lands, Many Lands, Many Stories: Asian Folktales from Children* (Tuttle, 1987, grade 4 and up) by David Conger, or *African Tales: Folklore of the Central African Republic* (Telcraft, 1992, grade 4 and up) illustrated by Rodney Wimer.

For the students interested in Western cultures, "the most familiar mythology outside the Judaic-Christian tradition is that of ancient Greece and Rome," writes David Russell (1991), instructor in languages and literature at Ferris University. Indeed, it seems that the daily lives of Americans are filled with references to the ancient Greeks and the heroes of that civilization. To show this, invite students to add to the following list their own references: Achilles tendon, Aires, Atlas, Herculon, January, Mercury, and Olympics.

Activity #19: "What Can a Journey-and-Return Pattern Tell Us?"

To reinforce not only what students know about the names from ancient Greece and Rome, but also what they can learn about history and human nature from some of the familiar myths of any culture, read aloud *Children of the Fox* (Farrar, 1978, grade 5 and up) by J. P. Walsh, a story of three young people who meet Themistokles, the Athenian leader. Godfrey (1980) maintains that only one pattern in the myths—a journey-and-return pattern—needs to be introduced to students in grade 4 and older. To do this, point out to students that a *journey-and-return pattern* is the pattern of a main character's journey to find something. In addition, the main character can (1) change something, (2) learn something, (3) prove themselves, and (4) defeat an adversary.

With the students, discuss a journey-and-return pattern in a myth such as *Theseus and the Minotaur* (Holiday House, 1988) by L. E. Fisher, and ask students what information they gained about the people (their human nature) and their culture (history) from the story. For other analyses, you can introduce single versions of myths such as *Two Queens of Heaven: Aphrodite and Demeter* (Viking, 1974) by D. Gates, *Prometheus and the Story of Fire* (Troll, 1983) by I. M. Richardson, and *The Adventures of Hercules* (Troll, 1983) by I. M. Richardson.

Ask the students to identify the characters (or the combination of characters such as seven sisters) as either heroines or heroes who are helpers (helpers can be parents, animals, or supernaturals) or characters who are hinderers (hinderers can be opponents such as nature, spirits, or monsters). Further, ask the students to identify the character's goal and what was achieved. Then review the journey-and-return pattern again by writing the students' ideas about the story in a graphic web on the board so they can see the important features in the pattern in Figure 4–2.

Activity #20: "Agree or Disagree"

Ask students to agree or disagree with the following statement: Myths and epics of different cultural groups have similar "journey-and-return" patterns. If needed, distribute History Master 12, "Journey-and-Return Stories," as a reading aid to help the students locate some classical Greek and Roman myths, Norse stories, or other hero and heroine tales to read before they agree or disagree. Additionally, a variety of myths with a journey-and-return pattern is available for students in such collections as *Myths of Greece and Rome* (Penguin, 1981, grades 6–8) by T. Bullfinch and *The Olympians: Great Gods and Goddesses of Ancient Greece* (Holiday, 1984, grades 6–8) by L. E. Fisher.

Quests of Early People

"Myths are stories with a special status," states Perry Nodelman (1992), author of *The Pleasures of Children's Literature.* "For those who believe in them, they are true—not symbolically true or allegorically true, but absolutely true, a factual accounting of the nature of the world as it is. If we accept their truth, furthermore, myths tell us how to live; what to believe and how to behave." Realizing that myths—people's stories with special status—can be another enriching dimension in historical study, you can help students further identify the concept of the

journey-and-return pattern as a *quest* that is found in stories of different cultures—by pointing out that the quest is a literary feature used often by writers. To do this, Cohen (1985) emphasizes that a quest be subdivided into four major components that will help the students identify its characteristics: the problem, the struggle, the realization, and a final peace or truth. Cohen points out that the problem(s) that main characters face often are *external* ones (with family, peers, and communities) that become *internal* obsessions and begin the quests.

Activity #21: "Journey-and-Return Patterns as Quests"

After discussing examples of quests in stories, small groups of three or four students can review a character's struggles during a quest—especially the struggles that involve the character's understanding of what is needed to deal with his or her problem(s). Additionally, encourage the students to give their views about the *understanding* that occurs when the character's struggle wanes and the character's inner strength (realization) emerges. Point out that this understanding/realization often leads the character to a final sense of peace or truth that ends the quest. Ask students to give examples of how this happened in any myths they have read. Further, ask them to tell what they learned about the people in the culture where the story originated, since respected cultural myths are often believed to be truth by the people who tell them and hear them.

Activity #22: "Problems of Characters"

For a study of the similar problems of characters then and now, introduce any one of the 12 tales that have a modern-day setting in *Bury My Bones But Keep My Words: African Tales for Retelling* (Holt, 1992, grades 4–7) by Tony Fairman. In the tales, there are fictional children who interrupt the story and allow the author to contrast the folktale world with today's modern world. Further, Fairman has invented some songs that he suggests be sung to the tunes of popular American and British children's songs that help identify the specific and diverse cultures from which the retold folktales originate. This serves as another way to acquaint the students with music as a feature of the civilizations of different cultures.

Engage the students in comparing the quest problems of the main characters in historical fiction with the problems faced today by main characters in contemporary realism. Have them record their comparisons on a data sheet. (See History Master 13, "Then and Now." This reproducible has suggestions

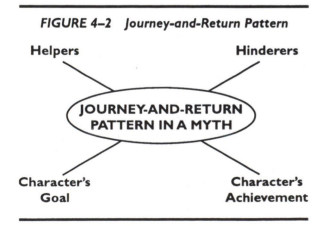

FIGURE 4–2 *Journey-and-Return Pattern*

Helpers   Hinderers

JOURNEY-AND-RETURN PATTERN IN A MYTH

Character's Goal   Character's Achievement

for the study of a main character on a quest and includes a chart for taking notes about what is read.)

People in Tales with Problems

"Among the many purposes of folktales," states Robert J. Whitehead (1984) author of *A Guide to Selecting Books for Children*, "is the purpose of helping children better understand the origins and values of the various cultures of the world, including their own; simplifying moral questions, as the stories sort out the good and bad; and allowing children to identify vicariously with heroes." To help students better understand these purposes in the classroom, engage students in solving a problem in a folktale from a selected culture. Examples of related activities follow.

Activity #23: "Solving a Folktale Problem"

With the students in a total group, point out that problems and puzzles of all kinds in folktales have intrigued people in all parts of the world for as long as anyone can remember. To demonstrate, read aloud a puzzle tale from *Standing on One Foot: Puzzle Stories and Wisdom Tales from the Jewish Tradition* (Holt, 1993 grade 4). Just before revealing the outcome of the tale, pause and sum up the dilemma. Ask the students what they would do if they were in the same situation. With the students, draw stick-picture diagrams and scenes on the board or on an overhead transparency to work out a solution to the story's problem. Encourage them to suggest more than one way to solve the problem.

Activity #24: "A Story to Solve"

Read aloud a tale from *Stories to Solve: Folktales from Around the World* (Greenwillow, 1985, grade 5 and up) by George Shannon. Distribute to each small group of students a folktale that includes a problem to solve. When each group has received a folktale with a mystery or a problem for the character to solve, leave it up to the members of the group to read it, discuss the problem, and suggest ways the character can solve the problem. Next, read aloud and discuss how the problem was solved in the story. As examples for the students, the following folktales from different cultures can be selected from Shannon's *Stories to Solve*:

- *African Heritage:* "Crossing the River" (African Hausa)
- *Asian Heritage:* "One Word Solves a Mystery" (China)
- *European Heritage:* "Dividing the Horses" (Jewish folklore)

Just in case some of the students can't find the clue(s) to solve the problem, an answer is available at the end of each story in Shannon's book. With the whole group together, discuss the problem in the story read by the small groups, the way it was solved, and what the students learned about the nature of the people and their culture that came from the story they read and discussed.

Stories of Health Care Awareness

"Children need books that present what is real," advocates Iris Tiedt (1979) in her book *Exploring Books with Children*. "They need stories about people interacting with all the stress and emotion that accompanies human relations. They need to read about children like themselves who are coping with situations that are real to a child growing up." Related to books that present what is real to students, early civilizations made contributions to the health care of their people and cured their illnesses just as America's society today is focusing on increased health care for its citizens. Children's books, such as those on History Master 14, "Stories about Health Care," document the contributions.

Activity #25: "Health Care"

If you think it will be difficult for some students to collect information themselves about the topic of health care awareness because suitable resources are not readily available, you can guide them toward analyzing and developing ideas from resources you give them rather than ask them to spend their time searching for information that is difficult to find. For interested students researching this topic, display *Medicine: A Treasury of Art and Literature* (Museum of Fine Arts, Boston, 1989) to provide examples of art related to medicine along with writings from Hippocrates, Chinese healers, contemporary healers, and *From the Earth to Beyond the Sky: Native American Medicine* (Houghton Mifflin, 1993, grades 5–8) by E. Wolfson. Wolfson's book is an overview of the practices of many Native People that include plant medicine, the training of a medicine man, ceremonies, and sacred objects.

A study of health care awareness can be introduced by reading aloud Barbara Esbensen's *Ladder to the Sky* (Little, Brown, 1989, grades 4–5) and then distributing a Book Map of Health Care for a discussion. A book map contains entries of children's literature that is put together by a teacher or a group of students. Reading the annotated book map, the students are asked to draw some conclusions about health care awareness and then discuss some of the attitudes and values of the people of a particular time period based on the annotations they have read about the books on the book map. History Master 14, "Stories about Health Care," also supports the topic of health care awareness and lists selected stories set in different time periods. For example, contemporary times are represented by *The Fire Curse and Other True Medical Mysteries* (Walker, 1994, grades 4–6) by David Lee Drotar. In the book, medical mysteries and documented occurrences (including photographs) from human combustion to premature aging are explored, and related theories are developed to explain what happened.

CHAPTER FIVE

500-1 B.C.

What was going on in 500-1 B.C.?

Multicultural Perspectives

By studying this period, students have the opportunity to move outside themselves and explore the lives and thoughts of different people. Such a study allows students to see faces and places they have never seen and to think about ideas they may not have reflected on before. For example, the students can:

- • Gather data about what life was like for Rome's leaders, invaders, and the recorders of Biblical stories. Colorful student-made display boards in the class can feature the people on different continents as well as the environments in which families lived, ways they traveled, and some colorful maps depicting the routes of on-the-go trade merchants.
- Read about the philosophers in Asia and retell the stories of storytellers in Africa and Australia.
- Research the work of building engineers in Asia, Central America, and Egypt.
- Sketch scenes of the ancient people in the area now Mexico and of Chichen Itza and Tulum with its temples, plazas, trades, and marketplaces. Scenes from *Maya Dioramas to Cut and Assemble* (Dover, 1989) by M. Kalmenoff can also be displayed. Gathering information about Chichen Itza, Mexico's great City of the Gods, and its people can lead to a larger thematic unit about "Great Constructions" throughout different periods of history.

If students need additional references, suggest some of the perspectives of the people for this time period, 500–1 B.C., found in Figure 5–1.

Unselfishness, Compassion, and Nonviolence, Circa 500 B.C.

"Biographies, historical fiction, and fiction set in specific various regions of the United States and other countries add much to students' understanding of history and geography," states Iris Tiedt (1979). "Good books can serve to make people who lived in earlier times seem real, to come alive for children reading about them today." To help make this time period come alive through books, guide the students, in small research groups, to different books to collect quotes from their reading that support the similarity of a selected value across different cultures and time periods. For instance:

- Students interested in values introduced in India around 500 B.C. by Siddhartha Guatama, the Buddha, will find that Guatama's life and teachings included the values of unselfishness, compassion for the suffering of others, tolerance and nonviolence, as well as prohibition of lying, stealing, killing, finding fault with others, and gossiping.
- Students interested in values in later India can gather data about Asoka, a great philosopher-king, who unified almost all of the country and established Buddhism as the state religion. Doing this, Asoka also renounced violence as a national policy; this policy can be compared to our government's policy against violence today.

While engaged in a comparison study of literature related to this time period, students will be able to find similar values in stories about people of other cultures (see Figure 5–2), and if interested, in other time periods.

FIGURE 5–1 Children's Books about 500–1 B.C.

PERSPECTIVES FOR 500–1 B.C.

African Heritage

Macaulay, D. *Pyramid*. Ill. by author. Houghton Mifflin, 1975. Discusses and illustrates the process of building an ancient pyramid, a "manmade mountain of stone," that protects the burial chamber of a pharaoh. Includes black-and-white detailed drawings of workers, their tools, and steps in the construction process. Nonfiction. Grade 6 and up.

Asian Heritage

Ashabranner, B. *Land of Yesterday, Land of Tomorrow: Discovering Chinese Central Asia*. Cobblehill/Dutton, 1992. Discusses the Silk Road trade and the accompanying politics. Nonfiction. Grades 4–7.

Confucius. *The Wisdom of Confucius*. American Classical College Press, 1982. Collection of sayings attributed to Kong Fuzi, a great Chinese philosopher and teacher. Nonfiction. Grade 6 and up.

Fisher, L. E. *The Great Wall of China*. Ill. by author. Macmillan, 1986. This is a subsequent history of the Great Wall, with facts about the political climates of the times and the magnitude of its construction. The Great Wall of China was built approximately in 221–207 B.C. during the Ch'in Dynasty, from which the name China was taken. Nonfiction. Grades 4–8.

European Heritage

Hernandez, X., & Comes, P. *Barmi: A Mediterranean City Through the Ages*. Ill. by J. Ballonga. Trans. by K. Leverich. Houghton Mifflin, 1990. This details the way a city in southern Europe in the fourth century B.C. would have evolved as told through the growth of a fictional city named Barmi. Grades 5–7.

Corbishleyk, M. *The Ancient World*. Peter Bedrick Books, 1992. Describes chronological order from the start of the ancient period to the end of the Roman empire and gives an overview of events in the world during this time period. Nonfiction. Grades 5–8.

MacDonald, F. *A Roman Fort*. Peter Bedrick, 1993. Shows the construction of a Roman fort and its use between 50 B.C.–A.D. 200. Includes drawings and diagrams and cutaways of the inside and outside of the buildings. Shows the living conditions of the soldiers and the weapons they used to defend the fort. Includes a glossary of English words derived from Latin. Nonfiction. Grades 4–8.

Moessinger, P. *Socrates*. Creative Education, 1994. This is a fictional letter written by Socrates from prison to his sons before his death (399 B.C.) It explains his view of life and his philosophy. Grades 5–8.

Latino/Hispanic Heritage

de Trivino, E. B. *Here Is Mexico*. Farrar, Straus & Giroux, 1980. Discusses pre-Columbian history, the colonial period, revolution, geography, arts and economics. Nonfiction. Grades 4–6.

Wood, T. *The Aztecs*. Viking, 1992. Describes ancient Aztec civilization from the beginning of the first civilization in Mexico to the vast Aztec Empire. Highlights the palace of Montezuma, the Great Temple of Tenochtitlan, a typical Aztec house, and the temple of the Aztec Knights. Nonfiction. Grades 4–6.

Original Native American Heritage

Oliphant, M. *The Earliest Civilization*. Facts on File, 1992. Explains human evolution, early farmers and settlers, the rise of early empires, and ends circa 200 B.C. Includes time lines, maps, and diagrams. Nonfiction. Grades 4–7.

FIGURE 5–1 Continued

Differently Abled Heritage

Sutcliff, R. *Warrior Scarlet*. Oxford, 1958. In the Bronze Age, it was believed that Drem, who had one good arm, would never become a warrior. However, he was determined to wear the warrior's scarlet cloak that would tell others he was a man of his people. Fiction. Grade 6 and up.

Female Image Heritage

Stanley, D., & Vennema, P. *Cleopatra*. Ill. by D. Stanley. Morrow, 1994. Portrays Cleopatra (69–30 B.C.) as an intelligent, personable, warm, and politically astute leader who first married her brother Ptolemy XIII and later attracted Caesar and Mark Anthony. Anecdotes from the Greek historian, Plutarch, pronunciation guide, and bibliography are included. Biography. Grades 4–6.

Walsh, J. P. *Crossing to Salamis*. Heinemann, 1977. This story tells of a family's hasty departure from Athens in 479 B.C. to escape the invading Persians. A young girl, Aster, her mother, a friend, and a servant escape to Salamis. Fiction. Grade 6 and up.

Religious Minority Heritage

Miller, L. *The Black Hat Dances: Two Buddhist Boys in the Himalayas*. Putnam, 1987. In Sikkim, a boy novice in a monastery lives a lifestyle that contrasts sharply with the son of a poor farmer. Fiction. Grade 6 and up.

Van de Wetering, J. *Little Owl: An Eightfold Buddhist Admonition*. Houghton Mifflin, 1978. Stories about animal characters introduce aspects of the Buddhist religion for children. Each of the eight chapters emphasizes one aspect, such as "Right Insight" or "Right Talking." Fiction. Grade 4.

FIGURE 5–2 Stories with Values of Early People

Brown, M. *Once a Mouse*. Ill. by author. Scribners, 1961. A fable from India about a mouse who wanted to be a larger animal. Folk Literature. Grades 4–5.

De La Mare, Walter. *The Turnip*. Ill. by Kevin Hawkes. Godine, 1992. A generous man prospers and his greedy brother does not. Folk Literature. Grades 4–5.

De Paola, T. *The Legend of the Bluebonnet*. Putnam, 1983. Unselfish actions of a young girl are rewarded in a Comanche legend. Folk Literature. Grade 4.

De Roin, N. *Jataka Tales: Fables from the Buddha*. Houghton Mifflin, 1975. Thirty fables from India teach a moral lesson and include Buddha as a noble example. Folk Literature. Grades 4–5.

Gray, J. A. B. *East Indian Tales and Legends*. Oxford, 1989. This is a collection of tales, fables, and the epic, the *Ramayana*. Folk literature. Grade 4 and up.

The Value of Friends. Ill. by E. Meller. Dharma Pub. Co., 1986. A Buddhist tale from the *Jataka Tales*. Folk Literature. Grade 4.

Williams, J. *Everyone Knows What a Dragon Looks Like*. Macmillan, 1976. Features of the story are similar to Taoist principles. Folk Literature. Grade 4.

Activity #26: "Values"

In a class meeting, challenge students to live one day at school according to the values of being unselfish, showing compassion for the suffering of others, being tolerant and nonviolent, avoiding lying, stealing, and finding fault with others, and gossiping. At the end of the day, have students meet again to self-evaluate and determine how they did and what effect, if any, following the values had on their lives during the day.

Activity #27: "Values of Buddhist Children"

Since Asoka's time, the values of unselfishness, compassion for suffering, and nonviolence have been accepted by various people in different cultures in different time periods, and several children's books verify this. To broaden students' perspectives about this historical feature, the students may begin with the tales from the Buddhist monks in Cambodia that portray the teachings of Buddha in *Cambodian Folk Tales from the Gatiloke* (Tuttle, 1987, grades 4–7), a collection edited by Muriel Carrison. Additionally, read a companion book that will add to their perspectives, *The Cat Who Went to Heaven* (Macmillan, 1930, grades 4–6) by Elizabeth Coatsworth. The story portrays the compassion for all creatures in the teachings of Buddhism. If other books are needed, suggest some of the entries listed on History Master 15, "Values of People in Early India and Other Cultures in Different Time Periods." Ask the students to report what they found after reading the stories they selected and invite them to tell *why* they think compassion and the other values have been respected by people in different cultures across time periods.

Ancient Mexico, 100 B.C.

To direct the students' attention on historical evidence of an ancient culture in the 7,000-foot-high plains of central Mexico that grew from 100 B.C., thrived, and then suddenly died about 750 A.D., show the Great Temple of Tenochtitlan in *The Aztecs* (Viking, 1993, grades 4–6) by T. Wood. The name, meaning City of the Gods, was given to the culture's pyramid and temple ruins by the Aztecs. Recent evidence indicates that the population was as large as Athens in this time period (150,000) and covered an area as large as ancient Rome (Kay, 1993). Several features of this early culture, however, are incomplete and are considered "mysteries"

by archaeologists. Ask students to locate the high plains in Central Mexico on a map and find out what the students can determine about the region of this early culture from the map's legends and symbols. Ask them to search for reference material about early Mexico and browse, read, or scan pages before they make their predictions on reasons why such a thriving culture might have suddenly died out.

Activity #28: "Mysteries of an Early Culture"

Since several features of this early culture are considered unsolved mysteries by archaeologists, ask students to bring the reference material they found to work with partners and predict (guess, hypothesize) about any or all of the following:

"What Can You Hypothesize…"

1. About the lives of the early residents on the high plains of central Mexico? Why do you think this way?

2. About what the residents called themselves?

3. About what the residents called the city?

4. About the reasons the Aztecs called the place the City of the Gods?

5. About the language(s) the residents spoke?

6. About the culture of the residents? (Point out that the artifacts and relics found indicate the culture resembled *neither* the culture of the Aztecs nor the Mayans.)

7. About what finally happened to the residents in this great urban city for it to suddenly die out around 750 B.C.? (Evidence indicates the city did *not* die out because of disease, drought, famine, or slow disintegration of the area.)

8. About the meaning of the massive decorations on the residents' temples and pyramids? (Consider these decorations: (a) a serpent's head, (b) a basalt skull with an open mouth and spaced teeth, (c) a carved mask that shows facial muscles tense with anger, (d) a mask with a smile, (e) a mask with flower patterns on its cheeks, and (f) a mask that shows an open mouth and open eyes to display surprise.)

9. About the importance or value of the residents' small pottery figurines? (What might be the value of (a) a pottery figure who sits on the ground and touches its toes and (b) a figure who looks as if its hair is in curlers.)

Ancient Briton, 100 B.C.

"To accept then, a biography for children as simply the life story of a famous personage is somewhat naive," states Dewy Woods Chambers (1971), author of *Children's Literature in the Curriculum.* "We need to ask ourselves what the author intended to say as he [she] told the life story. What large truth does the biography offer?" Chambers goes on to point out that a biography can do the following things for students as they study history: (1) give the story of a people and a social movement in history, (2) reflect cultural evolution, (3) personalize a cause, (4) give meaning to faith, (5) give body to an idea, (6) give motion to facts, (7) mirror the personalities of great people in history, and (8) reflect a way of life.

Moore (1985) writes that errors and inaccuracies in biographies seem to "reflect a potentially dangerous attitude held by authors, editors, and publishers: that it's OK to make mistakes." Indeed, as you and the students examine biographies carefully, you both may find omissions, inaccuracies, or dialogue in a biography that are "too fictionalized." Instead of excusing errors and inaccuracies in biog-raphies, you can invite the students to write to publishers, asking them to account for books the students found in their topic of study that fail to "measure up" on a point or two.

Activity #29: "Biographies That Measure Up"

As part of an action to stamp out mistakes they find in biographies, students can take the role of book reviewers and select some facts found in a juvenile biography and check the facts at that time against other data sources. Further, they can examine the books on a regular basis (perhaps every Friday afternoon) and cross-check certain facts by providing documentation from magazines, newspaper articles, pamphlets, or photocopies of pertinent information from encyclopedias and almanacs. Figures for a biographical study for the "Top Five Newsmakers" in this time period include:

Confucius	Socrates
Montezuma	Cleopatra
Buddha	

CHAPTER SIX

A.D. 1–1399

What was going on from the first century through the fourteenth century?

Multicultural Perspectives

"Reading historical fiction provides the experience of living somewhere else, with strangers, smelling exotic foods over wood fires, seeing flashes of color in costume and personality," state Glazer and Williams (1979). "These are alien sensations. Sampling alien worlds is one value of historical fiction. Another value is the readers' discovery during the exploration that there are similarities behind characters populating historical fiction and characters we all live with—and are—today. They are not strangers after all." Related to this point of view, Egan (1983, 1989) suggests that reading stories with characters similar to us and an emphasis on the way people responded to historical events can be the beginning of historical understanding for students (see Figure 6–1).

A unit about pre-Columbian settlements and other people in this time period between the first and fourteenth centuries can offer possibilities of getting

FIGURE 6–1   Children's Books about A.D. 1–1399

PERSPECTIVES FOR 1–1399

African Heritage

Hamilton, V. *The Time-Ago Tales of Jadhu*. Ill. N. Hogrogian. Macmillan, 1969. Has tales about a powerful mischief maker. Folk literature. Grade 5 and up.

Kurtz, J. *Fire on the Mountain*. Ill. by E. B. Lewis. Folktale from Ethiopia about Alemayu, a shepherd, who accepts a challenge from his sister's rich employer to spend a night alone on a mountain without a fire and wearing minimal clothing. He survives by concentrating on a shepherd's fire he sees on a nearby mountain. Folk literature. Grade 4.

Asian Heritage

Lamb, H. *Genghis Khan and the Mongol Horde*. Ill. by E. Fax. Repr., 1954. Linnet, 1990. Tells life of the successful military leader Genghis Khan (1167–1227) and his boyhood on the plains of the Yakka Mongols, his title of chief of his tribe at age 13, and his old age and death. His accomplishments led him to claim vast territories in the East that included northern China, Korea, Mongolia, Siberia, Turkestan, Afghanistan, and the former Soviet Union. His grandson was Kublai Khan, who was described by Marco Polo in *Travels*. Nonfiction. Grade 5 and up.

FIGURE 6–1 Continued

San Souci, R. D. *The Samurai's Daughter.* Ill. by S. T. Johnson. Dial, 1992. In Ancient Japan, Tokyo, the daughter of a noble Samurai, is trained in the traits of courage, discipline, and endurance. When her father is banished to the Oki Islands, she starts the long, dangerous journey to join him. Historical Fiction. Grades 4–5.

Latino/Hispanic Heritage

Arnold, C. *City of the Gods: Mexico's Ancient City of Teotihuacan.* Ill. by R. Hewett. Clarion, 1994. Introduces cultural and social history of ancient Teotihuacan, a city that influenced other Mexican and Central American people. Includes full-color photographs. Nonfiction. Grades 4–6.

Greger, C. S., reteller. *The Fifth and Final Sun: An ancient Aztec Myth of the Sun's Origin.* Houghton Mifflin, 1994. This is a creation myth where the first four suns are destroyed by jealous gods but the fifth sun is created through an act of sacrifice. Humankind now lives in the age of the Fifth Sun. Folk literature. Grade 4.

Original Native American Heritage

Carrick, C. *Whaling Days.* Ill. by D. Frampton. Clarion, 1993. Depicts development of whaling, including Native American hunters, and discusses modern whaling methods and pleads for the preservation of whales. Nonfiction. Grades 4–6.

Highwater, J. *Anpao: An American Indian Odyssey.* Lippincott, 1972. A Blackfoot legend of Scarface and Native American life in North America. Folk Literature. Grade 6 and up.

Young, R., & Young, J. Dockery, editors. *Race with Buffalo: And Other Native American Stories for Young Readers.* Ill. by W. E. Hall. August House, 1994. Over 30 tales grouped thematically as to ancient times, humor, magical beasts, spirit world, trickster tales, "Why" tales, and young heroes. Folk literature. Grade 4 and up.

European Heritage

Bernhard, E.. reteller. *The Girl Who Wanted to Hunt: A Siberian Tale.* Ill. by D. Gernhard. Holiday, 1994. When Black Death kills Anga's mother, her father takes a new wife to teach Anga womanly skills. In the Amar River region of Siberia, Anga wants only to be a hunter like her father and eventually her father's magical carvings allow her to escape her situation. Folk literature. Grade 4.

Bulla, C. *Viking Adventure.* Ill. by D. Gorsline. Crowell, 1963. Young Sigurd joins a ship's crew and sails to verify Ericson's discovery of Vineland. Fiction. Grades 5–7.

Dillon, E. *Rome Under the Emperors.* Thomas Nelson, 1974. Portrays life in Rome in 110 A.D. and portrays the lives of four boys of the times. Fiction. Grade 6 and up.

Haugaard, E. C. *Hakon of Rogen's Saga.* Ill. by L. & D. Dillion. Houghton Mifflin, 1963. When Hakon's island home is invaded, he flees until he can regain his birthright. Fiction. Grades 5–6.

Pushkin, A. *The Fisherman and the Goldfish.* Ill. by V. Konashevich. Trans. by P. Tempest. Moscow Progress Publishers, n.d. Ask students who are familiar with "The Fisherman and His Wife" to ascertain the similarities with this Russian version of the old man who asked a goldfish for favors. Folk literature. Grade 4 and up.

Pushkin, A. *The Tale of the Dead Princess and the Seven Knights.* Ill. by V. Konashevich. Trans. by P. Tempest. Moscow Progress Publishers, n.d. Ask students who are familiar with "Snow White and the Seven Dwarfs" to ascertain the similarities with this Russian version of the Tsarita's jealousy over the Tsar's young beautiful daughter. Folk literature. Grade 4 and up.

continued

FIGURE 6–1   Continued

Sutcliff, R. *Blood Feud*. Dutton, 1976. Jesstyn, an English boy, has to wear the detested thrall ring of a Viking slave. Later, he discovers that his Viking master is good and becomes a friend. Fiction. Grade 6 and up.

Differently Abled Heritage

de Angeli, M. *The Door in the Wall*. Doubleday, 1949. Robin, an English lord's crippled son, learns to accept his situation and becomes a hero. Fiction. Grade 6 and up.

Female Image Heritage

Brooks, P. S. *Queen Eleanor: Independent Spirit of the Medieval World*. Lippincott, 1983. Portrays the life of Eleanor of Aquitane and the politics she faced as a queen in the twelfth century. Biography. Grade 6 and up.

San Souci, R. *Young Guinevere*. Doubleday, 1993. Portrays Guinevere before she married Arthur. She turns to Arthur for help when her father's castle is under attack. Biography. Grade 5 and up.

Religious Minority Heritage

The Irish: A Treasury of Art and Literature. Museum of Fine Arts, Boston, 1989. Provides overview of Irish culture that includes writings from the Celtic sacred texts and reviews the centuries of foreign invasion, famine, and civil war. Nonfiction. Grade 8 and up.

Speare, E. G. *The Bronze Bow*. Houghton Mifflin, 1961. In land now Israel, Daniel Bar Jamin meets Simon's friend, Jesus, during a time of war against the harsh Romans and wants to avenge his parents' deaths. He learns the password phrase for Israel's liberating army as it fights against the Romans: "He trains my hands for war, so that my arms can bend a bow of bronze." Fiction. Grade 7 and up.

---

acquainted with the lifestyles of such people as Chinese Emperors, people in communes, Charlemagne, and religious monks. Children's literature also presents Maya leaders, Aztec warriors, and the native people and their leaders in the Americas. For students interested in the perspectives on Figure 6–1, guide them to several of the books so they can reflect on the way the perspectives are portrayed for this time period.

A.D. 1–99: Life in the First Century

"Children's literature is certainly one of the better ways to provide this [emotional] dimension," writes Dewey Woods Chambers (1976). "Emotional identification becomes highly possible when a good story is provided, be it realistic or historic fiction, with its setting in the time and place of the social studies unit." Related to this, you can provide an emotional dimension of the times through independent reading for older students about the lives of the people in the Iceni tribe in Early Britain (about 62

A.D.)—they revolted against early Roman Invaders—with Rosemary Sutcliff's *Song for a Dark Queen* (Crowell, 1978, grade 7 and up). The novel focuses on the dilemmas faced by Boudicca, the legendary Iceni queen. In a one-to-one student/teacher conference, discuss any problem of the past found in the novel that could be a current problem for people today. Would the method(s) used to solve the problem in the novel work today? Why or why not?

Activity #30: "People in the First Century"

After a student has read Sutcliff's novel independently, schedule a one-to-one conference and begin with a discussion of whether it is right to fight "if you think something is wrong." Ask the student to discuss his or her point of view about whether the early Romans were right/not right to invade the Iceni people in early Britain. After listening to excerpts from Sutcliff's story, ask the student to recall information about this early battle and write brief paragraphs in which he or she takes a position about the Roman invasion.

A.D. 100–199: Life in the Second Century

"For students, historic fiction may not be immediately appealing because it is not *now*," states John Warren Stewig (1988). "Children live in the present and more readily respond to books of contemporary realism. When first introducing historic fiction to students, teachers need to find books that speak clearly and compelling of problems that could be current ones but happen to arise in other times." Certainly, some writers of historical fiction do write about problems that could be current ones and can develop within students an awareness of the past, an appreciation for history, and a feeling of indebtedness toward people of the past. Reading these accounts, the girls and boys may begin to value and appreciate the contributions of people before their own times and realize that they also have obligations to future generations.

Historical fiction, exemplified by Stephen Trimble's *The Village of Blue Stone* (Macmillan, 1990) is an excellent genre to develop students' interest in history and begin an appreciation for the contributions of people before their own times. In Trimble's story, a fictionalized Anasazi village called the Village of Blue Stone is named after the turquoise stones found nearby. In the book, Trimble tells about the villagers, their clothing, and the customs and beliefs true to what could have happened. His narrative is based on the current research of artifacts and historical data. Further, the lives of the people in early Britain can be compared with what was going on in other areas of the world. If literature sources are needed, suggest some of the books listed on History Master 16, "Life in the First Century."

Additionally, the book shows one year in the village and includes codes of behavior and the rituals of the people living there. In the illustrations, the structure of the village, the work, and the way pottery was made are shown. Additionally, the author's notes mention the scientific events that correlate with the fictional story and include a list of Native American ruins to visit in Colorado, Arizona, New Mexico, and Utah. Charts, maps, a glossary, and index are included and are useful reference tools for the students' reports as they reflect on the contributions made by the Blue Stone villagers before the students' contemporary times.

Activity #31: "Contributions"

After listening to excerpts from Trimble's *The Village of the Blue Stone*, ask the students to suggest problems the people of the village could have had that might be similar to a problem today and any

contributions they made to improve their lives. Write the heading "Contributions from the Past" on the board and record the students' ideas. Elicit comments from the students about the contributions that Native Americans from the past have made and write the contributions on the board. Ask the students to make predictions (guesses, hunches) about the way that contributions from the past could indicate an obligation to a future generation. Write the heading "Obligations to Future Generations" on the board and record the students' ideas. Ask the students to write the two lists in their history journals and add their own individual ideas to the lists.

Contributions from Past Generations	*Obligations to Future Generations*
1.	
2.	

A.D. 200–299: Life in the Third Century

"At its best, historical fiction demands that the reader do some imaginary traveling to a different place and time," explain Glazer and Williams (1979). "Sometimes it will put readers on horseback, cantering through the green forests of England. Sometimes it will carry them to the pitching deck of a Viking ship.... Like any form of travel, historical fiction demands adjustment to new surroundings and strange faces. Like travel, it can lead to new understandings about similarities and differences between people." To guide students to the similarities and differences of people and their problems of this time period, read selections from *The Vikings* (Macmillan, 1992, grade 5 and up) by Hazel Mary Martell that portray the "facts" of the times. In her book, Martell describes the lifestyle of the Vikings, their clothing, families, farms, feasts, government, and society in an early settlement called Jorvik near the area now York, England. Students can locate this area on a world map. Ask students to get information from the map's legend and symbols and determine the geographical features of Jorvik and the nearby area. Ask them to determine what features would be reasons why the Vikings would settle there.

Activity #32: "Schematic Map and Research Journal"

Related to the study of the Vikings, ask the members of the group to make a schematic map on the board to show the different areas of research they are working on and then discuss any relationships between the areas being studied. As each topic is written on the map, invite the students to relate information they have discovered about their topics. Then ask them to try to pull the information together in a "serendipity." This accumulating narrative might feature a mythical character such as one named "the raiding, trading Viking." They may begin an ongoing "sense or nonsense" narrative that weaves in all of the research topics that the girls and boys are studying with sentences such as "While conducting research, I found...." For other activities, engage students in the following:

1. *Demonstrate Thinking out Loud*. A way to provide another focus for research about the Vikings is to read aloud from any material related to one of the subjects a student is studying. Demonstrate to the students the way *you* think out loud as you decide what information is important in the material. With the overhead projector, show the students the way you take notes from a reference and write down your ideas about the topic and show how you organize the ideas in groups (clusters, categories) on the transparency. Demonstrate the places where some information you have can be cross-checked by facts elsewhere and lead you to make some "therefore" statements aloud about the topic. Further, diagram a web, write an outline, or draw a graphic visual (spokes of a wheel) on the board to show the way some of the facts are related to the topic.

2. *Keep a Research Journal*. Another way to help the students see some relationships between new and old information is to ask them to keep a research journal and write their observations (hunches, guesses, predictions) each day. For an activity, read aloud material related to a subject a student is studying each day and ask all the students to make a fact web to show what they learn as they listen to the reading. Follow up by asking all to draw pictures about any information that interests them. Further, ask the students to evaluate their own progress by keeping a portfolio that shows their research notes, projects, and papers. At the end of the research project, meet with the students to review their original purpose for their research and discuss the insights, information, and skills they have gained in their studies.

3. *Culminating Activity*. Have students review their journals for the purpose of preparing a table of contents, numbering the pages, adding illustrations, and making a glossary and index. Additionally, the students can write their own brief autobiographies titled "Something about the Journal Author."

A.D. 300–399: Life in the Fourth Century

"Stop and imagine the simplest things—the significance of nightfall when there was no good artificial light, the misery of winter for the same reasons, as well as many others; conversely, the tremendous liberation of May Day and the lengthening days," suggests Geoffrey Trease (1972), a historical novelist, as he tells what he has to think about when he writes a historical story about a specific place in another time period. Trease says he has to "imagine the bodily sensation of cluttering clothes; wet weather before the invention of rubber and plastics. Think of the different sense of time before we had watches with minute hands." With students together as a group, you can present some of the "simplest things" that Trease is talking about and show them some of the details about the Middle Ages that can bring the people in this time period to life with *Life in the Middle Ages* (Nelson, 1967, grade 4) by Jay Williams.

Activity #33: "The Lantern Bearers"

To emphasize details about the people in this time period (about 337 A.D.) and their related values to older students, briefly discuss the plot in Rosemary Sutcliff's book, *The Lantern Bearers* (Walck, 1959, grade 6 and up). In the book, Sutcliff describes the effects of the presence of the Roman auxiliaries in Britain—the internal strife, the menace of invasion by the Saxons—and relates the story of a Roman officer who eventually gives his loyalty to Britain when all that he loves is finally destroyed. Confronting the Roman invasion, the people in Britain face danger, are terrified of capture and enslavement, and try to survive. For interested older readers, two of Sutcliff's prequels, *The Eagle of the Ninth* (Walck, 1954, grade 6 and up) and *The Silver Branch* (Walck, 1959, grade 6 and up) provide important background for this story about ways Romans ruled in Britain.

In a study of *The Lantern Bearers*, Adamson (1981) examined the novel along with other novels by Rosemary Sutcliff and looked for positive values found in western contemporary society. Adamson found that the six values most often demonstrated by Sutcliff's protagonists were:

Knowledge	Recognition
Dominance	Independence
Aggression	Generosity

Students in grade 6 and older can examine selections from Sutcliff's story for the values found in the society of this time period and then discuss the extent to which these same values are found in their own contemporary experiences. To connect this story about the past with the present, ask the students to relate the values in the story to similar happenings in current news events by finding news headlines and articles that show ways the people of today value or do not value knowledge, recognition, independence, generosity, and aggression. Discuss and display the articles that are found in an arrangement designed by the students.

A.D. 400–599: Life in the Fifth and Sixth Centuries

"Supplementing history textbooks with historical fiction brings advantages not possible by using a single textbook," states Bernice Cullinan (1981), children's literature specialist. "First of all, access to multiple resources enables learners to make choices about what they learn, and empowers them to make judgments about what they read. Secondly, a single textbook can provide only limited coverage of a topic; the array of trade books is virtually unlimited."

Cummings (1987), a middle-school teacher, also recommends the use of trade books with students, as Cullinan does. Cummings uses a whole language approach to develop reading skills and mentions that his class uses a highly integrated literature-based approach to reading, an approach useful in history study. To do this, the students select a theme, divide into groups, and choose books to read. They work out a time line for the reading. Each student keeps a reading journal and writes notes for discussions about such features as the foreshadowing of the character and the events in the plot.

Cummings and the students compare and contrast their notes about the plot, character(s), language, style, and the authors technique. The students examine the illustrations and make predictions about what is read. They write essays first with rough drafts and make revisions in their journals. The unit ends with a day of discussing the reading experiences to close the theme. The students give dramatic interpretations, display creative art, prepare book talks, and play tape recordings of their discussions. Cummings's suggestions certainly are suitable for introducing elementary and middle-school students to literature-based reading about this time period.

Activity #34: "Knowledge, Aggression, Independence, and Generosity"

In a manner similar to Cummings's (1987) suggested approach, values such as knowledge, aggres-

sion, independence, and generosity can be discussed with the students after reading aloud selected lines from Robert Browning's *The Pied Piper of Hamelin* (Derrydale Books, 1985, all grades) and showing the illustrations on an opaque projector. With the students in a total group, ask them to identify selected actions in the story and identify which value—generosity, independence, aggression, and so on—is demonstrated. Some examples of the values that are represented by the people's actions in the story that the students might mention are:

> *Generosity*. The town of Hamelin has a plague of rats until a Pied Piper generously offers his music to rid the town of rats.
>
> *Aggression*. When the Piper rids the town of rats and claims the offered reward of 1,000 gilders, the mayor becomes verbally aggressive and offers the Piper only 50.
>
> *Knowledge and Independence*. In return, the Piper knows he has the knowledge to play music no child can resist. He is independent (and retributive) in his thinking and actions, so he plays his music and the children follow him to the open side of Koppelberg Hill, where they all disappear inside.

For students interested further in this event, Gloria Skurzynski's *What Happened in Hamelin* (Four Winds, 1979, grade 4 and up) is another version that introduces students to the role of the serfs and the noblemen in the feudal system of this period. In this version, the setting is 1284 and Geist, a baker's apprentice, is befriended by a flute-playing stranger, Gast. Gast convinces Geist to use tainted flour to bake treats for the town's children. Gast then eases their pain with his music and lures them away to be sold as serfs to a distant nobleman. After reading the story, engage students in talking about the economy of the times, the need for labor, and this early version of today's warning often given to children by their parents—don't talk to strangers.

Follow up with creative drama and decide who will play the part of the narrator, the baker's apprentice, and the flute player. All of the students can engage in the drama and speak lines they select as a chorus. Select simple props—perhaps a flute and a baker's apron—and, as an option, portray the other characters with face masks on paper plates made by the students. These can be held up as the character speaks. Paste the speaking parts on the back of the masks and have students read them aloud when it is their turn. Take the "show" on the road and perform it for younger students at school.

Activity #35: "Values in People's Lives"

Values such as the ones found in Sutcliff's *The Lantern Bearers* can be selected as themes for a literature-based approach for reading about the Romans. Students, each working with a partner, can select a value as a theme and track a value from this time period forward. Students can write what they find about the values in their literature journals (their spiral-bound notebooks). With the students, elicit their suggestions about what themes they want to study across other time periods and write them on the board. Discuss the students' reasons *why* they think these values may be found across time periods and record their reasons. Students can be guided to several examples of stories reflecting these values, such as those listed on History Master 17, "What People Value."

Encourage the students to record some examples of the themes/values that they find in stories they read through the year. A list similar to History Master 17, "What People Value," can be kept by the students to keep a record of what they have read related to these values.

With the whole group, select another value, such as *knowledge*, and ask the students to make a list of alternative ways that shows how individuals can use the value of knowledge to help other people. After students develop the list, discuss each of the alternative ways and any consequences that might happen if the alternatives were put into practice. Engage the students in selecting three of the alternatives that they think are the most practical for them and ask them to tell their reasons for their choices. This activity can be repeated with the other values listed previously.

A.D. 600–699: Life in the Seventh Century

"Elementary school students are capable, at their level, of analyzing literature to better understand how an author uses language to produce a work of art," explain Dewey W. Chambers and Heath W. Lowry (1976) authors of *The Language Arts*. Their words point out that students can examine the variations in folktales such as *Cinderella* because of the influence it may have on their understanding of the culture from which the literature comes. Additionally, Cullinan and Carmichael (1977), authors of *Literature and Young Children*, mention that illustrations are an integral part of the book experience for children, and that several versions of traditional tales "can be compared to see which version carries the most impact in "its depiction of characters and events."

For example, a Chinese version of "Cinderella" that has had a good deal of impact on readers is *Yeh-Shen: A Cinderella Story from China* (Philomel, 1982, all grades), translated by Ai-Ling Louie. This story portrays China's culture circa 618–907. It describes the young girl this way: "Yeh-shen, the little orphan, grew to girlhood in her stepmother's home. She was a bright child and lovely too, with skin as smooth as ivory and dark pools for eyes." In this story, the lovely girl is treated badly by her stepmother, and when a festival approaches, she is left weeping at home while her stepmother and stepsister go off to the dance. The magical bones of a fish grant her wish for beautiful clothes and she receives a blue-feathered cape to wear to the festival. At the dance, she loses one of her golden slippers and her clothes turn back into rags. The lost slipper is presented to the king, who is determined to find the woman to whom the shoe belongs. During a search of the kingdom, the king discovers Yeh-Shen as his true love. The stepmother and stepsister, however, are sent to live in a cave as punishment and meet their fate in a shower of flying stones. After reading the story aloud, encourage students to tell what they learned about the Chinese culture through Ai-Ling's version of "Cinderella."

Activity #36: "A Culture's *Cinderella*"

Indeed, students can learn more about other cultures through various versions of "Cinderella." To do this, they may hear/read a selected tale, get together in writing groups and write/draw what they learned. If the students prefer to sketch, they can form illustration groups and create pictures to "read" the illustrations aloud to others. Have them review the story and identify information about the people's belongings, family patterns, food, shelter, and tasks in the culture. After reading the tale, they can collect information on a data sheet or shape chart entitled "What We Learned about the Culture of _____." For instance, they might conduct an inquiry about Cinderella with questions such as those shown in Figure 6–2.

The students also can collect information about the places that are important to the cultural group as well as the group's special language or vocabulary. They may also point out the facts that tell about the people in the tale. The activity can be repeated with other stories from History Master 18, "Cinderella: Different Cultures."

FIGURE 6–2 *Inquiry about Cinderella's Culture*

Cinderella's belongings?

Belongings used by Cinderella alone?

Belongings Cinderella used often?

Stepsisters' belongings?

Belongings used by stepsisters alone?

Belongings stepsisters used often?

WHAT DOES THIS TELL YOU ABOUT CINDERELLA'S CULTURE?

Anything special about the belongings?

Which belongings helped?

Belongings done without?

Belongings to be replaced?

A.D. 700–799: Life in the Eighth Century

"History is what we choose to recall," states Erik Christian Haugaard (1979), author of historical fiction for children. "If this were not true, all history books would be alike, and the only difference among them would be the latest discovery of some ancient facts. But the study of history, like everything else, changes with fashion; and what one generation thinks is important is considered insignificant by the next." To introduce students to what some authors have considered significant about the people's lives in the eighth century, read aloud descriptive excerpts from appropriate historical fiction and informational books to portray Viking life, European life, and other lifestyles in the eighth century. As examples, there are reference sources such as *ABC: The Alef-Bet Book, The Israel Museum, Jerusalem* (Abrams, 1989, all grades) and *ABC Musical Instruments from the Metropolitan Museum of Art* (Abrams, 1988, all grades), both by Florence Cassen Mayers, that will show children some of the possessions owned and valued by the people in this period. For instance, they will see a mold-made blue glass bowl, a Peruvian flute (*quena*), an instrument used since pre-Columbian days, and ancient beads of carnelian, glass, agate, and silver from caves near Jerusalem.

Activity #37: "What Do You Suppose... ?"

After seeing the illustrations in the two books by Mayers, ask students to "suppose" something about an item seen in the pictures. For example, show the picture of the eighth-century Peruvian flute and ask them to make a "suppose" statement such as "I suppose this is made out of wood." Ask them to elabo-

rate further on the first statement and make additional "suppose" statements such as, "Since it is made of wood, I suppose there were wood carvers who made it" and "Since it is a musical instrument, I suppose there were musicians who composed tunes for it." Ask students to elaborate still further and make other "suppose" statements such as "I suppose there were craftspeople who taught ways to carve flutes and teachers who taught people how to play the instrument."

List the "suppose" statements on the board to show the students how many predictions they can make from observing a single item. Repeat the activity with other items and then ask the students to work with partners and look at additional illustrations as they make "suppose" statements to one another about the eighth-century items they see. Have them select a favorite item of the period, sketch it, and record all of the "suppose" statements they can generate around the sketch.

A.D. 800-899: Life in the Ninth Century

"Young children love riddles as well as jokes," says Eileen M. Burke (1990), author of *Literature for the Young Child*. "Many of the collections of jokes include riddles and many of the riddles themselves have a good deal of humor in them. A number of the collections of riddle-joke-puzzle books have the older child as the target audience but they do include entries that the young child will ponder and enjoy." As Burke points out, riddles not only offer humor but also show students some examples of the inventiveness of people. Many riddles from Africa are in Aardema's *Ji-Nongo-Nongo Means Riddles* (Four

Winds, 1978, all grades). Riddles in 20 different languages of the Original Native Americans, including Aztec, Comanche, and Pawnee, are found in *Lightning Inside You: and Other Native American Riddles* (Lothrop, 1992, all grades) by John Bierhorst. Both are suitable for students in all grades. In keeping with the Native American tradition, Bierhorst's collection of riddles offer mystery and humor for interested readers.

To share some of the riddles with students, project a riddle on an overhead transparency and divide the class into cooperative groups to work together to solve the riddle. Additionally, invite each student to read and browse through riddle books and select a riddle to ask others in the class. When someone answers the riddle, have the students state what they think the riddle tells them about the inventiveness of the people who created the riddle.

Activity #38: "A Ghatawi/Riddle"

In *Traditions: The Folklore of Women and Children in Kuwait* (Kuwait Bookshops, Ltd., 1987, all grades) by Baza al Batini and Suzi Wells, there are *ghatawis* (riddles) and proverbs known by Kuwaiti children from well before the oil era. The riddles have been collected by the authors for anyone who

believes in the Kuwaiti proverb and say, "*Illi makah awal malah tallf*," which means in its transliteration "Without the past there is no future." Some students will be interested to read the author's explanation that the Arabic word *ghatawi* comes from the verb *ghata,* which means "to cover." Indeed, several different types of Kuwaiti riddles "cover" (or hide) the answers to questions related to the people's lives. The different types of riddles, and what they are about, can tell the students something about the lives of the Kuwaiti people—inferred information that they can discuss in the whole group (see Figure 6–3).

The students can keep a list of the titles of the books in which the riddles are found—and if interested, refer to History Master 19 "Book Selection Committee." This History Master encourages students to write information about books they would recommend to others in the class and make it available for others to read.

A.D. 900–999: Life in the Tenth Century

"The disparity in the quality of books now being published in the United States about Hispanic people and cultures will not surprise many critics,"

FIGURE 6–3 *Ghatawis-Riddles*

GHATAWIS-RIDDLES

1. **Answer Type**. A ghatawi that includes the answer in the words. Example: "Look at the word *riddle*: Can you spell that without any *r*'s?" (t-h-a-t).
2. **Descriptive Type**. A ghatawi that is a brief description of something without a question being asked. This type of riddle was developed by the Aztecs and Original Native Americans. Example: "A bowl on top of a bowl/ Sinking in the sun/" (a sunset).
3. **Interrogative Type**. A ghatawi that begins or ends with an interrogative or questioning word. Example: "What do you throw away in order to use?" (an anchor).
4. **Lyrical Type**. A ghatawi told in prose or in a tale that has a problem to be solved; see *Standing on One Foot Puzzle Stories and Wisdom Tales from the Jewish Tradition* (Holt).
5. **Rhymed Type**. A ghatawi with ending words that rhyme. Example: "Elizabeth, Lizzie, Betsy, and Bess,/They all went together to seek a bird's nest./They found a bird's nest with five eggs in,/They each took one, and left four in."
6. **Tongue Twister Type**. A ghatawi that contains alliteration. Example: "Peter Piper picked a peck of pickled peppers."
7. **Word Play Type**. A ghatawi that contains plays on words. This is the type often seen in the comic strip "Frank and Ernest," created by Thaves. Example: Frank, in the role of Malaprop Man, tells Ernest that he is going to attend a Shakespeare Festival in Stockholm and says, "It will be a smorgasBARD."

writes Isabel Schon (1990), author of several articles and books about Hispanic books for children. "A great number of these books still contain a very limited or one-sided view of Hispanic people, customs, or countries." Keeping Scholn's concern in mind, select a book that is particularly good in presenting the Toltec people, circa A.D. 26, in a fair and accurate manner. One choice can be *My Song Is a Piece of Jade: Poems of Ancient Mexico in English and Spanish* adapted by Toni de Gerez (Little, Brown, 1981, grades 4–6). "Escucha! Yo soy el cantor (Listen! I am the singer)" are the words that introduce one of the poems from the Toltecs, people who were prominent in the 1300s in the valley of Mexico. With the students, elicit the information they know about the Toltec who conquered other tribes in the region and also contributed a great deal to the Aztecs. For example:

• Students can discuss present-day findings about the great Toltec city of Tollan (also called Tula), which was about 60 miles from present-day Mexico City.

• Students can paint scenes of the great pyramids of rocks and temples that honored the chief god, Quetzalcoatl the Plumed Serpent, who was also recognized as a teacher, leader, and ruler. They can gather data about the stone tools used to carve the decorated stone panels on the temples.

• Students can read aloud the Toltec poems that encourage readers to look "long and wisely" at nature—the narrative voices extol such things as birds, cotton, sunflowers, fish, fireflies, water lilies, and pumpkins. For example, one of the poems shows a relationship between creatures and the beauty of nature with word pictures about a little golden fish that has no song and a turtledove that has "bells of gold/ in his throat."

• Students can discuss their perceptions about "What do we do in America today to show that we value the beauty of nature and creatures as the Toltecs did?" What poems about nature have been written that we know about? In what ways are the poems of today similar or different to the Toltec poetry?

Activity #39: "Nature Poetry"

The students can compare the Toltec poetry to some other verses about the environment from other cultures and start a "Nature Poetry Journal" of poems they find from parallel cultures throughout their study. Have them label a left-hand column with the heading "Toltec Nature Poetry" and a right-hand column with "Nature Poetry from Other Cultures."

Sensitive poets from different cultures have selected nature and living creatures as topics for their verses, and the students can find out about some of them by reading a variety poetry books to compare and contrast the poets' ideas as they write poetic words under the headings on the board. As a source, Amy Zerner and Jessie Spicer Zerner have compiled classical haiku (nature poems) in *Zen ABC* (Charles E. Tuttle, 1993, grade 4 and up), a book that guides readers to the rich background and sensitivity to nature that is Zen. Students can record the nature poems they like in their journals, draw accompanying illustrations, and give their journals as gifts to someone in their home or neighborhood at the end of the unit of study.

A.D. 1000–1099: Life in the Eleventh Century

To initiate interest in the life of the Incas, read aloud excerpts from Pamela Odijk's book *The Incas* (Silver Burdett, 1989, grade 6 and up) and from Anne Millard's *The Incas* (Watts, 1980, grade 6 and up) to the students. In presenting facts about the Inca customs, language, and religion, both Millard and Odijk describe the people and their history clearly. Additionally, mention the pre-Inca cultures—the Tishuanaco, Nasca, and Chinu—and identify on a globe or world map the Andean area where they lived.

Activity #40: "Pre-Inca People"

Engage students in discussing what the ancestors of the Incas might have been like and in guessing (predicting) what they can discover about the people from what they find in data resources. Mention that in 1992, Izumi Shimada, an anthropologist and associate of Harvard University's Peabody Museum, excavated a nobleman's tomb near the town of Batan Grande in the Lambayeque Valley of northern Peru. It is considered one of the biggest finds of pre-Inca artifacts. It appears that sometime in the eleventh or twelfth centuries, a middle-aged pre-Inca aristocrat from the Sican people in Peru, a regional culture that held power in this time period, was buried face down in a gold death mask with emerald eyes, along with many finely made gold and silver body ornaments, turquoise and lapis lazuli stones, textiles, seashells, and beads. Ask students to suggest what this information tells them about the pre-Inca people (e.g., they had mask makers and goldsmiths, appreciated gems such as emeralds, turquoise, and lapis, wore body ornaments, and valued seashells and beads).

Ask the students to work in small groups and find references from which to list some characteristics of the pre-Inca civilization (see the references listed on History Master 20, "The Maya, Aztec, and Inca"). Ask one of the students in each group to report to the whole class what the group found. Write the findings on the board as the students mention them. As each characteristic is listed, ask the students to give some cross-checking evidence from one of the references that they have used that verifies and documents this characteristic or item.

Life in Early Africa

With the objective of understanding that diversity among people is natural while they still have things in common with many other people, engage students in listening, noting details, and making comparisons about the Ashanti people and others in the early African kingdoms. Ask students to gather together to hear several Anansi stories (the Spider man stories), just as the Ashanti people in Ghana might have done at the end of the day. Develop a mood for the story and set the background for storytelling by reading the preface from *A Story, A Story* by Gail E. Haley. This is an Anansi story about a small man who tricked others and brought stories to the world from Nyame, the sky god. If desired, invite the students to listen and watch the entire story on a filmstrip (Weston Woods). Ask them to read other legends about Anansi and then discuss what the stories tell them about the Ashanti people who listened to the story.

Activity #41: "Early Kingdoms"

In grade 6 and up, students can be guided to selections from Basil Davidson's *African Kingdoms* (Time-Life Books, 1966, grade 6 and up), or to another reference about early African states to initiate an inquiry about the people in this time period. Read aloud Davidson's descriptions of the great early African cultures and show the accompanying illustrations by the African artist. Point out that the three empires of Ghana, Mali, and Songhay flourished in Central Africa in this period, and add related information with Daniel Chu's *A Glorious Age in Africa: The Story of Three Great African Empires* (Doubleday, 1965, grade 6 and up) and Lester Brooks's *Great Civilizations of Ancient Africa* (Four Winds, 1971, grade 6 and up). The information in the books add to the idea that Ghana and Mali were states of great wealth and exercised cultural and political power over a large part of

Africa. Later, the Muslim conquest of Ghana ended in its destruction, and subsequently, Mali's rulers were converted to Islam. One of their leading cities, however, established a university known throughout the Muslim world as a center of learning—Timbuktu. Some of the events of the great African Empires in this period can be highlighted by the students when they create a time line for a classroom mural or create their own individual time lines in the shape of mini-accordion-folded booklets.

Anglo-Saxons and Normans

Students in grade 6 and older can listen to excerpts read aloud from Eloise McGraw's *The Striped Ships* (McElderry, 1991, grade 6 and up) to initiate research about what was going on at this time and to study the Normans who invaded England on September 26, 1066. McGraw's story portrays Anglo-Saxon and Anglo-Norman emotions and lifestyles during the Norman invasion of England. Additionally, show the pictures from *The Bayeux Tapestry: The Norman Conquest of 1066* (Parkwest, 1988, grade 6 and up) by Norman Denny and Josephine Filmer-Stankey. This is a pictorial narrative that describes the 200-foot-long tapestry that illustrates the invasion. Elicit from students some features of the illustrations that show details in the lives of the people during this time period. Using a Venn Diagram, ask the students to compare and contrast the lifestyles of the two cultures.

Activity #42: "Norman Invasion"

After independent time to read fiction and nonfiction on the topic, engage students in discussing what the lives of the people were like during the Norman invasion of England and in predicting what they can tell about the lives of the people—kinship relationships, economics, employment, education, health care, politics, authority, and achievements—from the information they found in their reading. Ask students to sketch some of the characteristics of England's civilization during the Norman invasion and show their sketches to others in the whole group. As each sketched item is shown, ask them to give evidence from a resource that documented or showed this item.

A.D. 1100–1299: Life in the Twelfth and Thirteenth Centuries

"Picture books, like short stories and certain poetic forms, are perfect for sharing in classroom situations," says Rovenger (1987), who maintains that picture books should be introduced to as wide an audience as possible. Indeed, not only older students but some younger ones, too, can be introduced to views of the Middle Ages and other time periods with a particular type of picture book—the wordless book. As an example, select Mitusmasa Anno's *Anno's Medieval World* (Philomel, 1980) and use an opaque projector to show the blue-clad traveler in the book that challenges the students to think about how ideas take hold of a society and the ways the ideas grow and change. The scenes ask students to think about the value of ideas and beliefs, the human cost of these ideas, and the suffering of the people who struggled to give life to new ideas. How many examples of these ideas can the students find as you project the illustrations? What examples are happening in the United States today that illustrate these same ideas? What shows that people value ideas and beliefs, that there is a human cost to new ideas, and that people suffer today as they struggle to bring new ideas to life?

Activity #43: "From the Middle Ages Forward through Wordless Books"

To focus the students' interest on a sequence of historical events in illustrations, Roberts (1992) suggests that history can be shown through wordless books with the work of two authors-artists: Mitusmasa Anno and John Goodall. The books listed in Figure 6–4 can be springboards for further study and writing, and are a way to invite a student to sit and talk about an overview of history. Additionally, the illustrations in the wordless books can be shown as an advance organizer to help students prepare a web or word cluster about the history shown in the illustrations.

Also, wordless books can be a summarizing tool to help students write summary paragraphs about historical events. For example, you can project a transparency of a scene from the history in one of the books and ask the students to study the visual and make as many conclusions as they can before they write summary paragraphs. Each word-

---

FIGURE 6–4   *Wordless Books about the Middle Ages and Later Time Periods*

Anno, M. *Anno's Britain*. Ill. by author. Philomel, 1982. Anno features a "John Doe" traveler, clothed in blue, who tours the British Isles in detailed scenes that show period costumes, anachronistic objects, and fictional characters. There are scenes from *Romeo and Juliet* and from paintings by John Constable and Jean Millet. Historical monuments, thatched roof cottages, St. Paul's, Stonehenge, Big Ben, and other historical moments are seen.

Anno's Flea Market. Ill. by author. Philomel, 1984. Anno shows a lifestyle that begins on a Saturday morning in a town square where an elderly couple with a filled cart arrive at the massive city walls to go inside to set up their wares. As more and more tradespeople arrive, the market becomes more and more crowded. Gradually the spaces on the page show that the tradespeople have a collection of objects from around the world and from different periods of history.

Anno's Italy. Ill. by author. Collins, 1980. This wordless book starts with scenes of Adam and Eve cast from Eden, the travels of Mary and Joseph, the birth and death of Christ, and then shows later time periods and the cities of Rome, Florence, and Venice as they become more populated.

Anno's Journey. Ill. by author. Philomel, 1978. Has detailed scenes with hidden pictures that show folktales and stories (plots) during a journeyman's travels through northern Europe and give rich impressions of the land, the people, and their heritage.

Anno's USA. Ill. by author. Philomel, 1983. Explores various dimensions of American history, geography, cultures, and offers scenes from the Golden Gate Bridge and the Grand Canyon to the Alamo, Independence Hall, and the Statue of Liberty.

Goodall, J. *Before the War, 1908–1939: An Autobiography in Pictures*. Ill. by author. Atheneum, 1981. Goodall presents his autobiography in pictures beginning with his birth in 1908 and ending with England's declaration of war in 1939.

continued

FIGURE 6–4   Continued

An Edwardian Holiday. Ill. by author. Atheneum, 1979. Shows an Edwardian family arriving at the seaside, crossing the English Channel to France, and finally departing by train. This book may be paired with Goodall's *An Edwardian Christmas* (Atheneum, 1978), *An Edwardian Summer* (Atheneum, 1976), and *An Edwardian Season* (Atheneum, 1980).

The Story of a Castle. Ill. by author. McEldererry/Macmillan, 1986. Begins in 1170 A.D. when Normans built a castle for protection, and ends in the 1970s when the castle is opened as a public attraction.

The Story of a Farm. Ill. by author. Macmillan, 1989. Shows an English farm from its beginnings in the Middle Ages to the present.

The Story of an English Village. Ill. by author. Atheneum, 1979. Shows six centuries of history in changing landscape scenes from pastoral settings in the fourteenth century to urban congestion in the twentieth century.

The Story of a Main Street. Ill. by author. Macmillan, 1987. Moves through several time periods—from Elizabethan, Restoration, and Georgian to Regency, Victorian, and Edwardian—and shows the changes caused by commerce and trade that begins with some local trading at a stone market cross in a path (a "main street" in the Middle Ages) and ends with bustling shops on an Edwardian main street at Christmas time.

The Story of the Seashore. Ill. by author. McElderry/Macmillan, 1990. Begins in England with George III's arriving in Weymouth in the early 1880s and continues through the prewar and World War II days when coastal artillery protected the shore lines.

less book listed in Figure 6–4 shows actions that can be explained and described in a student's words, phrases, and brief paragraphs. Additionally, the students can name characters, develop dialogue, interpret actions, and make comparisons. Some of the references in the illustrations, however, may not be known to all students and will need to be discussed.

Castles and Castle Times, A.D. 1250

"Often, teachers and librarians are interested in locating several books on the same topic," states John Warren Stewig (1988). "Reading books that give different accounts of the same event or books about different aspects of a single topic can give children a richer understanding of the event or topic." To provide a richer understanding of this period for her students, Downs (1993) used two major strategies to bring history alive in a unit about "Castle Times" through (1) exploration and (2) activities based on children's books.

To do this, the students first selected children's books to research a topic related to "Castles and Castle Times." Second, the students participated in whole class activities that were connected to all areas of the curriculum based on the trade books. For example, after listening to *Sir Gawain and the*

Loathly Lady (1987, grade 4 and up) by Selina Hastings and several ghost stories from *Castles* (1988, grade 4 and up) by Beth Smith, the students met in small groups to brainstorm everything they knew about castles. Back in a whole group situation, the students dictated their information and recorded their ideas on the board. Further background information was gained by listening to additional excerpts from *A Journey through History: The Middle Ages* (1988, grade 4 and up) by Maria Ruis and *Castle Times* (1982, grade 4 and up) by Robyn Gee.

Next, the students went to the library to collect sources related to the topics they had chosen and read, browsed, and explored the topics. They recorded the interesting facts they found and shared the information with the total group when they returned to the classroom. On the board, the facts were written under headings and were turned into a data diagram similar to Figure 6–5.

As the students became engaged in studying the topic of their choice, they worked individually and in small groups. They each wrote a paper about their topics and prepared a final project that related to their findings. Examples of the final projects included singing a song from the time period, drawing a map, writing a book, creating a visual display, designing a costume, and teaching a game from the period.

FIGURE 6–5 Data Diagram about People and Castles in the Knockabout Middle Ages

The activities based on the trade books connected to different areas of the curriculum. The students participated in creating a time line (social studies), in making comparisons of novels of the periods (reading), in estimating foods needed for a feast (math), in designing and building a model of a castle (science and math), in listening to music of the era (music), in designing shields and bulletin board displays (art), in designing a replica of a tapestry (art), and in participating in a culminating activity that included role-playing a person from the time period (drama).

Activity #44: "Linking the Middle Ages to the Present"

Read selected descriptions from Bradley Steffans's *The Children's Crusade* (Lucent, 1991, grades 4–7) about an early religious journey and some of the beliefs during the Middle Ages. The students can talk about the religious troubles that formed a major part of the European politics in the Middle Ages (just as they have been a part of Middle Eastern pol-

itics in contemporary times). The book is suitable for a discussion about the idea that "history does *not* repeat itself, it's just people who repeat previous mistakes," and about Steffans's final section that connects the past to the present when he compares the Seventh Crusade in 1248 to the Israeli Six-Day War in 1967 and then again to the Gulf War of 1991. For other aspects of the Middle Ages, the students can be guided to books such as the ones listed in History Master 21, "Castles" and History Master 6, "Heroes and Heroines."

A.D. 1300–1399: Life in the Fourteenth Century

"When that Aprille with his shoures soote/ The droghte of March hath perced to the roote/ ..." are the first two lines of the rhyming verse written in Middle English known as *The Canterbury Tales* by Geoffrey Chaucer. The tales tell about pilgrims—city women, country men, priests, and tradespeople—who set out on a rainy April morning to travel to Canterbury around 1387 to visit the shrine of St. Thomas, a shrine named for the martyred Archbishop of Canterbury, Thomas à Becket. To entertain themselves during the long journey, Chaucer wanted to have each pilgrim tell two stories on the way to Canterbury and two on the way back but he never finished his work. Each story—be it about magic, a trickster, animals with flashing eyes, love, death, or the Devil—has the name of the pilgrim who told it, and Chaucer wrote a prologue for almost all of the stories.

Chaucer collected his stories about exciting chases, embattled knights, battles, and other topics from wherever he could—especially from ancient stories from the East and Europe. In Geraldine McCaughrean's version, *The Canterbury Tales* (Rand McNally, 1985, grade 7 and up), there is a great deal of humor though the retelling still keeps the flavor of the original and is suitable for independent reading. After hearing or reading some of Chaucer's tales, students can:

1. Develop a brief story for one of Chaucer's pilgrims to tell on the "way back."
2. Write a brief prologue for one of the stories.
3. Read one or two ancient stories found in the folk literature of a selected culture and transform it into a story that one of Chaucer's pilgrims might tell.

If desired, replicate the storytelling of the pilgrims' journey on a field trip, bus ride, or other educational outing, and engage the students in telling two brief stories on the way and two more on the way back.

Activity #45: "Knockabout World"

In this activity, about the fourteenth century, ask students to see what is plausible in a guess and what is not, and to verify and confirm a guess with their observations. With an opaque projector, show them an illustration from McCaughrean's *The Canterbury Tales*. Assure students that it is all right to

"guess" but that each guess, however uncertain, should be *verified* by what is seen in the picture. As an example, show the picture of Brother Palm in a "laboratory" after he visited an alchemist who announced he could turn all matter into silver. Brother Palm, somewhat greedy, purchases the alchemist's "secret" of turning matter into silver but, of course, waits in vain for silver to be made. The pot on the table can provide the first opportunity for students to give a best guess: "I guess it might be iron—it might be pottery." Continue:

1. If the students assume it is iron, elicit their next guess about the pot—perhaps a guess about the materials needed to make the pot and the tools used and the method of creating it.
2. If they assume that the pot is pottery, what would be their next guess about needed materials, tools, and how it was made?
3. Ask students to describe each object they see in the picture and then "give a guess" about what they described.

To provide another opportunity to give a "best guess," use an opaque projector and show the scene of the friar mixing something.

1. If the students think the friar is mixing chemicals, then ask them to make their next best guess based on the assumption that the friar is mixing chemicals.
2. If some students think the friar is cooking, ask them to make their next best guess on that assumption.

With the students, summarize this activity and ask them what they think they learned from observing and "guessing" (e.g., gathering information as historians do, expressing their own ideas, and observing carefully). Have them write their thoughts about what they learned on a page in a history journal or dictate what they learned for a classroom chart.

CHAPTER SEVEN

A.D. 1400–1499

What was going on in the fifteenth century?

Multicultural Perspectives

Wizards with long hair, knights in armor, royalty in expensive clothing, and serfs in workers' garb, as well as tales about what happened in the Age of Exploration are all a part of a unit about the 1400s that can suggest inquiry possibilities. Africa's diverse people, Asia's Emperors, settlers, and explorers, peacekeeping Native People and their leaders in Australia and the Americas, as well as Europe's rulers and explorers are also a part of this period. For students interested in the perspectives on Figure 7–1, suggest some of the books to help them get background information about how different topics are portrayed for this time period.

FIGURE 7–1   Children's Books about A.D. 1400–1499

PERSPECTIVES FOR 1400s

African Heritage

Bryan, A. *Lion and the Ostrich Chicks and Other African Folk Tales*. Atheneum, 1986. There are Hausa tales that include Ananse stories such as "The Foolish Boy." Folk literature. Grades 4–5.

Musgrove, M. *Ashanti to Zulu: African Traditions*. Ill. by L. & D. Dillon. Dial, 1976. Introduces customs from 26 different cultures in Africa with representations of food, clothing, and shelter. Nonfiction. Grades 4–6.

Asian Heritage

Lauber, P. *Who Discovered America? Settlers and Explorers of the New world Before the Times of Columbus*. Random House 1970. Overview of pre-Columbian explorers. Nonfiction. Grades 4–6.

Latino/Hispanic Heritage

Jacobs, F. *The Tainos: The People Who Welcomed Columbus*. Putnam, 1992. Native people living on a Bahamian island in the late 1400s. Nonfiction. Grade 4.

continued

FIGURE 7–1   **Continued**

Original Native American Heritage

Fradin, D. *Hiawatha: Messenger of Peace.* Margaret K. McElderry/Macmillan, 1992. Hiawatha, an Iroquois Indian, preached peace and helped unite Iroquois tribes—Seneca, Onondaga, Oneida, Mohawk, Tuscarora, and Cayuga—into the Iroquois Confederacy. Biography. Grades 4–5.

Pennington, D. *Itse Selu: Cherokee Harvest Festival.* Ill. by D. Stewart. Charlesbridge, 1994. In pre-Columbian North Carolina, a Cherokee boy's activities show the last day of *Itse Selu* with its theme of Thanksgiving and renewal during the Green Corn Festival. Includes Cherokee words and pronunciations. Grade 4.

European Heritage

Fritz, J. *Around the World in a Hundred Years: From Henry the Navigator to Magellan,* Ill. by A. B. Venti. G. P. Putnam's, 1994. Details the heroic aspects of the voyages (1421–1522) as well as such human traits as arrogance, cruelty, and greed of the explorers. Maps at chapter beginnings show explorers' routes. Biography. Grades 4–6.

Fritz, J. *Where Do You Think You Are Going, Christopher Columbus?* Ill. by M. Tomes. G. P. Putnam's, 1980. Details the voyages to the new lands and presents an egotistical, bullheaded Columbus who was talented and determined. Biography. Grades 4–6.

Hooks, W. H. *The, Legend of White Doe.* Macmillan, 1988. This is the legend of Virginia Dare, the first European child to be born in the colonies. Fiction. Grade 5 and up.

Levitin, S. *Roanoke: A Novel of the Lost Colony.* Atheneum, 1973. Portrays the colonists' relationships with the Native People through the experiences of a 16-year-old runaway. Fiction. Grade 5 and up.

Differently Abled Heritage

Trease, G. *The Red Towers of Granada.* Vanguard, 1967. Robin is declared a leper by the village priest and he sails to Spain to find a cure during the reign of Edward I. Fiction. Grade 6 and up.

Female Image Heritage

Burch, J. J. *Isabella of Castile: Queen on Horseback.* Watts, 1991. Portrays the life of the queen who sent Columbus to the New World, and, with her husband, Ferdinand, drove the Moors (the people who adopted Islam as their faith and Arabic as their language) out of Granada and united Spain. During this period, some Moors returned to North Africa, Granada was captured, and financing a route to the Indies was begun. Biography. Grades 4–8.

Churchill, W. *Joan of Arc: Her Life as Told by Winston Churchill.* Dodd, 1969. Portrays life of Saint Joan of Arc (1412–1431), a French heroine in white armor, who led the soldiers to victory at the Siege of Orleans in the Hundred Years War. Joan was a gentle peasant girl who did not read or write. She had visions that led her to leave her family and present herself to the uncrowned King Charles VII of France. In an attack on Paris, she was captured, sold to the English, condemned as a witch and a heretic, and burned at the stake in May 1431. Biography. Grade 6 and up.

Religious Minority Heritage

Finkelstein, N. H. *The Other 1492: Jewish Settlement in the New World.* Scribner's, 1987. Sephardic Jews in Spain were exiled and journeyed to a world that was "new" to them. Nonfiction. Grade 6 and up.

Student-selected "sight bytes" (informational lines similar to sound bytes, as seen in Figure 7–2) about people living on different continents, some explorers' voyages, the Middle Ages, and Europe's Renaissance can guide the students to inquire about ways people adjusted to their physical and social environment in this period. The students can contribute their discovered "sight bytes" (e.g., informational lines from trade books about this period that can be displayed in the class to interest others in additional research).

A.D. 1400: Life in the Fifteenth Century

"Storytelling is an exciting approach to developing multicultural awareness," states Ruth Stotter (1993), director of the Dominican College Certificate-in-Storytelling Program. She goes on to explain, "Cultures vary in their world view—not only do they have different clothing, houses and rituals, they also perceive reality through different lens....In addition, we acquire self-knowledge by hearing stories from other cultures, discovering cultural differences and how others view us. A story allows us to step into another life experience, to develop understanding and psychological insights."

With Stotter's point of view in mind, you can develop some background information about the life and works of Michelangelo and let the students "step into another life experience" with the book, *Introducing Michelangelo* (Little, Brown, 1992, grades 4–5) by R. Richmond. After reviewing the illustrations of the Sistine Chapel and its recent restoration as well as some of the reproductions of Michelangelo's art in Richmond's book, ask the students, "What do you notice?" and "Do any of these art works seem to belong together?" Help the students find similarities as a basis for grouping the art works and ask them to suggest a label or title for each of the groupings. Invite volunteers to say in

one sentence something about each one of the groups and then a final sentence for *all* of the groups the students have made.

After reading excerpts from Richmond's book, discuss the contrasts between Michelangelo's name and in his personality. Do students think he was really angelic? Discuss the idea that Michelangelo's imaginative interests in heavenly things added emphasis to his works of art, and invite students to look again at his art works to find any features that relate to heavenly things. Have them record their data in two columns on a sheet of paper with the left-hand column labeled "Heavenly Things" and the right-hand column labeled "Art Works."

Activity #46: "Artists and Their Art"

Using an opaque projector, show Michelangelo's works of art with the illustrations in *Michelangelo* (Harper & Row, 1975, all grades) by Howard Hibbard. Discuss some of the art works and ask the students what they noticed and *why* they think Michelangelo's art reflects the subjects it does. Ask them to think about the art and what it tells them about what people valued in this time period. Ask them to look at the art again and to think of a title for the collection. For students interested further in this topic, mention that they can explore the topic of artists and their art in other time periods with the additional reading found on History Master 22, "Artists and Their Art."

Master Inventor da Vinci

"1492 was a very good year," write Alice and Martin Provensen to begin their paper-engineered biography entitled *Leonardo da Vinci* (Viking, 1984, grades 4–6). "Things were happening all over. In Spain, Christopher Columbus was about to be famous. In Florence, a pretty town in italy, Leonardo da Vinci (1452–1519) was teaching his apprentices to play the lute, sing sweetly, to do their

---

FIGURE 7–2   *Example of a Sight Byte*

Sight Byte of the Week

What evidence is there?

In 1492, when King Ferdinand and Queen Isabella gave Jews four months to get out of Spain, Jewish property and wealth were confiscated to help finance Columbus's voyages to the New World (from *The Jews of New Amsterdam* [Atheneum, 1988] by E. Deutsch).

arithmetic, to mix paint and plaster, and to create masterpieces." The pop-up pages of da Vinci's inventions will help focus the students' attention as they discuss their ideas about ways the inventions affected people's lives and some of the changes the inventions influenced in later periods of history.

Have students in grade 4 and up select excerpts from various books to collect information about achievements of other inventors in this time period and show them some of the sketches from Leonardo da Vinci's notebook that are duplicated in Richard McLanathan's *Leonardo da Vinci* (Abrams, 1990, grades 4–6). Let them discuss the ways the inventions could (and did) affect this time period as well as later events in history. Additionally, write on the board the inventions by inventors that the students know about. With students' input, connect the "cause" of the inventions in this period to some subsequent "effects" with the additional sources in History Master 23, "Inventors, Inventions, and Discoveries." After gathering data about a particular invention, ask the students to present arguments for and against the invention.

Activity #47 "Touching People's Lives"

Review the illustrations again in *Leonardo da Vinci* and discuss other features—the birds that flutter across the page when Leonardo experiments with flight; the sight of the heavens and his discoveries of the stars and planets; his drawings of anatomy; and his painting of the famous *Mona Lisa*. Discuss the possible effect his contributions had on people's lives as well as the materials from which some of da Vinci's inventions were made. To pursue the topic of inventors further, ask for names of any historical figures commonly associated with this particular time period and show the children references that portray the inventions. Again, see History Master 23 for additional sources.

If desired, list da Vinci's contributions as the students review them. Once the list has been made, have students group them according to common characteristics and suggest a title for each group. The students can arrange the items on the list in groups and label them, then tell what they learned about his contributions. For students interested further in this topic, suggest some of the books on the previously mentioned History Master 22, "Artists and Their Art." With those books, the students can follow their individual inquiries about their favorite artists, collect examples of their work through references and photocopies, and create bulletin boards to teach others in the class about the artists. If appropriate, the students' oral reports about the lives of the artists and their work can accompany the unveiling of the bulletin boards.

Explorers: A Simulation Activity

"Simulations and games are highly motivating," state Jarolimek and Parker (1993). "Children enjoy participating in these activities and do so without much urging from the teacher. The fact that learners show increased interest in the subject when they are involved in simulation games is well documented." A simulation that is suitable for supporting a study of the Greenland settlement of Erickson, the Unlucky, or other explorers, is an activity called "Explorers."

In Eugene, Oregon, teacher Jay Reese (Shirts, 1972) created a game board for this simulation and drew a grid of 3/4-inch squares on a 3" × 4" sheet of cardboard. Each vertical line of the grid was numbered and each horizontal line was identified with a letter. On a similar smaller grid, Reese drew an imaginary continent, which he kept out of sight from the students. The class was divided into small groups that represented explorers from different nations. To "explore," the students started on the right-hand side of the grid and "explored" the unknown region to the left. As "explorers," each group could move three squares on the grid per day. At the end of each day, the teacher drew on the large map (using the smaller master grid as a guide) what the students would have seen in their travels that day—locales with water, coastline, or nothing. This gave the students a data base for the next day. For instance, when the students "discovered" a coastline, they had to decide whether to stop and settle the nearby area or to continue exploring the continent. The groups that decided to settle the area were asked to obey the laws imposed on them by the country who financed the explorations. Inevitably, there were disputes with the other exploring countries and the financing country.

Activity #48: "What's Your Choice?"

After a simulation activity related to exploring such as that discussed in the previous section, engage the students in dialogue about the choices they would make among the laws related to what the authorities of the financing country would accept (e.g., the king's fifth). For example, ask students to choose between following the rules and regulations that seem "right" to the explorers or being punished when the rules and regulations are not in line with the financing country. Ask them to choose between accepting the religion and culture of the financing country as being "right" or suffering a consequence such as ostracism or imprisonment. To bring more insight into this, read aloud excerpts from *The King's Fifth* (Houghton Mifflin, 1966, grade 6 and up) by Scott O'Dell, a story of an explorer's imprisonment and trial because his king had not received his "fifth" of the valuables found.

Earth's World in 1492

"Despite the way you may have learned about Columbus in the classroom, the rest of the world was not on some cosmic hold button," states Manning (1992), a children's librarian in Eastchester, New York. "Most of us have a peculiar view of history—it's vertical....Students are rarely aware that anything is going on elsewhere unless it has relevance to the subject at hand." To give students, grades 4 and older, a view of the working world in 1492, Manning (1992) suggests selecting and displaying books to try to encompass the fifteenth-century world and its architecture, geography, climate, cuisine, folklore, myths, and legends. For example, discussing a limited number of events about an overview of the world in 1492 from the book *The World in 1492* (Holt, 1992, grade 4 and up)—with contributions from writers such as Fritz, Highwater, the McKissacks, Mahy, and others—can enhance the students' understanding of what was going on at the time. This is a world history picture book that gives an overview of Europe, Asia, Africa, Australia, and the Americas. It shows the first voyage of Columbus in a world perspective.

From the information in this book, the students can discover that some of the world's ancient civilizations were more advanced than Europe during the Renaissance, and in some ways, more tolerant of others. For instance, mention to students that by 1492, China's Ming fleet had already explored faraway seaports and the medical doctors in Africa's kingdom of Songhai (now Western Sudan) were removing cataracts from the human eye. Indonesians had trade routes all over Asia and Arabia, and Mehmet II, a scholarly conqueror of Constaninople, allowed Christians and Jews to worship freely in his Muslim empire. As you discuss these events and others in this period, ask students to locate the geographical places on a large map or globe. They can sketch selected scenes on a mural or on pages of a student-made history booklet to show a horizontal "slice" of history rather than a vertical one.

Activity #49: "Time Line"

Since 1492 identifies the year that Columbus landed in the Americas, the students can get an idea of just how many years have gone by (through the 1990s)

by measuring a time line outside on the school grounds. A time line like this offers students an opportunity to develop their understandings of chronology and a structure for reading aloud excerpts from trade books that match events on the line. Additionally, students in the class audience can develop their skills in asking questions about people and their difficult decisions, places, and events by using the line. Begin this activity by asking a student to stand at one end of the "time line" that the students will be measuring. If needed, ask the student to label a sign that reads "Columbus, 1492." That point on the "time line" will represent 1492, the year Columbus sailed to the Americas. Now walking one step for each year (or 10 years), you and the students can walk abreast and go ahead in time 128 steps to reach the time of the pilgrims. Ask a student to stand there to mark the spot (or hold a sign). Then walk ahead 156 steps to reach the time of the American Revolution and have a student stand there. Walk ahead 80 more steps to mark America's Civil War days. Finally, walk ahead enough steps to take the students to the current year.

Back in the classroom, invite the students to focus on happenings in the fifteenth century. Use references to collect information about it, and illustrate a scene about it to make another time line. Remind the students that the classroom time line can show how related events are arranged in chronological order in this time period and show the relative amount of time that separates them. A time line also will help students arrange the happenings in proper sequence. Encourage them to select only a limited number of events that are clearly a part of a study of the fifthteenth century to enhance their understanding of this period.

Activity #50: "European Minorities in 1492"

With students, review the reasons why Isabella and Ferdinand drove the Moors out of Granada in 1469, as well as the perspective of the Sephardic Jews in Spain who were exiled in 1492 with *The Other 1492: Jewish Settlement in The New World* (Scribner's, 1987, grades 5–8) by Norman H. Finkelstein. Since some of the exiled Jews journeyed to the New World, ask students to predict what aspects of their lives—clothes, food, health care, education, view of royalty—the families would (or would not) take with them into exile. With Barbara Brenner's *If You Were There in 1492* (Bradbury, 1991, grades 4–8), review additional facts about life in late fifteenth-century Spain—the kinship relationship, education, economics, employment, politics, and the royal authorities. Ask students to infer what each of the topics tells them the most about the world in which Columbus lived.

Additionally, ask students to prepare a list of objects that Jewish families of the old world might take into exile and ask students to rank the items according to usefulness (value) to families leaving their homes. With the list of items that would be taken, engage the students in writing with their partners about an "ideal life" for the exiled Jews if they could have the best of both the "old" world in Spain and the "new" world. Ask student partners to read their narratives to other partner pairs.

Problems of Native People

The words "I don't know who this Indian is,/ A bow within his hand," begin the poem entitled "Indian" from *A Book of Americans* (Holt, 1986, all grades) by Rosemary and Stephen Benet. The verses can be reread aloud and dramatized because the lines have actions that can be visualized or imagined or sketched by the students (e.g., hiding by a tree, watching white men land). Select different lines for individual speaking parts and let all of the children chime in on the last four lines: "But, just remember this about/ Our ancestors so dear:/ They didn't find an empty land./ The Indians were *here*./ Discuss the last line with the children and ask them what meaning and feelings the words have for them and for descendants of Native Americans. Substitute the words *Native Americans* for the word *Indians* in the verses and reread it aloud. Discuss what meaning the word change might have for today's society.

Activity #51: "The Taino People"

To focus the students' attention on the Native People's point of view when Columbus landed in San Salvador, read aloud *Encounter* (Harcourt, 1992, grades 4–6) by Jane Yolen. It is a story about a Taino Indian boy who retells the story of the arrival of Columbus's ships and how the boy tried to warn his people not to accept the strange, white visitors. After hearing the story, ask children to tell their ideas of what they have learned about the Taino people on San Salvador and what they think the Native People were like in this time period. Ask, "What problems do you think the Native People of San Salvador had once the Europeans arrived?" Record their responses on the board. Ask them to select one or more of the items listed on the board and transform the words into a sketch to illustrate what went on. Display the sketches, select a few

problems that are shown, and discuss some alternatives that might have resolved the problems.

Activity #52: "History of the Tainos"

Additional data about the Tainos can be obtained by older students from such historical sources as *Morning Girl* (Hyperion, 1992, grades 4–6) by Michael Dorris. In *Morning Girl*, a close Taino family on a Bahamian island in the late 1400s includes Morning Girl and Star Boy, a sister and brother who are opposites in their natures: Morning Girl wakes up early and her younger brother likes the night. One day while swimming, Morning Girl sees a "canoe" being paddled toward shore by people who had "wrapped every part of their bodies with colorful leaves and cotton." In the epilogue, readers learn that the "canoe" belonged to Columbus.

Morning Girl's encounter can introduce older students to what happened when Columbus met the Tainos living on the island. The devastating results are portrayed further in Francine Jacobs's *The Tainos: The People Who Welcomed Columbus* (Putnam, 1992, grades 4–6). Relying on archaeological and anthropological findings and Columbus's own writings, Jacobs reconstructs the native culture of the gentle people who populated the Lesser Antilles. Her book gives students an impression of the greed of the explorers and of their annihilation of a trusting people whose name meant peace.

To get acquainted with the stories of the Taino people, the students can read tales from the Taino culture: *Atariba and Niguayama: A Story from the Taino People of Puerto Rico*, (Childrens Press, 1988, grades 4–6), a story adapted by Harriet Rohmer and Jesus Guerrero Rea, and *How the Sea Began: A Taino Myth* (Clarion, 1993, grades 4–5) retold by George Crespo. In the first story, Niguayama searches for a tall caeimoni tree and its fruit because he knows that it will save Atariba's life. In the second story, the origin of the island of Puerto Rico begins when ocean creatures and salt water pour from the burial gourd of the best hunter in the village.

To link the past with the present, discuss with students that although some people in the United States organize annually to recognize the arrival of Columbus in the western hemisphere around October 12, other people wonder why this is done and look critically at the deeds that followed the Europeans' arrival. For example, critics of Columbus say that he may have his reputation as a man who was remarkable for his vision and courage but he also bears the burden of initiating the demise of several thriving cultures in the New World. Good or bad, the impact of Columbus cannot be ignored (Hopkins, 1992). To some, he was a competent navigator whose encounters with Native People brought the disastrous results of disease, slave labor, and the *encomienda* system (a system based on European feudalism where Europeans received plots of land along with the right to force all resident people to stay and perform the work the owner required). The effects of these three factors were part of Columbus's "cargo" and changed history in ways that can be suggested by interested students. For additional resources on this topic that will guide interested students in independent library searches, distribute History Master 24, "Christopher Columbus."

Debates about Columbus

"My men grow mutinous day by day/ My men grow ghastly wan and weak," are descriptive words in the poem "Columbus" from *Joaquin Miller's Complete Works* (J. Miller, 1936, grade 4 and up) by Joaquin Miller. Engage students in dramatizing actions or drawing sketches that can be imagined from the verses. As an example, discuss the meanings of words that might be unfamiliar to some students such as "shoreless seas," "gray Azores," "Gales of Hercules," "swarthy," and "the mad sea shows his teeth tonight." This is a poem that lends itself to individual speaking parts and has a chorus of "Sail on! Sail on! and on!" for groups of students to speak aloud as a refrain. Invite the students to give their suggestions for ways to orally interpret the poem as you show it on an overhead transparency. Distribute individual copies to students and use it as a choral reading.

Activity #53: "Issues about Columbus"

Christopher Columbus: Recognizing Ethnocentrism (Greenhaven Press, 1992, grade 4 and up), by Bonnie Szumaki, offers informational material for student debates on several issues: (1) Columbus did/ did not discover the New World; (2) Columbus Day should/should not be celebrated; and (3) the Spaniards, in some instances, did/did not mistreat the Native People.

As background for a debate, point out to students that in a recent social action demonstration, a Native American group read aloud in public the names of native tribes exterminated by the European sword or by European diseases. In this demonstration of the 1990s, the Native Americans traveled in protest canoes as a symbol of sailing "to Europe to discover Spain." In their view, Columbus is blamed for genocide, slavery, colonialism, the plundering of tons of gold and silver, environmental destruction, legalized exploitation, economic exploitation, racism, and moral decadence. With interested students, return to the views in Szumaki's book and engage students in selecting material for debates on one or more issues related to Columbus. Further, after the students have read/heard biographical material about Columbus, ask them to record the explorer's actions taken toward Native People as having a positive or negative impact. Ask students to rank the impact from 1 (having highest impact) to 10 (having least impact). See Figure 7–3.

After this ranking, ask students to read the items again and talk about the pros and cons related to the advantages and disadvantages of explorers who encountered native groups of people. Invite students to discuss the merits (or lack of merits) of selected explorations and then write with partners about the positive behaviors that the members of an exploring group could have emphasized when they met the Native People.

For further discussion to link explorations of the past to modern explorations, ask students to recall what they know about U.S. astronauts and the first moon landing on July 20, 1969. Discuss the

---

FIGURE 7–3 *Impact of Actions*

	Impact of Columbus's Actions		
Positive-Impact	**Ranking of Force of Impact**	**Negative Impact**	**Ranking of Force of Impact**
1. action	1.		

ways in which the astronauts "claimed the land" and were/were not similar to Columbus and other early explorers. Ask open-ended questions, such as:

1. If you were in charge of space explorations, how would you decide who the "owners" of the moon and other planets should be? What else would you want to do?
2. If you were in charge of U.S. resources, under what circumstances would you agree that the United States should "mine" some of the resources on the moon and other planets?
3. In what ways should earthlings use other planets in the universe? Why do you think this way?

Columbus's Story in Drama

Morgan and Saxton (1988) maintain that a teacher can develop and enrich the language of students with drama in the classroom through the strategies of questioning, time to reflect, synthesizing the drama experiences, and role-playing different roles. By reading an introduction to content about the journeys of Columbus, the descriptions of navigation tools, and building ships in *Christopher Columbus: How He Did It* (Clarion, 1992, grade 4 and up) by Charlotte and David Yue, you can enrich the students' understanding of his first voyage and demonstrate some of the different roles important in the event (as shown in Activity #54).

Activity #54: "Points of View"

Pointing out that the students' purpose in role-play will be to defend a point of view, to argue for or against something, to make a decision, or to come up with a solution or plan, you can model different roles:

1. Being the authority (in role as Queen Isabella with class in role as Columbus)
2. Being second in command (in role as the first mate on the ship with Columbus and the students as the crew)
3. Being one of the group (in role as a sailor with the students as other sailors)
4. Being one of the helpless (in role as the son of Columbus who is placed with friars who have agreed to look after him during the expeditions)
5. Being an authority opposed to a group (in role as leader of Native Americans with the class members as Columbus and crew)

After demonstrating the various roles, you can engage the students in working with partners to take the roles themselves, play out a scene, and then switch roles.

In a role-playing situation in front of the whole class, the students in the *audience* can take the roles of members of observation teams to collect different kinds of information about the different feelings shown by the main "actors." During role-play, the students in the audience can be encouraged to observe the actors carefully and take notes on how many times a certain feeling is expressed.

After the role-playing, each student in the audience can make a report about how a certain "actor" reacted and showed his or her feelings. As a further example, the students can tally their information on a chart to show how many times feelings of friendship or unfriendliness were shown in the role-playing. As a follow up, invite students to check the accuracy of their "report" on the chart with the information each student got *independently* from watching the role-playing. Point out that when social scientists do this, they call it *checking the reliability* of their observations. Finally, Bolton (1993) suggests that at the end of the drama, the teacher and students evaluate the experience, discuss what was learned, and reflect through a discussion, writing, art, music, or anything that prompts the students to use the knowledge and feelings related to the role-play.

How History Is Made: Artifacts

"The emphasis is on understanding the past, the people who lived during those times, their problems and ways of living and their struggles to meet basic needs," explain Jarolimek and Parker (1993) in their elaboration on history's contribution to the social studies curriculum. "History taught in this way helps the child develop a better understanding and appreciation of human growth through the years— not only along political lines but in all ways—that contribute to a richer and more abundant life." Related to this point of view, Ramsay (1992), author of *Voyages to Discovery,* suggests that teachers help students discover that history is a process of discovery and interpretation. For instance, you can point out to students that in this process three things happen: artifacts disclose information, original documents give up their secrets, and various sources add new information to old events.

You can mention that writers of history use these things to write about what happened in the past and make decisions about what meaning the things have for the historical story they are writing. Indeed, much of what is written about in history arrives in a book written the way the writer believed or interpreted things to happen. Ramsay (1992) also recommends several activities for students—writing personal histories, doing hands-on activities related to artifacts and archaeology, seeing another's point of view, discerning different interpretations, and recognizing historical symbols—as ways to help students discover how history is "made."

Activity #55: "Artifacts Disclose Information"

Ask students to pretend that they have lost something and someone in the future will discover it 500 years from now (Ramsay, 1992). Engage them in working with partners and recording what they lost and what the lost item will tell someone in the future about their lives now. Ask them to transform their words into a drawing and sketch the scene they envision where someone in the future discovers the lost item. Invite volunteers to show their drawings and discuss their sketches and writing with others. Suggest independent reading with books about artifacts (see Figure 7–4) as clues to the past.

How History Is Made: Events

"Marian called it Roxaboxen," begins the story of a hill covered with rocks and wooden boxes that becomes an imaginary town for Marian, her sisters, and their friends in *Roxaboxen* (Lothrop, Lee & Shepard, 1991, grades 4–5) by Alice McLerran. This is a narrative based on the author's mother's childhood manuscript about a pretend-town. "There across the road, it looked like any rocky hill—nothing but sand and rocks, some old wooden boxes, cactus and greasewood and thorny ocotillo—but is was a special place." McLerran tells about her mother's friends who played in the imaginary town of Roxaboxen in their childhood as a part of her family's history. Round black pebbles were used as the town's money; houses and streets were edged with white stones; boxes were anything the children wanted and pieces of pottery were dishes. Something round was the steering wheel of a car and the floor of the jail had cactus on it to make it uncomfortable if you had to go there for speeding. If you had a stick and some kind of bridle, you imagined a horse and could gallop anywhere. After reading *Roxaboxen*, discuss with students any or all of the following:

1. Point out to students that history is not only studying artifacts—such as pieces of pottery children can use for dishes as they did in Roxaboxen—but it is also an accounting of events that happened in the past. Invite them to create, as McLerran did in her story, an event from their own personal histories by starting with a description of themselves as babies or young children (Ramsay, 1992).

2. Point out that history can include individual personal histories that students make. Distribute construction paper (12" × 18" sheets) and ask students to fold a sheet in half to make an individual "two-page" personal history. Ask them to think of titles for their histories and write their names as the authors. Tell each to write his or her "history" on the inside right-hand page and to illustrate the events on the left-hand page.

3. Point out that history can be part of a record kept by a writer who keeps adding pages to a personal history for a more detailed account of his or her life. Ask the students to select a part from their personal histories where they "learned something important" in their childhood and read it aloud to a partner.

FIGURE 7–4   *Books about Artifacts as Clues to the Past*

Conrad, Pam. *My Daniel*. Ill. by author. Harper and Row, 1989. Grades 5–8.

Cooke, J. *Archaeology*. Watts, 1987. Grade 4 and up.

James, C. *Digging Up the Past*. Wafts, 1990. Grades 4–6.

Porell, B. *Digging the Past: Archaeology in Your Own Backyard*. Harper & Row, 1979. Grade 4 and up.

Pryor, B. *The House on Maple Street*. Ill. by Beth Peck. Morrow, 1987. Grade 4.

Activity #56: "My Journal"

To have students take the role of historians, read aloud excerpts from *I Columbus* (Walker, 1990, grade 4 and up), a translation of the sailor's first voyage by Peter and Connie Roop, and discuss the value of a journal—a type of primary source material that a historian reads and uses before writing about a selected topic. Engage the students in writing a page in a "daily journal" that tells about their activities and lifestyle during the current school day for a specific year of your choice. Ask them to imagine being a historian and finding this journal in the future. Students should trade their pages with others and use this information just as an historian would to find out about life in that year. Ask them to read the information and make inferences (guesses, hunches, predictions) about what life was like for that day and year.

With students, mention that there usually are differences in the points of view about an event. Show this by reading excerpts from several biographies about Columbus such as *Columbus: Finder of the New World* (Morrow, 1952, grade 4 and up) by Ronald Syme and *The Quest of Columbus* (Little, Brown, 1966, grade 5 and up) by Ferdinand Columbus and edited by R. Meredith and E. B. Smith. With the students, organize two columns on the board labeled "Plus" and "Minus" to record both the positive and negative aspects of Columbus's voyages that have been recorded by the writers. The titles of the data sources may be listed on the left-hand side, as seen in Figure 7–5.

FIGURE 7–5   Aspects of Columbus's Voyages

Title	Plus (Positive)	Minus (Negative)
1. *The Quest of Columbus*	Brave	Greedy
2.	Discovered continent	Made mistakes
		Mistreated people
		Unable to govern

CHAPTER EIGHT

A.D. 1500–1599

What was going on in the sixteenth century?

Multicultural Perspectives

For an introduction to this time period, invite students to hear or read about the the thriving civilizations of the Native People and the European explorers in the area now known as the Americas, as well as the explorers' effects on the Native People. For the students interested in multicultural perspectives of the period, suggest some books from Figure 8–1, and invite the students to report what was going on in this time period through brief book talks.

FIGURE 8–1   Children's Books about A.D. 1500–1599

PERSPECTIVES FOR 1500s

African Heritage

McEvedy, C. *Atlas of African History*. Penguin, 1980. Provides an informative supplement in format of an historical atlas. Nonfiction. Grade 7 and up.

Asian Heritage

Li Shufen. *Stealing the Magic Fruit*. Ill. by Zhang Jianping and Qi Jun. Beijing Foreign Languages Press, 1985. This is the seventh of a 34-part series of books telling the story of resourceful, brave, and humorous Monkey, the irrepressible disciple of a Tang Priest, Xuanzang, found in the ancient Chinese fantasy novel *Journey to the West* that is over 400 years old. This adventure tells what happens when Monkey and Pig steal and eat some magic fruit of immortality. Monkey's ingenuity saves the day. Folk literature. Grade 4 and up.

Haugaard, E. C. *The Samurai's Tale*. Houghton Mifflin, 1984. Captures the times of the feudal warlords of the sixteenth-century Japan and portrays the life of the samurai, the professional soldiers, who fought under the *daiminos* (the nobles) and the *shoguns* the commanders, Fiction. Grade 5 and up.

Latino/Hispanic Heritage

Berler, B. *The Conquest of Mexico: A Modern Rendering of William H. Prescott's History*. Corona Pub., 1988. Retells episodes of the conquest by Cortes that includes the Native People's rebellion, Montezuma's death, and other events. Nonfiction. Grade 7 and up.

continued

FIGURE 8–1 **Continued**

Burrell, R. *Life in the Time of Moctezuma and the Aztecs.* Ill. by A. McBride. Steck-Vaughn, 1993. Gives an overview of the Aztec society, including human sacrifice, and a nonflattering view of Cortes. Nonfiction. Grades 4–8.

Dujovne, M. *La Conquista de Mexico Segun las Ilustraciones del Codice Florentino.* Mexico City: Nueva Imagin, 1978. Portrays view of the conquered Nahuatl people and includes Spanish explanations of the illustrations. Nonfiction. Grade 7 and up.

Fisher, L. E. *Pyramid of the Sun, Pyramid of the Moon.* Ill. by author. Macmillan, 1988. A time line shows a history of Mexico with each period identified by a symbol. Symbols show the periods on subsequent pages and the text describes ways Toltecs used pyramids and how the Aztecs built the Great Temple Pyramid. Illustrations (including one of human sacrifice) are in black and white. Nonfiction. Grade 4 and up.

Herzog, B. D. *Cortez & the Conquest of Mexico by the Spaniards in 1521: An Eyewitness Narrative by Bernal Diaz Del Castillo.* Repr, 1942/Linnet, 1988. Diaz, a soldier with Cortez, wrote his account, *The True History of the Conquest of New Spain,* and this text is based on his writings. Also includes drawings by Native artists of the period. Nonfiction. Grade 7 and up.

Los Aztecas: Entre el Dios de la Lluvia y el de la Guerra. Madrid: Anaya/Biblioteca Iberoamericana, 1988. Spanish language text that reviews the history of the Aztec people. Montezuma II ascends the Aztec throne in 1502 in the ancient capital, Tenochtitlan, now Mexico City. Nonfiction. Grade 7 and up.

McKissack, P. *Aztec Indians.* Children's Press, 1985. Describes the Aztec people and their customs, history, language, and religion. Nonfiction. Grade 7 and up.

Marvin, I. R. *Shipwrecked on Padre Island.* Ill. by L. Miller. Hendrick-Long, 1993. Marooned in 1554, 13-year-old Catalina loses her bracelet, which is found 400 years later by 13-year-old Jilliane. Fiction. Grades 5–7.

European Heritage

Hunter, M. *You Never Knew Her as I Did!* Harper, 1981. Will, a young page at Lochleven Castle, writes his memoirs of 1542–1587 about Mary, Queen of Scots. Fiction. Grade 5 and up.

Middleton, H. *Everyday Life in the Sixteenth Century.* Silver Burdett, 1983. Gives descriptions of daily life in the 1500s and shows the extremes—the devastating poverty and the wealth—that contrast the lifestyles that existed side by side in Europe. Nonfiction. Grade 7 and up.

Stanley, D., & Vennema, P. *Good Queen Bess: The Story of Elizabeth I of England.* Ill. by D. Stanley. Four Winds, 1991. Portrays the life of Elizabeth (1533–1603) and her influence on religion, politics, and exploration of the New World. Biography. Grades 4–5.

Original Native American Heritage

Goble, P. *The Gift of the Sacred Dog.* Bradbury, 1980. Coronado's men on horseback introduce the horse to the Plains people, an event told in other ancient tales. Folk literature. Grades 4–5.

Realm of the Iroquois. Time-Life Books, 1993. This is one in the American Indian Series that discusses the history of the Five Nations Confederacy from early in the sixteenth century up through the mid-1800s. Nonfiction. Grade 8 and up.

Yolen, J. *Sky Dogs.* Harcourt Brace Jovanovich, 1990. "A Blackfoot Indian tells how he, a young motherless boy, saw a horse for the first time and was called He-Who-Loves-Horses back in the time when the Plains Indians were given horses. Folk literature. Grades 4–7.

Differently Abled Heritage

Foreman, M., & Seaver, R. *The Boy Who Sailed with Columbus.* Arcade, 1992. Leif, an orphan, is left behind as punishment after he runs the *Santa Maria* aground. He is taken captive by Native People,

FIGURE 8–1 *Continued*

renamed Morning Star, and trained to help a blind wise man who teaches him to be a medicine man. Becoming a mystic years later, he sees European ships anchored offshore, remembers how Columbus captured people to take back to Spain, and with his family, his sons and grandchildren, he begins a long walk to the west to evade the Europeans. Fiction. Grades 4–5.

Female Image Heritage

Duran, G. *Malinche, Slave Princess of Cortez.* Linnet/Shoe String Press, 1992. Portrays life of Malinali/La Malinche, the Aztec princess and slave devoted to Cortez. Having an ability with languages, she also became an interpreter during the Spanish conquest of Mexico. Some facts are based on the *True History of the Conquest of New Spain* by Bernal Diaz del Castillo. Biography. Grade 7 and up.

Smith, L. *Elizabeth Tudor: Biography of a Queen*, Little, Brown, 1977. Takes a chronological look at the reign of Queen Elizabeth and shows the diplomatic and political aspects of her character. Biography. Grade 6 and up.

Religious Minority Heritage

O' Dell, S. *The Feathered Serpent*, Houghton Mifflin, 1981. With the Maya people, a young priest believes in the teachings of Augustine and concludes that evil exists because God wills it. If God wills evil, then the worship of idols and the sacrifice of humans must be beyond the Jesuit's control. With this rationalization, he has to make decisions about taking the role of the Mayas' mythical Kukulcan in order to save his own life, about responding or not responding to the Maya rites of sun worship, and about making his beliefs known to people who are steadfast in their own ancient beliefs. Fiction. Grade 7 and up.

A.D. 1502: Montezuma II and the Aztecs

Related to studying the Aztec culture and others, educators Touscay and McDermott (1993) suggest challenging the class to see how many countries the students can list, find, and talk about with others. Appropriately, the locales of the ancient Maya, Aztec, and Inca civilizations can be included when students gather information about various cultures, (e.g., Montezuma II ascended the Aztec throne in 1502 in the ancient capital, Tenochtitlan [now Mexico City]). An ongoing activity would be to ask students to keep track of all the places the class has visited in the books they are reading. Have students place stickers (colored dots) on a world map or a globe to identify the places. Engage them in looking for books about different places that they have not visited vicariously and in adding another colored dot to the map or globe. Invite your students to respond to the challenge of seeing how many countries related to their history study they can find, list, and talk about with others in small groups and in whole group situations.

Activity #57: "What Civilization Means to Me"

Organize students in identifying features (concepts in themselves) of a particular civilization with the purpose of studying similar features in other civilizations. As an example of this, Hyde and Bizar (1989) suggest asking the students to brainstorm some of the key features from either the Maya, Aztec, or Inca civilizations with the goal of identifying some of the features/concepts that are common to almost all civilizations. For example, the story of *White Hare's Horses* (Atheneum, 1991, grades 5–8) by P. K. Spinka will help the students identify some features as they hear about the young Chumash girl who finds her village threatened by the Aztecs and flees north on horses stolen from the Conquistadors. The girl's flight from the Aztecs might suggest that a feature/concept to study that is common to all civilizations is *authority*. Additionally, the pyramids in the Yucatan might suggest that another feature to study that is common to all civilizations is *architecture*. The bright ornaments of a ruler might suggest another—jewelry and body ornaments. Record on the board or a chart all of the features the students suggest.

To assist students further in identifying features, show pictures of L. E. Fisher's *Pyramid of the Sun, Pyramid of the Moon* (Macmillan, 1988, grade 4 and up). It includes illustrations of the Aztec civilization (including one of human sacrifice that make Shakespeare's words meaningful: "There's nothing good or bad, but thinking makes it so"). In Fisher's pictures, the students can see the method the Aztecs used to build the Great Temple Pyramid and can compare the methods with the Egyptian methods shown in other references books. Point out to students that Fisher's time line delineates the history of Mexico and identifies each time period with a symbol. The symbols are useful additions and show the students the different periods of history on subsequent page—they serve as time period reminders for readers.

To clarify the passing of time further, you might mention the great span of time of over 1,000 years between the pre-Columbian pyramids and the culture of the Aztecs, and point out that the Aztec temples are not physically near the earlier pyramids but are in a different location in Mexico. Mention that the earlier pyramids are part of a civilization that was different from that which built the Aztec temples. On the temples, the Aztec-Toltec god Quetzalcoatl (ket-SAHL-ko-AHT-l) has been shown in sculptures represented by a snake called the Plumed Serpent and part of its history mentions that his rule included love, beauty, poetry, flowers, life, and death (Adams, 1993). Additionally, record on the board or chart what the students observe in data sources and continue to make a list of features to study from the civilization that the students decide to study first (see Figure 8–2).

Provide students with data from a variety of materials about the Maya, Aztec, and Inca—children's literature, a brief essay, a journal—and then have the students add the things referred to in the material to their collection of facts on the chart about the concepts of civilization to be studied. Supplement what the students know about the Aztec civilization with the arts and crafts projects in *Aztecs* (Watts, 1993, grades 4–8) by Ruth Thomson. The directions for the projects are clear and accompanied by photographs. Additional data are found in the books about the Maya, Aztec, and Inca civilizations on the previously mentioned History Master 20, "The Maya, Aztec, and Inca."

To assist in further identification of more features of civilizations, consider using History Master 25, "Civilization: Explore a Concept," an activity that is based on concepts exemplified by the letters KEEPHRA, which refer to such features of civilizations as kinship patterns, economics (work/jobs/employment), education, politics, heath, religion, and authority, and is the work of Dr. Amando Ayala (1989), California State University, Sacramento, and other scholars. It will guide interested students in exploring the concept of civilization in additional depth.

Early Cities

Provide a glimpse of an early community by reading aloud T. Strasser's *The Diving Bell* (Scholastic, 1992, grades 4–7). In a storm, the ships of the Spanish conquistadors sink and Culca's brother and other native divers are sent down to recover gold. Culca devises a plan to save her brother's life while he is doing the dangerous diving. With students, discuss ways Culca's community could have been a better place for her, her brother, and the other inhabitants to live. Also, have students find out more about the issues referred to in the story—the role of

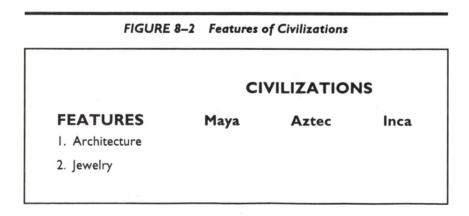

FIGURE 8–2   *Features of Civilizations*

CIVILIZATIONS

FEATURES	**Maya**	**Aztec**	**Inca**
1. Architecture			
2. Jewelry			

the church, the colonial exploitation of the native people, and the role of women.

Activity #58: "Making Life Better"

Working with partners, ask students to design (and write about) a model city for a Maya, Aztec, or Inca civilization from their points of view and show their ideas on paper or through model building. As an example of a way for the students to tell their ideas to the whole class the students can take the roles of people living in a Maya, Aztec, or Inca city, and play a scene where they ask about a needed service or improvement—such as Culca's brother's need related to safe diving, Remind the students *observing* the role-play that they have a responsibility to identify the information they gain from each role-play situation and to write down or sketch what they learn as they listen and watch. After the role-play, ask students in the audience to give examples of what information they received and to show their notes or their sketches to the group.

Once the differences are noted, ask students which list has the most items on it and *why* they think this is so (they probably know more about the topic). Ask students to think about the way the Native People might have felt about the horse when they first received it—and elicit the idea that different people can feel differently about a happening such as this.

A.D. 1541: Native People in Area Now Mississippi

"Hernando De Soto was Spanish,/an iron-clad conquistador" is the way the biographical story poem about De Soto begins in *A Book of Americans* (Holt, 1986, all grades) by Rosemary and Stephen Benet. Ask the students to suggest when individuals will read separate dialogue lines for a choral reading and when the group will speak as a chorus and repeat the poem aloud several times, changing the reading roles of the students each time. Discuss any vocabulary that may be new to some students (e.g., *conquistador*, *knightly*, *the sack of Peru*).

Activity #59: "Meeting between De Soto and Native American Leader"

Have the students imagine the setting De Soto saw as he marched to Quizquiz on the Mississippi River, the capital of a rich province of the Tunica Indians. Ask students to read the map legends and symbols on a map to infer what the area was like in the Mississippi River valley. Tell them to close their eyes and imagine the scene (or to use their pencils and sketch the image) that comes to their minds. Mention that the Tunica capital had mounds and a great fortress-like layout with an earthen embankment around it. This was a great Native American civilization on the Mississippi River and it sent a great chief to meet De Soto's expedition. It seems the Native Americans were carefully mobilized, had a formidable display of power, and showed themselves to be a highly organized kingdom. This is documented by the writings of a member of the expedition, known as the Gentleman of Elvas, who described the first time he saw the great native leader:

> A great chief arrived, with two hundred canoes filled with men, having weapons. They were painted with ochre, wearing great bunches of white and other plumes of many colours, having feathered shields in their hands, with which they sheltered the oarsmen on either side, the warriors standing erect from bow to stern. The barge in which the great chief came had an awning at the poop, under which he sat, and the like had the barges of the other chiefs; and...where the chief man sat, the course was directed and orders issued....All came down together, and arrived within a stone's cast of the bank. (Stuart, 1976, p. 81)

On the bank, De Soto had his crossbow-men hidden and tried to persuade the chief to come ashore, wanting to take him captive, but the chief sent up three barges loaded with fish and persimmon bread as gifts. De Soto ordered the men to fire and they struck down five or six Indians but the Native People did not panic, according to the Gentleman of Elvas's journal:

> They retired with great order, not one leaving the oar, even though the one next to him might have fallen....These were fine-looking men, very large and well-formed; and what with the awnings, the plumes, and the shields, and the number of people in the fleet, it appeared like a famous armada of galleys.

The excerpt written by the Gentleman of Elvas highlights the invasion of De Soto's expedition into the lives of the Native People in North America and documents some of the achievements of Native People. Ask students to tell or show their sketches of what they imagined about the meeting scene between De Soto and the chief.

With the whole group, review what took place between the two groups, and engage the students in working with partners and writing their ideas about an "ideal meeting" between De Soto and the Tunica chief. What could have happened at an ideal meeting? Ask the partners to return to the whole group and read aloud what they suggested for an ideal meeting. To further develop an awareness of some of the positive and negative actions that can occur when explorers meet Native People, engage the students in looking for further data sources that document the meetings of De Soto (or other explorers) with Native People.

Activity #60: "A World New to Europeans"

To prepare for drawing scenes on a mural about a world "new" to Europeans, guide students to books such as those on the reading list in Figure 8–3. Ask students to use the books as sources to obtain background knowledge about this time in history and use their knowledge as a stimulus for drawing scenes on a mural about the world "new" to Europeans explorers.

FIGURE 8–3   *Books about a World New to Europeans*

Native American Life Before Columbus

Martin, P. *Indians Before Columbus: Twenty Thousand Years of North American History Revealed by Archaeology.* University of Chicago Press, 1975. Illustrations provide useful resource for students. Nonfiction. Grades 5–8.

Early Legendary Exploration

Fritz, J. *Brendan-the Navigator: A History Mystery about the Discovery of America.* Putnam, 1979. Recounts life of Saint Brendan and his legendary voyage to North America before Viking explorations. Biography. Grades 5–8.

Early Viking Explorations

Humble, R. *The Age of Leif Erikson.* Watts, 1989. Gives background about European explorations and includes a time line. Nonfiction. Grades 5–8.

Lauber, P. *Who Discovered America? Settlers and Explorers of the New world Before the Time of Columbus.* Random House, 1970. Story of the new world in pre-Columbian times. Nonfiction. Grades 4–6.

Schiller, B. *The Vinlanders' Saga* Holt, 1966. Reviews period of exploration five centuries before Columbus. Nonfiction. Grades 6–8.

Sources for Time Line for Age of Explorers

Alpeer, A. F. *Forgotten Voyager: The Story of Amerigo Vespucci.* Carolrhoda, 1992. Discusses Vespucci's (1451–1512) early life, his contributions to cartography and navigation, and his voyages. Includes section on the historical method. Biography. Grades 4–8.

Asimov, I. *Ferdinand Magellan: Opening the Door to World Exploration.* Gareth Stevens, 1991. Ill. by J. R. Karpinski. Gives details about Magellan's (1480-1521) early voyages. Biography. Grade 6 and up.

Asimov, I., & Kaplan, E. *Henry Hudson: Arctic Explorer and North American Adventurer.* Gareth Stevens, 1991. Recounts Hudson's attempts to find a passage to the east around North America in 1607 and 1611 and the crew's mutiny. Includes a glossary and labeled drawings of the ships. Biography. Grades 4–5.

Blackwood, A. *Ferdinand Magellan,* Bookwright, 1986. Retells voyage from Spain to the Pacific and Magellan's first circumnavigation of the world. Biography. Grade 6 and up.

Goodnough, D. *Francis Drake, Sea Pirate.* Troll, 1979. Portrays life of Drake, a famous English navigator. Biography. Grades 5 and up.

FIGURE 8–3 **Continued**

Hill, K. *And Tomorrow the Stars: The Story of John Cabot*. Ill. by L. Kubinya. Dodd, 1968. Portrays Cabot's explorations to find a shorter route to the Spice Islands in the East Indies in 1497. Biography. Grade 6 and up.

Marrin, A. *Inca and Spaniard: Pizarro and the Conquest of Peru*. Atheneum, 1989. In 1532, the Incas, led by their prince Atahualpa, fought Francisco Pizarro and his men in territory now present-day Peru. Part of the text comes from the accounts of Guaman Pomo, a Native of Peru who served the Spaniards as a minor official. Nonfiction. Biography. Grade 7 and up.

Stein, R. C. *The Story of Marquette and Jolliet*. Children's Press, 1981. Recounts the exploration of these two Europeans. Biography. Grade 6 and up.

Stott, K. *Columbus and the Age of Exploration*. Watts, 1985. Discusses such explorers as Columbus, Vasco da Gama, and Francis Drake. Nonfiction. Grade 6 and up.

Syme, R. *Balboa, Finder of the Pacific*. Morrow, 1956. Portrays the explorations of Vasco Nunez de Balboa (1475–1517), the first European to discover the Pacific Ocean. Biography. Grade 6 and up.

Syme, R. *De Soto, Finder of the Mississippi*. Morrow, 1957. Portrays such events as leading an expedition from Florida to Oklahoma and discovering the Mississippi River and traveling with Francisco Pizarro to Peru. Biography. Grade 6 and up.

Thompson, K. *Pedro Menendez de Aviles*. Ill. by C. Shaw. Trans. from English by A. F. Ada. Hispanic Stories Series. Raintree, 1990. Portrays the life of this sixteenth-century explorer who established the first permanent settlement in the U.S. Biography. Grades 5–8.

Werner, E. *The Story of Henry Hudson: Master Explorer*. Dell, 1991. Discusses the voyages to the North as Hudson tried to find a waterway through North America to Asia. Biography. Grade 5 and up.

CHAPTER NINE

A.D. 1600–1699

What was going on in the seventeenth century?

Multicultural Perspectives

A unit about this period can offer possibilities of learning about Africa's people, Asia's peacekeepers, Australia's Native People and settlers, Europe's immigrants, as well as the encounters of the Native People of the Americas with Europeans. With chil-

dren's books as resources, the class environment and lessons can be carefully planned to help the students develop concepts and generalizations as they inquire about what was going on in other parts of the world. To assist in this, suggest some of the books in the perspectives in Figure 9–1.

FIGURE 9–1   Children's Books about A.D. 1600–1699

PERSPECTIVES FOR 1600s

African Heritage

Petry, A. *Tituba of Salem* Village. Crowell, 1964. Tituba, an intelligent black slave, is vulnerable to suspicion and attack from the witch-hunters in Salem. Historical fiction. Grade 6 and up.

Asian Heritage

Namioka, L. *The Coming of the Bear*. HarperCollins, 1992. In the 1600s, Japanese colonists were trying to settle the island of Ezo (now Hokkaido), which caused tension with the Aimu who lived there. Two samurai help ease the tensions of war. Historical fiction. Grades 5–9.

European Heritage

Bowen, G. *Stranded at Plimoth Plantation, 1626*. HarperCollins, 1994. Fictional diary of a young Plimoth settler, Christopher Sears, who records the trials and tribulations living at Plimoth Plantation in 1626. Detailed woodcuts show shelters, fencing, and daily activities. Historical fiction. Grades 4–7.

Kurelek, W. *They Sought a New World: The Story of European Immigration to North America*. Tundra Books, 1985. Depicts the various groups of people who settled on the North American land. Nonfiction. Grades 7–8.

Rinaldi, A. *A Break with Charity: A Story about the Salem Witch Trials*. Harcourt Brace Jovanovich, 1992. In Salem, Susannah English wants to join the girls who meet to have their fortunes told by the

---

FIGURE 9–1   Continued

slave Tituba. She observes the mass hysteria where people are named as witches and gets the courage to help end the "crying out" that threatens to tear apart her community. Nonfiction. Grades 5–8.

Walters, K. *Samuel Eaton's Day: A Day in the Life of a Pilgrim Boy*. Scholastic, 1993. Set in 1627 at Plimouth Plantation (note authentic historical spelling), the book portrays a hard day in the life of 7-year-old Samuel as he gets dressed, checks his animal snare, and gathers wood before he eats his breakfast of curds, mussels, and parsley. During the day, he helps the men harvest rye despite the pain of his blisters. Historical fiction. Grades 4–6.

Latino/Hispanic Heritage

Hoobler, D., & Hoobler, T. *South American Portraits* Ill. by S. Marchesi. Steck-Vaughn, 1994. Chronologically portrays 12 South Americans who became prominent after the arrival of the conquistadors. Discusses Garcilaso de la Vega, a Spanish-American writer, Rose of Lima, a girl from Peru who was the first American saint, Antonio Francisco Lisboa, a sculptor, liberators Simon Bolivar and Jose de San Martin, and others. Grades 5–8.

Rohmer, H., Chow, O., & Vidauke, M. *The Invisible Hunters*. Children's Book Pr., 1987. Portrays the impact of the first European traders on the life of the Miskiot Indians in seventeenth-century Nicaragua. Historical fiction. Grades 4–6.

Original Native American Heritage

Brebeuf, Father Jean de. *The Huron Carol*. Dutton, 1993. This is the story of the birth of Christ as set in the Huron world that was written by a missionary, Father Jean de Brebeuf in the 1600s. Folk literature. Grade 4.

Fritz, J. *The Double Life of Pocahontas*. Ill. by E. Young. Putnam, 1982. Details life of a Native American princess and her journey to England as the wife of John Rolfe. Biography. Grades 4–6.

Sewall, M. *People of the Breaking Day*. Atheneum, 1990. Portrays the Wampanoag people as a proud industrious nation in southeastern Massachusetts before the settlers arrived. Shows the life in the tribe and the place of each member in the society and gives details about hunting, farming, survival skills, and the value of a harmonious relationship with nature. Includes recreational and spiritual activities. Nonfiction. Grades 4–5.

Differently Abled Heritage

De Trevino, E. B. *Nacar. The White Deer*. Farrar, Straus & Giroux, 1963. A mute Mexican shepherd boy protects a white deer and presents it to the King of Spain in 1630. Historical fiction. Grades 4–6.

Female Image Heritage

Fritz, E. I. *Anne Hutchinson*. Chelsea, 1991. Details Anne's early life and gives an historical context for her banishment from the New England colony. Biography. Grades 4–5.

Nichols, J. K. *A Matter of Conscience: The Trial of Anne Hutchinson*. Ill. by D. Krovatin. Steck-Vaughn, 1993. Describes religious climate in which Anne lived and mentions the difference between a "Covenant of Works" and a "Covenant of Grace"—two views that help readers understand her words and actions before and after her trial. Biography. Grades 4–6.

Speare, E. G. *The Witch of Blackbird Pond*. Houghton Mifflin, 1958. Kit, raised by a loving grandfather, is encouraged to read history, poetry, and plays. Historical fiction. Grade 6 and up.

continued

FIGURE 9–1   Continued

Religious Minority Heritage

Aliki. *The Story of William Penn*. Prentice Hall, 1984. William Penn (1644–1718), a Quaker, establishes the colony of Pennsylvania as a refuge for religious nonconformers and he treats fairly the Indians who named him Onas, which meant quill or pen. Biography. Grades 4–6.

Ammon, R. *Growing Up Amish*. Atheneum, 1989. Portrays the history of the Amish movement and shows the Amish lifestyle in a Pennsylvania Dutch area. Nonfiction. Grades 4–6.

Costabel, E. D. *The Jews of New Amsterdam*. Atheneum, 1988. Recounts the struggles of the Jews who journeyed to America from Brazil during the colonial period and discovered that the United States did not hold equality for all its people. Nonfiction. Grades 4–5.

Rice, E. *American Saints and Seers: American-born Religions and the Genius Behind Them*. Four Winds, 1982. Describes America's various religions, including the religions of Native American Indians, Shakers, Mormons, and Christian Scientists. Nonfiction. Grades 7–8.

Europe's Immigrants to North America

"It is grateful we were to reach any land safely, and thus we came to New England, first landing on the point of Cape Cod" is the way Marcia Sewall describes the feelings of the Pilgrims in her book, *The Pilgrims of Plimouth* (Atheneum, 1986, all grades; point out the spelling in the title). Sewall continues, "While still on board ship, in preparation for life in America, we agreed upon laws of behavior." Today, students visiting Plymouth, Massachusetts, can see Plymouth Rock on Water Street along with *Mayflower II,* a replica of the original ship, before they visit Plimouth Plantation, a re-creation of the newcomers' seventeenth-century village. Today, Plymouth Rock is about 6 feet across and rests under a protective canopy, surrounded on three sides by granite and on a fourth side by an iron grill facing the waves of the Atlantic Ocean. This is said to be the very spot on which the Pilgrims came ashore in 1620 and it has withstood the erosion of centuries as a symbol of the beginning of European civilization in the land now called the United States of America.

Invite students to meet in small groups and tell others what they know from their experience studying the Pilgrims.

Activity #61: "Settlers at Plymouth Rock"

Cullinan (1981) suggests that students can get further involved in the study of the settlers at Plymouth Rock with the following: Ask students to listen to parts from *Who's That Stepping on Plymouth Rock?* (Coward, McCann & Geogehan, 1975, grade 5 and up) by J. Fritz and then think about what they would tell today's tourists visiting Plymouth Rock if *they* were the rock. Invite students to write a draft of the speech to tell what has happened to the rock over the years and then deliver it from the rock's point of view to others in the class.

Thanksgiving's Beginnings

"Harvest festivals go back to ancient times when most countries of the world celebrated a bountiful harvest. The Thanksgiving holiday, as students know it, was brought to this country by the Pilgrims. In the fall of 1621, the Pilgrims celebrated their first harvest with a bountiful feast and shared the food—turkey, deer, roast corn, Indian pudding, and fruit—with the Native Americans who lived nearby. To enrich students' further understanding of the meaning of Thanksgiving day, read aloud selections from *Thanksgiving Poems* (Holiday House, 1985, all grades) edited by Myra Cohn Livingston, a collection of traditional and contemporary poems that commemorate this day of celebration.

Students in all grades who are interested in the origin of Thanksgiving can review the topic independently or with the whole group. A place to begin is with the belief of some specialists who maintain that the Thanksgiving celebration descended from the British Custom called Harvest Home. In the celebration, villages joined together to bring in the grain from the fields and share a feast when the work was completed. This custom may have been continued by the English pilgrims with Massasoit, the leader of the Wampanoag tribe, and his people who joined with the Pilgrims for what was called "thanksfiving." In documentation of this, Edward Winslow, Pilgrim father, wrote several words in his journal that could be reproduced *as he spelled them* on a chart for the class: "Our harvest being gotten in, our Govenor sent four men on fowling, so that we might after a special manner rejoice together after we had gathered the fruit of our labor" (Morissey, 1991).

After reading or hearing Winslow's words, discuss with the class, "Just what is Edward Winslow, a Pilgrim father, saying to you? Can you tell us more about the meaning of 'four men on fowling' and the 'fruit of our labor'? What does Winslow say to you personally?"

Activity #62: "Colonists' Families and Homes"

Invite students to look at illustrations about the colonists and identify items they see in the homes of the colonists. Record their suggestions on the board in a list with the heading, "In Colonists' Houses." Ask the students to meet with partners and identify the objects on the list that the students do not have in their houses today and make a list of the items. Then, return to the original list on the board and ask the students to tell the objects that they have now that the colonists did not have in their houses. Invite the students to return to this last list, and as a whole group, suggest items that they could do without if they had to do so today.

If You Lived Series

Show the cutaway diagram of the *Mayflower* and ask students what they wonder about when they hear about the *Mayflower*. Write their questions on the board. Read aloud excerpts from *If You Sailed on the Mayflower in 1620* (Scholastic, 1991, grade 4 and up) by Ann McGovern. Discuss the children's questions in the whole group to see how many of their questions were answered by the reading. Review several of the book's questions with the students. Ask the students to search for other books that could answer any of the questions unanswered by the book.

Activity #63: "If You Lived..."

Ask the students to divide into groups to make connections from this time period to other periods and to study life in different periods with the stories in the *If You Lived…* series. After reading and discussing a selected story in small groups, ask the students to regroup as a whole class and report what they learned about people and their problems in their time period and any connections to this period that

they discerned. For the reporting, the students can begin with reports about the latest time period and go back in time as "time-travelers" or begin with reports about the earliest time period and go forward in time as "Back to the Future" adventurers. For students interested further in connections, guide them to History Master 26, "Historical Periods in *If You Lived* Series."

North Americans' Encounter with Europeans

For older students, read aloud excerpts from James E. Knight's *Blue Feather's Vision: The Dawn of Colonial America* (Troll, 1982, grades 4–6). In the story, Blue Feather, aged chief of the Algonquin nation in the Massachusetts tribe, fears that the English white men who have killed two warriors will return and destroy the Native American way of life. Discuss with students the contrast of the words of Blue Feather with the words of his youngest son, who thinks that the warriors and their arrows will drive away the white-skinned man. He does not believe the words and vision of his father. Ask such questions as:

1. What do you think the youngest son should do? Why?
2. How do you think the other Native People will react if he used warriors and arrows? Why?
3. Has something like that ever happened to you (where you did not believe the words of a parent or an authority figure)? What did you do?
4. As you reflect on that now, do you think that was a good thing to do? Why or why not?
5. Is there anything you would have done differently? What could the youngest son do differently in the story?

Activity #64: "Sharing the Earth"

With students, reread excerpts from *Blue Feather's Vision* or from *People of the Breaking Day*, and ask students the meaning they receive from "It is Kiehtan, the Great Spirit, who made us all." Discuss some of the differences (similarities) between the Native People's view of life, which was in harmony with nature, the spirits, and the land, and the European settlers' apparent desire to conquer their natural surroundings. Write the ideas of the students about these differences/similarities on the board, under the headings, "Native People's View of Nature" and "European Settlers' View of Nature."

With the students' input, elicit their views about Blue Feather's fears about the English white men.

Were his fears justified? Unjustified? Ask the students to consider the point of view of the chief's youngest son, who thought that the warriors and their weapons could drive away the white-skinned men. Discuss the alternatives to this situation that are suggested by the students before asking them to write their own positions on the matter as if they had been there with the chief and his son.

A "Voyce Allso"

In 1648, Margaret Brent argued that she should have a seat in Maryland's Assembly with "a vote in the howse for herselfe and voyce allso." She was the attorney for the Lord proprietor in St. Mary's City (the capital of Maryland founded in 1634 by Governor Leonard Calvert). Lord Baltimore, the governor, denied her request, but the assemblymen told him that his affairs were "better for the Collonys safety...in her hands than in any mans (sic) else in the whole Province" (Stuart, 1976, p. 137). With students, explore the feelings that Margaret Brent might have had when she was denied "a vote" by Lord Baltimore: How do they think Margaret felt? Why do they think she felt that way? Who has a different idea about how she felt? What do the students suppose the feelings of the assemblymen were in this situation? Have the students ever had something like this happen to them? What happened? What did they do? As they think back now, was that a good thing to do? Why or why not? Is there anything they could have done differently? Is there anything that Margaret could have done differently? How many students agree or disagree with the Colonial governor's actions? Why?

Activity #65: "Women Who Wanted a 'Voyce'"

Elicit from students names of women who wanted a "voyce allso" in matters during this period. Have them identify what recognition, if any, the women received. Mention that many famous women have asked for a "voyce allso" today and have achieved recognition in different ways. Their lives can be studied by interested students and the information they find can be placed in a personality file to be used for writing biographies and as reference material in research and discussions. Engage students in finding out more about any or all of the following famous women who have asked for a "voyce allso":

Helen of Troy	Cleopatra
Queen Isabella	Catherine of Russia
Mary, Queen of Scots	Queen Elizabeth I

Jane Addams	Anne Marbury
Julia Lathrop	Hutchinson
Clara Barton	Florence Nightingale
Lucretia C. Mott	Sarah M. Fuller
Margaret Sanger	Elizabeth Cady Stanton
Dr. M. Carey Thomas	Margaret Olivia Sage
Annie J. Cannon	Marie Curie
Jane Austen	Florence Sabin
Christina Rossetti	Edith Wharton
Ethel Barrymore	Edna St. Vincent Millay
Clare Booth Luce	Eleanor Roosevelt
Frieda Miller	Frances Perkins
Madame Lucie Aubrac	Fusaye Ishikawa
Emmeline G. Parkhurst	Sarah Bernhardt
Mary Cassatt	Pearl Buck
Susan B. Anthony	Maria Mitchell
Mary Ann McClintock	Martha Wright

Link the past to the present and mention that some famous women have asked for a "voyce allso" and achieved recognition recently by being inducted into the national Women's Hall of Fame. The students can find out more about these women and place the information they find in a personality file as a resource for writing biographies. These are the contemporary American women who have been nationally recognized for having a "voyce allso:" Ethel Percy Andrus, founder of American Association of Retired Persons; Antoinette Blackwell, America's first ordained minister; Emily Blackwell, physician and pioneer women's medical educator; Shirley Chisholm, political and civil rights leader; Jacqueline Cochran, Director of Women's Air Force Service Pilots; Ruth Colvin, founder of Literacy Volunteers of America; Marian Wright Edelman, founder of Children's Defense Fund; Alice Evans, microbiologist; Betty Friedan, feminist strategist and author; Ella Grasso, first woman elected govenor of a state; Martha Griffiths, former lieutenant govenor of Michigan; Fannie Lou Hamer, civil rights and political leader; Dorothy Height, President of National Council of Negro Women; Dolores Huerta, co-founder of the United Farm Workers' union; Mary Jacobi, physician and leader in medical education for women; Mae Jemison, first African American woman in space; and Gloria Yerkovich, founder of Child Find to locate missing children.

Colonial Heritage Concept Box

Rinehart (1980) suggests making heritage and concept boxes to arouse the interest of nonreading students or those reluctant to read. A heritage box is a collection of items that shows several distinctive characteristics of a time period. To catch the interest of a reluctant reader or a nonreader you can introduce the life of the Pilgrims by reading aloud a favorite book and then engaging students in creating heritage boxes to hold a collection of items and drawings that show some of the characteristics of the Pilgrims' cultural heritage and their time period. Rinehart and other librarians made the original boxes, but similar ones can be created by interested students.

Activity # 66: "Brainstorming"

Ideas for a colonial heritage box can be brainstormed by students at any grade level. Perhaps the box can contain sketches of wooden toys, a corncob, dried apple head dolls, a hornbook replica, a simulated paper lantern, and drawings of other unusual items or some articles of clothing of this period. With students, discuss items for the colonial heritage box and list on the board or on an overhead transparency things that could be included. To assist in questioning during a brainstorming activity, use the letters in the word *brainstorm* as guides for the types of questions to ask students:

> **B** is for *brainstorming* with questions about the ABCs—ask the students for words in alphabetical order that are related to the topic (in this case, the characteristics of colonial time period).
>
> **R** is for the student's *reactions* to the topic.
>
> **A** is for any *alliteration, antonyms* (and synonyms) related to the topic.
>
> **I** is for *items* or *individuals* related to the topic.
>
> **N** is for *new* descriptions the students want to contribute.
>
> **S** is for *Similarities* and what students *see* and *smell* that is related.
>
> **T** is for what students *taste* and *touch* that is related.
>
> **O** is for *objects* related to the topic.
>
> **R** is for *rhyme, rhythm,* and *repitition* related to the topic.
>
> **M** is for the students' *moods* (and feelings) about the topic.

Draw out the students' ideas for creating objects for the heritage box. Then group the students' ideas on the board or transparency to help them organize their thoughts. Suggestions from the students can include a guessing game about the period, with the answers given somewhere on a paper in the box. There can be a bibliography for further reading, a song sheet, the students' original books, and a page of recipes. Further, the students can put a list of the contents inside the lid of the box for a checklist to account for the items. Donated to the school library, the classroom book corner, the children's wing of a local hospital, or a nearby children's home, the boxes can provide a meaningful introduction or a summary to the time period.

Pocahontas and Other Native Americans

"Princess Pocahontas/ Powhatan's daughter,/ Stared at the white men/come across the water" begins the biographical story poem of "Pocohantas" in *A Book of Americans* (Holt, 1986, all grades) by Rosemary and Stephen Benet. After reading the poem and other books about Pocahontas aloud, ask students as a group to dictate or write what they know about Pocahontas. Write their suggestions on the board. With the children's help, arrange their suggestions into a new free-verse poem about her. Ask the students to draw illustrations to accompany their free-verse poem when it is transferred to a permanent chart for the classroom. Affix the illustrations as a border for display and rereading.

Activity #67: "Being a Biographer"

The students can get involved with some of the research approaches used by biographers when they re-create an event in the lives of Original Native American girls and women such as Pocahontas, Sacajawea, Maria Tallchief, Nancy Ward, Daisy Hooee Nampeyo, Susette La Flesche, Sarah Winnemucca, and others. To gather information about a personality, ask students to read information from a biography, take notes, and rate the information about the girls or woman in one of the following ways: it supports a positive female role; it supports a negative role; and it supports a neutral one (Haupt, 1984). Their page of notes can be arranged in a manner similar to the following:

Information I Selected about

	Positive	Negative	Neutral
1. _____			
2. _____			

After taking note of some of the events in the biography, students can discuss their information and ratings:

1. What information did you get about the physical appearance, dress and body ornamentation, and personality of the woman? What were the interests and activities of the woman and her role in the family?
2. Which women, if any, were evaluated as the Indian princess stereotype or the white man's helper stereotype?
3. What were your findings about the Native American females in biographies?

According to Haupt, it appears that the Native American Indian females in biographies published after 1972 have been portrayed more accurately and objectively than in earlier publications.

Significance of Diaries and Journals

A well-written children's book where the character keeps a diary or journal will help increase an interest in writing by elementary and middle school students. Book characters who write also help increase an interest in the contributions made by primary sources such as diaries and journals. Related to this, Samuels (1989) reported that older students (grade 7 and up) enjoyed reading books with teen protagonists with problems that seemed real to them. Carlsen (1980) found that older students wanted to identify with characters like themselves and read about problems similar to their own. To offer stories about characters who had struggles similar to those of today's students, read aloud parts from historical fiction to show the students different ways in which the characters used reading and writing—literacy—to resolve their problems in life and to help students see ways that the characters' quality of life was improved through their interest in books and writing. As a follow-up to the stories, the students can discuss how the characters relied on their literacy to resolve situations they faced and then select additional books for independent reading that have additional characters who relied on their literacy to solve problems. Suggested books from various genres are found in Figure 9–2.

FIGURE 9–2   Significance of Diaries and Journals

1700s

Fritz, J. *The Cabin Faced West.* Coward, McCann, 1968. Anne Hamilton keeps a diary and writes letters to her friends back East. Historical fiction. Grade 6 and up.

1800s

Blos, J. *A Gathering of Days.* Scribners, 1979. Includes imaginary entries from the diary of a girl from New England for the years 1830–1832. Historical fiction. Grade 6 and up.

Nixon, J. L. *A Family Apart.* Bantam, 1987. Jennifer and Jeff listen to their grandmother read to them from a dairy kept by their great-great grandmother, Frances Mary Kelly. Frances Mary lived in New York City with her parents and five brothers and sisters, and her life changed from being simple, fun, and loving when Mr. Kelly died. In order for the family to survive, Mrs. Kelly and the two oldest children, Frances Mary and Mike, found any kind of work they could, and the entries tell what happened to the family. Historical fiction. Grade 6 and up.

1900s

Dekker, M. *The Nature Book: Discovering, Exploring, Observing, Experimenting with Plants and Animals at Home and Outdoors,* Macmillan, 1988. With information from the book, living things can be observed and a notebook of observations can be kept as a result of working with the pages labeled "Food Is Nature, Too." Informational. Grades 5–6.

Fitzhugh, L. *Harriet the Spy.* Harper, 1964. Eleven-year-old Harriet keeps her journal in a notebook and writes down her impression of her family, friends, and the people in her neighborhood in New

FIGURE 9–2 Significance of Diaries and Journals

York. To get her impressions, Harriet spies on the others and is ignored by her parents who are busy with their own activities. Contemporary realism. Grades 4–5.

George, J. C. *My Side of the Mountain*. Dutton, 1959. Sam Gribley keeps a diary about his adventures in the wilderness. Realistic fiction. Grade 6 and up.

Griffin, P. R. *Hobkin*, Margaret K. McElderry, 1992. This is a book best suited for individual reading because of its subject matter of abuse. Reading old diaries in her new home after escaping an abusive stepfather, Kay realizes that, for many years, the house has been the home of a helpful brownie (a hob) named Hobkin. Contemporary realism. Grades 6–7.

Heinrich, B. *An Owl in the House: A Naturalist Diary*. Little, 1990. Heinrich makes a realistic comment about a naturalist's interest in adopting a great horned owlet found in the Vermont woods and records the changes in the owl's appearance and its growing interest in food. Informational. Grades 4–6.

Sachs, M. *Dorrie's Book*. Doubleday, 1975. Dorrie, a seventh-grader, and her friends, are challenged by the teacher to write a "real book" with chapters, a plot, and characters. For this assignment, Dorrie writes about her perfect family where she is an only child her parents are like movie stars, and they live in a beautiful apartment that has a balcony. Contemporary realism. Grade 6 and up.

Snyder, Z. K. *Libby on Wednesday*. Delacorte, 1990. Libby, educated at home, goes to public middle school where she feels she is superior to her classmates; in contrast, they feel she is socially inferior to them. Libby takes refuge in writing and tells her story in her journal entries in a third-person narrative. Libby and others learn of the serious problems of their friends in their writers' club during Wednesday meetings. Contemporary realism. Grade 5 and up.

Activity #68: "Robinson Crusoe's Manuscript of 1659"

Discuss with older students some meaningful purposes for writing about different historical periods: (1) their notebooks can be used to record what they learned each day, (2) a diary and journal can keep their thoughts and (3) a sketchbook can hold their drawings. As an example to show students, present *My Journals and Sketch books by Robinson Cruso* (Harcourt, 1972, grade 5 and up) by Annie Poltzer, an account about a fictional hero based on a real-life adventure. The students will "discover" that Robinson Crusoe's "manuscript" has been found in a trunk in an old Scottish manor house. In Politzer's book, the students will see brief journal entries that date from October 3, 1659, to May 7, 1684. Along with drawings, there is a map of the island, and a plan of Crusoe's house with possessions such as a "basket of turtle eggs" and "snares for rats." The steps Crusoe used to weave baskets and to make a ship in a bottle are also included and can be followed by the students to reenact the activities supposedly faced by the stranded man on the deserted island. Point out that the student's own "manuscripts" and "sketchbooks" can include a plan of their own houses, a list of their possessions, sketches of items, and directions for "doing something" the students do at home.

Where Native Americans Lived

"The Abenaki lived along rivers and streams that stretched toward the rocky coast of the Atlantic Ocean," states Evelyn Wolfson in *From Abenaki to Zuni: A Dictionary of Native American Tribes* (Walker, 1988, grade 4 and up). "The Abenaki built small villages high above the water on bluffs, which offered them protection against attack." Wolfson also mentions that her dictionary of Native American communities is intended to inspire students to look further and "fill in the gaps" in Native American history. With a large map of America and information from Wolfson's book, ask the students to help locate the areas in which selected Native People lived.

Invite students to contact a representative from a local historical group to discover what Native Americans first settled in their area, what groups of people came later, and what parts of the culture of Native Americans and later groups are recognized in the community today. Additionally, ask students to do the following:

1. Survey the classroom(s) to find out the different languages, spoken and prepare a list that identifies the languages.
2. Survey the Yellow Pages in the local telephone directory and take notes for a report about business or services that appear to be serving particular groups of people.
3. Invite the parents, friends, or relatives of students to class to talk about their language, customs, and ways they maintain their heritage and communicate with their ancestors' original home country.
4. Make a historical scrapbook of the various ethnic groups in the area and note what they have contributed to the community.
5. Survey the White Pages in the local telephone directory and take notes for a multicultural report about names that appear to identify particular groups of people now living in the community.

Activity #69: "Native American Communities"

As a project to help "fill in the gaps" of Native American history with older students, discuss the entries in the two lists of tribal names on History Master 27, "What Are the Lists Describing?" Ask the students what they think the lists are describing (Hyde & Bizar, 1989). City names? Bodies of water? Indian chiefs? Discuss the names on the lists and ask, "Where did each tribe live?" and "Why do you think the communities are divided into groups on the list?"

Ask the students to work in groups of three or four and locate where these communities lived. Give each student a blank map that has some geographical features such as water, current states' boundaries, and so on. Ask them to write in pencil where each community of Native Americans may have lived. Students can then turn to reference material such as maps, atlases, dictionaries, encyclopedias, related texts, and trade books, and record what they find about the communities on the maps. Invite the small groups to return to the whole group and discuss what was written on the maps. Some of the students may point out that the differences in the lists are the locations of the communities. For instance, Group A lived along the western seaboard; Group B lived in the in area now Florida; Group C, the eastern seaboard; Group D, the plains; and Group E, the northeastern seaboard.

For further research, ask students to find the locations of the following communities using the small maps by William Sauts Book, a Native American artist, in *Abenaki to Zuni: A Dictionary of Native American Tribes* by Wolfson or in other sources:

Pequot	Oneida	Tuscarora
Abenaki	Onondaga	Others

With the students, mention the complexity of researching information about Native Americans in the available data sources. As an example of the complexity, the Europeans called the Lenni Lenape by another name, the Delaware. Information about these Native Americans, primarily farmers, is thus most often found when the name, Delaware, is discussed. This name difference also points out that communities often referred to themselves by one name, that other communities often referred to them by another name, and that Europeans often gave them yet another name. Thus, varying information about the names of the communities can be written on a Name Difference Chart and facts about them can be cross-checked very carefully.

As another example, a student may read in a source that the Pequot tribe is extinct and yet find another source that indicates that in 1983, the descendants of the Pequot, on the Mashantucket Reservation in Connecticut, were granted federal recognition and awarded $600,000 to acquire land and $300,000 to develop their economy. Sometimes, the students also will find that a name, such as the Algonquin, could be used to identify a group of people as well as a language family.

Since the English settlers had a great deal of contact with the Algonquin people, some of the words from their languages are included in American English today and some students will be surprised to learn that they know some Algonquin words that they can illustrate (e.g., *chipmunk, hominy, moccasin, moose, opossum, raccoon, skunk, squash, toboggan,* and *woodchuck*).

Government of Native People

"By the shores of Gitchie Gumee,/ By the shining Big-Sea-Water,/ Stood the wigwam of Nakomis,/ Daughter of the Moon, Nokomis" begins the verses to read aloud from "Hiawatha's Childhood" by Henry Wadsworth Longfellow found in *The Arbuthnot Anthology of Children's Literature* (1971, all grades). Ask students to close their eyes to imagine the scenes of the shining Big-Sea-Water, the wigwam, the pine trees, old Nokomis, and little Hiawatha, or ask them to sketch the scenes they think of while they are listening to the words. Mention that the Iroquois Confederacy (the League of Six

Nations) was a league founded by Deganawida and carried on by his disciple, Hiawatha, who, as a child, "learned of every bird its language,/ learned their names and all their secrets."

Activity #70: "Iroquois Confederacy"

The students studying this topic can begin with *Hiawatha and the Iroquois League* (Silver Burdett, 1989, grade 4 and up), by Megan McClard and George Ypsilantis, to get further information about the Hiawatha's life, the Iroquois, the Indians' council, and the European settlers. Discuss the idea that prior to the European settlers' arrival, six Iroquois communities around the Finger Lakes in today's New York had joined together into the Iroquois Confederacy, a group that also was called the League of Six Nations, a league founded by Deganawida and his disciple, Hiawatha. Wolfson (1988) has identified the six communities and described the meanings of their names:

> Cayuga (meaning where-the-boats-were-taken-out; also mucky land)
>
> Mohawk (man-eaters)
>
> Onondaga (on-top-of-the-hill-or-mountain)
>
> Seneca (people-of-the-big-hill)
>
> Tuscarora (hemp-gatherers)
>
> Oneida (people-of-the-stone)

In the Oneida tribe, the women made many important decisions for the people because the men hunted and fished away from the villages for lengthy periods of time. The Oneida and the other nations agreed to be governed by a common council of representatives from the communities and were allies when engaged in battles against the Algonquin and Huron people, longtime foes.

To simulate a government by a council as the Native Americans did, invite the students to a class meeting to discuss the idea of being governed by a common council of representatives from the students. If the students had a council government for their classroom, how would they select their representatives? How long would the representatives serve? What issues could be considered by the council?

For additional discussion, the students may review a map of the communities' locations and discuss how the location of the Confederacy might have influenced some of the things that happened during this time period. They can discuss/write reasons why the location of the Iroquois Confederacy might have influenced the following:

1. The Iroquois Confederacy bitterly opposed the expansion of the French into their world and they attempted to prevent the French from building trading outposts and forts south of the Great Lakes.
2. They bitterly opposed their longtime foes, the Huron people.
3. The Iroquois Confederacy supported the British.
4. The Iroquois Confederacy became allies of the British during the American Revolution.

Fate of Native People

After discussing the information related to a map activity about locating the communities of Native Americans, the students may inquire into the fate of some of the Native Americans in the Americas. Related to the locations of the communities, students can investigate the patterns of settlement of newcomers from different countries in the United States and give responses to the following: Who were the newcomers? Where did they originate? Why did they come? Where did they settle in America? Why there? For instance, different student groups could select books that discuss different parts of the country and investigate the diverse groups who settled there with History Master 28, "What Were the Patterns of Settlement on Lands Inhabited by Native Americans?" To do this, the students can inquire into the fate of some of the Native American communities in the Americas and relate that to the patterns of settlement of various newcomers.

Activity# 71: "Native People"

To aid in the investigation about Native Americans who lived in different regions and newcomers who settled in those regions, ask students to review additional information from different sources with audiovisual materials. Several titles of videos related to this topic appear in Figure 9–3 and are matched to the names of Native communities that are representative of many of the people who lived in different geographical regions. Engage students, working with partners, to write original stories about Native Americans and newcomers after they research the history of Native People in their regions and the settlers who moved into the regions. Point out that some of the regional names of Native Americans may not be found in Figure 9–3.

FIGURE 9–3   *Patterns of Newcomer Settlement Affecting Native Americans*

U. S. REGION	MAJOR GROUPS AFFECTED AND RESOURCES	NEWCOMERS
Northwest	Bella Coola, Chinook, and Haida: *The Drum* (New Dimension Media, 1987) was produced by Alaska Native Resource Development Project and shows how a Native American tribe reaffirms its heritage. Grade 4 and up.	(to be identified by students)
Plains	Apache, Blackfoot, Cheyenne, Crow, Lakota, Comanche, Kiowa, Omaha, Pawnee, and Teton: *Contrary Warriors: A Film of the Crow Tribe* (Direct Cinema, 1986) gives tribe's history as well as portrayal of contemporary Crow leader, Robert Yellowtail. *Ghost Dance* (New Day Films, 1991) commemorates the 1890 Wounded Knee Massacre with poetry, art, or Lakota artists. Advanced grade 6 and up.	
Southwest	Apache, Hopi, Navajo, Papago, and Zuni: *Letter from an Apache* (Barr Films, 1985) is an adaptation of a letter written by the Apache, Wassajah, in 1905, who was taken at age 5 by raiding Pima Indians and later sold to a white man. Wassajah, in adulthood, became America's first male Native American physician. Grades 4–6. *Monument Valley: Navajo Homeland* (Finley-Holiday Film Corp., 1991) shows tribe's homeland, a religious ceremony, and other customs and crafts. Grades 3–6.	
Southeast	Cherokee, Choctaw, Natchez, and Seminole: *Indians of the Southeast* (Video Dialog/Barr Films, 1991) shows Cherokee customs, their daily activities, and organization of tribe. Grades 3–6.	
Northeast	Abenaki, Chippewa (Ojibwa), Mohawk, MicMac, Seneca, Shawnee, Wampanoag, Winnebago, and Onondaga: *Moyers/ Oren Lyons the Faithkeeper* (PBS Video, 1991) offers stories of the Onondaga, one of the six nations in the Iroquois Confederation as told by Oren Lyons. Advanced grade 6 and up.	
Hawaii	Native Hawaiians: *Voices of the Land* (Bullfrog Films, 1991) features interviews with native Hawaiians who are critics of using geothermal energy near the home of the goddess Pele and other Native People about why certain places are held sacred by Native People and how wilderness can link humans to their place in nature's cycle. Grade 5 and up.	

Settlers in the Colonies

Give students an opportunity to hear *The Thanksgiving Primer* (Plimoth Plantation, Inc., 1987, all grades) and poetry from, *A Book of Americans* (Holt, 1986, all grades) by Rosemary and Stephen Benet. Elaborate on the hard lives of the Pilgrims and Puritans who "were English to the bone" and settled in New England with the poem "Pilgrims and Puritans." You can discuss the settlers in the area now New York with the poem "Peter Stuyvesant" (Stuyvesant) was a sturdy govenor with a famous "timber toe"). Also, ask students to imagine the ships southern settlers journeyed in while listening to the verse "Southern Ships and Settlers."

Activity #72: "Life in the Colonies"

With students and a map of the United States, point out the regions of settlements by certain newcomers and discuss what life in the colonies was like (e.g., what was going on in the Virginia settlement, the colonial life in New England, and the people's lives in the middle colonies). With various sources as ref- erences to obtain background information, engage students in working in small groups and contribut- ing to a roller theater movie that represents some of the events in the lives of the people in the settle- ments. If needed, the sources that follow in Figure 9–4 can provide a background of information for the groups.

FIGURE 9–4   Books about Life in the Colonies

Life in the Colonies

Aldeman, C. L. *Rum, Slaves and Molasses: The Story of New England's Trianguar Trade*. Crowell-Collier, 1972. Details early years of trade of some New Englanders beginning with selling slaves for molas- ses to convert into rum. Describes the horrors faced by the slaves and the viewpoints of the slavers. Grade 6 and up.

Aldeman, C. L. *The Story of the Thirteen Colonies*. Random House, 1966. This one-chapter-per-colony approach offers facts about key people and their heritage, the economy, and agriculture. Grade 6 and up.

Carter, A. *The Colonial Wars*. Watts, 1992. Portrays conflicts during the years 1689–1763. Grade 4–6.

Fisher, L. E. *The Schoolmasters*. Watts, 1967. See the other books by Fisher in this Colonial American Craftsmen Series that include *The Blacksmiths* (1976) and *The Tanners* (1966). See also Fisher's other books by Watts that portray colonial America: *The Architects* (1970), *The Peddlers* (1968), *The Doctors* (1968), and *The Homemakers* (1973). Grade 4 and up.

Glubok, S. *The Art of Colonial America*. Macmillan, 1970. Shows art work of the colonies in black-and- white illustrations. Grade 4 and up.

Smith, C. *Battles in a New Land: A Sourcebook on Colonial America*. Millbrook, 1991. Has reproduced paintings and drawings that illustrate the French and Indian Wars and the battles among the French and British colonists. Nonfiction. Grade 7 and up.

Tunis, E. *Colonial Craftsmen: the Beginnings of American Industry*. Crowell, 1965. Reviews the crafts related to agriculture, commerce, handicrafts, and manufacturing goods. Grade 6 and up.

Life in Virginia Settlements

Anderson, J. *A Williamsburg Household*. Clarion, 1988. Portrays life in colonial Williamsburg in a slave- holding family. Grades 4–6.

Benezet, A. *Views of American Slavery, Taken a Century Ago*. Ayer, 1969. A history of enslavement, importation, and purchase of Africans in 1760 time period. Grade 7 and up.

Campbell, E. *Jamestown: The Beginning*. Little, Brown, 1974. Portrays different view points of people living in the region (e.g., Native Americans, sailors, and settlers). Grades 5–6.

O'Dell, S. *The Serpent Never Sleeps*. Houghton Mifflin, 1987. After a shipwreck and a 4,000-mile jour- ney, Serena Lynn and others arrive in Jamestown to find people starved and listless and the set- tlement almost abandoned. Fiction. Grades 6–8.

Life in New England Settlements

Anderson, J. *The First Thanksgiving Feast*. Ill. by G. Ancona. Clarion, 1984. Has first-person accounts of life at Plimoth Plantation in 1620s. The photographs are taken at Plimouth Planation, a Living His- tory Museum. Nonfiction. Grades 4–6.

continued

FIGURE 9–4   Continued

Barth, E. *Turkeys, Pilgrims and Indian Corn: The Story of the Thanksgiving Symbols.* Clarion, 1975. Details the dress and customs of the early Pilgrims and discusses foods at the harvest festivals. Nonfiction. Grades 4–6.

Brown, M. W., ed. *Homes in the Wilderness: A Pilgrim's Journal of Plymouth Planation in 1620 by William Bradford and Others of the Mayflower Company.* Linnet Books, 1988. This is an edited version of the Pilgrim diaries that tell how the Pilgrims survived their terrible first winter. Adaptations include the names of the passengers on the *Mayflower,* glossary, drawings, and maps. Grade 5 and up.

Daugherty, J. *The Landing of the Pilgrims.* Random House, 1987. With excerpts from primary documents from the Pilgrims' journals, this narrates the history of the settlers who landed by Plymouth. Grade 6 and up.

Feenie. *Squanto.* Repr., 1965/Linnet, 1988. Biography of Tisquqntum, sold as a slave, who returns to New England and acts as an interpreter. Grades 6 and up.

Fisher, M., & Fowler, M. J. *Colonial America: English Colonies.* Gateway Press, 1988. Show black-and-white photographs portraying daily activities in settlements in New England. Grades 4–6.

Fritz, J. *Who's That Stepping on Plymouth Rock?* Coward, 1975. Describes the history of Plymouth Rock, an American monument that now is displayed on the waterfront in Plymouth, Massachusetts. Grades 5–6.

Fradin, D. B. *The New Jersey Colony.* Childrens Press, 1991. Recounts differing views of settlers as well as Native Americans, loyalists, and revolutionaries. Grades 5–8.

Leob, R. H. *Meet the Real Pilgrims: Everyday Life on a Plimouth Plantation in 1627.* Doubleday, 1979. Portrays life in early New England through photographs of the reconstructed village of Plymouth. Grades 4–6.

Morrison, S. E., ed. *Of Plimouth Plantation.* Knopf, 1953. Presents the journal of William Bradford who wrote about the landing of the Pilgrims and their life in the colony. Grades 6–10.

Perl, L. *Slumps, Grunts, and Snickerdoodles: What Colonial America Ate and Why.* Clarion, 1979. Portrays a brief history of edibles from the American Colonial era. All grades.

Life in the Middle Colonies

Cousins, M. *Ben Franklin of Old Philadelphia.* Random House, 1963. Useful source of information about this patriot from Philadelphia. Grades 4–6.

Dolson, H. *William Penn.* Random House, 1963. Depicts life from boyhood in England and Ireland and becoming a Quaker, whose followers were not tolerated in England. Grades 5–6.

The Colonists' Almanac

In the settlements of the middle colonies, most families that could afford an almanac bought one. Show students an example of an almanac—an all-purpose book that has a calendar, information about the predicted weather, the tides, moon changes, and some listed dates of historical events to remember. Sometimes, the almanac includes health hints, proverbs, popular sayings, recipes, and humorous notes. Mention that in 1732, Benjamin Franklin published *Poor Richard's Almanac* (Peter Pauper Pr., n.d., all grades) and included some of his brief sayings such as "Waste not, want not" and "A stitch in time saves nine." As students to suggest contemporary sayings of today that they can contrast to Franklin's sayings.

Invite students to transform the written lists into a visual format for a room display and illustrate pairs of comic strip-style pictures with a word bubble to show Franklin's saying on the left-hand side of the paper and a word bubble to show contemporary words on the right-hand side.

Activity #73: "An Original Almanac"

With students, invite them to begin pages for an original almanac for their own families (or significant others in the home) and engage them in collecting sayings, proverbs, and quotes that they like. Of course, they can make up their own sayings. Ask them to include the important dates in the lives of their family members, to make some weather predictions, to write their favorite recipes, to illustrate the pages and sayings with small illustrations, and to add anything else they think should be in their almanacs for their families.

Constance: A Story of Early Plymouth

Reading selected text from *Constance: A Story of Early Plymouth* (Lothrop, 1968, grade 5 and up), by Patricia Clapp, can give older students a view of the daily activities of a young girl in New England. After reading descriptions from the story, ask the students to review some of Constance's responsibilities and her recreation. Group the comments on the board and have students compare their work and recreation today with those of Constance:

Constance's Work	*Constance's Recreation*
1.	1.
My Work	*My Recreation*
1.	1.

Activity #74: "Gender Stereotyping in 1600s"

Constance: A Story of Early Plymouth (Lothrop, 1968, grade 5 and up) by Patricia Clapp, can interest students in gathering data about the lives and contributions of women and girls (as well as men and boys) who traveled to the colonies. Discuss some of Constance's diary entries and talk about what entries could be added to her diary (such as those related to her life before she left England for America.) Related to this, ask students to write an entry for Constance before she leaves for America. Other class projects can include:

1. Students can plan a career presentation day in the classroom to learn of the opportunities available for women and men in the 1600s in the colonies and compare with today's opportunities.
2. Students may take the role of pilgrims to speak of their occupations and then bring in speakers in contemporary careers such as female cab drivers and male nurses.
3. Students may find newspaper ads, count the sex roles shown, and discuss the implications in today's world and compare what was found with the times of the colonies.
4. Students may watch favorite TV shows—such as "Little House on the Prairie" reruns—and analyze the characters. With the whole group, students should discuss any bias and stereotypes found.
5. Students may examine the roles of women and girls in TV sitcoms or count the men and women on TV news. After reporting the data to the class, the students should discuss the implications.

The Seventeenth Century

Hepler (1979) points out that close to many schools are potentially available sites to take students back into different time periods—old cabins, nineteenth-century homes, historic school houses, as well as tools, craftsmen, and imaginative colleagues to help make history a potential language experience for students of all ages.

Activity #75: "Products"

As an example of this type of meaningful language experience, the students can get involved in:

1. Mixing and frying oat cakes to eat along with cheese, broth, and jam to make up their lunch
2. Eating lunch on wooden plates
3. Weaving on a small loom
4. Mixing lotions—making hand creams, pomanders, and sachets that were popular in this time period
5. Making candles and dyeing cloth
6. Identifying plants by making an inventory of the plants in seventeenth-century gardens and mapping an example of a garden

Invite the students to raise questions and follow their interests about a study of seventeenth-century home life, the politics, crafts, occupations, and so on. They can become engaged in related activities that consist of sketching, carving (with soap and plastic knives), sewing, writing with quill pens, making lavender bags, doing lace work, and trying their skills at quilting. They also made corn dolls for good luck and assemble the brooms needed for good housekeeping.

CHAPTER TEN

A.D. 1700–1799

What was going on in the eighteenth century?

Multicultural Perspectives

Bulletin boards can make a unit of this period an exciting one when they feature the crafts people made, the different geographical locations where they lived, and the ways they traveled. Colorful related maps can show the population centers of their parallel cultures. Some students will realize that the coldest days of the Little Ice Age were still going on and affected the people in the northern hemisphere—their food, clothing, shelters, and activities. For instance, during the early 1700s in Europe, many northern rivers still repeatedly froze every winter, and when the River Thames froze annually, the people in London, warmly dressed, adapted and held Frost Fairs on its thick ice. For students who are interested in the perspectives in Figure 10–1, suggest some of the selected books for further reading.

FIGURE 10–1 *Children's Books about* A.D. *1700–1799*

PERSPECTIVES FOR 1700s

African Heritage

Burke, D. *Black Heroes of the American Revolution.* Harcourt, 1976. Depicts the contributions of African Americans during the Revolutionary War. Includes drawings, etchings, bibliography, and index. Nonfiction. Grades 4–6.

Felton, H. W. *Mumbet* Dodd, Mead & Co., 1970. With the help of a young lawyer, Theodore Sedgwick, Elizabeth Freeman wins her freedom in 1781 in the courts of the state of Massachusetts. Biography. Grade 6 and up.

Hamilton, V. *Many Thousand Gone: African Americans from Slavery to Freedom.* Ill. by L. & D. Dillon. Knopf, 1993. Portrays portraits of Sojourner Truth and other freedom fighters—some unknown, some well known. Nonfiction. Grade 5 and up.

Hansen, J. *The Captive.* Scholastic, 1994. Based on a journal written in the late 1700s, this is about Kofi, the 12-year-old son of an Ashanti chief. Kofi is sold and sent to America after his father is murdered by a family slave. Kofi and others escape and return to Africa. Historical fiction based on fact. Grades 5–8.

FIGURE 10–1 Continued

Haskins, J. *Get On Board: The Story of the Underground Railroad.* Scholastic, 1993. Depicts the history of the network of people who helped slaves make their way to freedom. Includes photographs, index, and bibliography. Nonfiction. Grades 5–8.

McKissack, P. & F. *Soiourner Truth, Ain't I a Woman?* Scholastic, 1993. Portrays Sojourner Truth's times and the trial when she goes to court to regain her son. She preaches for human fights and quotes the Bible. Biography. Grade 6 and up.

Millender, D. H. *Crispus Attucks: Black Leader of Colonial Patriots.* Macmillan, 1983. Portrays the life of a Colonial African American and his contribution to America's Revolution. Biography. Grade 5 and up.

Rappaport, D. *Escape from Slavery: Five Journeys to Freedom.* Ill. by C. Lilly. HarperCollins, 1991. Includes true stories of slaves who acquired their freedom. Nonfiction. Grade 8 and up.

Richmond, M. *Phillis Wheatley.* Chelsea House, 1988. Reviews the life of an early African American poet and includes primary source materials. Biography. Grade 6 and up.

Sullivan, G. *Slave Ship: The Story of the Henrietta Marie.* Cobblehill, 1994. This is a re-creation of the slave ship's final voyage before it sank in the Gulf of Mexico in the early 1700s. Describes slavery, the discovery of the wrecked ship, and the memorial placed at the site by black divers. Maps included. Grades 5–8.

Yates, E. *Amos Fortune, Free Man.* Aladdin, 1950. At age 60, Amos (At-Mun) buys his freedom, establishes a business, and buys the freedom of others, including that of his three wives. Biography. Grades 4–8.

Asian Heritage

Fleischman, P. *Path of the Pale Horse*, Harper & Row, 1983. A young apprentice doctor, Lep, has his faith in medicine shaken during a Yellow Fever epidemic in Philadelphia. Historical fiction. Grade 6 and up.

Latino/Hispanic Heritage

Anderson J. *Spanish Pioneers of the Southwest.* Ill. by G. Ancona. Dutton, 1989. Depicts a pioneer family in a Spanish community in New Mexico in the eighteenth century and the family's hard work, harsh conditions, and their traditions. Nonfiction. Grades 4–6.

de Varona, F. *Bernardo de Galvez.* Raintree, 1990. Bernardo de Galvez, a Spanish soldier, becomes a popular governor in the Louisiana territory and joins the United States in its revolt against England. Biography. Grades 4–6.

Original Native American Heritage

Clark, E. *Cherokee Chief: The Life of John Ross.* Crowell-Collier, 1970. Portrays the life of John Ross (1790–1866), a Cherokee leader, who confronts the persecution of the Cherokee people by others. Biography. Grades 5–6.

Hudson, J. Dawn Rider. Putnam, 1990. Sixteen-year-old Kit Fox, a Blackfoot, is forbidden to ride horses. She disobeys and her riding skills help her people when their camp is attacked. Fiction. Grade 4 and up.

Differently Abled Heritage

Neimark, A. E. *A Deaf Child Listened: Thomas Gallaudet, Pioneer in American Education.* Morrow, 1983. A fictionalized account of Thomas Gallaudet (1787–1851), who advocates treatment and education of the deaf. Biography. Grades 5–8.

continued

FIGURE 10–1 Continued

European Heritage

Blumberg, R. *The Remarkable Voyages of Captain Cook.* Bradbury, 1991. James Cook (1728 to 1779), the British navigator, mapped the South Pacific region and endured the hardships of the voyages. Includes the material of a scientist and an artist who traveled with Cook. Biography. Grade 6 and up.

Kinsey-Warock, Natalie. *Wilderness Cat.* Illustrated by Mark Graham. Scarsdale, NY: Cobblehill, 1992. In the 1700s, Serena is heartbroken because her family is moving to Canada and her parents say she must leave her beloved cat, Moses, with a neighbor. Historical fiction. Grades 4–6.

Meyer, K. A. *Father Serra: Traveler on the Golden Chain.* Huntington, IN: Our Sunday Visitor Publishers, 1987. Discusses the phases of Father Serra's life as well as the founding of the California Missions, 1769–1798. Biography. Grade 4.

Female Image Heritage

Banim, L. *A Spy in the King's Colony.* Ill. by T. Yuditskaya. Silver Moon Press, 1994. In 1775 in Boston, 11-year-old Emily Parker suspects 18-year-old Robert Babcock of being a spy for the Loyalists. She gets involved in the delivery of a secret-coded note to General Washington about the movement of cannon from Fort Ticonderoga to Farmingham. Grades 4–5.

DePauw, L. G. *Founding Mothers: Women in America in the Revolutionary Era.* Houghton Mifflin, 1975. Discusses the contributions of women during the Revolutionary War. Nonfiction. Grade 7 and up.

Hoople, C. G. *As I Saw It: Women Who Lived the American Adventure.* Dial, 1978. Details contributions of colonial and pioneer women from diaries, journals, letters, and speeches. Includes struggles of a frontier doctor, a Union spy, and others. Nonfiction. Grades 4–7.

San Souci, R. *Cut from the Same Cloth: American Women of Myth, Legend and Tall Tale.* Philomel 1933 Has stories of women from different cultures who were "larger than life" and did extraordinary deeds to save themselves, their friends and families, and to "pay back" deserving victims. Includes map with the characters sketched in locales. Folk literature. All grades.

Religious Minority Heritage

Faber, D. *The Perfect Life: The Shakers in America.* Farrar, 1974. Mother Ann escapes from Manchester, England, with several followers who voyage to America and set up the first settlement in upstate New York in 1776. Details the Shaker influence on furniture construction, their mechanical inventions, and their religious beliefs as well as their overall achievements. Nonfiction. Grade 6 and up.

Klots, S. *Richard Allen: Religious and Social Activist.* Chelsea House, 1990. Details life of Richard Allen who becomes the founder of the African Methodist Episcopal Church and speaks for African Americans in post-revolutionary Pennsylvania. Biography. Grades 6–8.

Yolen, J. *Simple Gifts: The Story of the Shakers.* Viking, 1976. Details a history of the Shakers in America. Points out that the Shakers were successful as they established communal living and grew to 22 communities until the sect's later final decline. Nonfiction. Grades 5–7.

Values and Beliefs Can Be Altered

Moore (1992) states that some children's books demonstrate how values and beliefs can be altered through the power of the environment—no matter the historical or geographical setting. As an example, discuss with the class the idea that cultural conflict has been known to precipitate animosity and violence, but it also has been known *not* to precipitate hatred. In this time period of the 1700s, mention that the feud for land between the Native People in the United States and the encroaching white settlers led to the documented cases of white children being captured by Native Americans and taught tribal ways.

Two books are based on documented cases, *A Circle Unbroken* and *I Am Regina*. In *A Circle Unbroken* (Clarion, 1988, grade 6 and up) by S. Hotze, Rachel Porter lives with the Dakota Sioux for seven years. In her environment, she is known as Kata Wi and shares moments of fondness with her Indian family. Discovered by her father at age 17, she finds she cannot adjust to the white lifestyle and so chooses to return to the Dakota Sioux, which is the "circle unbroken."

In *I Am Regina* (Philomel, 1991, grade 6 and up), Regina Leninger is kidnapped from her Pennsylvania home by Allegheny Indians in 1775 at the start of the French and Indian War. In her environment, she is forbidden to speak English or talk about her past life while she learns the ways of the tribe. When she is reunited with her mother, she has little memory of her life with her white family but she chooses to return to that life—which, to Native Americans, represents a "circle that is broken." After reading one of the books, engage students in discussing ways beliefs can be altered through one's environment.

Activity #76: "Beliefs, Values, and Environment"

With students, discuss the idea that a person's values can be changed through the environment. Point out that some stories in children's literature, based on real-life experiences, document this idea. As the students read through the academic year, invite them to display the title and the name of the author of any story related to this idea on a class bulletin board with the heading of "Values Can Be Changed." Related readings can include *The Ice Trail* (Metheun, 1980, grade 4 and up) by A. E. Crompton, the story of Daniel (also called Tanial) who escapes from the Abenaki; *Indian Captive: The Story of Mary Jemison* (Frederick A. Stokes, 1941, grade 7 and up) by L. Lenski, a narrative based on a true event; and *Calico Captive* (Houghton Mifflin, 1967, grades 7 and up) by E. G. Speare, a young girl's story based on a diary kept in 1754.

War for America's Independence

"Learning stations or centers are one variation of small-group learning and lend themselves well to thematic instruction," states Patricia L. Roberts (1993), author of *A Green Dinosaur Day: A Guide for Developing Thematic Units in Literature-Based*

Instruction, K–6. "A variety of learning activities can be made available to the students across different content areas through learning stations." A teacher, with the students, can create a learning center where the students discover some special items related to U.S. independence by working with partners or individually. In a center, poems and tape recorders can be made available so the students can record and listen to their own voices. For example, a student can record facts discovered about the Liberty Bell for others to hear along his or her painted interpretation of the bell and invite others to add more background information:

> *Kept in Philadelphia, the Liberty Bell was so big that it had cracked and been repaired for years before it rang on July 9, 1776. It rang for the first public reading of the Declaration of Independence. The next year, it was hidden because people were afraid the British would melt it down for ammunition. The bell was taken back to Independence Hall and it rang its last time in 1846 when the Abolitionists adopted it as a symbol and called it the Liberty Bell. Today, it is in its own glass pavilion across from Independence Hall.*

Activity #77: "America's Struggling Revolutionists"

As background for America's Revolutionary War, engage the students in discussing the struggles of the people that led them to America's revolution after reading excerpts from *The Story of the Boston Massacre* (Crowell, 1976, grades 4–6) by Mary Kay Phelan, a description of one of the early events where men and boys threatened British soldiers and led toward America's revolution against England. Another view, *The Fifth of March: A Story of the Boston Massacre* (Harcourt, 1993, grades 6–8) by Ann Rinaldi, is told through the life of Rachel Marsh, an indentured servant, who was a nursemaid to John Adams's children. This portrays the political unrest, the contrasting views of the loyalists and patriots, and the fermenting danger of mobs. Follow up with *Boston Tea Party, Rebellion in the Colonies* (Troll, 1982, grades 4–6) by James E. Knight and read aloud the description given by a Boston merchant about the colonists' protest against the East India Company and the taxation by England. More about the excitement and the events that led up to the Boston Tea Party are in Walter Oleksy's *The Boston Tea Party* (Watts, 1993, grades 4–6). Engage students in using the information they gained in making "The Story of the Boston Massacre" diorama, or a panorama scene on a mural, or a 3-D shoebox scene, or posters of the event.

Common People and Uncommon Leaders

"The important thing resulting from the American Revolution is not just that we got our freedom, but we became a nation with a balancing act...and the balancing act is going on to this very day," states Carlos Cortez, a professor from the University of California at Riverside's history department who was the key speaker for a recent teachers' conference (Bettinger, 1993). Emphasizing that people need an identity other than just being an American, Cortez goes on, "It's the same reason there is a religious revival in the United States. It is the same reason there is an Association of Pomona Teachers—because people need identities. The larger society gets—the more you need these little identities to give you a spot on the map of humanity." He explains further, "And that's why ethnicity is with us to stay. The issue is, do we make the best of it, or do we make the worst of it?"

Reflecting on Cortez's words, you will realize that students can study what it means to be an American and also help build bridges between ethnic groups when they understand that multiculturism is not going to disappear. It seems that some students are not going to be just "plain Americans" because in our contemporary times, some of them need an identity other than "just" being an American. Help students understand what it means to be an American as well as what it means to have an additional identity by having them write their names and their identities of daughter, cousin, student, friend, and so on, on stickers (colored dots) and placing the dots on a map of their state. Help them better understand each other through cooperative work and other activities in the classroom.

Some suggestions for cooperative activities are discussed in the following section. Roles of women and girls are found in stories listed on History Master 32 and 33.

Activity #78: "Biographies"

Ask students to divide into small groups and introduce sets of Jean Fritz's biographies about figures in America's Revolutionary Days *(What's the Big Idea, Ben Franklin?* [Coward McCann, 1978] and others). Establish interest in each one with brief book talks that include using the overhead and transparencies of the book covers as a billboard to advertise the stories. The books can be read by students interested enough to sign up to read three more of the books and to participate in discussions about them (Smith, 1992). In groups based on their book choices, the students can talk about their reactions to the historical characters, plot, setting, and theme, and then relate what happened in the book to other books or to experiences the students have had. They can discuss the illustrations, raise questions they have about the writing, and discuss examples of powerful words they liked. While reading, each student can take notes on a "Response Assignment" sheet and bring the notes to the group each day for further discussion with the members. When the discussion comes to a close, invite interested students to do some of the following:

1. Reread a selection to review a character's motivation, the reactions of certain character or review the author's use of words.

2. Reread a portion to develop the meaning of the title and review the ways the illustration tell more than the text.

3. Write in a literature response journal, select a favorite page to talk about or write about, and sketch an illustration that showed the student's response to the story.

America's Revolutionary Times

"Listen my children, and you shall hear/ Of the midnight ride of Paul Revere.../It was two by the village clock/ When he came to the bridge in Concord town/ "are words from Henry Wadsworth Longfellow's poem "The Midnight Ride of Paul Revere" (in *Paul Revere's Ride* [Dutton, 1991] by Ted Rand). This poem can lead students to discuss "Did Paul Revere really ride to Concord and warn the colonists that the British were coming?" and "What was a Man-of-War really like?" The night rides of Revere, Dawes, and Prescott are detailed in *The Battle of Lexington and Concord* (Four Winds, 1992, grade 4 and up) by N. Johnson. Facts about a Man-of-War are found in Richard Platt's *Man-of-War* (Dorling Kindersley, 1993, grade 4 and up) and in Stephen Biesty's illustrated cross sections of Admiral Nelson's flagship *HMS Victory*. Facts about the past found by students in references similar to *Man-of-War* can help answer the questions they have as well as answer the following ones (examples of information about history that have become distorted through time):

1. Did Betsy Ross *really* make the first flag for America?
2. Did George Washington *really* chop down a cherry tree?
3. Did George Washington *really* cross the Delaware in the daylight with the "Stars and Stripes"?

Activity # 79: "Essence of America's Revolution"

Students, may hear/read current material and data sources to find the latest information about some of the legends mentioned previously and report back to the whole group what they found. For example, some students may report about:

1. *The legend of Betsy* Ross. *The American Flag* (Simon & Schuster, 1973, all grades) by Thomas Parish discounts the idea that Ross made America's first flag. Another source, *A Flag for Our Country* (Steck-Vaughn, 1993, grades 3–4) by Eve Spencer, mentions that the story comes from the oral tradition handed down from one generation to another and there is no supporting factual data that Ross, a young war widow, designed the first flag of the United States.

2. *The legend of George Washington and the cherry tree. Washington's America* (Grosset & Dunlap, 1961, all grades) by Robin McKown calls the cherry tree tale fanciful.

3. *The legend of Paul Revere. Paul Revere's Ride* (Houghton Mifflin 1988, all grades) by Henry Wadsworth Longfellow and illustrated by Nancy Winslow Parker) points out that Paul Revere was captured and never reached Concord, but two other men, William Dawes and Samuel Prescott, warned the colonists that the British were coming.

Washington: Presidential Fox or Hedgehog

Thomas Mann (Dobbin, 1993) of Washington's Brookings Institution says there is a political science theory that all presidents can be classified either as a fox or a hedgehog, based on the kind of politician the president was while in office. To be classified as a fox, a president is seen as one who knows many small things and is driven by events. A "fox" president also gropes and seems less interested in governing than in politics and is one who prepares for change that is usually accomplished by a successor. Additionally, a "fox" president goes about things in an incremental way that leaves many people dissatisfied and does not give people the big story that would help them understand how the pieces fit together in what is going on.

To be classified as a hedgehog, a president is seen as one who leans toward larger conceptual thinking and has an overall focus on a major issue, such as fighting to make a country independent or confronting communism called the "evil Empire." Often, a "hedgehog" president will put forth important and farseeing initiatives (e.g., foreign policies in response to the realization that the world can be a treacherous place). Ask students to give examples of presidents, some of their actions, and label each as a fox or a hedgehog from their points of view.

Activity #80: "Foxes and Hedgehogs"

Ask students in partnerships to select a biography about George Washington or another U.S. president, read it together, and take notes to find evidence to present a point of view that the president could be classified either as a fox or a hedgehog. A president who is classified as a fox is one who does things in an incremental way. A president who is classified as a hedgehog is one who shows larger conceptual thinking.

When the partners report to the class, ask them to tell others their final generalization (e.g., "We decided that President Washington could be classified as a _____") and then give several sentences from the biography that support their view. Keep a record of the partners' decision on an overhead transparency or on the board so students can see any patterns that are emerging from their data. For instance, does it look like the majority of U.S. presidents the students studied were foxes who did things in an incremental way or hedgehogs with larger conceptual thinking?

Tories and Whigs

"Why this will never, never do!/ It is a rebel orgy,/ And we are loyal subjects, who/ Will fight for good King Georgie!/" are words that portray the views of a Tory in the poem, "Oliver De Lancey" in *A Book of Americans* (Holt, 1986) by the Benets. With the students, discuss the times during the American Revolutionary War, when some people, such as the British General Oliver De Lancey and his "noted" landowner family, were loyal subjects of the British King George and were called Tories, along with other British supporters of the time. Discuss the poets' view in the poem about what would have happened if the Tories and British *had won* the war and why the author wrote that the the United States would then have "rulers regal, No Stars and Stripes! No July Fourth! No bold American eagle!" Ask students to meet in small groups to make their own speculations about what would have happened and how their lives would have been changed if the Tories and British had won the war.

Activity #81: "Points of View"

With students, discuss the idea that during the Revolution, some colonists supported the Tory point of view, which was the view that the colonists' revolution was an "unjust" revolution against King George III of England. The Whig point of view was that the revolution was a "just" one. In the Revolution, an early battle between the British troops and the colonists was the Battle of Lexington and Concord, west of Boston. Review the events that led up to this battle and discuss them along with the late-night rides of Paul Revere, John Dawes, and John Prescott, and the apparent disorganization of both sides with the descriptive excerpts from *The Battle of Lexington and Concord* (Four Winds, 1992, grades 4–6) by Neil Johnson. Point out that the British troops in the Battle of Lexington and Concord are not shown as villains in the book.

Choose further selections from My *Brother Sam Is Dead* (Four Winds, 1974, grades 6–10) by Christopher and James Collier to demonstrate to students what it felt like for a family to be divided over the two views. Ask the students to meet together and discuss which view they would have supported if they had lived in this time period. A closer look at military life is shown in *The Revolutionary Soldier 1775–1783: An Illustrated Sourcebook of Authentic Details about Everyday Life for Revolutionary War Soldiers* (Globe Pequot Press, 1993, grade 7 and up) by C. K. Wilbur.

As a whole group, review some of the major causes of the Revolutionary War with the students with such sources as *George Washington: Leader of a New Nation* (Dial, 1991, grades 4–7) by M. P. Osborne and *Guns for General Washington: A Story of the American Revolution* (Harcourt, 1990, grades 4–7) by S. Reit. Have them record the causes in their history journals after discussion.

Decision-Making Situations

With the whole class, engage the students in examining choices and alternatives in problem situations related to the Revolutionary War. Ask the students to make decisions for the following situations and discuss possible consequences of the decisions that are made:

1. A man in the group begins to make slanderous remarks about the local colonists who want to break away from England. A crowd of colonists calling themselves patriots gathers and begins to threaten the man. A nearby colonist militiaman approaches the group. The man continues to make his remarks about being loyal to the King of England and the crowd becomes angrier. Someone shouts a threat of violence. The militiaman decides to take the man away to a nearby military barracks. What do you think the militiaman should have done?

2. You see a colonist militiaman being pelted with stones and sticks by a small group of young people whose families are loyal to the King of England. The militiaman is trying to arrest one of the young men. What would you do if you were there?

3. Your English government is trying to pass a law in your colony that would allow the British Soldiers to enter your home without a search warrant if they believed that there might be weapons in the home. You have to decide what you think about this law. What would you decide?

Activity #82: "Political Buttons"

Read aloud excerpts from the text about the estrangement between Benjamin Franklin and his Loyalist son, William, presented in *The American Revolution: "Give Me Liberty or Give Me Death!"* (Enslow, 1994, grades 4–6) by Deborah Kent. Ask the students to meet with partners and discuss again which view—Tory or Whig— they would have supported if they had lived in this time period as Franklin and his son did. Invite them to think carefully about a message to show their views and make a lapel button as a personal way to show their views to others in the class. Students can make their own buttons by using a piece of adhesive-backed white shelf paper and crayons or felt marking pens. They can add pictures if they wish, pull off the adhesive backing, and wear their lapel buttons to show their views—Tory or Whig.

People Who Risked Their Lives

Suggested books for this theme are found on History Master 29, "Those Who Risked Their Lives For Others." Have the students scan newspapers and magazines to locate articles and illustrations of contemporary people who have risked their lives for others. Ask them to cut out the articles and illustrations to create a large collage on mural paper and display the art work in the room.

Activity #83: "Helping Others"

Introduce students to people who were everyday citizens in history and who made significant contributions as they risked their lives to help others. Read excerpts on this theme from the chapter biography about Lydia Darragh, who spied for George Washington during the Revolutionary War, in *Secret Missions* (Scholastic, 1988, grades 4–6) by Ellen Levine. Ask students to make connections from this time period to other periods by listening/reading the biographies of others who risked their lives to help others—Alexander Ross and William Still, who helped slaves escape from southern plantations, and Leesha Boos, who worked for the Resistance Movement in Holland to save Jews from Nazi deportation during World War II. Have students search through newspapers to locate contemporary articles about people today who have risked their lives to save others and display the articles on a chart.

Paul Revere and Others

"Listen my children, and you shall hear/ of the midnight ride of Paul Revere" introduce Longfellow's poem. *Paul Revere's Ride* from the version illustrated by Adrian J. Lorio and Frederick J. Alford (Houghton Mifflin, 1971, all grades). Review what is going on and draw stick figures on the board to show the scene in Boston of the British Man-o-War ships in the harbor and Revere watching the North Church Tower in the night to see his friend's coded signal—one light if the British were leaving their ships and marching by land, two lights if they were arriving by sea. Distribute copies of the poem and have the students orally interpret (low voices, high voices, one-line-per student, lines for small groups, unison) lines for several readings. For an optional rereading, have students suggest sound effects (e.g.: "You shall hear of the midnight ride of Paul Revere" [slap side of leg]). Write the students' suggestions on an overhead transparency of the poem so all can see the cues as the poem is reread.

Activity #84: "Biographical Writing That Crackles"

With students, introduce the idea of biographical writing that "sparkles" and read aloud some excerpts from biographies as examples. Carr (1981), instructor of children's literature classes, from the Univer-

sity of Virginia, points out that when authors include little-known details that enhance the daily life of the past, it leads to lively biographical writing for readers. Examples of this are found in the writing of Jean Fritz as she tells about Paul Revere writing in his day book with "This is the day for me to…" and never finishing the sentence because he was always in too much of a hurry *(And Then What Happened, Paul Revere?* [Coward, McCann & Geoghegan, 1973, grades 4–6]). Another example is about John Hancock, who kept writing his signature over and over so it would look imposing in *Will You Sign Here, John Hancock?* (Coward, McCann, 1976). Still another is about Patrick Henry, who imitated a mockingbird that imitated a jay in *Where Was Patrick Henry on the 29th of May?* (Coward, McCann, 1975, grade 4 and up). Read aloud selected excerpts.

Activity #85: "Actions"

Lively writing about these figures can bring the past to life for readers. For instance, the students can visualize Patrick Henry as he pushed his glasses back on his head (pantomime the action)—something he always did when he was ready to use "fighting words":

> *I know not what course others may take…but as for me…" Patrick dropped his arms, threw back his body and strained against his imaginary chains until the tendons of his neck stood out like whipcords and the chains seemed to break. Then he raised his right hand in which he held an ivory letter opener. "As for me," he cried, "give me liberty or give me death!" And he plunged the letter opener in such a way that it looked as if he were plunging it into his heart.*

Review this piece of writing with the students and ask them to consider the actions of Patrick Henry. Elicit from them the actions and words that were peaceful and those that appeared aggressive. Write their suggestions on the board in two lists, labeled "Peaceful" and "Aggressive." With the students, review the two lists and then engage them in putting a plus sign (+) by the entries they think would have led to a peaceful meeting with the British and putting minus sign (–) by the entries they think would have caused an aggressive meeting between Patrick Henry and the British. With this information about peaceful actions, ask the students to join with partners and write a paragraph describing an ideal meeting between Patrick Henry and a British soldier on the other side. Ask the students to return to the whole group and read their paragraphs aloud. From the discussion, develop a list of guidelines on the board for future "representatives," such as Patrick Henry, to use when the meet with soldiers of an aggressive force.

Benjamin Franklin and Others

Myra Zarnowski (1988) states that she integrated reading and writing with biographies in her fourth-grade class. To begin, she read aloud from a fictionalized biography of Benjamin Franklin every day for three weeks. Then, for a two-month period, the students turned to Franklin's life as a topic and independently read several biographies about him and recorded their reactions in journals. Later, the students wrote original fictionalized biographies about Franklin. In a similar way, your student's can integrate reading, writing and children's literature in the classrooms with an historical figure and related biographies.

Activity #86: "Research the Subject"

Students interested in contributions from the heroes and heroines represented in this time period can research the historical figure and discuss what they find. Suggest some of the following as ways to guide their research over several days:

1. First, make a question map with the name of a historical figure in the center that the student considers to be the greatest hero/heroine in the American Revolutionary War. Discuss the focus question that needs to be answered: Who was the greatest hero/heroine in the American Revolutionary War?

2. Next, discuss any related questions and write those around the center of the question map.

3. Third, talk about any type of information that is related to the questions. Each student will want information that will convince others in the class of the validity of his/her choice. For example, a student might want a list of what the person did that made a contribution during America's Revolutionary War and then collect some information on the significance of the contribution.

4. Then, introduce the students to different types of reference from which to collect information.

1783: The Constitution

Introduce Jean Fritz's book, *Shh! We're Writing the Constitution* (Scholastic, 1987, grades 3–6), and discuss some anecdotes about the people involved in the writing of the constitution that begins, "We, the people..." words that made Patrick Henry see

"red" because it wiped out the states' "thirteen separate identities." Once the citizens of the colonies read the Constitution, they were quick to take sides as the states were asked to ratify it. Those who were for it called themselves the Federalists and those against it became known as the Anti-Federalists. Ask students which view they would have held in this time period and why.

Activity #87: "The Constitution's Balancing Act"

With the students, provide copies of the text of America's Constitution that is included in Fritz's *Shh! We're Writing the Constitution*. Invite students to work in small groups together to find evidence of the "balancing act" designed by our nation's founding leaders. The words successfully balance the forces of unity and pluralism, individualism and conformity, freedom and authority, commonalities and diversity. Engage students in locating words and phrases that they believed address these forces and noting what they found on a reference sheet such as the following:

What Our Constitution Says about:

1. Unity
2. Pluralism
3. Individualism
4. Conformity
5. Freedom
6. Authority
7. Commonalities
8. Diversity

For students interested in reading further about the topic, guide them to *The Bill of Rights: How We Got It and What It* Means (HarperCollins, 1990, grades 4–6) by M. Meltzer for a discussion about the states as they ratified the Constitution and the way citizens argued about the need for a Bill of Rights. It also describes the events that led up to the writing of the Bill of Rights and the meaning of the amendments and has a bibliography for further reading.

Bringing the Past into the Present: The Bill of Rights

In support of using the Constitution as a focus in the classroom, McEwan (1989), State University of New York at Cortland, says that the Constitution can help a teacher's classroom management through an approach called *judicious discipline,* which was developed by Dr. Forrest Gathercoal of Oregon State University. It is based on constitutional law and rulings of the Supreme Court to present the rights related to property loss and damage, legitimate educational purpose, health and safety, and disruption of the educational process. Some are rights that students are guaranteed in their school and some represent the times when students can be deprived of those rights.

To introduce this in the classroom, students may discuss these topics and generate guidelines that help them fulfill their obligations as citizens,(e.g., the teacher will give a receipt for items confiscated from the students that have disrupted the educational process). For example, fighting on the playground could begin with arbitration and mentoring and then result in an apology or loss of privileges as well as a supportive aspect to help students to learn to control their anger that leads to fighting. Classroom meetings can relate the students' problems to a constitutional interest—property loss and damage, legitimate educational purpose, health and safety, and disruption of the educational process, and so on—before an analysis of the problem begins and alternatives to the problem behavior is discussed. If you are interested further in this type of discipline, you should turn to Forrest Gathercoal's *A Judicious Discipline: A Constitutional Framework for School Rules and Decisions* (Prakken Publications, 1989).

Activity #88: "America's Bill of Rights"

Show the whole group a copy of the Bill of Rights and ask the students to rank the rights beginning with the most important and ranking down to the least important from their points of view. With the purpose of trying to reach a consensus, ask the students to divide into small groups and discuss the reasons why they feel the way they do about the rankings. They may change their rankings during the group discussion. Have a reporter from each group report the rankings back to the whole group. Have student volunteers record the rankings of the groups on the board.

People's Rights

"We, the people of the United States, in order to form a more perfect union..." are phrases to guide students to books that review the U.S. Constitution, the basic law by which our country is governed. Discuss the meaning of the Bill of Rights, the first 10 amendments written to support the concept of equality in the Declaration of Independence, and to emphasize the basic freedoms of citizens in the United States. In addition to the books about the Bill of Rights that students might check out from a school library, two books by Warren Coleman, *La Carta de Derechos (The Bill of Rights)* and *La Con-*

stitucion (The Constitution) (both Childrens, 1989) are available in Spanish.

After reading selected parts from these books and others, ask the students to discuss some of the rights guaranteed under the Bill of Rights. Point out that some of the rights were controversial at the time and arguments almost cost the unity of the colonists in this time period. Ask students to think why someone would argue *for* or *against* the following rights and record their remarks on the board: right of freedom of religion, right of freedom of speech, right of freedom of the press, right to peaceably attend meetings, right to petition the government, right to keep and bear arms, right to fair treatment when accused of a crime, right to privacy, right of an accused person to be free on bail until tried, right to a public trial by a jury, and right of freedom from cruel and unusual punishment when guilty.

	For	*Against*
Freedom of religion	1.	1.
Freedom of speech	2.	2.

Activity #89: "Linking the Past to the Present"

Invite students to suggest ideas for a special Students' Bill of Rights for the classroom. Record their ideas as a visual graphic on the board with headings similar to the ones in Figure 10–2. Ask students to make brief "speeches" for each heading in the graphic and ask their friends in class to vote on a proposed new "right" they support. The students can design one-page broadsides about the new rights (posters were called broadsides in Revolutionary days) and keep a record of the voting pro-

FIGURE 10–2   *Students' Bill of Rights*

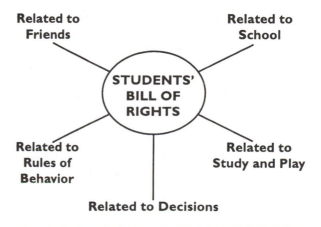

cess. Findings can be reported orally to other classrooms and in writing in a class newspaper.

History Mysteries and Ghost Stories

"Like sports stories, mysteries often combine action with suspense about how things are going to come out. Who outsmarts whom?" ask Glazer and Williams (1979). "Again, the child character has a major effect on the outcome, sometimes confounding adults with deft deduction. Again, children reading the stories can find young heroes or heroines who master the world of their neighborhoods." Indeed, the heroes and heroines in history mysteries and ghost stories not only master the world of their neighborhoods but also master the different worlds in different time periods. You can introduce your students to some of these history mysteries and ghost stories with the titles given in Figure 10–3.

FIGURE 10–3   History Mysteries and Ghost Stories

Pre-Columbus Time Period

Fritz, J. *Brendan the Navigator: A History Mystery about the Discovery of America.* Putnam, 1979. Discusses the Irish monk who might have been the first European in North America and some evidence about this "history mystery" from different sources. Nonfiction. Grades 4–8.

1200: Days of Ancient Maya Cities

Meyer, C. & Gallenkamp, C. *The Mystery of the Ancient Maya.* Atheneum, 1985. In the jungles of Central America, recent discoveries show evidence of ancient Mayan cities that remain one of history's mysteries. Nonfiction. Grade 7 and up.

1400: Days of America's Discovery

Lauber, P. *Who Discovered America? Mysteries and Puzzles of the New World.* HarperCollins, 1992. Discusses such mysteries such as "Were early Irish priests and Vikings discoverers of America?" and "Who were the 'Indians' Columbus met?" Nonfiction. Grade 6 and up.

1533: Days of Queen Elizabeth I

Hilgartner, B. *A Murder for Her Majesty.* Houghton Mifflin, 1986. Sixteenth-century English life and political intrigue are seen through the eyes of 11-year-old Alice Tuckfield, who hides in the Workshire cathedral disguised as a choirboy while searching for her father's murderer. Fiction. Grades 4–8.

1600: Days of Roanoke Island

Bosco, P. J. *Roanoke: The Story of the Lost Colony.* Millbrook, 1992. Portrays life of Elizabethan England and native people in the colonies based on journals of two colonists. Nonfiction. Grades 4–8.

Hubbard-Brown, J. *The Secret of Roanoke Island.* Avon, 1991. The first settlers of Roanoke Island mysteriously disappeared. Nonfiction. Grade 5 and up.

1693: Days of Seventeenth Century New England

Reiss, K. *Pale Phoenix.* New York: Harcourt, 1994. In 1693, 13-year-old Abby is caught outside of time when her family home burns and she is doomed to go on living for centuries without growing older. She appears as a lonely new student at Miranda Browne's school and is asked to stay with the Brownes. Miranda observes Abby's strangeness when she disappears for periods of time, when she cries, and when a stone whistle plays a part in Abby's life. Finally, a journey back in time resolves Abby's problems. Fiction. Grades 6–9.

1700: Days of Area Now San Diego

O'Brien, E. F. *Anita of Rancho Del Mar.* Fithian Press, 1991. Twelve-year-old Anita and her brother Tonio find a map of their land grant, which leads to the mystery of who is plotting to take over

---

FIGURE 10–3   Continued

the rancho. Shows the children attending a fiesta, learning a new dance called the waltz, being taught by a tutor, and facing a mountain lion. Dangers of rancho life include stopping horse thieves, solving problems with Native People, buying supplies in Santa Barbara, and facing a storm at sea. Fiction. Grade 5 and up.

1800: Days of Butch Cassidy

Steward, G. B. *Where Lies Butch Cassidy?* Crestwood, 1992. Discusses the mystery concerning Cassidy's death. Nonfiction. Grades 4–8

1800: Days off Nineteenth-Century Massachusetts

Voight, C. *The Callendar Papers.* Atheneum, 1983. In the summer of 1894, 13-year-old Jean Wainwright organizes the papers of Mr. Thiel's deceased wife at their estate in the Berkshire Mountains. Jean uncovers a mystery that brings danger. Fiction. Grade 5 and up.

1800: Days of Edgar Allen Poe

Avi. *The Man Who Was Poe.* Orchard, 1989. A mysterious writer (who is really Edgar Allen Poe) offers to help Edmund when his mother, aunt, and sister disappear. Fiction. Grade 7 and up.

1842: Days of Charles Dickens

Curry, J. L. *What the Dickens!* McElderry, 1991. In a Harrisburg bookstore in Virginia, 11-year-old Cherry Dobbs overheads a plot to steal Dickens's manuscript in progress, *American Notes.* Cherry foils the scheme. A reader learns about American history of the time period and may be inspired to read the authentic *American Notes.* Fiction. Grades 4–6.

1837: Days of Nineteenth-Century London

Garfield, L. *The December Rose.* Viking, 1987. "Her name was Donia Vassilovas. She was known as an enemy of the country and a grave risk to the security of the state." With these words, a mystery begins as Barnacle, a young chimney sweep in Victorian London, is caught up in murder, espionage, and political intrigue. Fiction. Grades 5–8.

1845: Days of Nineteenth-Century Artic

Beattie, O., & Geiger J. *Buried Ice: The Mystery of a Lost Artic Expedition.* Scholastic, 1992. In England in spring of 1845, Sir John Franklin's expedition sets sail in two ships, the *Erebus* and the *Terror,* to look for a northwest passage. Luke Smith, a stoker on board the *Terror,* narrates the story of the harsh winter and a mysterious illness that affects the crew. In this expedition mystery, none of Franklin's party ever returned. Years later, in 1930, some explorers find the remains of two of his campsites, a few records, and skeletal remains of some party members. The author, an anthropologist, uses the evidence and hypothesizes about the fate of the Franklin expedition. Nonfiction. Grade 4 and up.

1864: Days of Battle of New Market

Alphin, E. M. *The Ghost Cadet.* 1991. In Virginia, the ghost of a Civil War soldier from the Military Institute moves into the present to visit Benjy Stark and tells him the battle of New Market from the cadet's southern point of view. Fiction. Grade 5 and up.

1872: Days of Nineteenth-Century England

Pullman, P. *The Ruby and the Smoke.* Knopf, 1985. "Her name was Sally Lockhart; and within fifteen minutes she was going to kill a man." So begins a mystery about the opium trade and a search for a missing ruby in Victorian London. Fiction. Grade 6 and up.

continued

FIGURE 10–3   **Continued**

1900: Days of Twentieth-Century St. Louis

Peck, R. *The Ghost Belonged to Me*. Viking, 1975. In a setting of the early twentieth century, Alexander Arnsworth befriends Blossom Culp and discovers that her mother, Mrs. Culp, knows about the ghost in his barn. Fiction. Grade 5 and up

1900: Days of Twentieth-Century Washington State

Beatty, P. *Sarah and Me and the Lady from the Sea*. Morrow, 1989. The Abbot children and their mother are trying to live through a harsh winter on the peninsula in Washington. When a lady is washed ashore tied to a mast and unable to speak any language they know, they take on the mystery. Fiction. Grade 6 and up.

1910: Days of Twentieth-Century Medicine

Hahn, M. D. *Time for Andrew: A Ghost Story*. Clarion, 1994. In 1910, 12-year-old Andrew, who is dying of diphtheria, finds himself in 1990 in his own room, now occupied by his great-great-nephew Drew. Identical, the two boys change places and modern medicine saves Andrew's life. Fiction. Grades 4–8

1930: Days of Judge Crater

Stewart, G. B. *What Happened to Judge Crater?* Crestwood, 1992. Discusses the mysterious disappearance of Judge Crater, a state Supreme Court Justice in New York in the 1930s. Nonfiction. Grades 4–8.

1950: Days of the Rosenburgs

Larsen, A. *The Rosenbergs*. Dial, 1992. There is a mystery about whether the available evidence supports the idea that the Rosenbergs were guilty of the crimes for which they were executed. Nonfiction. Grade 5 and up.

1990: Days of Gold

Pople, M. *A Nugget of Gold*. Holt, Rinehart and Winston, 1988. Sally Matthews finds an old nugget that had been fashioned into a woman's brooch. Inscribed on the back are the words *Ann Bird Jem Ever*. This gold piece leads her into a mystery and love story nearly 100 years old that become part of a family's history for generations. Fiction. Grade 6 and up.

1990: Days of Mystery about a Burial

Tate, E. E. *The Secret of Gumbo Grove*. Watts, 1987. Raisin is interested in African American history and she wants to track down the big mystery of a famous person who is buried in the Calvary County cemetery. Fiction. Grade 5 and up.

1990: Days of Mystery about a Keepsake

Precek, K. W. *The Keepsake Chest*. Macmillan, 1992. In the attic of a house in Ohio, Meg Hamilton discovers an old cherry chest carved with the date 1774. Inside were quilts, old papers, baby clothes, and an old blue uniform coat. The chest helps her find clues to prove her family had a legal right to the land before a developer moves in to build a housing development. Fiction. Grades 4–6.

1990: Days of the Legend of Red Horse

Paulsen, G. *The Legend of Red Horse*. Dell, 1994. The ghost of Red Horse, a Native American legend, helps the law-abiding children as Apache Will Little Bear Tucker and his friend, Sarah Thompson, are kidnapped by villains who want the children's discovered treasure. Will and Sarah escape, wander in caves underground, and solve the legend of Red Horse. Fiction. Grades 4–6.

Activity #90: "A Ghost of the 1700s"

Read aloud to students a story set during America's Revolutionary War such as *A Witch Across Time* (Atheneum, 1990, grade 6 and up) by G. B. Cross. In the story, Hannah Kincaid goes to Martha's Vineyard to live with her great-aunt in a house 250 years old to recuperate from anorexia and to adjust to her new stepmother. Hannah makes contact with a young ghost who shares her sadness with Hannah. After the story, discuss:

1. How does the writer describe the 1700s?
2. What points made an impact on you in the book?
3. What evidence does the author have to document the story?
4. What would you say to a younger student who asked you what the American Revolution was like?

John "Appleseed" Chapman (1774–1845)

"The maples, shedding their spinning seeds,/ Called to his appleseeds in the ground,/ Vast chestnut trees, with their butterfly nations,/ Called to his seeds without a sound,/ describes Appleseed's observations of nature in "In Praise of Johnny Appleseed" by Vachel Lindsay in *Story and Verse* (Macmillan, 1946) by Miriam Blanton Huber. After reading aloud the poem, pair a companion story about Johnny Appleseed (now considered a folk legend) such as the one in *Johnny Appleseed* (Morrow, 1988, all grades) by Steven Kellogg. Kellogg's book is a biographical retelling of John Chapman, the gentle healer, who always carried apple seeds and was known to have a tame wolf as a companion. Sometimes he dressed in ragged clothes and wore a cooking pot for a hat as he traveled through Pennsylvania, Ohio, and Indiana. Since Kellogg's book is the story of a famous man's life, it can be an inspiring way for students to learn history in this time period.

It has additional value because it can be used comparatively with other accounts that the students locate. Students can compare some of the different versions: *Better Known as Johnny Appleseed* (Lippincott, 1950, grades 4–5) by M. L. Hunt focuses on Appleseed as a humble eccentric man who was universally loved; and *Johnny Appleseed* (Little Brown, 1990, grade 4) by R. Lindbergh has poetic lines in rhyme. Books about Johnny Appleseed can strengthen a study about the history of pioneers and westward movement in the United States and lead some students on to inquiry about the types of

apples, the fruit's life cycle, where apples grow, the jobs apples provide, and ways they are used by today's families.

Activity #91: "Different Poems— Different Accounts"

"Of Jonathan Chapman/Two things are known,/ That he loved apples,/ That he walked alone./" These words describing Chapman's behavior introduce the poem "Johnny Appleseed" in *A Book of Americans* (Holt, 1986, all grades). In another poem, "The Ballad of Johnny Appleseed" by Helmer O. Oleson in *The Arbuthnot Anthology of Children's Literature* (Scott, Foresman, 1971, all grades), the setting is emphasized with the words: "Through the Appalachian valleys, with his kit a buckskin bag,/ Johnny Appleseed went plodding past high peak and mountain crag./" Different poems about Appleseed, such as these two, will give students different accounts of his life and become ways for them to compare and contrast the ways that history has been seen differently by poets who wrote at different times. As you read a poem aloud, ask the students to create a character diagram for Johnny Appleseed with headings of "Setting," "Clothing," "Travels," and other topics and add information they receive from the poems.

Appleseed Connects to Content

A study of the life of Johnny Appleseed (1774–1845) can be a bridge to a study of content about apples and to other types of literature about the topic. For instance, to relate a study about the topic of apples, you can introduce informational books about apples and related topics. Engage students in telling what they learned about the history of apples, life cycles, problems and solutions about growing and harvesting, as well as related economic principles from the books they locate.

Activity #92: "Johnny Appleseed and Native Americans"

Read aloud more verses from the lengthy narrative titled "In Praise of Johnny Appleseed" by Vachel Lindsay from Huber's *Story and Verse for Children* (Macmillan, 1966, all grades). Discuss what the students visualize during Appleseed's meeting with the Indian leaders when they brought him "magical trinkets and pipes and guns,/Beads and furs from their medicine lair—/Stuck holy feathers in his hair." Discuss the value of Appleseed's actions from their points of view and have students record their views in brief essays.

Tree in the Trail and Other Books

"The informational book seems to be especially designed for the young researcher. Many of these books have fine and accurate illustrations, a good meaty text, a detailed index, a table of contents, and often a glossary, bibliography, and possibly footnotes," explains Dewey Woods Chambers (1971). "It offers the youngster who does research a fine place to begin. A good informational book can expand and enhance the youngster's ideas about what books are and how they can be used." As an example, Chambers suggests *Tree in the Trail* by Holling C. Holling as a book that offers hours of "fruitful searching." *Tree in the Trail* is the story of a tree planted by an Indian boy many years ago in Southwestern United States. As the tree grows, events in history revolve around it and the Spanish come, the mountain men arrive, the wagon trains stop, and as time passes, the westward movement is illustrated clearly in this beautifully done informational book.

Realizing that not all books are as finely crafted as Holling's book, Kobrin (1988) has a motto of saying "No" to ugly informational books and suggests 10 ways for students to judge a book of facts: attractiveness, accuracy, appropriateness, authority of author, cautions, design of the book, format, rhetoric, stereotypes avoided, and tone. Kobrin indicates that educators should refer students to appropriate books that make reading and research an enticing task, to the print and pictures that reflect accuracy, to books written by someone who has a knowledge of the subject, and to authors who distinguish between fact and theory and opinion, make nonstereotypical presentations, and have an exciting tone that creates an excitement for the subject. Invite students to each bring an informational book related to the 1700s to class from the school library and review several of them in the whole group according to Kobrin's criteria.

Activity #93: "Making an Index"

Kobrin (1988) says that she became annoyed when she tried to find something in the Brown Paper School series and then decided to index the books. Then she thought, "Why me? Better my students," and she assigned paragraphs, pages, and chapters to individuals and groups and let them create an index. The students found key words, learned the value topic sentences and subheads, and developed an appreciation the way the author organized a chapter. Kobrin typed the index, had the students sign it, and put it in the book. As Kobrin did in subsequent years, you can "misplace" an index and have it created again and again.

Any time, students may index an informational book that lacks an index. For instance, girls and boys reading *The Wright Brothers* (Fawcett, 1992) by Becky Welch will discover no index, as is found in *The Wright Brothers* (Holiday, 1992) by Russell Freedman. With students, discuss the index as a reference tool and its ability to assist them as they search further on the topic.

Pecos Bill and Geography

After you read aloud the book *Pecos Bill* (Morrow, 1986, grades 4–5) by Steven Kellogg, guide students to the terms in the tall tale that relate to geography. For instance, the words, His kinfolk decided that New England was becoming entirely too crowded, so they piled into covered wagons and headed west," can encourage girls and boys to locate "New England" and "West" on a map of the United States. With blank maps of the United States, the older students can draw symbols or objects for other terms on the map as they listen again to the tall tale. They can research the history of the area with books that offer summaries. Other geographical places to identify include East Texas, Pecos River, and Hell's Gulch. As they listen to the words about Pecos Bill as he tries to corner the wild stallion, Lightning, the students can identify additional locales. Discuss the adventure where Bill chases Lightning to the Artic Circle and the Grand Canyon and returns to Pinnacle Peak—and find those places on the maps. Additionally, the map on the book's endpapers can motivate students to sketch and color original small scenes of Pecos Bill and his adventures on their maps.

Activity #94: "Pecos Bill and Sluefoot Sue"

Turn to another version of Pecos Bill, *The Legend of Pecos Bill* (Bantam, 1993, grades 4–5) by Terry Small, and mention that Sluefoot Sue's mother came from the Chickasaw people, a tribe from a Woodland tribe in the southeast, and that the plot takes place in the Washitaw Valley in Oklahoma and then in Texas. With their maps, ask students to identify these geographical places, too. For students interested further in the topic, invite them to study the cultures of the Chickasaw people and other Plains tribes in the southwest. Some students may be interested in the lives of the Eastern Apache, Comanche, Kiowa, Osage, Tonakawa, Waco, and Wichita.

Engage older students in drawing maps of the southwest region that include Oklahoma, Texas, and other states that were the stomping grounds of Pecos Bill and Sluefoot Sue. Using the maps, have students discuss reasons why ranchers wanted to raise cattle in the area and have them trace routes of trail drives and mark cattle raising areas.

Activity #95: "Frontier Characteristics"

With students, divide them into small groups to research the story of one of the tall tale heroes or heroines. Tell students that the group members will need to tell the whole class ways that their research supported what they read in the tale or did not support the writing in the story. Then, engage the students in discussing attributes of the western frontier they have discerned from such tall tales as those in

American Tall Tales (Knopf, 1993) by Mary Pope Osborn, in *Iva Dunnit and the big Wind* (Dial, 1985, grades 2–5) by Carol Purdy, and other stories about other heroes—perhaps *The Legend of John Henry* (Bantam Doubleday Dell, 1993, grades 1–3) by Terry Small. Ask the students to identify facts about the western frontier that they learned from the tall tales and write the facts in their notebooks. Then ask them to meet with partners and use the facts to write brief descriptive paragraphs about the frontier. Once the paragraphs are written and read to other partners, ask the students to transform their writing into drawings and refer to the descriptive words in their writing to sketch a scene of the frontier. For other tall tales, see History Master 30, "America's Tall Tale Characters."

CHAPTER ELEVEN

A.D. 1800–1899

What was going on in the nineteenth century?

Multicultural Perspectives

All types of books—historical fiction, informational books, biographies, and folk literature—can add an emotional dimension to this time period. The books can take students along the divergent paths taken by U.S. people during these days as well as along the convergent path toward a more perfect union (1850–1879) and the beginning of an industrial Union (1877–1899). Facts of the early years in this time period can be brought into a meaningful context by discussing the politics in the country's early republic.

With students interested in any of the following selected perspectives in Figure 11–1, you can guide them to a few selections of children's literature and to the way the perspectives are portrayed during this period.

FIGURE 11–1 Children's Books about A.D. 1800–1899

PERSPECTIVES FOR 1800s

African Heritage

Altman, S., & Lechner, S. *Many Voices, One Song, Followers of the North Star: Rhymes about African-American Heroes, Heroines, and Historical Times.* Children's Press, 1993. Tells a rhyming story about courageous people who followed the Northern Star as a way to a better life. Nonfiction. Grade 4 and up.

Bisson, T. *Nat Turner.* Chelsea House, 1988. This tells of Turner's life as a slave who persuaded others to rise up in a revolt of 1831. Turner felt he had no control over his destiny. Biography. Grades 7–8.

Cooper, M. L. *From Slave to Civil War Hero: The Life and Times of Robert Small.* Lodestar, 1994. Biographical material about Smalls, a slave in Charleston, S.C., who worked as a pilot on a cotton steamer and defected to the Yankees in 1862. He later became an African American hero and a representative in the U.S. Congress. Biography. Grades 5–8.

Haley, A. *A Different Kind of Christmas.* Doubleday, 1988. This is a Christmas season story set in 1855 that relates to the Underground Railroad. Historical fiction. Grade 7 and up.

Katz, W. L. *Breaking the Chains: African American Slave Resistance.* Atheneum, 1991. Discusses some myths about slavery and the idea that African Americans were satisfied with their lot and did little to free themselves. Nonfiction. Grades 6–8.

FIGURE 11–1   Continued

Katz, W. L., & Franklin, P. A. *Proudly Red and Black: Stories of African and Native Americans.* Atheneum, 1993. This contains six biographies of Americans who are of Native American and African descent. Most of the biographies—such as Paul Cuffe of New England; John Horse, a Seminole leader; Edward Rose, a frontier scout; and Bill Pickett, a famed rodeo rider—lived in the nineteenth century. Biography. Grades 6–8.

Lester, J. *To Be a Slave.* Ill. by T. Feelings. Dial, 1988. A collection of stories from slave living in the first half of the 19th century (1800–1850) and narratives and quotes from ex-slaves through a 1930 Federal Writers Project. Nonfiction. Grade 5 and up.

McKissack, P. C., and McKissack, F. L. *Christmas in the Big House, Christmas in the Quarters.* Scholastic, 1993. Offers a verbal picture of a way of life and the Christmas holiday in the South in 1859. Discusses Christmas preparations on a Virginia plantation. Nonfiction. Grades 4–7.

Merriwether, L. *The Freedom Ship of Robert Smalls.* Ill. by L. J. Morton. Prentice, 1971. Presents the life of Robert Smalls (1839–1919), the captain of *The Planter*, a freedom ship. Biography. Grade 4.

Paulsen, G. *Nightjohn.* Delacorte, 1993. Twelve-year-old Sarny tells the horror of her life as a slave on the Waller plantation in the 1850s. She learns reading and writing from Nightjohn, a new slave. Fiction. Grade 7 and up.

Sagarin. M. *John Brown Russwurm: The Story of Freedom's Journal, Freedom's Journey* Lothrop, Lee & Shepard, 1950. This is the story of Russwurm, a supporter of the National Colonization Society of America of 1816 and its goal of setting up a colony in Africa for free African Americans and having an independent government in Liberia. Biography. Grades 6–8.

Asian Heritage

Takaki, R. *Journey to Gold Mountain: The Chinese in 19th Century America.* Chelsea, 1994. Describes experiences of nineteenth-century immigrants and documents their contributions. Nonfiction. Grade 5 and up.

Yep, L. *Dragon's Gate.* HarperCollins, 1993. Otter, a 14-year-old Chinese boy, tells of the experiences of the Chinese laborers who built the transcontinental railroad in the Sierra Nevadas at the time of America's Civil War. The "Dragon's Gate" is his uncle's folktale about a fish who swims upstream to go through a river gate and changes into a dragon, which means a person can survive against obstacles and become one who changes things. Historical fiction. Grade 6 and up.

Yep, L. *Mountain's Light.* Harper, 1985. Portrays the repugnant conditions faced by Chinese immigrants who travel from Hong Kong to San Francisco during the days of the California Gold Rush and the promise of the gold fields and the fighting among the groups that carried over from China to America. Historical fiction. Grade 6 and up.

European Heritage

De Paola, T. *An Early American Christmas.* Ill. by author. Holiday House, 1987. Shows the spirit of the winter season is spread from a German family to a whole town. The customs that are enjoyed are ones seen in a contemporary season—singing carols, placing a tree inside, and putting bayberry candles in the windows. Historical fiction. All grades.

Fix, P. *Not So Very Long Ago: Life in a Small Country Village.* Dutton, 1994. Students whose ancestors came from Central Europe will be interested in the life of a single family in a European village and their dependence on the potter, the weaver, the tinker, and the apothecary. Historical fiction. Grades 4–6.

continued

FIGURE 11–1   Continued

Lee, K. *Tracing Our Italian Roots.* John Muir Publications, 1993. Describes life in Italy, particularly the economic hardships in southern Italy, and the conditions that led people to emigrate as well as the prejudice they faced and their working conditions in the United States. Discusses Geraldine Ferraro and other famous Italian Americans. Nonfiction. Grades 4–6.

Moscinski, S. *Tracing Our Irish Roots.* John Muir Publications, 1993. Describes life in Ireland, particularly the potato famine, and the conditions that led people to emigrate as well as the prejudice they met in their working conditions in the United States. Nonfiction. Grades 4–6.

West, T. *Mr. Peale's Bones.* Silver Moon Press, 1994. Eleven-year-old Will and his father help energetic Charles Wilson Peale with his excavation of mammoth bones discovered in a marl pit near their uncle's farm in Ulster County, New York. Fiction. Grades 4–6.

Latino/Hispanic Heritage

Finley, M. P. *Soaring Eagle.* Simon & Schuster, 1993. Rumors of war between Mexico and the United States send Julio Montoya and his father to Fort Bend. This story is best for individual reading by mature readers because of emotional and sensitive material. Fiction. Grades 7–8.

Krumgold, J. *And Now Miguel.* Ill. by J. Charlot. Crowell, 1953. Miquel claims his pride in his family when he is considered old enough to go with the men who worked on the ranch. Fiction. Grade 6 and up.

O' Dell, S. *Carlota.* Houghton Mifflin, 1981. Spanish-speaking Carlota, daughter of a native California, Don Saturnino, joins her father in ambushing English-speaking settlers who are trying to annex California to the United States. Historical fiction. Grade 5 and up.

Original Native American Heritage

Bealer, A. *Only the Names Remain: The Cherokees and the Trail of Tears.* Little, Brown 1972. This informational book depicts the hardship of the Native Americans forced leave their lands. Many died when they were marched miles to a relocation site. Nonfiction. Grades 5–8.

Brown, M. M. *Sacagawea: Indian Interpreter to Lewis and Clark.* Children's Press, 1988 Recounts life of the Shoshone woman who was the guide and interpreter for the expedition. Biography. Grades 5–8.

Diamond, A. *Smallpox and the American Indian.* Lucent, 1992. Recounts a national tragedy of an epidemic among Native People of the upper Missouri River in 1837–1840. Nonfiction. Grades 5–8.

Farnsworth, F. J. *Winged Moccasins: The Story of Sacajawea.* Ill. by L. Bjorklund. Messner, 1954. This is an authentic account of 19-year-old Sacajawea (1786–1884), sister of an influential Shoshone chief and wife of a French guide, who guided the Lewis and Clark expedition to the Pacific. Biography. Grades 5–8.

Hudson, J. *Sweetgrass.* Philomel, 1989. Sweetgrass, a 15-year-old Blackfoot girl sees the effects of smallpox, the whites'disease, and cares for her family. Historical Fiction. Grades 4–6.

Oppenheim, J. *Osceola, Seminole Warrior.* Troll, 1979. Portrays life of leader of Native Americans. Biography. Grades 5–8.

Roop, P. & Roop, C. *Ahyoka and the Talking Leaves.* Ill. by Y. Miyake. Lothrop, Lee & Shepard, 1992. Together, Seequoyah and his daughter, Ahyoke, create a written language for their Cherokee people. Fiction. Grades 4–5.

Sanford, W. R. *Chief Joseph: Nez Perce Warrior.* Enslow, 1994. Introduces the Native American leader with documented information and quotes. Black-and-white reproductions and index included. Biography. Grades 4–6.

Schwarz, M. *Cochise: Apache Chief.* Chelsea, 1992. Details the story of the Chiricahua Apache leader along with a background of the history of his people and their battles. Biography. Grade 6 and up.

FIGURE 11–1   Continued

Stewart, E. J. *On the Long Trail Home.* Clarion, 1994. Nine-year-old Meli is separated from her family as they are driven by soldiers from their homes in North Carolina and marched to government lands in Oklahoma. Historical fiction. Grades 4–6.

Taylor, C. *What Do We Know about the Plains Indians?* Peter Bedrick, 1993. This book covers topics such as daily life, clothing, languages, and beliefs about the diverse people and cultures of the Native Americans of the Great Plains. Nonfiction. Grades 4–6.

Wallin, L. *In the Shadow of the Wind.* Macmillan, 1984. This is a story of a white boy and a Native American girl, both teenagers, who fall in love in 1835, a time when the Creek People struggled to save their land from white settlers. Historical fiction. Grade 7 and up.

Wallin, J. *Trails of Tears: American Indians Driven from Their Lands.* Hendrick-Long Pub., 1992. In 1832, President Jackson ordered troops to march 1,600 Cherokee people to the West. Nonfiction. Grade 4 and up.

Differently Abled Heritage

Howard, E. *Edith Herself.* Atheneum, 1987. In the late nineteenth century, orphaned Edith faces a new life and comes to terms with her epilepsy as she copes with the ways others react to her illness. Historical fiction. Grades 5–7.

Kudlinski, K. V. *Facing West: A Story of the Oregon Trail.* Viking, 1994. In 1845, Ben's asthma is the reason his family takes him West. Pete, a mountain man and guide, helps Ben learn self-reliance on the trip, a characteristic Pete calls facing "the elephant." Historical fiction. Grades 4–5.

Markham, L. *Helen Keller.* Watts, 1992. Portrays Keller's life and focuses on her friendship with Alexander Graham Bell and her brief excursion into vaudeville. Biography. Grades 4–6.

Sanders, J. *Brothers of the Heart.* Scribners, 1985. In the Michigan wilderness in the 1800s, a developmentally different boy learns survival skills and gains self-esteem with the help of a Native woman. Historical fiction. Grade 7 and up.

Whelan, G. *Hannah.* Ill. by L. Bowman. Knopf, 1991. In the West in 1887, 9-year-old Hannah copes with her blindness and proves she can learn at school by listening and discovers she can read books in Braille. At the closing, the children, under the class bully's, leadership, earn money and buy her a Braille writer. Historical fiction. Grades 4–5.

Female Image Heritage

Atkinson, L. *Mary Jones: The Most Dangerous Woman in America,* Crown, 1978. Portray life of Mary Jones (1830–1930), devotee to the labor movement. Biography. Grade 6 and up.

Avi. *The True Confessions of Charlotte Doyle.* Orchard Books, 1990. In 1832, Charlotte sails from England to the United States and changes from a prim lady into one who climbs the rigging and joins the crew. Historical fiction. Grade 5 and up.

Berleth, R. *Mary Patten's Voyage.* Albert Whitman, 1994. Fictionalized account of an actual event in 1856 when the 18-year-old wife of the captain of the ship *Neptune's Car* took over for her sick husband. She piloted the ship around Cape Horn in a race with other ships to reach California first. Historical fiction. Grades 4–5.

Blumberg, R. *Bloomers!* Bradbury, 1993. In 1851, Libby arrived in Seneca Falls, New York, wearing bloomers—gathered pants—covered by a skirt that barely reached her knees. This shocked everyone but intrigued her cousin. Eventually, wearing bloomers was the new symbol of the women's movement. Fictionalized biography. Grade 4.

continued

FIGURE 11–1   Continued

Fleischman, P. *The Borning Room*. HarperCollins, 1991. This is a story of four generations of Ohioans whose important events—births and deaths—take place in the home's borning room. Georgina Caroline Lott, born in the room in 1851, tells about her family to a painter who is painting her portrait toward the end of her life. Historical fiction. Grade 6 and up.

Greenfield, E., & Little, L. J. *Childtimes: A Three-Generation Memoir*. Crowell, 1979. Each of the book's three parts contains the experiences of a grandmother, a mother, and daughter—three generations of African American women. Biography. Grade 6 and up.

Holland, C. *The Bear Flag*. Houghton Mifflin, 1990. Catherine Reilly, a widow, survives the frontier and earns the respect of others. Includes historical events such as the Kelsey-Bidwell-Bartleson Crossing of the Great Basin and the Sierra (1841), the John Fremont and Kit Carson Winter Crossing (1844), and the Bear Flag Revolt (1846). Historical fiction. Grade 7 and up.

Johnston, J. *Harriet and the Runaway Book: The Story of Harriet Beecher Stowe and Uncle Tom's Cabin*. Ill. by R. Himler. Harper, 1977. In Ohio, Stowe sees slaves escape to freedom and is determined to write a book, *Uncle Tom's Cabin* (Bantam, reissue 1981) to show how terrible slavery was. Biography. Grades 4–5.

Levenson, D. *Women of the West*. Watts, 1973. Beginning in 1818, facts about the lives Native American women, African American women, and European American women are detailed. Nonfiction. Grade 7 and up.

Meade, M. *Free Woman: The Life and Times of Victoria Woodhull*. Knopf, 1976. Present the life of Victoria Woodhull (1838–1927), the first woman to run for president of the United States. Biography. Grade 6 and up.

Meigs, C. L. *Jane Addams: Pioneer for Social Justice*. Little, 1970. Portrays the life of Jane Addams (1860–1935), who became a social reformer. Biography. Grades 5–7.

Religious Minority Heritage

De Angeli, M. *Thee, Hannah*. Doubleday, 1949. Hannah, a young Quaker girl, helps an African American mother and child to safety. Historical fiction. Grade 4 and up.

Historical Stories in Songs

"Work songs, often developed as a diversion from boring work, capture the rhythm and spirit of the labor in which their creators were engaged," writes Cullinan (1981). "The songs sing of the values and the life styles of the people who laid the railroads, dug the tunnels and canals, and toted that bale. In addition, ballads were used to inform and to persuade, to foster agreement, and unify people." Related to this period, introduce an event through a folk song and discuss historical information about the song (see History Master 31, "Selected Story Songs"). Reviewing a historical event through the song, the students will benefit in other ways as they develop musical skills they can build on in later musical experiences (Gregory, 1979). In support of this, Roberts (1992) maintains that folk songs give students a context for a particular event or time period and that the historical notes in song books are helpful since folk songs have a history and the notes tell the students more about the song. Invite the students to participate in this activity to highlight some of the events in U.S. history. By singing "Yankee Doodle" and some of the other early songs from the 1700s and other time periods, the students can review and present periods of history through music.

Activity #96: "Singing through History"

If appropriate, engage the students in researching a book of U.S. songs from the school library or public library. With the book, sing and discuss some of the songs (e.g., "What does the song tell us about what the people were doing/thinking in the time period?") and select the songs that the students think best represent people and events that they want to emphasize in a song medley. They can "value vote" for their favorites and give their reasons for wanting to include or exclude any song. After the songs are selected, rehearse the historical songs and then, if desired, rehearse a presentation with a narrator who briefly describes the event, historical figure, or place related to each song before it is performed.

As a repeat performance on subsequent days, have students select different songs to represent the same historical periods and produce a different performance of "Singing through History." With a variety of story songs and song books from History Master 31, the students can learn a multitude of songs from different time periods, which can be followed by independent reading of the picture song books and more discussion of the historical notes that are included. Additionally, if your students are interested in listening to humorous stories about some selected folk songs, you can find them in *Hear the Wind Blow: American Folk Songs* (Bradbury, 1985) by Scott R. Sanders. The authors invented stories offer students several models for writing their own original humorous stories about traditional folk songs.

Lewis and Clark: 1804

Read the verses about the trip "up the Missouri River" that took "one year and a half" from the poem "Lewis and Clark" in *A Book of Americans* (Holt, 1986, all grades) by the Benets. To remember of the expedition that opened the wilderness further, invite the students to suggest ways to orally interpret the verses (loud voices, soft voices, with motions, with sound effects) and read them aloud as a choral reading. The words tell how about Lewis and Clark suffered from the croup, escaped a grizzly's chase, and felt that their teeth were "full of moss."

Activity #97: "Lewis and Clark"

With students, divide a large blank mural of butcher paper into sections to represent the timeline of the 7,000 mile journey discussed in *Merriweather Lewis and William Clark: Soldiers, Explorers, and Partners in History* (Children's Press, 1988, grade 5 and up) by David Petersen and Mark Coburn and in *The Incredible Journey of Lewis and Clark* (Lothrop, 1987, grade 5 and up) by Rhoda Blumberg. Blumberg's book gives another account of the expedition led by Lewis and Clark as they traveled into the then unknown western regions of America in the early 1800s.

The journals of Lewis and Clark have been edited to focus on the expedition's high points in *Off the Map: The Journals of Lewis and Clark* (Walker, 1993, grades 5–7) by P. & C. Roop. The explorers

wrote in their journals that they saw the plains black with buffalo, rocks twisted into mysterious shapes, and snowy mountains that stretched far into the horizon. Invite students to illustrate each section of the mural with their drawings of the rivers, mountains, and wildlife, and to write captions from their notes about events on the expedition that they heard when the biography was read aloud or read when they browsed independently for further information. Books suitable for adding more information are *Bold Journey: West with Lewis and Clark* (Houghton Mifflin, 1985, grades 4–6) by B. Bohner and *Who'd Believe John Colter?* (Macmillan, 1992, grades 4–5) by M. B. Christian. *Bold Journey* is a fictionalized view of the expedition is told by Private Hugh McNeal; *Who'd Believe John Colter?* depicts the adventures through the eyes of John Colter, a fictionalized hunter-trapper who went along.

Daniel Boone

Engage students in sharing their prior knowledge about contributions made by pioneers in settling the Trans-Appalachian West, and write their suggestions on the board. Read excerpts the about lives of the children living in the 1800s from *Pioneer Children of Appalachian* (Clarion, 1986, grades 5–6) by Joan Anderson. As an example of the trailblazing that was required to open paths in the wilderness, introduce the students to Daniel Boone by reading aloud: "Daniel Boone at twenty-one/ Came with his tomahawk, knife, and gun/ Home from the French and Indian War/ To North Carolina and the Yadkin shore." The words are Arthur Guiterman's way of introducing Boone's adventures on the Wilderness Road in his poem "Daniel Boone" in *Story and Verse for Children* (Macmillan, 1965, all grades) by M. B. Huber. After reading the poem aloud, have students locate on a map North Carolina and other locales that are mentioned. Ask them what facts about settling the West they heard in the poem and compare their new ideas with the former suggestions on the board. Engage them in sketching some of the facts in original scenes of the West.

Activity #98: "On the Frontier"

Have the students select partners and discuss what they know about the lives of frontier men and women, their work, the clothing they wore, and the tools they needed. Ask them to compare the trailblazing frontier people with the forest rangers of today and write notes about their comparisons (similarities). Additionally, invite a forest ranger to visit the class and discuss his or her work, clothing, and tools needed. Schedule time for the student partners to ask questions of the visitor, and then ask each other questions related to some of the comparisons they made.

Further, use some sample generalizations to stimulate thought about the people who lived in this time period. For instance, present a general statement, such as one of the following, to the students and ask them if they agree or disagree with the statement and then explain why. Encourage them to find additional sources that support their views.

1. All men were frontiersmen like Daniel Boone.
2. All women stayed home and took care of the children.
3. Native American Indians were always fighting with American European settlers.
4. Many people with an African heritage have made contributions to the United States.
5. Many people with a Latino/Hispanic heritage have made contributions to the United States.
6. Many people with an Asian heritage have made contributions to the United States.

America's National Anthem

"Then conquer we must,/ when our cause it is just/ And this be our motto, 'In God is our Trust,'/ And the star-spangled banner in triumph shall wave/ O'er the land of the free and the home of the brave/" are the final words of the last verse of the poem that Francis Scott Key wrote in his Baltimore hotel room the night of September 14, 1814, after he watched the English bombard Fort McHenry. The previous day, Key had arrived on board a British prisoner exchange vessel in Baltimore Harbor in 1814 to intercede for a friend who was a prisoner. He watched the English battle the defenders of Baltimore and wrote his impressions the next night.

After students have discussed some of the causes of the War of 1812, read aloud *The Star-Spangled Banner* (Doubleday & Co., 1975, all grades) by Peter Spier. Discuss how our current version of the flag came to be. Reviewing the illustrations in the book on an opaque projector, ask the students what meaning(s) the pictures and the words have for them today.

Activity #99: "Francis Scott Key"

With the whole group, discuss the reasons for the War of 1812 between the United States and England and draw stick figures on the board to represent scenes of what was happening. Talk about Key's involvement in the events. Read aloud the selections about the events and ask students to tell in their own words what was read. After discussing the points of the War of 1812, read aloud Key's poem and, on the board, write the heading, "The Star-Spangled Banner." Beneath the heading, write and discuss some of the phrases from the poem dictated by the students.

1. twilight's last gleaming
2. perilous fight
3. O'er the ramparts
4. foe's haughty host
5. in dread silence reposes
6. morning's first beam

Engage students in sketching scenes to illustrate some of the selected words and phrases on the board. After the students finish their art work, discuss it and display the illustrations in sequence in the room according to the sequence of the words of Key's poem. In small groups, ask students, "What changes, if any, happened to Americans after the War of 1812?" Ask a volunteer from each group to report on the group's discussion to the whole class.

The Alamo: 1836

Showing geographical locations with a large map of the United States, mention to students that in 1836 near the San Antonio River in Texas, Davy Crockett, James Bowie, and William Travis led 186 men in a hopeless battle during the war for the independence of Texas from Mexico. The Alamo (Spanish for cottonwood) was built in 1727 as a mission with a church and convent and it stood alone in the battle surrounded by brush and 4,000 Mexican troops led by General Santa Ana. All of the defenders at the Alamo were killed; however, some members of the defenders' families survived. John Jakes's book, *Susanna of the Alamo* (Gulliver, 1986, grade 4), tells how Susanna Dickinsen, a young widow, survived along with her young daughter and played a part in this event. Students can research more about the war against Mexico with G. C. Wisler's *Piper's Ferry: A Tale of the Texas Revolution* (Lodestar, 1991) and search further for points of view of both sides of this war. Also, they can read more about others who have made heroic contributions from books listed in Figure 11–2.

Activity #100: "Two Generals"

Assist older students as they learn more about the two generals, Santa Ana and Sam Houston, with biographical material, and engage them in reviewing the generals' points of view about the Alamo battle in San Antonio. Students researching more about Sam Houston may want to read biographical

FIGURE 11–2 *Children's Books about the Alamo*

Hoff, C. *Johnny Texas*. Ill. by B. Meyers. Hendrick-Long Pub., 1992. This is the story of a pioneer German family and their experiences in the exciting days of early Texas. Grade 5 and up.

Jakes, J. *Susanna of the Alamo*. Gulliver, 1986. Depicts the battle at the Alamo during the war for the independence of Texas from Mexico and Susanna Dickinsen, one of the few survivors. Grades 4–5.

Lawson, D. *The United States in the Mexican War*. Harper, 1976. Reviews the fall of the Alamo and ways President Polk continued America's expansion to include Texas, California, and New Mexico. Grade 7 and up.

Pinchot, J. *The Mexicans in America*. Lerner, 1989. Discusses the causes and effects of the Mexican War. Grade 6 and up.

Rickerby, L. A. *Ulysses S. Grant and the Strategy of Victory*. Silver Burdett, 1990. Includes section on the reasons for the Mexican War and the battles and people involved. Grade 7 and up.

Stern, P. *Henry David Thoreau: Writer and Rebel*. Crowell, 1972. Includes Thoreau's position that the Mexican War was an unjust war and his refusal to pay his taxes to support it. Grade 7 and up.

Westridge Young Writers Workshop. *Kids Explore America's Hispanic Heritage*. John Muir Pub., 1992. Presents the view of the Mexican soldiers who fight for a just cause at the Battle of the Alamo. Grades 4–6.

Wisler, G. C. *Piper's Ferry: A Tale of the Texas Revolution*. Lodestar, 1990. Portrays the danger in Texas in the 1930s for a teenage boy, his family, and friends as they run the ferry. Grades 5–6.

material about Davy Crockett, James Bowie, and William Travis, also defenders at the Alamo. Invite the students to write on a paper strip two sentences—one each about Santa Ana and Sam Houston. Suggest that they write what they know about the two generals. Then have them take turns reading their sentences. Read aloud selected information about the two generals from the biographical material. Ask the students to check their paper strips to see if their information is similar to what the biographical material says. If their information is similar, they can mark a check ($\sqrt{}$) by the sentence. If they think their sentence is not correct, they can write a correct sentence on the back side of the strip. Display the students' sentence strips on a chart under a heading of "Two Generals at the Alamo."

John Sutter: 1839

Provide initial background about Native American lifestyles in the area now California in 1839 (a time when Sutter arrived) by reading aloud a Yosemite Indian legend such as *Tul-Tok-A-Na: The Small One* (Council of Indian Education, 1991, all grades) by Kathleen Allan Meyer. Meyer's retelling tells how the great rock, now called El Capitan, grew to be the tallest rock in the Yosemite Valley of Califor-

nia and how Tul-Tok-A-Na (meaning the small one) was a tiny inch worm that rescued two small Indian boys stranded on the top. Ask, "If you had been in the story, what would you have done? How might the legend be different if the two boys were not rescued? How has life changed in Yosemite since the days of this legend? What is there in California today that relates to this legend?"

Activity #101: "Before the Gold Rush"

After reading aloud a story about Tenaya, the dedicated leader of the Indians of California's Valley, in *The Tragedy of Tenaya* (Council for Indian Education, 1991, grades 4–6) by Allan Shields, ask the students to consider other activities going on in 1839 in the area. With facts printed on index cards, engage the students in gathering facts and documenting information about the days before the Gold Rush. They can begin with the times of John Sutter, an energetic, garrulous man with blond hair and blue eyes, and his travels as he journeyed over 30,000 miles in five years and conducted his entrepreneurial activities in the Southwest, Northwest, Hawaii, and Alaska.

To discuss the parts played by John Sutter and John Marshall in the discovery of gold at Sutter's Mill, ask the students to identify events related to

Sutter's arrival in California or the discovery of gold for point-and-counterpoint (two points of view) creative dramas for role-playing. List their topics on the board. Have students research facts to role-play the event. The points of view can be a springboard to motivate students to write their own point-and-counterpoint situations for the brief classroom dramas.

The Gold Rush

Jarolimek and Parker (1993) mention the value of asking open-ended questions—ones that elicit more than one point of view from the students. To elicit several points of view about reading/hearing about Sutter, ask the students questions similar to the following:

1. If you had been John Sutter, what route would you have taken to Sacramento and why would you have gone that way? (Provide map of California that shows the rivers and delta areas).
2. How might the history of California been different if John Sutter had found *very* hostile Indians near Sacramento instead of the friendly ones?
3. How has life in the Sacramento area changed since the days of John Sutter?
4. What is there about California today that relates directly to the discovery of gold started by John Sutter, James Marshall, and the others?
5. Ask students, "What is there about California's history in this time period that could also be played out in other roles?"

Activity #102: "Famous Figures"

Engage students in different groups to dramatize other situations similar to those described in sources, such as *Famous Builders of California* (Dodd, 1987, grades 4–6) by Edward F. Dolan, a narrative about Sutter and others who contributed to California's history—Father Junipero Serra, John Fremont, Henry Wells, William Fargo, John Muir, and Luther Burbank (See Figure 11–3). An additional group in the classroom can take on the responsibilities of being a check-out-the-facts group. This means the group members will verify some of the facts about the famous figures in this time period. (Perhaps a student will discover that Sutter left Switzerland ahead of his creditors, who wanted Sutter to repay his debts after his dry goods business failed.)

The Cumberland Road: 1850

Through children's literature, students can relive vicariously what happened on one of America's early main roads from the East to the Ohio Valley—a rough, dusty road that went from Cumberland, Maryland, to Pittsburgh, Pennsylvania, through rough and difficult country. Daniel Boone blazed the Wilderness Road through the Cumberland Gap in 1769. Called the Cumberland Road, it snaked around through the Allegheny Mountains and weary travelers had to ford many fast-moving creeks and rivers.

Read aloud several excerpts about the lives of children who went along from *Children of the Wild West* (Clarion, 1983, grades 4–6) by M. Meltzer, and

---

FIGURE 11–3 *Children's Books about Gold Rush Days*

Blumberg, R. *The Great American Gold Rush*. Bradbury, 1989. Discusses the people who arrived—Chinese, African Americans, Chileans, Mexicans, and others—and the methods they used to recover gold. Grade 5 and up.

Coerr, E. *Chang's Paper Pony*. Harper & Row, 1988. In a gold-mining camp, Chang wishes for a pony, a reward he receives from Big Pete when Chang gives him some gold nugget he finds on Pete's cabin floor. Grade 4.

Egan, F. *The Taste of Time*. McGraw, 1977. Jedediah Wright, widower, heads west in 1859 to seek gold. Grade 7 and up.

Kasky, K. *Beyond the Divide*. Macmillan, 1983. Fourteen-year-old Meribah Simon, an Amish girl, and her father, journey over 3,000 miles by wagon train from Pennsylvania to California. Grade 7 and up.

Murrow, L. K. *West Against the Wind*. Holiday House, 1987. In the 1850s, Abigail Parker travels with her mother and brother on a wagon train to join their father. Grade 6 and up.

ask students to think about (or sketch in a comic-strip format) what is going on as you read aloud. For example, ask them to picture certain details such as the swaying wagons, plodding animals, and the walking people. Ask them to imagine the smell of the dust in the air and hear the sounds of pesky buzzing mosquitoes, snorts of oxen, moos of cows, the crack of an oxen whip, and the coughs of dusty children and adults. Invite students to tell about their thoughts and show their sketches to others in the class. The sketches may be categorized in groups by the students, given labels for the categories, and placed in a class book (one category per chapter) to reflect trail travel during this time period.

Activity #103: "Children of the West"

Ask students to point out examples of ways people tried to overcome the danger, deprivation, and drudgery of life on the trail in the 1800s. Record their suggestions on the board. Ask them to think of their own experiences today and ways they have overcome danger, deprivation, and drudgery in contemporary times.

> *Ways to Overcome Danger,*
> *Deprivation, and Drudgery*
>
> *On the Trail in the 1800s   Today in the 1900s*
> 1.   1.

Have students turn this list of contrasting suggestions into drawings. Have them fold a sheet of art paper in half. On the left-hand side, they should sketch a way people on the trail coped with deprivation, drudgery, or danger; on the right-hand side, they should sketch a way that people today cope with the same adversities.

The Oregon Trail: 1845–1851

Read aloud "Squishing through the mudholes, drunken with the rain;/ Turn your face to heaven, boy—and punch those bulls again. These words reflect a part of the pioneers' lives from Jim Marshall's poem, "The Oregon Trail: 1851," in *Northwest verse* by H. G. Merriam. Marshall writes descriptive phrases that can entice students into further discussion about life on the trail (e.g., "whips cracking," "white sails of schooners," "keep y'r musket handy," "wagons bogged in prairie mud, teams stuck fast," and "trail's pinched out").

After reading the poem, add a 10-year-old girl's details about a 2,000-mile journey from Arkansas to Oregon with descriptions from *Bound for Oregon* (Dial, 1994, grades 4–6) by Jan Van Leeuwen. This historical novel tells about the preparation for the

journey, the difficulty of leaving behind other family members, and the hardships that were met—always pushing past endurance to beat the early snows in the mountains, the sacrifices people made, bad weather, little or no food, fast-moving rivers to cross, little or no medical assistance, sickness, and even death. Best for individual reading because of sensitive material, display *Patty Reed's Doll: The Story of the Donner Party* (Tomato Enterprises, 1989, grades 4–6) by R. K. Laurgaard, a historically accurate account of a pioneer tragedy on the trail that caused the deaths of pioneers camping in the Sierra Nevada range.

Activity #104: "The Trail"

Ask students to imagine a flashback to 1843 and set a scene on the Oregon Trail. Use *The Oreaon Trail* (Holiday House, 1990, grade 5 and up) by L. E. Fisher as a reference and point out that the trail was "littered with broken wheels, smashed or burned wagons, and dead animals." To elaborate further, read aloud some of the pioneers' diary pages and letter selections that Fisher includes and ask students to visualize what is going on as they mark the trail on a map and listen to your description of what was going on.

Activity #105: "Survivors on the Trail"

Since over 35, 000 people died on the Oregon Trail, the photographs and paintings from historical societies show the courage of the people through their journals, diaries, and letters. To give students examples of journal entries, read aloud selections from *The Way West: Journal of a Pioneer Woman* (Simon & Schuster, 1993, grades 4–6) by Amelia Stewart Knight or *The Prairie Traveler* (Corner House, reprint 1969) written by Captain Randolph Marcy in 1859, and make them available for individual reading. *The Way West* is an authentic account of Amelia's overland journey with her large and resourceful family as they faced illness, hunger, and discomfort during the spring and summer of 1853; *The Prairie Traveler* is a wagoner's guidebook and almanac.

Have small groups of student's imagine themselves in the role of overlanders on the trail and determine how Amelia's family powered their wagon. Ask them to draw a "three-legged decision bug" (see Web 11–1) and write the available choices of wagon power—horses, mules, or oxen—at the end of each leg.

Ask the student's to gather facts about the animals to determine their suitability on a wagon trail and then list on the "bug" the advantages and disadvantages of choosing a particular animal to power a

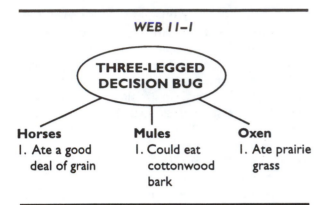

WEB 11–1

THREE-LEGGED
DECISION BUG

Horses
1. Ate a good
deal of grain

Mules
1. Could eat
cottonwood
bark

Oxen
1. Ate prairie
grass

wagon on the trail before they decide on a final choice for their wagon. What will they choose? Horses? Mules? Oxen? Why? Ask a student from each group to report on the group's choice of power for their wagon. Write the choices on the board and add a plus or a minus by each choice during the discussion as the students give reasons for their choice of wagon power.

Horses
1. ate a good deal of grain
2. costs the most
3. fastest

Mules
1. could eat cottonwood bark
2. cost less than horse
3. faster than oxen

Oxen
1. ate prairie grass
2. cost less than mule
3. slower than mule

Stereotypes

"Librarians, teachers, and parents must make a special effort to compensate for the inbalance on the library shelves of today," states Kathy Byrne de Filippo (1984). "They should take the trouble to search for those books which contribute to a nonstereotyped image for little girls and which serve to balance the existing male dominance." To develop the idea of nonstereotyped images with students, encourage them to express their ideas, opinions, beliefs, and attitudes about the things that women and men from history, unknown or little known, have achieved and contributed (Hyde and Bizar, 1989). To confront stereotypes of women during the westward expansion time period and to present the

difficulties of women traveling on the wagon trains, ask each student to write down his or her initial ideas about the roles, work, and responsibilities of women and girls who traveled west. Use sentences beginning with *"Before* I listened to diaries about women traveling on wagon trains to the west, I thought...."

Activity #106: "I Think..."

After the students have written down their initial ideas about the roles, work, and responsibilities of women and girls who traveled west before reading or listening to women's diary entries, have students listen to excerpts from the diaries about women and their lives on wagon trains. Read aloud selections from *Women's Diaries of the Westward Journey* (Schocken, 1982) by Lillian Schissel or another suitable source. Engage students in reflecting about what they heard and in writing any ideas they had that changed. Use a sentence such as *"After* listening to the diaries about women traveling on wagon trains to the west, I think...." Have students read their before-and-after ideas in small groups and report back to the whole class about the changes in their thinking about the roles of women and girls. In a whole group discussion, ask the students their ideas about:

- "How could we define the problems of women and girls on wagon trains from your notes and the discussion?"
- "What patterns about women and girls and wagon train travel can you see?"
- "What other questions could you ask about this?"

Students interested in related topics can be guided to the sources about individuals or women's groups shown on the previously mentioned History Master 32, "Role of Women and Girls" and History Master 33, "Women's Rights."

Minority Stereotypes

"Stereotypes are identified by a lack of individual distinguishing characteristics. Instead, they conform to a fixed oversimplified patterns, as found in many blanket views of blacks, Native Americans and other 'labeled' groups," maintains Katharine Everett Bruner (1988), a school librarian in Harrison, Tennessee. "They affect attitude and are perpetuated long beyond whatever original validity they may have held." As Bruner suggests, stereotypes can become expressions, and when actions go unchallenged, then injustice is given a seal of approval. Older students can react to this by challenging stereotypical expressions and actions in the discussions of stories they read. To get students involved:

1. Read aloud excerpts from an early publication of historical fiction and engage the students in finding out all they can about one of the characters or historical figures. They should note the date of the publication of the book and then identify the characteristics of a stereotyped character.

2. Have students suggest a list of questions about the character's history, interests, and values to use during their research for facts.

3. After gathering facts, ask them to draw some conclusions about the character and support their conclusions with evidence from their research.

4. Discuss the idea of fairness or unfairness when a student makes a conclusion about a person without knowing a lot about her or him. Additionally, the students can compare stereotypes in another book that was published later and point out the ways the story perpetuates or does not perpetuate the stereotype of minority groups (Bruner, 1988).

Activity #107: "Stereotypes"

After listening to excerpts about Amos Fortune in *Amos Fortune* (Dutton, 1967, grade 6 and up) by Elizabeth Yates, have students talk about stereotypes they recognize in this setting of the 1800s. In the story, At-Mun, an African prince, becomes the man Amos Fortune in America and credits his success to his master's wife who taught him to read. Have students talk about the stereotypes they recognize. As the students discuss Amos and his life, ask for their views about Amos's willingness to credit his success to another.

Portrayals of Native Americans

In some early stereotypes of Native Americans, the students may find that the word *savage* is used to depict the original people of the Americas. As an example published in the 1950s, the white characters in *Flaming Arrows* (Harcourt Brace Jovanovich, 1957, grade 6 and up) by William O. Steele see the Native People as savages and defend their fort against the "red devils."

To gain additional perspective into other stereotypes, have students talk about any other stereotypes they recognize. Ask students to compare additional examples from other books about Native Americans

published in earlier years with those published recently. For example, students may find that some of the terms found in earlier writings are still found today whereas other terms have been excluded.

Considering these stereotypes and others, Bruner (1988) suggests that students search for stories that recognize the dignity and intelligence of the sexes and of people of exotic origin, unfamiliar appearance, and different development. Indeed, students need to know that the one-sidedness of stereotypes is not the whole picture. When stereotypes are found in books from the past or the present, they can be invited to challenge them and to speak out for the common values that exist in all people of all cultures.

Activity #108: "Personality Portfolios"

To help students connect history further with reading, writing, biographical research and alphabetizing, Ark (1984), a media specialist at Spinning Hills Middle School in Dayton, Ohio, suggests that personality files (folders) be developed about contemporary personalities to provide biographical information. To put this idea into action in the classroom, the students can develop folders about famous contemporary Native American leaders to provide up-to-date biographical information. To develop the folders, have students write letters and contact the personalities to ask for biographical information and a photograph. When received, the material can be filed in a folder for others in the class to use. Independent readers can use the folders to read about notable Native Americans who once lived in the area, people who live in the community now, or those who are known worldwide. Additionally, reluctant readers can use the material for browsing when they are guided to the personality files.

To elaborate further on the contributions of leaders, ask the students to listen to some material read aloud about historical figures in this time period. (Select some examples of general statements about the figure that may or may not be true.) Discuss the statements with the whole group. If appropriate, tell the students that they will be studying about some of these people and that they are to find out the extent to which their ideas about the people are right or not. To get questions to guide the study, ask the students to tell what they would like to know about certain historical figures and turn their ideas into questions.

Have each student make several general statements about the historical figure of this time period that he or she wants to inquire about in this activity. Have the students record their statements. Engage each student in researching the general statements they made about the famous person and using several references. Students should then return to the whole group to state the general statements about the historical figures that they previously made. Ask the students to meet in pairs and compare their previous general statements with their research to determine if their research documented their previously made general statements. Ask them to report to the whole group about the ways in which they changed their generalizations.

Orphan Trains

Linda MacDonell and Eldon McNabb (1993) point out the magnitude of the number of children and families suffering today from the phenomena of hopelessness because of their homelessness. They state this "was brought into public view at Christmas, 1992, when over 1300 homeless children gathered at a Convention Center in a central city in a large Western state." The children were there to celebrate the holiday at a party sponsored by Project Homeless, a project funded through the state's department of education. This contemporary support is in contrast to what happened to homeless youngsters in the 1800s as told in I. Holland's *The Journey Home* (Scholastic, 1990, grades 6–8), a story of two young sisters who journeyed from New York City to Kansas on one of the Children's Aid Society's orphan trains. One sister, Maggie, tried to adjust to her new life as an orphan, believing that nothing in life is certain.

Another story of homeless children is told in K. Karr's *It Ain't Always Easy* (Farrar, Straus, Giroux, 1990, grades 6–8), where two New York orphans flee from the Children's Aid Society. Rather than be shipped west, the children set out by themselves on foot. The perils that they meet and the eventual resolution of their problems make this an a novel for older students. Also discuss with students, the idea of whether the solution used for homeless children in the 1800s would work today. Discuss why or why not.

Activity #109: "The Homeless"

Since findings currently indicate that the number of homeless families with children is growing at an alarming rate—sometimes tripling in one year. The students can get involved in a project to ensure that identified homeless children have access to books by donating some of the original books they make at school to help bring some joy to children and their families. Through the students, many homeless and unnoticed children, who might otherwise go without books and reading and a chance for literacy, can be helped. Engage the students in telephoning for information and talking to people about homeless projects sponsored by the county office of education and the state department of education in their area.

The Pony Express: 1860

To focus student attention on historical mail service, read aloud excerpts from *The Pony Express: Hoofbeats in the Wilderness* (Watts, 1989, all grades) by J. J. Dicerto that explain how the Pony Express began service in 1860 and carried mail along the Oregon-California Trail in all kinds of weather between St. Joseph, Missouri, and Sacramento, California. In a cause-and-effect situation that students can explore, the express ended a short time later in 1861 because the telegraph finally made connections from the east to the west coast. To elicit several points of view about the Pony Express, ask the students open-ended questions such as:

1. If you had been a rider for the Pony Express, what route would you have taken to Sacramento from St. Joseph and *why* would you have gone that way? What geographic features would you expect to see along the route? (Provide map.)

2. How might the history of California been different if there had been no telegraph and the Pony Express had continued to Sacramento instead of ending as it did?

3. How has life in St. Joseph (or Sacramento) changed since the days of the Pony Express?

4. What is there about California or Missouri today that relates directly to the Pony Express?

Activity #110: "Riders"

Review with the students some of the history of the Pony Express with selected parts from Linda Van Der Linde's book, *The Pony Express* (Macmillan, 1992 grades 6–8), and provide students with information about the riders, their horses, and the routes they took. Help the students compare and contrast how the mail travels today with the way mail traveled on the Pony Express and ask them to weigh letters and parcels, estimate postage costs, and determine distribution routes for classrooms in the school with a school map. They can choose pen pals in other grades and select volunteers as mail carriers, and determine zip codes for the various classrooms.

Before the Civil War: 1862

"Readers' Theater is an oral presentation of written text," states Gallagher (1993). "It can be informal, without any prereading or rehearsal, and is one of the few literature-based activities that works with any age group and with mixed age groups." To begin Readers' Theater related to the pre-Civil War period, select books that enrich the students' history curriculum, just as a fourth-grade teacher did when she engaged the children in scripting a version of *Nettie's Trip South* (Macmillan, 1989, grades 4–8) by Patricia McKissack during a study about slavery.

In the story, 10-year-old Nettie travels from Albany to the South, where she witnesses a slave auction. Writing back home, Nettie describes her inward struggles about the experience. Have students develop a scripted version about Nettie's struggle. The narrators can sit in chairs in pairs with their backs to each other in front of the room. For dramatic effect at various points in the script when the role of a narrator changes, the narrator can stand to read while the others let their heads drop down.

Activity #111: "Script a Story"

To introduce the students to the Civil War period, select *Mine Eyes Have Seen the Glory* (Museum of Fine Arts, Boston, grades 4–8) with paintings, sculpture, and prints of the harsh reality of this war. If desired, discuss some of the wrenching events in *Pink-and-Say* (Philomel, 1994, grade 4 and up) by Patricia Polacco. Polacco's story is about Sheldon Curtis (also called Say), age 15, who lies badly wounded in a field in Georgia. Pinkus Aylee, an African American Union soldier, also a teenager, carries Say home to his mother, Moe Moe Bay. Say, who once shook Abraham Lincoln's hand, is nursed back to health. After Moe is killed by marauders, the boys return to their units, are captured, and taken to Andersonville where Pink is hanged. Before his death, Pink begs to "touch the hand that touched Mr. Lincoln…just one last time." Motivated by some of the scenes of battle art in *Mine Eyes* or the specifics in *Pink and Say*, the students can be invited to script a brief story related to one of the events. Scripting can include the following steps (Gallagher, 1993):

1. In a group, ask students to choose a excerpt from a story or an event.
2. Read related text about it aloud to students and ask them if they can "hear' different voices (or things to be said by different readers.)
3. Write on the board the numbers 1, 2, 3, and so on for the number of narrators, and indicate when a different reader should read aloud. Iden-

tify the page or place in the text for the narrator beside the number.
4. Sometimes, the text will need to be retyped or rewritten by the students in a script form and then highlighted with pen markers.
5. Engage students in the group to review copies of the text and decide which narrator should read each line. As an option, invite two or three students to read a line together, or ask one student to "echo" the line of a previous narrator, or let the whole group read the same line, as a Greek chorus does.

Underground Railroad

In Ann Petry's book, *Harriet Tubman: Conductor on the Underground Railroad* (Crowell, 1955, grade 4 and up), published in the 1950s, Harriet Tubman's father, Ben, taught her how to pick a path through the woods without making a sound and "neither of them ever discussed the reasons why it was desirable to be able to go through the woods soundlessly." After the story, ask open-ended questions that can elicit more than one point of view from the students:

1. If you had been Harriet Tubman, how would you have walked in the woods soundlessly? How would you pick a path through the woods without making a sound? How can a person move soundlessly?
2. How might the history of African Americans been different if Harriet Tubman had not been a conductor on the Underground Railroad?
3. How has life changed for African Americans since the days of Harriet Tubman?
4. What is there about your state today that relates directly to the contributions of Tubman and others?

Activity #112: "An Escape Route"

Instead of asking students to brainstorm about the features of the Underground Railroad, present the students with excerpts that are word pictures about the system from your favorite source or from Patricia Beatty's book of the 1960s, *Blue Stars Watching* (Morrow, 1969, grades 4–8). This is a story about unsuspecting Will Kinmot who discovers that his father's farm is really a station on the Underground Railroad. Though the book is out of print, it can be found in the children's collection at a large public library. Begin a discussion with students about the network of African Americans, European Americans, and others who helped slaves make their way to freedom and what the network was like. Additional word pictures of the network written by different authors can be found in related readings in Figure 11–4.

The Civil War: 1863

"Across Five Aprils is as meaningful today as it was when it was first published in 1964," states Eileen Van Kirk (1993), author of fiction and nonfiction for young people. "It tells the story of a family torn apart by the Civil War. Jethro and Ellen Creighton are clearly living in 19th-century rural America, where hard, honest work was the mark of a man; book learning, while cautiously respected, was not considered important; where women often worked alongside the men in the fields, but were still solely responsible for the household chores, and would not have been able to conceive of a different order." Van Kirk's description portrays the time period when slavery became a burning issue in the United States that attracted many personalities in the days before and during the Civil War period. For example, the president of the Confederate States of American during the Civil War was Jefferson Davis (1808–1889). The military and political events of the war are presented along with Davis's interesting quotes in *Jefferson Davis* (Children's Press, 1993, grades 4–5) by Zachary Kent. Questions that arise from the book can be recorded on an overhead transparency for a class discussion:

1. "From your point of view, is it ever right to be in favor of slavery?"
2. "What rights did the northern Yankees think were important? The southern Confederates?"
3. "What was life like for people in the South during this time period? The North?"
4. "How does that life compare with ways you live today?"

Activity #113: "Creative Drama"

Additional facts about the effects of the Civil war on individual soldiers are found in *Behind the Blue and Gray: The Soldiers life in the Civil War* (Lodestar, 1991, grades 6–8) by D. Ray. Primary sources such as anecdotes, period photographs, and quotations are included, along with useful research features—a Table of Contents, Glossary, Bibliography, and Index. Demonstrate ways to show that all of these features are useful as reference aids for the students' research.

To set the stage further with the students about what was going on at the Battle of Bull Run during

---

FIGURE 11–4   *Children's Books about the Underground Railroad*

Collins, J. *John Brown and the Fight Against Slavery.* Millbrook, 1991. Details information about Brown's raid on the arsenal at Harper's Ferry in 1859. Grades 4–6.

Everett, G. *John Brown: One Man Against Slavery.* Ill. by J. Lawrence. Rizzoli, 1992. Sixteen-year-old Annie Brown worries over her father's decision to join the raid. Grades 5–7.

Fritz, J. *Brady.* Ill. by L. Ward. Coward, 1960. Brady's father has strong antislavery feeling and Brady helps him assist a slave. Grades 5–7.

Hamilton, V. *Anthony Burns: The Defeat and Triumph of a Fugitive Slave.* Knopf, 1988. This is the story of a 20-year-old slave who was reclaimed under the Fugitive Slave Act and his trial. Excerpts from the autobiography of William Parker, a former slave, are included. Grade 6 and up.

Lester, J. *This Strange New Feeling.* Dial, 1982. Based on true accounts, this portrays the lives of three slave couples as they struggled for freedom. Grade 8 and up.

Rappaport, D. *Escape from Slavery: Five Journeys to Freedom.* Ill. by C. Lilly. HarperCollins, 1991. Recounts true stories of slaves who achieved freedom with help from both whites and African Americans. Grades 4–7.

Winter, J. *Follow the Drinking Gourd.* Knopf, 1988. Peg Leg Joe, a one-legged sailor, sings a song with directions to the Underground Railroad to the slaves on the plantations in the South. Music included. Grades 4–5.

the war, give a brief book talk about some the events in Paul Fleischman's *Bull Run* (HarperCollins, 1993, grade 6 and up) as you sketch a map of the site on the board or mark a replica of the site on a sand table. Fleischman's fictionalized interviews make verbal pictures of some of the participants of the times—a brave young soldier, fearful parents, Confederates, and Yankees—and portrays their actions and fears at the battle where General McDowell's Union troops outnumbered General Beauregard's Confederate soldiers. This was known in the Union as Bull Run and in the Confederacy as the Battle of Manassas. The sequence of several battles can be listed on a time line and reviewed through the children's literature in Figure 11–5.

FIGURE 11–5   Children's Books about Civil War Battles

Battle of Vicksburg, May 14–July 4: The Union Gains Control of the Mississippi

Clapp, P. *The Tamarack Tree*. Lothrop, Lee & Shepard, 1986. A teenage British girl visiting in the South feels the North is right and experiences the siege of Vicksburg. Grade 7 and up.

Monjo, F. N. *The Vicksburg Veteran*. Ill. by D. Gorsline. Simon, 1971. General Grant's son participates in the Union victory that gains control of the Mississippi. Grades 4–5.

Battle of Gettysburg, July 1–3: Between Lee's Army of Northern Virginia and General George G. Meade's Army of the Potomac

Coffey, V. J. *The Battle of Gettyburg*. Silver Burdett, 1985. Portrays the actions of the Civil War that leads to this battle and describes the aftermath. Grade 7 and up.

Collier, J. L., & Collier, C. *With Every Drop of Blood: A Novel of the Civil War*. Delacorte, 1994. Fourteen-year-old Johnny joins a wagon train to take food to Confederate soldiers and is captured by a black Union soldier who eventually saves him from imprisonment. Includes a Foreword that discusses the use of the word *nigger* in the book. Grades 6–9.

Gauch, P. L. *Thunder at Gettysburg*. Ill. by S. Gammell. Putnam, 1975, 1990. Portrays the scenes, sounds, and feelings about the horror of one of the war's worst battles. Grades 6–8.

Johnson, N. *The Battle of Gettysburg* Four Winds, 1989. Includes full text of Lincoln's Gettyburg Address and has black and white photographs of a reenactment in 1988. Grade 7 and up.

Murphy, J. *The Long Road to Gettysburg*. Clarion, 1992. Eighteen-year-old Confederate Lieutenant John Dooley (who is a staunch defender of the South) and 15-year-old Union soldier Thomas Galway (who faces anti-Irish prejudice) are two participants of the battle. Their narratives tell about the march North through Virginia and Pennsylvania and the Battle of Gettysburg. Grades 4–7.

Perez, N. A. *The Slopes of War*. Houghton Mifflin, 1984. Buck Summerhill returns to Gettysburg as a soldier in the Army of the Potomac and loses his leg in the fight for Little Round Top. Grade 7 and up.

Battle of Chattanooga, November 23–25

Steele, W. O. *The Perilous Road*. Ill. by P. Galdone. Harcourt, 1958. Chris Brabson, almost 12 years old, lives in Tennessee, hates the Union troops, and is determined to fight them. Grade 7 and up.

Battle of New Market, May 15

Beller, S. P. *Cadets at War: The True Story of Teenage Heroism at the Battle of New Market*. Betterway, 1991. On May 15, 1864, about 250 cadets from the Virginia Military Institute stood beside Confederate soldiers under the command of General John C. Breckenridge. They helped drive back a superior Union force and suffered a casualty of 24 percent. Grade 5 and up.

Young People during the Civil War

"How cold is an empty room, / How sad a deserted house,/ O, how melancholic is an empty room./ I roam around looking, looking./" is part of a verse entitled "Song for Someone Who Is Absent," from *A Crocodile Has Me by the Leg: African Poems* (Walker, 1967) edited by Leonard W. Doob, former Chairman of the Council on African Studies at Yale. After reading this verse or similar verses, discuss with students the idea that, in all cultures, war and other situations cause loved ones to be absent and affect the emotions of everyone involved—just as the words of the verse convey. Point out that in any war situation, such as that for the young people in Janet Hickman's *Zoar Blue* (Macmillan, 1978, grade 6 and up) during the Civil War, there are personal sacrifices and sometimes grave and serious situations that cause a great sadness in families. If appropriate, ask volunteers to tell of their feelings when loved ones were absent.

Activity #114: "Emotions"

Discuss the idea that war affects the emotions of people, and that in any war situation, there are conflicts between a person's principles and his or her loyalty to the country, as well as a time of personal sacrifices and much grief felt for the men and women in the armed forces. To focus on such feelings, read excerpts aloud from *Zoar Blue* and discuss them. For example, discuss the thoughts of a young member of the Separatists, a nonviolent religious group in Zoar, Ohio, who says, "A Separatist could not murder any enemy, much less, one supposed, a countryman."

In Zoar, a community of German immigrants share their property and adhere to a strict "sense of community" and religious principles. However, John Keffer and other young Separatists enlist in the Union Army in defiance of the community elders. In the army, the young men struggle to keep their personal values and realize the values are not in keeping with those around them. They are loyal to the country and respect Lincoln's call for troops, but the teachings of their church emphasize that people of conscience do not fight each other. The young men are caught in a conflict between killing and not killing other people and they long for the former days of life in their religious community before they went to war. A similar view is held by young Joseph King in *The Deserter* (Herald Press, 1990) by R. Koch, and King stays true to his religious beliefs when he walks away from battle.

Further, discuss the themes (big ideas) students have found in different stories about the Cvil War and then point out any similarity of the themes in other stories about wars in other time periods. List the titles of the stories and themes that the students mention during the discussion. For instance, the themes and the stories might be written on the board in a format such as the following:

1. People realize that freedom is worth fighting for at all times.
   This theme is similar to the big idea I found in the story of _____.
2. Women and men, girls and boys, want freedom from political and religious persecution.
   This theme is similar to the big idea I found in the story of _____.
3. People want freedom from the destruction of hatred and prejudice.
   This theme is similar to the big idea I found in the story of _____.

After collecting and recording the data from the students, point out the similarity of the themes in other stories about wars in other time periods. Make some "therefore" and "thus" types of statements to show students a way a reader can generalize from the data.

The Blue Ridge Mountains

To bring the life of a Civil War soldier closer to older students, discuss the character of Charley in Patricia Beatty's *Charley Skedaddle* (Morrow, 1987, grades 4–6). Leaving the Bowery Boys gang on the rough streets of New York City in 1864, Charley rejoins the Army of the Potomac in Virginia to avenge his brother's death. During a battle, when he takes a rifle and shoots a Rebel soldier, Charley goes into shock with the terror of seeing death all around him and he runs, ("skedaddles"). Charley is not given the punishment of being shot as a fleeing soldier but he receives the contempt of his comrades and he feels ashamed and guilty. Journeying through the Blue Ridge Mountains to get away, he meets Granny Jerusha Bent and works for her on her isolated farm so he can hide. Discuss Charley's actions and ask students what meaning his behavior has for them today.

Activity #115: "Courage"

With students, discuss the word *courage* and what it means to them. Compare their definitions with the definitions given by others (Hemingway defined courage as "grace under pressure"). Discuss the way Charley proves to Granny that he is not a coward but a person of great courage. Talking with the students, help them understand some of the aspects of war, and if desired, draw a diagram on the board that contrasts two points of view between America's Revolutionary War (sometimes called America's First Civil War because some British subjects in America fought other British subjects in America) with America's later Civil War, the war between the states in the North and South (Moir, 1978).

Value of Letters

"Letters in literature are highly important within the story themselves, to the reader in their enhancement of character and plot, and to the teacher as a creative means to several ends," writes Laurie Maxwell (1993), an intermediate school teacher in Virginia. "Letter writing today, while no longer essential, ties us in a subtle way to all of history. In fact, its permanence is made obvious even in the number of letters, notes, and paper we choose to leave in time capsules." Maxwell further points out the significance of letters in the days when no other way of communication was readily available—when the telephone, computer, and fax more not even realistic dreams for humans. Indeed, letters were valued in this time period and are very significant in some of the historical stories that the students will read.

For instance, ask the students to listen to excerpts from the letters between the brothers in *Across Five Aprils* by Irene Hunt, a story of John, a young man during the Civil War. His family in Illinois waits for news from him through letters. In fact, his brother, Jethro, realizes that John's letters tell him more about the Civil War in a closer way than the newspaper accounts of what was going on. With the letters, students can begin to understand that the writer of historical fiction who includes such letters must make choices about the material he or she includes in the correspondence. With examples of a few letters, discuss with the students, "What aspects of life in the time period could a writer have included in the letters? What aspects, if any, do you think a writer should have out? Aside from letters adding to the story, what are some of the things that the author can reveal about the life of a person, and what he or she stands for, in a letter?"

Activity #116: "Letters"

Engage the students in discussing which one of the following activities they want to choose for a study about ways people communicated with letters in historical periods. When the students have finished their activities, invite them to meet as a whole group and discuss their points of view about ways communication changes between people when they can talk face to face as contrasted with writing words on paper in a letter. Indeed, the students can see this for themselves when they participate in telephone conversations to one another in the classroom and then switch to writing and sendng letters to classmates. After students read historical fiction that have letters as a significant part of the story, suggested activities are:

1. You can work with a partner to develop a dialogue between the two of you to talk about any subject brought up in a letter from the story. One of you will be the one who wrote the letter and the other will be one who received the letter in this conversation.

2. Respond to the letters in the story as if you were the actual recipient. If desired, work with a partner to write a response.

3. Respond to the letters in writing as if you were the character living currently. Talk about which problems from the past would be the same today and which might be different in today's world.

With books that include letters in the narratives, the students can see various ways that the characters in books used letters and postcards to communicate with others. If needed, guide them to the stories in Figure 11–6.

Abraham Lincoln

"Lincoln was a long man,/ He Liked out of doors/ He liked the wind blowing/And the talk in country stores" are words that begin the poem "Abraham Lincoln" in *A Book of Americans* (Holt, 1986, all grades) by the Benets. The verses tell children that Lincoln liked telling stories and jokes, carried his letters in his tall black hat, and wore a shawl around his shoulders to keep warm. After reading the verses aloud, select lines about Abraham Lincoln for the children to interpret orally. Use their suggestions for line-a-student, unison reading, low voices only, and others, to orally interpret the words and reread the lines aloud for a choral reading.

Activity #117: "Contrasting Statements"

With the whole group, present contrasting statements made by President Abraham Lincoln (or another famous figure) and invite students to explain why Lincoln might have made two very different

FIGURE 11–6   Children's Books That Reveal the Significance of Letters

1800s

Forman, J. *Becca's Story.* Scribner's. 1992. Becca Case's two beaus, Alex and Charlie, go off to fight for the Union. Their letters to Becca tell about army life, their thoughts about the battles, and the southerners they are fighting. Based on family letters and journals. Grade 7 and up.

Lyons, M. E. *Letters from a Slave Girl: The Story of Harriet Jacobs.* Scribner's, 1992. This adaptation is based on Jacob's own autobiography and shows what the hardships of slavery meant for a young black woman in the middle 1800s. Grades 5–6.

Hesse, K. *Letters from Rifka.* Holt, 1992. Rifa, a young Jewish girl, writes to her relatives in Russia about her battles with disease and official red tape before she joins her family in America. Grades 4–7.

1900s

Brisson, P. *Kate on the Coast.* Bradbury, 1992. Kate writes to her friends after her family moves to Seattle, and she tells about cruising the Alaskan fjords, camping at Yosemite National Park, exploring a Hawaiian island, and touring San Francisco, Honolulu, and Hollywood. Grades 4–5.

Cleary, B. *Dear Mr. Henshaw.* Morrow, 1983. This is about Leigh Botts, a boy who lives with his mother, misses his father, and writes letters to an author, Mr. Henshaw. Mr. Henshaw answers with lists of questions and encourages Leigh to keep a dairy. In his diary, Leigh tells his thoughts about his parents, the theft of food from his lunch bag, and his own writing problems. Grades 6–8.

Everett, G. *L'il Sis and Uncle Willie.* Rizzoli, 1992. Corresponding through letters begins for L'il Sis after her Uncle Willie visits her in her home in South Carolina. Her uncle is William H. Johnson, an African American painter, whose work is shown in the National Museum of American Art in Washington, DC. Grades 4–5.

statements. Related to this, review what was going on when the statements were made and ask the students to discuss what the statements tell them about Lincoln and how he felt about what was happening at the time. On the board or overhead transparency, write examples of quotes by Lincoln. The following are from *Great Quotations of Great Leaders*:

Discuss Statement #1: When you have got an elephant by the hind legs and he is trying to run away it's best to let him run.

Discuss Statement #2: If you would win a man to your cause, first convince him that you are his sincere friend.

After discussing the two statements, engage the students in discovering more about Lincoln in other books.

Information from Photographs

Withe the students, show a 1800s photograph of children (transferred to an overhead transparency) and ask them to look at the clothing and hairstyyles of the people in the photograph. After observing articles of clothing, hairstyles, and other objects in the photograph, ask them to predict what services, workers, and jobs were available at the time (e.g. people who made clothing, ribbons, and lace; shoemakers; workers in leather factories, etc.)and list the services on the board. Review the list and ask the students to suggest pantomime actions related to the workers and perform them for each of the words.

Activity #118: "Photographs from the Past"

With the students, show photographs of the 1800s on the opaque projector and help them examine real scenes from the past Ask them to transform the visual statements in the photographs about what life was like into their own oral statements for the whole group. Ask them to look for what is alike and what is different in today's lifestyle and the lifestyle of the 1800s. For those interested further in the topic of photography, guide them to some of the books listed in Figure 11–7.

FIGURE 11–7 **Photographers and Their Pictures**

1800

Ayer, E. *Margaret Bourke-White*. Dillon, 1992. Presents the professional life of a world-renowned photographer as she confronted gender prejudice of her times. Biography. Grade 5 and up.

1850

Conrad, P. *Prairie Visions: The Life and Times of Solomon Butcher*. HarperCollins, 1991. In the area now Nebraska, Butcher traveled and took photographs of families in front of their sod homes in a visual statement of what life was like on the midwestern prairie. Biography. Grade 6 and up.

1865

Hoobler, D., & Hoobler, T. *Photographing History: The Career of Matthew Brady*. Putnam's, 1977. Portrays the life of the photographer who recorded scenes from America's "Battle between the States" with his camera and film. Biography. Grade 4–7.

1900

Lawlor, L. *Shadow Catcher: The Life and Work of Edward S. Curtis*. Walker, 1994. A life story of the photographer who devoted 30 years to document in photographs, words, and sound recordings the state of the Indian cultures of North America in the 1900s. Biography. Grade 8 and up.

Price, A. *Haunted by a Paintbrush*. Children's Press, 1968. Gordon Parks, a famous African American artist and illustrator, tells of his sharecropping, poverty, and visits to a psychiatrist, and how drawing became highly important to him. Autobiography. Grade 4.

Turk, M. *Gordon Parks*. Crowell, 1971. Details Parks's boyhood of fishing and hunting, the death of his mother, and his life as an orphan. Parks's initial fame as a photographer (1912–   ) comes from his camera scenes in Harlem and his sensitiveness. Biography. Grade 4.

How the West Was Fun

When Senator Roscoe McCorkle has an important meeting in Washington with the president, he needs to travel from faraway Grass Valley by stagecoach and then by train in *Charlie Drives the Stage* (Holiday House, 1989, all grades) by Eric A. Kimmel. In the story, the senator is out of luck because there is no stage going anywhere because of several dangers—avalanches in the pass, bandits on the road, and Indians on the warpath. The senator is told that the river is rising, too, and the bridge may go out. Still insisting he leave right away, the Senator makes a deal with Charlie Drummond to deliver him to Washington. Charlie agrees but says, "Once we get going, we don't stop. And we don't turn back." The senator agrees. The story concludes with a humorous surprise ending. After hearing the story, the students can locate their own books of humorous views of history or select several books listed on Figure 11–8 (see also History Master 34).

Activity #119: "Charley Drives the Stage"

After the story, review objects in the illustrations (e.g., clothing, leather goods, hats) and ask students to determine what services, workers, and jobs were available in the stagecoach days (e.g., the workers who were needed to make the clothing, leather goods, hats, etc.) and list them on the board. Review the list and ask the students how they could really know that these services, workers, and jobs, were available in this time period and invite them to search for more information in other data references about each one and report what they learned back to the whole group (see also History Master 34).

How the West Was Serious: Historical Heroines by Patricia Beatty

Write the word *heroine* on the board and ask the students to suggest reasons for giving heroines in his-

---

FIGURE 11–8   *Children's Books about How the West Was Fun*

1700s: Davy Crockett

Quackenbush, R. *Quit Pulling My Leg, Davy Crockett.* Prentice-Hall, 1987. Portrays life of Crockett as a frontiersman and separates facts from fanciful stories. Biography. Grade 4 and up.

1800s: Artemis Bonner

Myers, W. D. *The Righteous Revenge of Artemis Bonner.* HarperCollins, 1992. As an African American in the Wild West in 1880, Artemis Bonner teams up with his friend, Frolic, to avenge a murder against the Evil Catfish Grimes and his friend, Lucy Featherdip. Grade 5 and up.

1880s: Stagecoach Driver on America's Western Frontier

Kimmel, E. A. *Charlie Drives the Stage.* Ill. by G. Rounds. Holiday House, 1989. In 1887, Charlie Drummond is the only stagecoach driver who has "a ghost of a chance of getting through" to take Senator Roscoe McCorkle to the train so the Senator can arrive in Washington for an important meeting with the president. Fiction. Grades 4–5.

1800s: An Elephant Chase

Cross, G. *The Great American Elephant Chase.* Holiday House, 1993. In 1881, a con man's daughter is helped by an orphan boy as they travel from Pennsylvania to Nebraska and try to keep her elephant away from a thief. Grades 4–6.

1800s: Theodore Roosevelt

Quackenbush, R. *Don't You Dare Shoot That Bear.* Simon & Schuster, 1984. Humorous introduction to the personality of Theodore Roosevelt (1858–1919). Grade 4.

1800s: Cowboys in America's West

Shepard, A. *The Legend of Lightning Larry.* Scribner's, 1993. Crooked Curt, Devilish Dick, Dismal Dan, Evil-Eye McNeevil, and Moldy Mike meet their match with Lightning Larry. Grades 4–5.

---

torical fiction wider attention. Write their suggestions on the board and then have them divide into small groups. Give some groups copies of one of Beatty's books and other groups copies of another. Assign the members to reading different chapters of the selected book by Beatty that their group has received. When discussing the heroines in a whole group setting, they will get to know some of Beatty's heroines in different historical settings. For instance, there's Kate Ann Scott in *Bonanza Girl* (Morrow, 1993), who travels with her widowed mother and younger brother from Oregon to the gold fields of Idaho in the 1880s, and Whitney Kimball in *The Nickel-Plated Beauty* (Morrow, 1993), who works with her five brothers and sisters to pay for an expen-

sive cookstove (a nickel-plated beauty) for their mother.

Activity #120: "Heroines"

In the whole group, ask members to introduce and discuss the heroines they read about. Return to the list of suggestions on the board that the students gave as reasons for giving heroines in historical fiction wider attention by readers and ask students if they agree or disagree with each of the reasons originally written after reading a sample of Beatty's historical fiction. If desired, distribute a duplicate of Figure 11–9 as a reference list for those who want to read more about heroines. Additionally, discuss several choices for a writing assignment about the historical

FIGURE 11–9   Children's Books about How the West Was Serious:
Heroines by Patricia Beatty

Invite students to join a literature group and read more about one or more of the following heroines:

Group 1: Truth Hopkins, a Quaker girl, in *Who Comes with Cannons* (Morrow, 1992) helps further the cause of freedom when a slaves takes refuge on her family's farm and she helps him escape to the North. Grade 5 and up.

Group 2: Hannalee Reed in *Turn Homeward, Hannalee* (Morrow, 1984) is sent North to work in a Yankee mill during the closing days of the Civil War. Grade 5 and up.

Group 3: Bethany Brant in *Behave Yourself, Bethany Brant* (Morrow, 1986) adjusts to the pranks of her tomboy cousin on her aunt's cattle ranch in nineteenth-century Texas. Grade 5 and up.

Group 4: Katie Ann Scott in *Bonanza Girl* (Morrow, 1993) travels with her widowed mother and younger brother from Oregon to the gold fields of Idaho in the 1880s. With the help of a new friend, Helga, they open a restaurant and become a part of the new mining town. Grade 5 and up.

Group 5: In *Hail Columbia* (Morrow, 1970), a suffragette in Oregon in 1893 stirs up the town of Astoria by her vigorous dedication to causes. Grade 5 and up.

Group 6: Fayette Ashmore in *Eight Miles from Monterey* (Morrow, 1982) helps her mother establish library outposts in the still-wild Monterey mountains in 1916. Grade 6 and up.

Group 7: Hannalee Reed in *Be Ever Hopeful, Hannalee* (Morrow, 1988) leaves home again to travel to Atlanta where her family wants to make a new start. Grade 6 and up.

Group 8: Lupita Torres in *Lupita Manana* (Morrow, 1981) journeys to the United States to find work and earn money to send back to her mother. Grade 6 and up.

Group 9: Whitney Kimball in *The Nickel Plated Beauty* (Morrow, 1993), works with her five brothers and sisters to pay for an expensive cookstove (a nickel-plated beauty) for their mother. Grade 6 and up.

Group 10: Thirteen-year-old Dorcas in *Red Rock over the River* (Morrow, 1973) goes with Hattie Lou Mercer, the Native American housekeeper, to Arizona Territorial Prison, to write letters for illiterate prisoners and sees Hattie's brother escape. Grade 6 and up.

fiction stories Beatty has written. As examples, students may select one or more of the following:

1. *Add a Character.* If interested, students can add another character (perhaps themselves) into a rewritten event of a selected story.
2. *Add a Conflict.* Students can add a different conflict to an event in the plot.
3. *Add a Conflict Resolution.* Students can change the outcome of the story.

History and a Story Lunch

Organize a story lunch for interested students during their lunch period, three or four days a week. Read aloud excerpts from historical fiction while the students eat lunch. Story selections should portray views of people from different time periods.

Activity #121: "Information Books and Biographies"

To engage students deeper in historical places and faces, Mueller (1991) points out that educators who suggest books for students can be facilitators and give students facts about history as well as suggestions for a related biography and an informational book. For instance, for a study of the Civil War, Mueller suggests Dybowski's *Robert E. Lee and the Rise of the South*, Rickarby's *Ulysses S. Grant and the Strategy of Victory,* and Shorto's *Abraham Lincoln* (all Silver Burdett, 1991, grade 6 and up) since the books provide varying views on the times for young adolescents. For other biographies and informational books to put together, see History Master 35, "Informational Books and Biographies to Pair Together."

Artists of the 1800s

Interested in integrating the paintings of artists with a study of the 1800s, a sixth-grade teacher reviewed the pictures of Alfred Jacob Miller's watercolors of the American West (Dalkey, 1992). The watercolors were displayed in a local museum and the teacher was surprised when she discovered that some of the details in the paintings were not authentic. For example, in the painting "Blackfeet on the Warpath" a Native American's clothing, heavily fringed on the leggings and sleeves, was not one that would have been worn into battle. Realizing that art is usually fiction, the teacher decided to point out to her students, some of the inaccurate views of the original Native American culture painted by Miller.

Miller, an European-trained artist who studied in France and Italy, joined Charles Drummond Stewart, a Scottish nobleman, in the summer of 1837, and traveled the Oregon Trail to become one of the first European artists to paint the Plains people, the fur trappers, and the Rocky Mountains. Miller's story and work, influenced by his culture's view of Native America people, can be relevant to a discussion by contemporary students since Miller's work points out that his viewpoint is one perpetuated today by some people as their version of what the "Old West" was like. See History Master 36, "Westward Expansion."

Activity #122: "Cross-Checking Art"

Older students interested in the idea that art is fiction can point out some of the accurate and inaccurate views of the Original Native American culture in a story such as *An Indian Winter* (Holiday House, 1992, grades 4–6) by Russell Freedman. Freedman's story is about a German prince, a Swiss artist, and others who explored the Missouri River valley in 1933. Learning about the territory and its inhabitants, the artist recorded the impression of his journey in pictures and the others wrote their impressions in words. After a review of the illustrations by Karl Bodmer in Freedman's book, interested students can cross-check the authenticity of some of the story's details with other data sources. For students pursuing the topic of artists and their art through historical time periods, guide them to some of the books on the previously mentioned History Master 25, "Artists and Their Art."

Perceptions of the 1800s

Paul Goble, an author and illustrator who has always been interested in the Native Americans, was watching a TV account of Custer's last battle and was struck by how biased the story was (Stott, 1984). When he tried to find a book with the Native Americans' point of view, he couldn't, and so the idea for his book, *Red Hawk's Account of Custer's Last Battle,* began. This is an account told by an Ogala Sioux, who was a 15-year-old in 1876. Goble's retelling treats both sides fairly. As excerpts from the story are read aloud, ask older students to listen for evidence that the native fighters had great respect for the bravery of their opponents.

Activity #123: "Mitakuye Oyasin"

Introduce Goble's retellings of legends that reflect a similar theme of "ways we are all related" (a theme expressed by the Sioux as *mitakuye oyasin*) from the Plains tribes. Some of the retellings are *The Girl Who Loved Wild Horses* (Bradbury, 1978), *The Gift of the Sacred Dog* (Bradbury, 1980), *Star Boy* (Bradbury, 1982), *Buffalo Woman* (Bradbury, 1984), *The Friendly Wolf* (Bradbury, 1974), and others. Goble further explains the theme of *mitakuye oyasin* in his notes in *Buffalo Woman:* "The buffalo was the source of life for the people, giving them food, hides for robes, and tipi covers, as well as many other things. The lives of both were closely interwoven, and the story teaches that buffalo and people were related... that these stories were not simply for entertainment; they had power to strengthen the people's bond with the herds, and to encourage the herds to continue to give themselves so that the people could live. It was felt that retelling the story had a power to bring about a change within each of us, that in listening we might all be a little more worthy of our buffalo relatives." Have students' discuss how this relationship is shown in the several legends of the Plains tribes by giving talks about books found on History Master 37, *"Mitakuye Oyasin:* We Are All Related."

Little Big Horn: 1876

The question "Who won the battle of Little Big Horn in 1876?" is important because it raises the issue of how many battles over Little Big Horn were fought and whose voices have been heard about the historical event. The question also raises the issue of whose historical perspectives are recognized and whose interpretations are considered today. It also raises questions for discussion by the students about the extent to which some voices have been ignored traditionally and excluded from published materials.

To provide background about Little Big Horn, discuss with the students the situation in 1876, when the Sioux and other Native Americans won the first battle as they defeated George Armstrong Custer's 7th Calvary at the Little Big Horn river camp. Led by the Sioux warriors under the leadership of Crazy Horse, the Native Americans fought the soldiers in a battle some know as "Custer's Last Stand." There was a "Second Battle" of Little Big Horn that took place when the federal government transformed the site of the battle into the Custer Battlefield National Monument and ignored the fact that Custer and his troops weren't out there alone. There was the "Third Battle" of Little Big Horn in 1989 that started when a group of Native Americans reclaimed their historical presence on the Little Big Horn battlefield. They erected a plaque to commemorate the Native American heroes of the battle and to include the perspectives of the Native Americans at the monument.

Activity #124: "Title for a Poem"

Without showing the poem's title, show students the body of the poem "Crazy Horse" from *A Book of Americans* (Holt, 1961, grade 5 and up) by Rosemary and Stephan Vincent Benet. Mask the title of the poem that is copied on a chart or the board. Ask students first to listen to the poem about the Sioux leader read aloud, to read it silently, to read it again as a whole group, and then to take turns with partners to read alternate lines. Invite students to give their predictions about the identity of the Native American leader from the information they got from the poem. Ask them to give reasons for their predictions. Reveal the title (masked at the foot of the chat) and show students various informational books in the classroom book corner that have events and dates related to the lives of Crazy Horse and to George Armstrong Custer.

Trail Drive: 1878

With the opaque projector, show students some of the advertisements, book reviews, news accounts, and articles about people of the time period from 1818 to 1876 that relate to the dusty Westward Movement, the fighting in the Civil War, the Reconstruction Period, effects of Slavery, and information about the Mexican War from *Annals of American History* (Bloch & Co., 1992, grade 6 and up) by L. M. Bloch, Jr. Ask the students to discern what they can about the trail drives of the period from the projected accounts in the book. Mention that before modern transportation, cowboys had to drive cattle many miles to market towns.

Engage students in discovering additional information about the cowboys and their work on the cattle drive by reading aloud parts about a lead steer on a trail drive in 1878 from *Old Blue* (Putnam, 1980, grades 4–6) by Sibyl Hancock. Ask them to imagine the cowboys living on the grazing range, roping a calf, branding the calves, and eating near a chuck wagon. At times, when unaware cattle were approached without warning and were startled, the whole herd could become frightened enough to stampede. When this happened, the cowboys worked with others to find the lead steer and turn the herd. Point out that at other times, cowboys often rode herd for many days, and often, their work was dull and boring. If they got lonesome out on the range, they sang songs to pass away the hours. Invite the students to tell ways they would pass the time as a cowboy/cowgirl on the range and suggest western songs they know for singing.

Activity #125: "On the Trail"

Ask the students to pretend that they have been invited on a trail drive in the West in the 1800s and that they will fly from their city to the starting point of the Cumberland Trail. Tell them to look at a map of the United States and to think what geographical features (bodies of water, mountains, rivers, small hills) they will fly over on their flight. They may draw/trace a large map of the United States and add lines to show the path of their flight to the trail drive. They also can add sketches of some of the tools used by the cowboys—horses, saddles, lariats, levis, chaps, jackets, and hats—as a border on the map. Ask them to look for additional books for descriptions of trail drive locations that could be drawn on their maps. Display all the maps and encourage students to explain to others what information they showed on their maps.

Ethnic Cowboys

"Prairie goes to the mountains,/ Mountain goes to the sky./The sky sweeps across the distant hills/ And here, in the middle/ Am I" are the first words in "Open Range," a poem written by Kathryn and Byron Jackson in *The Arbuthnot Anthology of Children's Literature* (1976) that can give students a sense of the vastness of the West and its great open ranges where ranchers let their cattle roam freely. To get another view of the frontier, Millhofer (1993) suggests that a teacher arrange for Cowboy Jack (a.k.a. Jack O. Hannah) and Dusty Trails (a.k.a. Gary R. Sells), two dynamic teachers in the Clovis Unified School District, California, to visit your school to help make history come alive. The two teachers give children an incentive for writing their own tall tales, cowboy stories, and poems. If the two are unavailable in your area, you might prevail on two parents, classroom aides, university student teachers, relatives, managers of western stores, or others to dress in full cowboy regalia and visit the classroom. You and the two visitors can show off the practical purposes of the bandanas (blindfolding a frightened horse), 10-gallon hats (to carry water), vests (for pockets), pants (pocketless for comfort in the saddle), boots (protection), spurs (to get the best work out of the horse), and rawhide chaps (protection against rope and brush burn) as you encourage students to learn and write about the American cowboy.

With your help, the visitors also can show students ways that cowboy poetry and songs, history, and multiculturism add to the study of this time period. You can display western items, play recorded songs, recite poetry, and point out that cowboys came from every ethnic background. Some students can research such topics as the invention of barbed wire in the 1880s, the introduction of the ancestors of the longhorns by Spanish settlers, and the discovery that disease-carrying ticks caused Texas Fever—a disease that caused milk and beef cattle to die. Others can inqure about the major cattle trails in the 1800s (e.g., the Chisholm Trail from San Antonio to Abilene) and the *remuda* (herd) of different horses (a circle horse, a brush horse, a cutting horse, a roping horse, a river horse) available for different jobs. Additionally, they can learn to read the brands used on cattle, an idea that dates back to the early Egyptians who used brands on their livestock. They can sing cowboy songs they have found and learn to dance "The Gal from Arkansas" and other cowboy square dances that were popular in Dodge City and other bustling places.

Activity #126: "Multicultural Cowboys"

Invite students to listen to "Vaqueros: The First Cowboys" (in *Cobblestone, 10,* 4 [April, 1989]: 21–23) by Sylvia Whitman to become aware of the history of the Mexicans who were the cow-herders (vaqueros) for Spanish settlers in the sixteenth century and gave today's cowboys the names of *corral, rancho, la reata* (lariat), and *bronco.* Introduce students to America's most famous cowboy, Will Rogers, the part-Cherokee Native American who entertained people with his humor and his roping abilities, by reading his life story from *Cowboys and Cattle Drives* (Children's Press, 1980, grades 4–8) written by Edith McCall or from *Will Rogers: Cherokee Entertainer* (Chelsea, 1993, grades 7–8) by Liz Sonneborn.

Give students a further picture of the Old West by reading excerpts from *Cowboy Country* (Clarion, 1993, grades K–3) by Ann Herbert Scott, where an old-timer takes a boy on a overnight trek to Devil's Canyon and tells tales of the Old West as he compares present-day ranching practices with those of the past. Also guide students to the fast-paced *The Story of Nat Love* (Silver Burdett, 1991, grades 4–5) by Robert H. Miller, to give them a glimpse of the role of an African American in the Old West. If desired, provide some scenes of Texas after the Civil War with descriptions from *The Black Mustanger* (Morrow, 1971, grade 5 and up) by Richard Wormser.

Students can find out more about other cowboys and their lives with any of the following: *American Cowboy in Life and Legend* (National Geographic, 1972) by Bart McDowell; *The Black West: A Documentary and Pictorial History* (Doubleday, 1973) by William Loren Katz; *Cowboys of the Wild West* (Clarion, 1985) by Russell Freedman; and *Cowboys and Cattle Ranching: Yesterday and today* (Crowell, 1973) by Patricia Lauber. Additionally, they can go back in time to learn about Hugh Glass (see Robert McClung's *Hugh Glass Mountain Man,* Morrow, 1991) and other mountain men who explored the western parts of North America long before the cowboys arrived, or go forward in time to learn about other cowboys and their activities with some of the references in Figure 11–10.

Effect on Native Americans in the West

"The Buffalo are gone./ And those who saw the buffalo are gone./" With children, read aloud "Buffalo Dusk" from *The Arbuthnot Anthology of Children 's Literature* (Scott, Foresman, 1971, all grades) and discuss the idea of America's frontier expanding westward and its effect by on the Native People who lived on the land. Ask students to imagine the buffalo in the herds by the thousands, pawing the prairie sod, with their great heads down. Ask them to tell what it meant to the Native People to learn that "the buffaloes are gone," and the meaning of the words "those who saw the buffaloes are gone."

Activity #127: "The West's Development"

Related to a study of 1800s, *Thunder Rolling in the Mountains* (Clarion, 1992, grade 5 and up) by Scott O'Dell and Elizabeth Hall portrays cruelty, heroism, and betrayal told through the voice of the daughter of Chief Joseph of the Nez Perce Indians. She tells about how his people prepared to leave

FIGURE 11–10 *Children's Books about Cowboys*

1700

Rounds, G. *The Cowboy Trade*. Holiday, 1972. Overview. Grades 4–8.

Sullivan, C. *Cowboys*. Rizzoli, 1993. Art reproductions by Remington and others. Grade 4 and up.

1800

Freedman, R. *Cowboys of the Wild West*. Clarion, 1985. Portrays the nineteenth-century West and the cowboys who lived there on cattle ranches. Grade 5 and up.

Marrin A. *Cowboys, Indians, and Gunfighters: The Story of the Cattle Kingdom*. Atheneum, 1993. Describes the arrival of horses and settlers and cattle from Spain, the cowboys, life without laws in frontier towns, economic reasons for near extermination of the buffalo with hunts, and the effect on Native Americans, particularly Comanche retaliation. Includes photographs, information notes, and index. Nonfiction. Grade 6 and up.

1880

Lightfoot, D. J. *Trail Fever: The Story of a Texas Cowboy*. Lothrop, Lee & Shepard, 1992. In 1880, George Saunders goes on his first cattle drive at age 5. In later years, he sees his first stampede at age 10. Becoming a Texas trail driver, he survives floods, droughts, and freezing nights, and confronts raiders and bandits. Includes interviews with Saunders's grandchildren. Nonfiction. Grade 4 and up.

1900

Greenlaw, M. J. *Ranch Dressing: The Story of Western Wear*. Lodestar, 1993. Details the history, construction, and style of hats, boots, chaps, and other western attire. Grades 4–8.

---

peacefully for the reservation in 1877. On their journey, the United States army attacked the Indians who were fleeing to Canada, and this caused Chief Joseph to pledge, "I will fight no more forever."

Invite students, in small groups, to select a line of inquiry about research topics such as the effect on the Original Native Americans of the following:

Going on a Wagon Train through the Wild West

Traveling by Railroad in the Wild West

Exploring in the Wild West

Daily Doings in the Wild West

Families Building Their Homes in the Wild West

The Blizzard of 1888

"Emotional identification is likely to occur when text and illustrations of the book radiate sincere human emotions, warmth and hope and when aspects of the human condition being depicted are comparable to the readers' own experiences or are within their ability to withstand them," writes Patricia J. Cianciolo (1989) of Michigan State University. "If emotional identification and enjoyment is experienced from the literary selection, readers may consciously (or more realistically, subconsciously) continue to read in order to find answers to basic human questions and concerns." For example, a story that can stimulate students to feel and to think is *Day of the Blizzard* (Coward, 1978, grades 4–8) by Marietta Moskin, a story of 12-year-old Katie, who goes out of her house on a special errand unaware that the storm of wind, snow, and cold will turn into "the Great Blizzard of 1888." After reading the story, have students compare their own experiences with those of Katie.

Activity #128: "My Point of View"

In Moskin's story, Kate is going to the pawnbroker to redeem a brooch that signifies a tradition in her family—every woman in her family has worn it on her wedding day. The day was the last day the brooch could be redeemed from the pawnbroker and her mother was too ill to go for it. Adding to the situation, Katie's father, a conductor on the New York Central Railroad, was delayed by the snowfall crippling the traffic in the city. After reading the story aloud, discuss with students their responses to questions related to Katie's concerns:

1. Like Katie, what hopes do you have? What were Katie's hopes?
2. What possession(s) in your family signify a family tradition?
3. Have you, like Katie, been caught unaware of coming events? What happened?

Casey at the Bat

"The outlook wasn't brilliant for the Mudville nine that day,/ The score stood four to two with but one inning more to play" wrote Ernest Thayer in *Casey at the Bat* (Coward, McCann, Cohegan, 1978, all ages). Robert Whitehead (1984), children's literature specialist, recommends *Casey at the Bat* as a poem to share with children as an example of quality verse that they can understand. It is a humorous poem about "Mighty Casey," who struck out in an important game. It can be just the way to introduce students to the historical popularity of baseball in America in the 1800s.

Activity #129: "Casey's Poem"

Invite older students to number off 1, 2, 1, 2, and so on. Ask the students who are is to be Casey's supporters on one side of the room and the students who are 2s to be Casey's critics on the other side. As the poem is read for the first time, ask students to identify places for the supporters and the critics to interact. During a second reading, ask the supporters to cheer when it is appropriate and ask the critics to boo each time the strikes are called on Casey. Plan to invite another class to be the audience and to listen to this interactive poem as a salute to the sport's World Series week in October.

Cause and Effect in the 1800s

Wooster (1993) recommends a cause-and-effect approach to help the students think critically about the material in Fisher's *Nineteenth-Century America Series* and the other history-related trade books they read. To do this, the students work cooperatively with partners and use two sets of index cards. Each set is in a different color; students write a "cause" on one set of colored cards and an "effect" on the other set of colored cards. They match the cards and use them to review events in the time period.

Activity #130: "Cause-and-Effect Events"

To study this time period further, engage the students in creating "cause" cards in one color and "effect" cards in another color (as mentioned previously). Ask the students to present the cards to other partnerships and use the cards in reviewing events about the time period. In a whole group situation, the students and teacher can cooperatively develop a cause-and-effect diagram on the board about a topic.

Topic

Cause _____ *Effect*

"America the Beautiful": 1895

"To Katherine Bates's New England eyes, the Rockies were a staggering sight; more than a sight, a felt presence—purple, brown, green, midnight blue under the moon, gold in the rising sun," stated Michael Drury (1993) when he wrote about Bates, the woman who wrote "America's Favorite song." To tell what she saw, Bates wrote these familiar words: "O Beautiful for spacious skies. / For amber waves of grain./ ...And crown thy good with brotherhood/ From sea to shining sea!" The words were set to music that are appropriate to sing when studying a unit on this time period. Provide an artist's interpretation of Bates's words by showing and discussing the illustrations in *America the, Beautiful* (Atheneum, 1993, grade 1 and up) by Neil Waldman with his acrylic paintings of sites that represent "purple mountain majesty" and "fruited plain" and other phrases. There is an explanation of the sites at the back of the book to elaborate on the print and pictures.

Activity #131: "My View of 'America the Beautiful'"

With copies of Bates's first verse, sing the words together as a group and ask students, "If Katherine Bates had been in our town and if you had been with Katherine Bates when she wrote those words, what beauty do you see in our area that she could have written about?" Ask students to meet with a partner and write a list or draw sketches of some of the beautiful things that they have seen in their area, town, or city. After the students have finished their lists or drawn their sketches, ask them to return to a whole group setting, and working together, turn their ideas into a free-verse poem about America.

Discrimination

With selected books, engage students in researching some of the various ethnic and cultural groups that have come to the United States and the discrimination that members of each group have faced. Talk about terms or names that are used to respect members of ethnic groups. Refer to the harmful effects on newcomers of denigration and discuss the resiliency needed by newcomers. A resource for this topic is *Developing Resiliency through Children's Literature: A Guide for Teachers and Librarians, K–8* (McFarland, 1992) by Nancy Lee Cecil and Patricia L. Roberts. If needed, the students can create a chart or diagram about ways to show respect to others and use it as the center for a discussion about the positive effects of respect as well as the harmful effects of discrimination. Invite the students to talk about the implications of name calling and why the use of certain terms is denigrating, and the various feelings that name calling evokes, especially in newcomers.

Activity #132: "Newcomers' Feelings"

Before role-playing some of the vignettes about newcomers from selected children's books, discuss the idea that children in all time periods of history who were newcomers have had difficulties in feeling "different," in being excluded, in being laughed at for having a language "accent," in facing name calling, negative labeling, and other prejudicial acts. Newcomers today also face these difficulties:

1. Family stress related to such things as fears of drug addiction, deportation, family separation, gang activity, unemployment, and unwanted pregnancies
2. Fear, tension, and hostilities between ethnic and racial groups
3. Stresses from being caught between two cultures and two worlds

As part of being caught between two cultures, students who speak English as a second Language (ESL) may be limited-English Proficient (LEP) and have Native languages of Spanish, Vietnamese, Cantonese, Mandarin and other Chinese, Cambodian, Filipino/Tagalog, Hmong, Korean, Lao, and Japanese. If desired, select a story from the several books listed on History Master 38, "Newcomers," read it aloud, and invite children to work in partnerships to role-play some of the incidents. The partners can take turns being the "newcomer" and the "native-born" child.

CHAPTER TWELVE

A.D. 1900-Present

What was going on in the twentieth century?

Multicultural Perspectives

Inquiring about this time period means that students can ask questions about their modern state, its immigration patterns, its technology, its people, and its cities. It means, additionally, that students can have an out-of-the-decade experience. When students are interested in any of the perspectives in Figure 12–1, suggest several examples of children's literature.

FIGURE 12–1   Children's Books about A.D. 1900–Present

PERSPECTIVES FOR 1900s

African Heritage

Armstrong, W. *Sounder.* Ill. by J. Barkley. Harper, 1969. A Black sharecropper's family endures injustice with dignity and courage. Historical fiction. Grade 6 and up.

Berry, S. L. *Langston Hughes.* Creative Education, 1994. Has brief biographical sketches to portray the life and writings of the African-American author who wrote to explain black Americans' conditions in America. Biography. Grade 6 and up.

Bertol, R. *Charles Drew.* Crowell, 1970. Recounts life of this distinguished African American doctor who became the first director of the Red Cross Blood Bank. Biography. Grade 4.

Hamilton, V. *W. E. B. DuBois: A Biography.* Crowell, 1972. Portrays DuBois's contributions as he works for justice and equal rights for African Americans, organizes the National Association for the Advancement of Colored People, becomes editor of *Crisis,* the association's magazine, and writes more than 20 books, including *Souls of Black Folks.* Biography. Grade 6 and up.

Haskins, J. *Ralph J. Bunche: A Most Reluctant Hero.* Hawthorn, 1974. Recounts life of Bunche, who became a professor of government at Harvard, a Director of the U.N. Trusteeship Division, and a mediator for the United Nations. Biography. Grade 6 and up.

Hoyt-Goldsmith, D. *Celebrating Kwanzaa.* Holiday House, 1992. Motivates readers to talk to family members and friends about African American traditions. Grades 4–8.

Hull, M. *Rosa Parks: Civil Rights Leader.* Chelsea, 1994. Details how Parks's act of not giving up her bus seat to a white person motivated the black community and leaders to respond nationally. Portrays Parks's suffering, the legal battles, and the subsequent civil rights actions. Biography. Grade 7 and up.

FIGURE 12–1 **Continued**

Lawrence, J. *The Great Migration: An American Story.* HarperCollins, 1993. Lawrence offers a pictorial essay—a sequence of paintings with captions—to show the 1916–1919 migration of African Americans from the South. Nonfiction. Grade 4 and up.

Levine, E., editor. *Freedom's Children: Young Civil Rights Activists Tell Their Own Stories.* Putnam, 1993. Includes first-person stories of people who, as children, participated in the civil rights events of the 1950s and 1960s. Nonfiction. Grades 7–8.

Porter, A. P. *Jump at de Sun: The Story of Zora Neale Hurston.* Carolrhoda, 1992. Portrays life of this African American writer (1903–1960). Hurston collected folktales and wrote about the lives of African American people in her novels. One of the most popular was *Their Eyes Were Watching God.* Biography. Grades 4–6.

Walker, A. *Langston Hughes, American Poet.* Ill. by D. Miller. Crowell, 1974. Portrays life of this important writer (1902–1967) who published his first poem, "The Negro Speaks of Rivers," at age 19. Biography. Grades 4–5.

Walter, M. P. *The Girl on the Outside.* Lothrop, Lee & Shepard, 1982. Set in Central High School in Little Rock, Arkansas, this is the story of two students, one white and one black, who support desegregation. Historical fiction. Grades 4–7.

Asian Heritage

Huong, D. T. *Paradise of the Blind.* Morrow, 1988. Originally banned in Vietnam, this story recounts grim realities in Vietnam under Communist rule in the 1970s through the eyes of a teenage girl. Historical fiction. Grade 8 and up.

Sook, N. C. *The Year of Impossible Goodbyes.* Houghton Mifflin, 1991. Portrays a firsthand view of how a family suffered under Japanese subjugation during World War II. Historical fiction. Grades 5–8.

Yep, L. *The Star Fisher.* Morrow, 1991. Joan Lee, a Chinese-American teenager, quarrels with her parents who stay with their Chinese traditions as Joan tries to fit in at her school in West Virginia. Historical fiction. Grade 7 and up.

Zheng, Zhensun, & A. Low. *A Young Painter.* Scholastic, 1991. Portrays the life and artistic skill of 16-year-old Wang Yani, a young artist whose style experts recognized as free form (xieyi hua) when she was 4 years old. Biography. Grade 5 and up.

European Heritage

Kerr, R. *The Texas Orphans: A Story of the Orphan Train Children.* Eakin Press, 1994. In 1904, orphans are put on a train in New York City headed for Sequin, Texas. They start new lives with new families. Historical fiction. Grades 4–5.

Murphy, E., & Driscoll, T. *An Album of the Irish Americans.* Watts, 1974. Discusses the contributions as well as the hurdles that Irish immigrants encountered in the United States. Nonfiction. Grade 7 and up.

Skurynski, G. *Good-Bye, Billy Radish.* Bradbury Press, 1992. In Pennsylvania, Hank Kerner and his friend nicknamed Billy Radish (really Bazyli Radichevych), though different, are best friends. Billy is a newcomer from the Ukraine and realizes he will work as a steelworker in contrast to Hank who objects to working in the mill. Historical fiction. Grade 5 and up.

Original Native American Heritage

Echo-Hawk, Roger C., & Echo-Hawk, Walter R. *Battlefields and Burial Grounds: The Indian Struggle to Protect Ancestral Graves in the United States.* Lerner, 1994. Discusses the current movement of Native

continued

FIGURE 12–1 **Continued**

Americans to protect the graves of their ancestors and Native American cultural beliefs. Focuses specifically on the Pawnee tribe and their struggles. Nonfiction. Grade 7 and up.

Kissinger, R. K. *Quanah Parker: Comanche Chief.* Pelican Pub., 1988. Recounts this great leader's life as he fights the encroachment of settlers on Indian lands and works for coexistence between the Native Americans and the settlers. Biography. Grade 7 and up.

Kroeber, T. *Ishi, Last of His Tribe.* Ill. by R. Robbins. Parnassus, 1964. During the early 1900s, Ishi, a Yahi Indian of California, realized most of his tribe had been killed or driven from their homes by the invading gold-seekers and settlers. Biography. Grade 7 and up.

Hinton, L. *Ishi's Tale of Lizard.* Farrar, 1992. Depicts Ishi's stories of Lizard and how he makes arrows, saves a friend, and leads women in dance. Folk literature. Grades 4–8.

Hoyt-Goldsmith, D. *Cherokee Summer.* Holiday, 1993. Portrays 10-year-old Bridge Russell, a member of the Cherokee Nation of Oklahoma, through a photographic essay. Includes Cherokee alphabet. Nonfiction. Grades 4–6.

Peters, R. M. *Clambake: A Wampanoag Tradition.* Lerner, 1992. Native American children dressed in tee shirts and jeans, prepare for a ceremonial clambake, an *appanaug.* Nonfiction. Grades 4–7.

Rand, J. T. *Wilma Mankiller.* Ill. by W. Anthony. Steck-Vaughn, 1993. Portrays the life of the first female Principal Chief of the Oklahoma Cherokees born in 1945. Biography. Grades 4–5.

Reggunti, G. *The Sacred Harvest: Ojibway Wild Rice Gathering.* Lerner, 1992. Glenn Jackson, a Native American boy, is old enough to participate in gathering wild rice to get the sacred food of his people. Nonfiction. Grades 4–7.

Siy, A. *The Eeyou: People of Eastern James Bay.* Dillon/Macmillan, 1993. Describes the Native People's contact with first Europeans up to the present. Includes photographs, maps, and fact outlines, and suggests activities such as exploring the Eyou's own system of writing. Nonfiction. Grades 4–7.

Latino/Hispanic Heritage

Goodwin, D. *Cesar Chavez: Hope for the People.* Fawcett Columbine Books, 1989. Life of Cesar Chavez (1927–1993), a labor leader supported by civil rights groups throughout the country. Biography. Grades 7–8.

Female Image Heritage

Fisher, M. P. *Women in the Third World.* Watts, 1989. Provides personal profiles of women that elaborate on contemporary issues. Nonfiction. Grades 6–8.

Freedman, R. *Eleanor Roosevelt: A Life of Discovey.* Clarion, 1993. Describes Roosevelt's active life and her large number of friends in a documented text with numerous quotes. Biography. Grades 6–8.

Giblin, J. C. *Edith Wilson: The Woman Who Ran the United States.* Viking, 1992. Has details about the years Edith was the wife of President Wilson as she supported her husband during America's entry into World War I in 1917. Biography. Grade 4.

Igus, T. *Great Women in the Struggle.* Just Us Books, 1991. Depicts profiles of over 80 African American women with photographs and quotes from the subject or other sources. Includes a bibliography and chronology of dates in African American history. Nonfiction. Grades 4–6.

Ransom, C. F. *Listening to the Crickets: A Story about Rachel Carson.* Carolrhoda, 1993. Describes Carson's love of nature and her difficulties in being a female marine biologist. Biography. Grade 4.

Peavy, L., & Smith, U. *Dreams into Deeds: Nine Women Who Dared.* Scribner's. 1985. Has profiles of women in the National Women's Hall of Fame that are introduced with fictionalized vignettes. Biography. Grades 4–7.

FIGURE 12–1   Continued

Rappaport, D. *Living Dangerously: American Women Who Risked Their Lives for Adventure.* HarperCollins, 1991. Portrays lives of adventurous women in a collective arrangement. Women mentioned are mountain climber Annie Smith Peck, taxidermist Delia Akeley, diver Eugenie Clark, and marathoner Thecla Mitchell, who overcomes handicaps to train for and compete in the New York City Marathon. Biography. Grades 4–6.

Roosevelt, E. *Eleanor Roosevelt, with Love: A Centenary Remembrance.* Dutton/Lodestar, 1984. Description of Eleanor's beliefs and her personal and public life as seen by her son. List of biographies and index included. Biography. Grade 5 and up.

Schneider, D. *American Women in the Progressive Era, 1900–1920.* Facts on File, 1993. Recounts women's struggle for equality. Includes primary sources such as diaries, letters, and photographs. Nonfiction. Grade 7 and up.

Stanley, S. C. *Women in the Military.* Messner, 1993. Reviews history of females serving in wars and the establishment of women's service units in the branches of the armed forces. Nonfiction. Grade 8 and up.

Warren, R. *A Pictorial History of Women in America.* Crown, 1975. Portrays the important contributions of women in America's history. Nonfiction. Grade 7 and up.

Religious Minority Heritage

Bial, R. *Amish Home.* Houghton Mifflin, 1993. Reviews history of the Amish, their language, the beliefs that are rooted in their religion, and the importance of family and community. Includes photographs and list for further reading. Nonfiction. Grades 4–6.

Blue, R. *Cold Rain on the Water.* McGraw, 1979. Depicts the struggles of Alex and his Jewish family who journeyed to the United States from Russia to find religious freedom. Historical fiction. Grades 7–8.

Rice, E. *American Saints and Seers: American-born Religions and the Genius Behind Them.* Four Winds, 1982. Recounts the various religions that have developed in the United States and includes information about the American Indian religions, Christian Scientists, Mormons, and Shakers. Nonfiction. Grade 7 and up.

Rosenblum, R. *The Old Synagogue.* Jewish Publication Society, 1989. Depicts history of the establishment, decay, and restoration of a synagogue and its surrounding neighborhood originally founded by immigrants from Europe. Nonfiction. Grades 4–8.

Differently Abled Heritage

Crutcher, C. *Staying Fat for Sarah Byrnes.* Greenwillow, 1993. A girl who is disfigured and an obese boy suffer emotionally from the mockery and teasing of their peers. The two become hard and callous in their view of the world, until their senior year in high school changes the directions of their lives. Contemporary realism. Grade 8 and up.

Riskind, M. *Apple Is My Sign.* Houghton Mifflin, 1981. Ten-year-old Harry Berger is nicknamed "Apple" because his family tends orchards. He goes to Philadelphia to a school for the deaf where he befriends others, learns football, and says he wants to be a teacher. Contemporary realism. Grades 4–8.

Trull, P. *On With My Life.* Putnam, 1983. In this portrayal, a reader learns that cancer and the amputation of a leg are not more traumatic than the unthinking reactions of those around you. Autobiography. Grades 4–8.

1900–1909

The 1906 Earthquake

When the students are studying the physical setting and the past of their state and local region, they may be interested on what has happened to people through the years. To show a western child's concerns and reactions to a frightening earthquake, read aloud *Earthquake: A Story of Old San Francisco* (Viking, 1993, grades 4–5) by Kathleen V. Kudlinski. In the story, 12-year-old Phillip wakes up early on April 18, 1906, because dogs are barking and horses are whinnying. When he is out in his father's stable doing his early-morning chores, he sees mice leaving the building and then Phillip feels the ground jump and tilt under his feet. In just a few minutes, everything changes for him as his family's home and stable is in ruins, many of the horses are injured, and San Francisco is on fire and burning rapidly. Everyone is afraid and concerned about the approaching flames—even the neighborhood bully.

Related to reading aloud a story about the 1906 earthquake in San Francisco, turn to *Earthquake at Dawn* (Harcourt Brace Jovanovich, 1992, grades 5–8) by Kristiana Gregory. The story is based on a letter written by a survivor's experience during the earthquake, photographer Edith Irvine and her 15-year-old assistant, Daisy. They saw a sense of togetherness as people shared with others; some risked their lives to fight the fire and rescue survivors; even some musicians assembled in Golden Gate Park to play for the people who gathered in the park. They also saw the havoc the fire caused—many people without homes walked the streets, others struggled for the basic needs of food and water, and still others looted and took what they could.

Smith (1993) at Utah State University suggests reading Laurence Yep's, *Dragonwings* to students, grade 6 and up, not only for its story of Moon Shadow, a Chinese boy, who helps his father build a successful motor-driven flying machine, *Dragonwings* but also for its vivid description of the 1906 earthquake. Smith points out that the description of the 1906 earthquake gives teachers an opportunity for several class activities. For example, the students can consider the effect of the quake on the buildings and sketch their ideas of Yep's description:

> *From all over came an immense wall of noise: of metal tearing, of bricks crashing, of wood breaking free from nails, and all. Everywhere, what man had built came undone. I was looking at a tenement house to our right and it just seemed to shudder and collapse. (p. 154)*

They can discuss what people were feeling and the effect of the quake on them:

> *And then the survivors started to emerge, and I saw that there were many hurts in mind as in body. Some people wandered out of the buildings almost naked, others still in their nightclothes. I saw one man with lather on one side of his face, the other side already clean-shaven. In his hand was a lather-covered razor. One woman in a nightgown walked by, carrying her crying baby by its legs as if it were a dead chicken. Father caught her by the shoulders and gently took the baby from her. (p. 174)*

Activity #133: "Natural Disasters"

Smith (1933) suggests guiding students to previously published newspapers and magazines to find accounts of natural disasters such as the floods in the Midwest, the hurricanes in Florida and Hawaii, the Loma Prieta earthquake in California, and the Mt. Pinatube eruption in the Philippines. Ask the students to read aloud information from the articles they find and then, for disscution, write the facts they find on the board, an overhead transparency, or a large class chart. Discuss the findings from the chart with questions such as, "In what ways were costs (damages, relief efforts), though different, also similar? What reasons can you think of for the high costs? Ways to reduce costs? Ways to improve relief efforts? and What can we do to help?"

1910–1919

World War I: 1914–1918

"Another book that rings true is Gloria Skurzynski's *Good-Bye Billy Radish* (Bradbury, 1992)," states Eileen Van Kirk (1993), author of the historical novels titled *A Promise to Keep* (Dutton, 1990) and *Silk* (Berkley, 1991). "Although somewhat episodic at first, it builds to a powerful and moving conclusion, and at the same time, creates a clear and fully realized picture of life in a harsh steel-mill town during the First World War." In the story, young Hank and older Billy work in the harsh conditions of the mills as Billy and his immigrant family struggle to be a part of America. They all face the horror of World War I and the onslaught of a flu epidemic. Van Kirk goes on to point out that historical novels like this one are all about giving students the "common thread of humanity that unites us" as well as an opportunity to know what life was all about growing up in another time period—and how the struggles of their parents and grandparents demanded in courage. Additionally, Van Kirk mentions that historical novels of this caliber provide students with a sense of heritage and can relive some of the fine things that happened—as well as the terrible things that happened in the name of progress and ignorance.

"Oddly enough, very few books for children about World War I have been published," write Huck and colleagues (1987). With this in mind, you may want to review with the students several main events of World War I. With a world map or globe, the sites of the following events can be discussed:

1. The deaths of members of the Austrian royal family at Sarajevo, Yugoslavia, in 1914 and Austria's need for expansion and a seaport on the Aegean Sea begins the war as Austria declares war on Serbia.

2. The alliance of two groups of countries takes place: Austria is allied with Germany, Italy, and others; France is allied with Great Britain, Russia, the United States, and others. Germany begins submarine blockade of the British Isles and Allied forces land at Salonika in 1915.

3. Tanks are first used in warfare as a series of battles take place in the Verdun area in 1916.

4. Unrestricted warfare in 1917 continues as the first U.S. troops land in France, the British capture Jerusalem, and Russia declares an armistice with Germany. During this time, the Russian revolution forces Czar Nicholas to give up his throne and the Bolsheviks seize control.

5. One year later, in 1918, President Wilson announces "Fourteen Points" that lead to an armistice. These include withdrawal and surrender of troops, the return of prisoners, payment for damage done in invaded territories, and the return of cash and goods taken from invaded countries. The allies set the final peace terms in the Versailles Treaty in 1919.

Activity #134: "World War I"

With students and a world map or globe, review some of the previous events and ask students to group the actions as "Pluses" and "Minuses" in international behavior. Write the actions in one of two columns labeled + and − on the board. Review the items in the Plus column and ask students to work in small groups to write a group paragraph about the "positive" events and actions. They also can write any other positive ideas they have that they think "would have avoided" World War I and led to peace. Review the items in the Minus column and ask students to work in small groups to write a group paragraph about the "negative" events and actions,

and to think of ways the negative actions could have been improved. Ask students to return to the whole group and read aloud what they wrote and discussed.

World War I: People's Lives

"Historical fiction is an important complement to history textbooks and other nonfiction historical accounts," write Sebesta and Iverson (1975). "Fiction that clearly depicts geographical regions that contrast with the environment of most readers can be an accessible way to geographical information. Accuracy is required—both of fact and perspective. But accuracy alone isn't sufficient. There must be, in addition, a good story with a theme appropriate to the time and place and authentic characters. The story must move along in a satisfying manner, synthesizing information without relinquishing its hold upon the reader." A story that satisfies the reader is G. Houston's *LittleJim* (Philomel, 1991, grade 6 and up)—the story of a young boy in Appalachia who pondered what it meant to be a "man" during 1917, the year that the United States reached into its storehouse of materials for its Allies and entered World War 1. In *LittleJim,* the boy and his father battled a conflict of their own—the boy's schooling versus the boy's working on the family farm. This story supports a study of life during the World War I period as well as study of Appalachian culture.

Activity #135: "Teenagers"

In Germany, Jan, a teenage boy, was adopted by German combat soldiers during the war after his village was destroyed by Russian and German armies in R. Frank's *No Hero for the Kaiser* (Lothrop, 1986, grade 6 and up). Jan knows that one of the "invisible" bullets can kill man or beast on the spot and thinks, "A dreadful feeling! But there was worse to come." An interesting fact for students is that this book was first published in 1931 and subsequently banned by the Nazis. In the United States, in the aftermath of World War I, 13-year-old Annie befriends a horribly burned and embittered young veteran at a veteran's hospital in Kansas, against the express wishes of her mother in M. L. Rostkowski's *After the Dancing Days* (Harper, 1986, grade 6 and up). Annie asks questions about peace, heroism, patriotism, and the physical and emotional casualties of war. Have students contribute their own questions about these subjects for discussion.

Activity #136: "Causes"

If appropriate, have students develop a fact-and-question sheet about World War I (or any conflict, war, or event) and ask them to work with partners to infer some of the causes from their points of view and from the facts on the sheet.

1920–1929

Decline of Native Americans

"The successful writer of historical fiction is aware that historical points of view change with time and that treatment of character and fact is inevitably affected by the way these things are viewed in the period in which the author is writing," write Sutherland and Arbuthnot (1986). "Thus the treatment of women, Blacks and Native Americans in historical fiction changed drastically in the 1970s and the writer should understand this change and see it in its historical perspective." As part of this historical perspective, discuss with the students additional examples of the impact of the Europeans' arrival on the Native People on North America's West Coast in the 1900s. Use a 1925 cultural conflict similar to the impact of the Europeans on the Tainos as an example. A. L. Kroeber, a noted authority on California Indians at the University of California in Berkeley, commented on the decline of the California Native American population due to the missions (Heizer & Whipple, 1967):

> It is established that the tribes that were completely devoted to mission life are gone, many of them are wholly extinct; the most fortunate may amount to one-hundredth of the original number.... It must have caused many of the fathers a severe pang to realize, as they could not do daily, that they were saving souls only at the inevitable cost of lives. And yet such was the overwhelming fact. The brute upshot of missionization, in spite of its kindly flavor and humanitarian root, was only one thing: death.

Discuss which (if any) points of view have changed over time.

Activity #137: "Data about the Topic"

Ask interested older students to look for more data to support Koebler's statement about the missions or to support/not support the problems facing Native Americans mentioned in other stories. Engage students in cross-checking information and using more than one source to arrive at a conclusion about Koebler's statement. Ask students to tell what they found that expanded and "rounded out" the statement. Point out the value of seeking several authorities through references to confirm or negate a statement such as the one Koebler made.

If conflicting evidence is found, lead students to examine a reference for clues of validity—copy-right date, background of the author, and knowledge presented. Point out the value of arriving at a conclusion based on the students' critical thinking—not just on accepting some words printed in a book.

1930–1939

The Rainbow People and *Tongues of Jade*

To focus student interest on historical storytelling, discuss the evenings of storytelling after a hard work day enjoyed by Chinese old-timers who picked fruit in the orchards near Sacramento, California, and other cities in the 1930s. In *Tongues of Jade* (HarperCollins, 1991, grades 3–7), also by Laurence Yep, short stories and folktales that were told by the Chinese working on a WPA Works Process Administration project are recorded for readers. The stories are based on the oral Chinese American tradition with sections such as "Roots" and "Family Ties." Yep's mini-essays introduce the sections. You can provide a contrast to the voices of Chinese old-timers with voices of contemporary young people in *American Dragons: Twenty-Four Asian American Voices* (HarperCollins, 1992, grade 8 and up) by Laurence Yep. This is another ancestral collection that has poems and short stories from contemporary Asian American students (attending the University of California) from several countries, including China, Japan, Korea, Vietnam, and Thailand. Engage students in simulating evening storytelling by meeting in groups and telling favorite short stories and folktales.

Activity #138: "Storytelling"

After reading aloud excerpts from *Tongues of Jade* and *The Rainbow People* (Harper & Row, 1989, grades 3–7) by Laurence Yep, discuss with the students the various characters—tricksters and fools—as well as the virtues and love reflected in the lives of Chinese Americans in the tales. Point out that the promise of a "good life" and a "golden mountain" in the United States attracted immigrants from China. Suggest Yep's other novels with this emphasis—*The Serpent's Children* (Harper, 1984, grade 6 and up) and *Mountain Light* (Harper, 1985, grade 6 and up). *The Serpent's Children* describes the life of a young girl in the 1800s in China who protects her family, and *Mountain Light* is a description of interactional fighting among groups in China and the terrible conditions of an immigrant ship sailing from Hong Kong to San Francisco in the 1850s. After reading one of the stories, have students discuss what promises attract immigrants today and compare them with the promises that attracted immigrants in the early 1900s.

Government Expansion

"A good book—a work of literary excellence—has the quality of speaking to its readers between the lines. It is this quality that makes a book *real*," writes Charles Reasoner (1975), a professor at New York University. "it is this quality that makes writers of good books seem to say more than they actually put down on paper. In between the lines are innuendoes, imagery, signs, and signals for perceptive readers to pick up, flash against a background of unique personal experiencing, and create *with writers* arresting moments of life which not only spring from, but transcend, characters and plot and go on living with them for a long, long time." Several stories about the government's expansion in the 1900s "speaks to their readers between the lines" and present different ways of dealing with people who lived on the land but few books discuss any outright battles—"any arresting moments"—between America's citizens and America's government. Carolyn Reeder's *Grandpa's Mountain* (Macmillan, 1991, grades 4–8), however, tells about the "battle" that 11-year-old Carrie faces when she visits her grandparents' home in the Blue Ridge Mountains one summer. That summer, Carrie finds her grandpa "changed" and fighting the government men who want to turn the land into the Shenandoah National Park. In the fight, he becomes as hard and intractable as the men he opposes, a behavior that shocks Carrie. After reading the story, have students compare their world with Carrie's world and her grandpa's fight against government expansion.

Activity #139: "Benefits for Many versus Disruption for Few"

Related to *Grandpa's Mountain*, encourage the students to discuss the reasons for various actions of the government, the beliefs of the people living in the Blue Ridge Mountains, and the consequences of the actions on both sides. Write headings on the board to organize the students' comments:

Government Actions	*Beliefs of the People*
1.	1.
Consequences	*Consequences*
1.	1.

Guide students to see that this set of events and its consequences during the Great Depression has relevance for situations today in which the government still pits projected benefits for the many against the disruption of a few. Engage students in discussing people they know in their lives today who are "fighting the government" about an issue. Ask the students to select one of the people and write a paragraph about the person and the issue.

1940–1949

World War II: 1939–1945

"The World War II literature for children certainly goes from the point of 'war is glorious' to somewhere within the 'war is hell' category," states Mary Maness (1976), an investigator into the treatment of war related to World War II, the Korean conflict, and the Vietnamese war in children's literature. "As we look at the literature of the present era, we certainly see illustrated the absurdity of war." Maness points out that an example of "war is glorious" is found in *Snow Treasure* (Dutton, 1942, grades 4–8) by Marie McSwigan, a story of school children in Norway who smuggled 13 tons of gold valued at $9 million on their sleds to a hideaway so it can be taken to America. In contrast, the idea that "war is hell" is shown in *Matthew, Mark, Luke and John* (John Day, 1966, grade 7 and up) by Pearl Buck, the story of four illegitimate children born of American soldiers and Korean mothers. And the idea that "war is absurd" is found in *Cross-Fire* (Pantheon, 1972, grade 8 and up) by Gail Graham, a story of an American soldier who is alone in the jungle and finds four Vietnamese children who hate Americans and have returned to their destroyed village. At the end, the soldier dies of wounds inflicted while trying to save the life of one of the children.

Activity #140: "Story Web"

Bromley (1991) suggests webbing activities for historical fiction that describe World War II and other events, and maintains that Bette Greene's *Summer of My German Soldier* (Bantam, 1973) is suitable for students in grade 5 and up who are studying units about World War II, prejudice, discrimination, and social awareness. Greene's story is about a 12-year-old Jewish girl who befriends and shelters one of the German prisoners of war in a camp in Arkansas. To involve students further in the story, Bromley (1991) suggests that students create a story web and contribute information for some literary elements—characters, setting, point of view, and themes—and write their thoughts on a web.

After the students read the story, engage them in discussing each of the categories listed on the web, the conflicts among the characters, and the reasons for the conflicts *they* discern from the story. Additionally, interested students can create another web for Greene's sequel, *Morning Is a Long Time Coming* (Dial, 1978, grade 5 and up), the story of the girl's journey to Europe at the end of the war to find the German soldier's mother.

Events that occurred during World War II affected children and adults for years afterward, and this is portrayed through 11-year-old Etienne in *The Shadow Children* (Morrow, 1994, grades 5–8) by Steven Schnur. When Etienne visits his Grand-Pere's farm at Mont Brulant for the summer, he sees refugee children in rags that no one else sees and finds artifacts in the nearby woods where railroad tracks used to be. He hears the whistle of the imaginary train and even meets the children's teacher, Isaac. Eventually, Etienne realizes that he is reliving some of the events that happened years before when the Jewish children in the town were turned over to the Nazis. Figure 12–2 suggests additional stories.

The Holocaust

"There are probably many teachers who will agonize over the place of literature in teaching about the Holocaust, " writes Cullinan (1981). "Valid questions for them are: Is mass murder a suitable subject for a children's novel? What is the place of an account of it in the school curriculum? What are the possible consequences of not informing people about one of the most bitter lessons in history?" Related to this, two teachers, Tunnell and Ammon (1991), taught an Anne Frank unit to eighth-graders, so they had an opportunity to appreciate *The Diary of Anne Frank* as literature and to make a connection between Anne's world and their world. The following steps were taken as part of the curriculum:

FIGURE 12–2   Books about World War II

Gehrt, B. *Don't Say a Word.* Margaret McElderry, 1986. The title points out the need for secrecy in Hitler's Germany and implies consequences to citizens who opposed Hitler. In one scene, a stranger refuses to speak to a mother when the children are around and says, "There are certain things that one should really not speak of at all. One extra pair of ears is already too many, not to mention three pairs" (p. 105). Advanced grade 6 and up.

Orgel, D. *The Devil in Vienna.* Puffin, 1988. In 1937, Lieslotte Vessely is required by her father to join the Hitler Youth movement since he held a high position in Hitler's political organization. Her friend, Inge Dornewal, realized that it was becoming too dangerous for her to continue her friendship with Lieslotte. Advanced grade 7 and up.

Orlev, U. *The Man from the Other Side.* Macmillan, 1993. A stepfather and his son take food to the Jews in the Warsaw ghetto by traveling through the city's sewers. Grades 5–8.

Ray, D. K. *My Daddy Was a Soldier.* Holiday, 1990. Presents what it is like for a child when a father is called to war and things change. Grade 6 and up.

Richter, H. P. *Frederick.* Holt, Rinehart and Winston, 1970. The story of Hitler's pogrom against the Jews is told through the story of Frederick, a German Jewish boy. Frederick's friends lacked the courage to stand up against what was going on. Advanced grade 7 and up.

Schellie, D. *Shadow and the Gunner.* Four Winds, 1982. Bobby's 18-year-old friend, Billy, falls in love with Bobby's sister. When Billy leaves for his military duty, Bobby finds it hard to accept the changed relationship. Grade 6 and up.

Van Kirk, E. *A Promise to Keep.* Lodestar, 1990. When a German pilot parachutes from a burning plane near the English farm, Curt, an Austrian refugee and farmworker, reveals that his heart and loyalty are with Germany, and he asks 14-year-old Ellie to help smuggle the pilot out of England. Ellie's choice is either to betray her country or refuse Curt's friendship. Grade 6 and up.

1. Students listened to *Terrible Things* (Harper & Row, 1989) by Eve Bunting.

2. Students discussed possible interpretations of the story and drew from their own experience of similar happenings.

3. Students received background information through trade books such as *Remember Not to Forget* (Watts, 1985) by Norman Finkelstein, an overview that provided the definitions of *anti-Semitism* and *Holocaust*. Students listened to excerpts from *A Nightmare from History* (Clarion, 1987) by Miriam Chalkin for background information about anti-Semitism and how Hitler supported it.

4. Students visited the library and were assigned research reports and read related stories in different research groups with the purpose that they would soon be reading the play, *The Diary of Anne Frank*. They knew that Anne lived during the time when anti-Semitism was high. For 10 days, the students worked in the library and in the classroom, organized their reports, and prepared their presentations to the whole class.

5. Each day, the teacher read to the students and showed pictures from resources to enrich their understanding of the Holocaust. Mini-lessons about organizing group work, how to use data sheets to collect information, and creative ways to make final presentations were taught to develop the students's library and organizational skills in writing research.

6. In cooperative heterogeneous learning groups, the students worked on different topics that included projects such as map making, time line constructing, and drawing. The topics included (a)The People Who Helped the Jews During the Holocaust; (b) Kristallnacht; (c) Causes of World War II; (d) The Lives of Famous People during World War II; (e) The Concentration Camps; (f) D Day; (g) The Nuremberg Laws and Trials; and (h) Dangers of Neo-Nazi Groups and Other Hate Groups to the American Way of Life.

7. The students' final presentations included skits, games, talk shows, and mock trials, and they discussed the parallels from this time period to events happening currently. Finally, the students evaluated what they had learned on an evaluation survey and suggested that the class invite speakers who had firsthand knowledge of the Holocaust.

Engage your students in discussing connections between their world and Anne Frank's World from their point of view.

Activity #141: "Anti-Nazi Youth"

Point out to students that recently, with the publicized violence of ethnic cleansing in Bosnia and rage against foreigners in Germany and other countries, the memory of the White Rose Anti-Nazi Youth Group is a powerful reminder of the importance of people standing up and speaking out against racial hatred. To make a connection between the world of the White Rose group and the students' contemporary world, ask students, grade 7 and up, to listen to excerpts from J. Foreman's *Ceremony of Innocence* (Hawthorn Books, 1967), a true story of Hans Scholl, his sister Sophie, and their friends who started the White Rose resistance group in Nazi Germany. Ask them to review additional information about the Scholls (Keeler, 1993) by discussing the decisions related to some events such as the following:

1. Before World War II began, Hans Scholl joins the Hitler Youth Group and Sophie joins the female equivalent, but their humanistic upbringing clashes with the regimentation of the group and their attitudes change from silent resistance to action.

2. The Scholls, Christoph Probst, Willi Graf, and Alexander Schmorell—all students at the University of Munich—become the vital core of the White Rose resistance, a name taken after a novel of the same name.

3. In February, the Scholls and Probst throw copies of the leaflet from a balcony at the university and are seen by a university janitor, who has them arrested. A few days later, the Scholls and Probst stand before Roland Freislter, a Nazi judge who spends the entire trial harassing them. In spite of this, it is reported that Sophie Scholl stood up in the middle of the trial and said, "Somebody had to make a start."

4. In Germany on February 22, 1943, Hans Scholl, his sister Sophie, and their friend, Christoph Probst were slain. This is the beginning of the Nazi attack on the White Rose resistance and the Nazis' sentencing of the rest of the White Rose members to death or to prison.

Children in Conflicts

Polese (1991), a Writer in Residence at Sunny Brae Middle School, Arcata, California, points out the value of reading an author's personal truths about war in quality books that look at war through a child's perspective. Such books can help a child face questions about war, the Holocaust, and the importance of freedom. Related to this, Milton Meltzer, in his book *Never to Forget* (Dell, 1977, grade 6 and up), shares his feelings about the Holocaust and the importance of freedom in people's lives. He writes, "The Holocaust was a measure of man's dimensions. One can think of the power of evil it demonstrated—and of those people who treated others as less then human, as bacteria. Or of the power of good—and of those people who held out a hand to others." Books such as Meltzer's and others (see Figure 12–2) can present war as it has been experienced by children and adults and can help your students examine their questions about war.

Activity #142: "Questions about War"

Several additional books will help older students examine questions about war raised by those who were affected by the experience of the Gulf War or living in military families. Some of the concerns of children that are brought about by war are separation, fear of separation, and a change in people's values (e.g., sometimes civil liberties erode, communities can polarize, and the innocent can suffer through no fault of their own). Additionally, there are the emotions of the returning service people that need to be recognized and appreciated. Books, for students in grade 5 and up, suitable for further independent reading on the subject can be located by interested students. See History Master 39, "Twentieth Century Conflicts."

1950–1959

Hawaii: 1950

"Recent studies of ways books affect children and ways cultural images are shown in children's books support a conclusion that some children can and do develop healthy perceptions about the heritage of others and can modify certain beliefs about the culture of others," write Roberts and Cecil (1993). To develop a multicultural image of life in the 1950s—a time when the Hawaiian Islands became the fiftieth state—read aloud *Blue Skin of the Sea* (Delacorte, 1992, grade 6 and up) by Graham Salisbury. It is the story of a father, a fisherman, and his teenage son who live in the quiet village of Kai-lua-Kona on the big island of Hawaii. The Mendozas love the sea, yet they realize its related dangers—the force of a hurricane, the appetite of a hungry shark, and the power of dangerous waters. One day, when the father's fishing boat fails to return, Sonny faces the fear of losing his father through a boating

accident. With this story, the students can develop a perception about the heritage of Hawaiians who live on and near the sea and can recognize the universal feeling of a son's fear of losing his father—a feeling found in the cultures of all people.

Activity #143: "Feelings and Family Ties"

Roberts and Cecil (1993) suggest that after reading the story, the students discuss the family ties between Sonny Mendoza and his father as well as some of the difficulties Sonny faced as he grew up. If desired, draw parallels from the story and the students' own experiences. On the board, start a "feelings" web with the label "Sonny's Feelings" in the center and ask for the students' suggestions for information to write under the related categories of Feelings about Family Ties, Feelings about His Childhood, Feelings about His Teenage Years, and Feelings about His Search for His Identity. Invite the students to make their own "feelings" web about their family and childhood from their own experiences.

After the students read *Blue Skin of the Sea*, ask them to discuss the purpose for journeys to the islands by explorers and others, trace sea routes, discuss hardships on the journeys, and estimate distances covered by sea journeys. Ask students if any of their reasons for the journeys to the islands are the same reasons people use to explore places today. Additionally, engage them in drawing a large map of the Pacific Ocean area and tracing different sea routes to Hawaii on it. As a border for the map, the students can add the titles of other books they find related to "Life in Hawaii" and tell others what they learned about what life was like for this Hawaiian family in this time period.

1960–1969

Vietnam

As background for any similarities of the Vietnam action with other conflicts, excerpts from *Always to Remember: The Story of the Vietnam Veterans Memorial* (Putnam's, 1992, grade 6 and up) by Brent Ashabranner can be read aloud and compared to other books such as *A Memorial for Mr. Lincoln* (Putnam's, 1992, grade 6 and up), also by Ashabranner, and *The American Revolutionaries: A History in Their Own Words* (Crowell, 1987, grades 4–8) by Martin Meltzer. All three books are filled with historical sources—photographs, prints, paintings, maps—and offer students an opportunity to discuss the impact of the three wars that have divided people of the United States in different ways—America's Revolutionary War, the Civil War, and the Vietnam action. With a map of Washington, DC, point out that the Vietnam Memorial is only a short distanc away from the Lincoln Memorial and the Washington Memorial, and that the closeness of the memorials can symbolize a meaning for any visitors who have the insight to recognize all three monuments and what they signify about the "close similarities" of three wars that affected America. Invite your students to offer their ideas about the meaning of the memorials.

Activity #144: "Wars That Divided Americans"

After a discussion with older students about the conflicts related to the Vietnam War that divided people in America, draw three large intersecting circles on the board or an overhead transparency. Label one circle "Revolutionary War," another "Civil War," and the last "Vietnam War." Write *America's Heroes and Heroines* in the intersection of the circles. With the whole group, ask students what they want to know about America's War heroes and heroines and list their ideas on the board. Some of their suggestions might include the extent of the role of women soldiers, the role of Asian Americans and other minorities, the Presidential responsibilities at the time, the way the government handled related situations, and the names of heroic people during the conflicts. To extend this further students can participate in any or all of the following:

1. Ask students to work in pairs and find facts about one of the war actions and take notes about Americans and their heroic actions. With the whole group, elicit further information about the students' facts and add them to the circles in the appropriate places.

2. Ask students what more they want to know about war heroes and heroines and list their questions on the board. Ask them to work in partnerships and research facts about any one of the three conflicts.

3. Ask students to record the information they find in data sources in the appropriate place on copies of the intersecting circles. Differences among the wars can be written in the circles and similarities can be written in the intersecting space.

4. With the students, view a television tape or video(s) of an address about Vietnam by President Lyndon Johnson and then distribute copies of Pres-

ident Lincoln's Gettysburg Address as well as Patrick Henry's brief exhortation given before the Revolutionary War that includes the words "Give me liberty or give me death." After seeing Johnson's address and taking notes on the former president's main ideas, the students can read excerpts from Lincoln's and Henry's material to discuss any similarities they think of among the three sources.

5. With partners, engage the students in taking the role of a soldier who has returned from Vietnam and writes a letter to the president, starting with "Dear President Johnson." In the letter, students should write their views using as much information as possible that they gained from seeing a video or reading documents or data sources. Repeat this activity after the students reread copies of Lincoln's Gettyburg Address and Henry's declaration by having the students take the roles of soldiers in both the American Revolution and in the Civil War who want to write the presidents. In the whole group, ask students to point out what they learned from this investigation and the use of the primary references.

Let Freedom Ring: Martin Luther King

A biography is "a vehicle for developing children's natural curiosity about people and the world around them to the point where they themselves investigate a particular life, and, through the artful use of language, tell that human story to others," states Milton Meltzer, a well-known biographer, in the Foreword in *Learning about Biographies* (Zarnowski, 1990). The problem of accuracy a writer has in investigating a particular life can be demonstrated to the students by asking them to look at three biographies (or more) of Martin Luther King, Jr.'s life. An easy biography, *The Picture Life of Martin Luther King, Jr.* (1968, grade 4) by Margaret B. Young, is easy to read and covers the tumultuous years of the Montgomery, Alabama, bus boycott in one sentence: "After a year the laws were changed." More difficult books, such as Ed Clayton's *Martin Luther King: The Peaceful Warrior* (Archway, 1964, grades 6–7) and *Meet Martin Luther King, Jr.* (Messner, 1982, grades 6–8) by Doris and Harold Faber, have more details about the violence during the boycott and raise questions about the concept of authenticity that older studen can explore further. As an example, ask students to consider which of the author's descriptions about what happened during the bombing attempt on King's house might be most accurate. Point out that the differences in the authors' descriptions to alert the students to the idea that few biographies are *totally* accurate because writers have to simplify facts for readers, and because sometimes they fail to complete the research they need.

Activity #145: "Dr. King's 'I Have a Dream' Speech"

Speaking out for freedom and justice on August 28, 1963, Dr. King delivered "goosebump" words in his "I Have a Dream" speech that still sends an emotional message to those that hear it. Elicit the children's interest in discovering that their speaking voices can be as effective as King's with a choral speaking activity using excerpts from Dr. King's speech. Demonstrate a line arrangement for the words the children select from the speech. To do this, ask a student or a small group to read the first line, another to read the second line, and so on through the lines. If appropriate, introduce this activity with a pattern similar to the following:

All: So let freedom ring....

First student or group: In the process of gaining our rightful place, we must not be guilty of wrongful deeds.

Second student or group: Let us not seek to satisfy our thirst for freedom by drinking from the cup of bitterness and hatred.

Third student or group: We must forever conduct our struggle on the high plain of dignity and discipline.

Discuss Dr. King's words about his dream, which included a vision that children would live one day in an America where they would "not be judged by the color of their skin but judged by the content of their character." Ask the students what these words mean to them today and invite them to draw/sketch their dreams about America today. With interested students, review King's goals in the struggle for civil rights from David Adler's biography, *Martin Luther King, Jr.: Free at Last* (Holiday, 1986, grades 4–8).

Additionally, read aloud parts about the struggle for civil rights for African Americans and show the photographs from the days of slavery up through desegregation found in Jim Haskins's *The Day Martin Luther King, Jr. Was Shot: A Photo History of the Civil Rights Movements* (Scholastic, 1992, grades 4–6). For those interested further in the lives of Coretta and Martin King, Jr., suggest *Coretta Scott King: Keeper of the Dream* (Enslow, 1992, grade 6 and up), a biography by S. Henry and E.

Taiz. The book traces the life of Coretta King as a civil rights activist beginning with her early life in Alabama, then her marriage to Martin, and finally, her ongoing work.

1970–1979

Women's History Week

"We need to break down the stereotypes of women just as we are trying to eliminate stereotypes based on race, for both racism and sexism are harmful to our total population," writes Iris Teidt (1979). "Sexism can occur in illustrations. It can also show up in language, in attitudes expressed toward women and their achievements, and the way they are characterized. Sexism can ever occur when women are ignored or omitted." Thus, the stereotypes of women in history in the United States should be studied during the year, not just during National Women's History Week.

National Women's History Week, commemorated every March, (1978) inspires teachers, college and university professors, community members, and students to review the contributions of women. In the classroom, posters from the National Women's History Project (P.O. Box 3716, Santa Rosa, CA 95402) can feature the photographs and brief biographies of women who are part of the wide spectrum of our country's history. Women who have been commemorated in the past years include Chien-Shiung Wu, Mary McLeod Bethune, Sarah Winnemucca, and Elizabeth Cady Stanton. Interested teachers and students may write the National Women's History Project for additional information and a current price list.

Activity #146: "Ideas, Opinions, and Attitudes"

Hyde and Bizar (1989) suggest that students should be encouraged to express and explore their ideas, opinions, and attitudes. To encourage students to express their opinions, you can confront some of the assumptions that students hold by reading aloud or having the students read stories about the role of women and girls and the way a stereotype has or has not occurred in different time periods. This can be examined in a discussion as the students read about the roles across time periods and compare with roles in their experience. If needed, the figures at the beginning of the chapters for each century and the previously mentioned History Master 32, "Role of Women and Girls," have suggested book titles for interested students.

Diverse Families

Beginning with the present, stories about multicultural families can launch a mural of America's diversity. Students may prepare a mural of common people doing uncommon things during different years in the 1900s.

Activity #147: "Families and Their Values"

With students in grade 4 and older, point out ways to link the past to the present by reviewing the diversity and plurality of Americans, "then" and "now." To do this, ask students to locate excerpts from different books over several days' time to emphasize America's richness shown through the diversity of families. Suggestions for books for a display to entice students to read further are found in History Master 40, "America's Culturally Diverse Families."

1980–1989

Human Understanding

James Banks indicates that older students, grade 5 and up, can come to know book characters as human beings, develop intense feelings for them, and even experience agony when they are exploited or mistreated. Banks explains that some of these fictional characters are Henry in Frank Bonham's *Durango Street* (Dutton, 1965), Jethro and Fess in Kristin Hunter's *The Soul Brothers and Sister Lou* (Scribner's, 1969), and Jimmy in Robert Cole's *Dead End School* (Little, Brown, 1968) because all the characters evoke deep feelings and concern. Banks also states that "since our major social problems grow from the negative attitudes...we must modify the racial attitudes if we are to create the democratic society that we say we have." When used effectively, Banks indicates that literature can help students develop racial tolerance and a commitment to eradicating social injustice.

Activity #148: "Empathy"

For 11- and 12-year-olds, Crystal (1972) suggests empathy-arousing role-playing to catch sudents' interest, involve them, and hold their attention on a topic. Crystal recommends short situations for enactment in pantomime and drama situations from children's literature that could be role-played:

1. Moving into a new house, as seen in Mohr's *Felita*
2. Assigned the part of a shepherd in the school's Christmas pageant, as seen in Lasky's *Pageant*
3. Others suggested by the students

1990-PRESENT

Our Area's History

"Questions may be used to check the child's comprehension of concepts, generalizations, or subject matter," state Jarolimek and Parker (1993). "Often such questions require the learner to reproduce or recall factual information that has been read or discussed in class.... In terms of the development of intellectual skills, the most important questions to ask are those that require elaborative, reflective responses." These higher-level questions often begin, "Why..." "How..."How do we know..." "Show that..." "If that is true, then..." With this in mind, encourage students to take the role of local historians and develop questions on a question map on the board as a guide for the historical research of their area, town, or city. The question map for this might have headings like those in Figure 12–3.

Activity #149: "Tale of Our Town"

Read aloud the memories about the great Dimpole oak that are part of a town's history in Janet Taylor Lisle's *The Great Dimpole Oak* (Orchard Books/Franklin Watts, 1987, grades 4–6). The people find their lives intertwined because of the tree standing in a field owned by an old farmer. Howlie and Dexter really believe the legends about its buried treasure, and a swami from Bombay believes that the tree has incredible power. The tree itself is saved when the farmer announces he has willed it to the town in hopes "that the children would play beneath the tree and keep its stories and memories alive with telling and listening." Students can find out about others who were just as interested in keeping memories alive for others.

To tell the tale of the students' town (neighborhood, city), encourage them to interview elderly citizens with written questions and audiotape recorders; to visit monuments and buildings; to read plaques and tombstones. They can read news from earlier time periods, visit the nearby library branch, and talk to people from the local historical society. When the students have the information they want for their questions, engage them in writing a historical story to tell the tale of their town. They may publish it in a class newspaper, send it to the historical, society, or mail it to the newspaper editor of the town paper.

Invite the students to show the information they have about their area and prepare a history exhibit of the area, town, or city for others to see for a Back-to-School night or an assembly presentation. Have students prepare foods reminiscent of the times—lemonade, popcorn, hot dogs, homemade ice cream,

FIGURE 12–3 Example of a Question Map

cakes and cookies—and distribute them dressed in clothes that reflect an earlier time. If desired, show displays of patchwork designs of quilts and pillows, set up reading booths where the students read brief stories to young children, and talk about old photographs they carry with them. The record player can play music popular of the times—perhaps some rag-time band music—and a display area can show some of the books about changes and continuity (listed in Figure 12–4).

Families as a Part of History

Ammon and Weigard (1993) also point out that an excellent way for students to learn about the process of history is to trace the history of their own families and to read children's books can help the children develop such projects. In support of this approach, Davis (1989), a middle school teacher, developed a genealogy lesson that placed the students and their families in history, gave them a clearer picture of their ethnic backgrounds, and provided an opportunity to see what their families had contributed to society. With parental permission to study their genealogies for four generations, the students discussed their genealogy and family histories and Alex Haley's *Roots* (Doubleday, 1976). They listened to excerpts from the record titled "Alex Haley Tells the Story of His Search for Roots" (Warner Brothers Records, 1977) and looked at some sample

genealogies. Diagrams on the board showed the students how to develop a chart of a family's history. They took time to sketch some preliminary genealogies and brought them in periodically to show them to the teacher and talk about any difficulties they were experiencing in doing this.

Suggest to your students that they search to discover what their families have contributed to their communities.

Activity #150: "Family History"

Working on a genealogy project, some students in grades 4–6 may be interested in listening to *Rosy Cole Discovers America* (Little, Brown, 1992) by Sheila Greenwald. In the story, Rosy learns about history through her own family history and realizes that it took all different kinds of families to build America. As Rosy did, students in grade 4 and older can create a chart for their family histories and number each person on the chart, with the number 1 assigned to the student. The chart can show aunts, uncles, grandparents, and great-grandparents. Additionally, the students can make a list of all the persons assigned numbers, their names, places and dates of birth, and if appropriate, the years of deaths.

Several books can help the students with their projects. For example, Lila Perl's *The Great Ancestor Hunt* (Clarion, 1989, grades 4–8) shows students how to create a family tree by conducting an interview and researching family momentos and avail-

FIGURE 12–4   *Changes and Continuity in the City and Country*

Mattingly, C. *The Miracle Tree*. Ill. by Marianne Yamaguchi. Gulliver, 1986. Because of a pine tree that was still alive 20 years after the atomic bombing of Nagasaki, a daughter, her husband, and her mother are reunited. A plea for peace in a sensitive story about the pain of war that was part of this family's history. Grades 4–8.

Provensen, A., & Provensen, M. *Shaker Lane*. Ill. by authors. Viking, 1987. Each family's history is different on Shaker Lane. When the Herkimer sisters sell off parts of their land, the housing developers arrive and cause modest income tenants to move when they are replaced by middle income owners. Grades 4–5.

Pople, Maureen. *A Nugget of Gold*. Holt, 1988. Sally Matthews finds an old nugget that had been fashioned into a woman's brooch. Inscribed on the back are the words *Ann Bird Jem Ever*. This gold piece leads her into a mystery and a love story nearly 100 years old that become part of a family's history. Grade 6 and up.

Pryor, B. *The House on Maple Street*. Ill. by B. Peck. Morrow, 1987. Shows changes over 300 years that could be sequenced with a mural of the scenes or with time lines. Grade 4.

able public records. Richard Rosenbloom's *My Block* (1988, grades 4–8) focuses on occupancy succession and features one block in Brooklyn three generations ago, and David Weitzman's *My Backyard History Book* (1975, grades 4–8) tells students how to gather information from cemeteries, obituaries, the Yellow Pages, and a realtor's office. Each student's completed project can be given as a gift to someone in the family as part of the history about the family.

To help the students discover information about their own families and enjoy family stories, have each of them write a letter to his or her grandparents asking them to write back and tell a story from childhood. The students can make family trees and organize an "Old-Fashioned Museum" with related artifacts and objects in the class.

Intergenerational Interviews

Another excellent way for students to learn about the process of history is to study the history and contributions of elderly people. Children's books can help the students enrich such learning. If they are curious about things an elderly person remembers from his or her childhood times, certain intergenerational stories can offer insights into a young person/elderly person relationship. The stories also can help students place certain families in history, give them a clearer picture of different ethnic backgrounds, and provide an opportunity for them to see

what elderly relatives in families have contributed to society. With interested students, engage them in recording an elderly person's personal history with a tape recorder (or video or film camera).

Activity #151: "Interview"

To get ready for an interview, students may work with partners to rehearse the following:

1. Write specific questions that ask for details. Ask questions to find out about where the individuals live, what their parents were like, what life was like in their childhood, what school was like for them, what their friends were like, what their interests were, and other things the student would like to know.
2. Write questions that are open-ended (e.g., "Tell me about…").
3. Write questions that respect the privacy of the elderly person.
4. Leave space on the paper for the person's answers.
5. Practice with a tape recorder.
6. Tell the adults in the home and the teacher about your proposed interview.
7. Have an adult go with you when you visit an elderly person in their own home.
8. Arrange your own transportation if it is needed and discuss this with the adults in the home.
9. Contact the elderly person the student wants to interview and schedule a time.

10. Rehearse the questions and gather everything you need for the interview—tape recorder, paper, pencils—into a bag.
11. Arrive for the interview on time and, during the conversation, accept the answers without expressing your own agreement/disagreement.
12. Read notes or listen to the tape after the interview and then write a summary of it.

Gulf War

"If it is true that understanding events of the past makes people better able to cope with problems of the present, the best historical fiction is making a singular contribution toward the development of today's children, who will be tomorrow's adults," state Sutherland and Arbuthnot (1986). As part of fostering an understanding events of the past, read the book characters' views of the Persian Gulf crisis and Desert Shield and Desert Storm from Patricia Giff's book, *The War Began at Supper: Letters to Miss Loria* (Dell, 1991, grades 4–6), Illustrated by Betsy Lewin. When the Gulf War begins in January 1991, five children—Alice, Jessica, Karl, Michael, and Sara—write to their former student teacher, Miss Loria. In their letters, they tell how each one is affected by the war and how they cope with what is going on. Invite the students to relate the book characters' experience with any of their own experiences affected by the Gulf War. In what ways do the students think that understanding the Gulf War event will make people better able to cope with a similar situation in the future?

Activity #152: "Gulf War"

With students who volunteer, discuss how they were affected by the war and ways they dealt with what was going on at the time. During the discussion, record some of their reflections on the board in a graphic visual that shows a way to organize the thoughts of the discussion.

Just as the children—Alice, Jessica, Karl, Michael, and Sara—in Giff's story wrote to their former student teacher, have the students write personal letters to a friend or relative about their views. In their letters, have them tell how they are affected by war and how they cope with something that bothers them.

A Historical Spread of Effect

Show the students a historical *spread of effect* about a social problem (Jarolimek, 1971)—a way to trace some main ideas back through different time periods through related readings about what has happened in similar situations in the past. To do this, discuss the headlines that represent some of the social problems and issues in a current issue of the local newspaper. Discuss some of the articles with the students and ask them to identify the main idea or the essence of what is discussed in the articles. The "essence" of an article can be identified with terms such as *justice, health, and housing,* or *conservation, education, and jobs* for everyone. After discussing what the students value in the situations presented in the articles, list their main ideas of the articles (the essence) on the board and invite students each to vote for two of the ideas that are most important to them. After the vote, ask students to make predictions about what the future *could* be for these situations. Encourage them to connect their main ideas back to different time periods and look for at least one related reading about what has happened in situations in the past that are similar to recent headline news.

Activity #153: "Spread of Effect about Fear of War"

Studying history that relates to a current newspaper headline helps the students understand the variety of factors that lead to historical events and, as Jarolimek (1971) states, to understand that certain points of major historical significance are generally identified by a single date but the points of significance have a *spread of effect* that extend *prior* to the point and *subsequent* to it. For example, in order for students to understand the Gulf War, they should go back to the events that led to the Korean war action or to the events that led up to World War II. To have additional knowledge of World War II, students will get more meaning if they go "back" to World War I and learn about the series of events that finally led to the fateful day of December 7, 1941.

Thus, history can be seen as a story of the activities of people and their relationships, and it is best viewed when it is *not* cut up into parts separated by dates. The past relationship(s) of people can help students understand their hopes and aspirations as well as their achievements and failures. Here is an example of how one class started this type of discussion: A sixth-grade class reviewed an issue of the city's paper and found the headlines and main ideas that are listed in Figure 12–5. With the students, the teacher discussed some of the stories from children's literature that related to the headlines and the main ideas. The sample headline helped guide the students back through historical periods as they considered a "spread of effect" related to the head-

FIGURE 12–5   Spread of Effect about War

News Headline: Yeltsin Tries to Ease U.S. Nuke Fears
Main Idea: Fear of war
Related Stories Portraying Different Time Periods:

Gulf War

Bratman, F. *War in the Persian Gulf.* Millbrook, 1991. Describes the history of conflict in the region reflecting the importance of oil in international politics, the rise of Saddam Hussein, the use of sanctions, the fear of war, and the war itself. Photographs and maps included. Grade 6 and up.

Vietnam War

Detzer, D. *An Asian Tragedy: American & Vietnam.* Millbrook, 1992. Depicts the background in chronological order and discusses the problems for the people of America and Vietnam. Includes points of view of other historians. Advanced grade 6 and up.

Korean War

Buck, P. *Matthew, Mark, Luke and John.* John Day, 1966. A story that tells the plight of illegitimate children born of Korean mothers and American fathers and of their rejection by the Koreans.

World War II

Bosco, P. *World War II.* Facts on File, 1991. Focuses on Belleau Wood and Argonne, effect of the war on women and minorities. Maps and index included. Advanced grade 6 and up.

World War I

Bosco, P. *World War I.* Facts on File, 1991. Discusses military logistics, politics, and battlefields. Has personal narratives, quotes, battle descriptions, index, and maps. Advanced grade 6 and up.

America's Civil War

Lyon, G. E. *Cecil's Story.* Ill by P. Catalanotto. Orchard/Watts, 1991. Through the changing seasons, a child worries and waits at a neighbor's farm for his mother to return with his wounded father. He feeds the animals and helps plow the fields. His parents return and his father is still the same (even with one arm missing). Easy to read. Grade 4.

America's Revolutionary War

Turner, A. *Katie's Trunk.* Ill. by R. Himler. Macmillan, 1992. The colonists dumped tea into the Boston Harbor and Katie's family, loyal to England, are disliked by former friends and neighbors. Warned that the rebel colonists are coming, the family hides in the woods but Katie returns to defend the family's home. Hearing the rebels'voices, she hides in her mothers wedding trunk. Easy to read. Grade 4.

Early Rome and Wars

Coolidge, O. *Caesar's Gallic War.* Repr., 1961. Linnet, 1991. Gives background, character of Caesar, and description and action of the war. A fictional narrator tells the tale of warrior chieftains, soldiers, politicians, and the supreme commander, Caesar. Grade 6 and up.

continued

FIGURE 12–5   Continued

Early Vinland and Wars

Haugaard, E. C. *Hakon of Rogen's Saga*. Ill. by L. & D. Dillon. Boston: Houghton Mifflin, 1963. Hakon's island home, Rogen, is invaded when his widowed father kidnaps a rival chieftain's daughter for a bride. Treated as a slave, Hakon is at the mercy of an evil uncle who wishes to take Hakon's birthright. Fearing for his life, Hakon flees and hides in a cave in the mountains and considers what he feels about freedom as he tries to overcome his fears. Rark and others loyal to his father come to Hakon's aid and he regains his birthright and assumes the island again, proclaiming: "That is everyone's birthright, his freedom, and the gods have only one message for us, that we must live" (p. 132). Grade 6 and up.

---

line and read excerpts from books portraying the different period.

In groups, ask students of one group to meet with another group and discuss the reasons for war they would support and tell why they would do so. Ask those opposed to war to discuss their reasons and present them, too. Invite each group to meet with each of the other groups.

Effect of Events

"Problem-centered, also known as issue-centered, education has long been one of the most popular approaches to social studies education among the very best teachers," state Jarolimek and Parker (1993). "The central focus of a problem-centered unit is a real public problem. It should be a problem that has challenged people throughout history and in many cultures." If the problem-centered unit has a focus on the concept of war, elicit some examples from the students with such questions as:

1. Who is responsible for war?
2. How should society punish war-makers? In what ways do you think there are or are not better ways than "an eye for an eye?"
3. When is or isn't a society justified to use violence to achieve its objectives?

Events related to wars in history generally are identified by a single date, but, as has been mentioned, the events also have a *spread of effect* (Jarolimek, 1971) that extends before the event and after the event. It was mentioned previously that in order for students to understand the Gulf War, for instance, students can go back to the events that led

to the war before it, or the Korean incident, or the events before World War II. To have some grasp of World War II, students need to go back to the topic of World War I and understand the series of events that led to December 7, 1941 in WWII. Doing this, students will realize that history is a story of the activities of people and their relationships. Emphasize to students that the past relationship of people can help them understand the hopes and aspirations of people as well as their achievements and failures.

Activity #154: "Headlines"

Discuss the idea of a spread of effect of an event and invite students to research a spread of effect for any one of the events shown in a newspaper's headlines. Each event is identified by a single date but the event has a *spread of effect* that extends before the event and after the event. Engage the students in searching for data sources in children's books that relate to an event in the headline and write the title, author, publisher, publishing date, and an annotation of the data source on index cards or on data sheets.

For example, when some sixth-grade students saw a recent news headline proclaiming "U.N. Stops Equating Zionism to Racism" and read the main idea that land was being claimed by different people, they suggested stories they had read that featured the same idea—land had been claimed by different people. The teacher made a contribution, too, and briefly related the plot of a story set in Early Britain, Rosemary Sutcliff's *The Lantern Bearers* (Walck, 1959). In the story, the last of the Roman auxiliaries leave in their galley and abandon Britain to the internal strife and menace of invasion by Saxons. To record data about this book and any other books that the students wanted to suggest, they completed an index card for a card catalog file of books in the classroom and wrote some information for others to read. Engage student's in compiling index cards for a card catalog in the classroom.

Great Floods

"Ole Man River,/That ole Man River,/ He just keeps rolling,/He just keeps rolling along" are words from a familiar song to sing together. The words can initiate a discussion about the terrible effects of the flood on people whose homes and businesses were inundated in America's Great Flood of 1993. In a parallel situation reminiscent of the 1993 flood, some heavy rains fell rapidly in 1898 and a dam east of Johnstown, Pennsylvania, burst, causing a torrent of water to devastate the city in less than an hour. The flood left over 2,000 people dead and created extensive property damage. To focus student attention on Europe's great flooding of 1993, discuss the effects of the December rains in Germany, France, and the Netherlands, and on over 13,000 people who had to leave their homes and businesses during the Christmas season. To discuss current weather conditions, clip a weather map from a current newspaper and make a transparency so student's can explain the day's weather conditions and terms and to predict any rain in the near future in the students' area.

Activity #155: "Flood Areas"

To focus student attention on a historical flood in the 1800s, read aloud excerpts from *The Day It Rained Forever: A Story of the Johnstown Flood* (Viking, 1990, grades 4–6) by V. Gross, and tell the effect the flood had on people through the eyes of the members of one family. Further, ask students to compare the effects of the flood of 1889 with the Great Flood of 1993 that left over 40,000 people homeless, put more than 16,000 square miles of land under water, and cost over $10 billion in damages to business and homes. Record the students' comparisons on a class chart and discuss.

Invite the students to consider the problems encountered by people during a flood and list them on the board. Ask students to meet in small groups to think of what is needed to help return people to their lifestyles and to think of which agencies, resources, charities, and so on that might supply the help. To prepare for a report to the whole group, they can record their ideas on a data sheet.

As an optional activity, the student's can determine the extent to which their families live (or do not live) on a flood plain, and if appropriate, suggest

ways they can prepare for a possible flood in the future. Encourage them to list the things they should have ready for a possible evacuation from flood waters. Invite them to make an informational chart for the home that shows their list, and encourage them to display the list in a prominent place for family members to see in case of a future emergency.

Inventors Create Change

To connect the concepts of change and continuity to inventors from the past to the present, point out to students that a large newspaper in a western state recently challenged students (grades K–8) to find a problem reported in the paper, or from their own experience, and develop an invention to solve it (Bojorquez, 1993). The newspaper's goal was to help youngsters apply critical thinking and problem-solving skills. The students responded with inventions that were practical, useful, environmentally related, and, in a few cases, profitable. The students invented homework machines, automatic bedmakers, sock clips, kid detectors, entertainment centers, and robots of all kinds. Here are some of the winners:

> A winning invention was the Trash Smasher made of nylon. It had pouches on the front with Velcro enclosures where students placed their leftover paper, plastic, and aluminum products. Students can put their wrappers in the smasher and take them home and recycle them.
>
> Another invention was an automatic water faucet. The water turned on when something was placed underneath the sensor.
>
> Still another was the Block Organizer, a container that compartmentalized all the different sizes and shapes of Logo blocks.

Activity #156: "Inventors Create Change"

Ask the students to identify problems they have experienced and meet with partners to draw sketches of inventions that would solve the problem(s). They can describe the invention on the back of the sketch. In the whole group, ask students to show their sketches and tell others about their inventions. Invite their comments about the inventions with a student-suggested criteria or the following: (1) being durable, (2) being practical, and (3) being useful. Display the sketches and invite interested students to write a group letter or individual request to order an information booklet about applying for patents from the General Information Concerning Patents, #003004006595, Superintendent of

Documents, U.S. Government Printing Office, Washington, DC 20402 (cost $2.25).

History and Poetry

Selections of poetry provide materials to summarize the study of U.S. life during any time period and can be placed on charts to display in the classroom. Working in partnerships, the students can also search for and locate poems that reflect different times.

Activity #157: "Poetry about Time Periods"

For a reading activity, "An Hour's Worth of Poetry," select poems heard before from favorite sources and ask students to rehearse and review poems that portray different historical time periods. Ask students to move into small groups. Provide each group with a poetry anthology and ask them to find a poem representing a particular time period beginning with the 1400s and ending with the 1900s. Examples of poems for this activity are in Figure 12–6 and History Master 41.

After reading their poems in small groups, students can join the total group and report any facts about the times that they learned from the poems, record facts on the board in an informational fact web, copy the web into their history journals, and return to their small groups to suggest lines for a free-verse poem about this period in history. After copying their group poem into their notebooks, the students can select individual lines to illustrate with sketches.

History and Concepts Across Time

Elicit concepts (or themes) from students—such as the ideas of newcomers, rebellion, democracy, freedom, and so on—and invite them to find examples of the concept across different periods in U.S. history. Ask them to collect information from some of the stories they have read and record what they find about their theme (or concepts) on a data collection sheet.

Activity #158: "Getting Information about a Time Period"

Ask students in small groups to use their data sheets to tell other members what they found and then report their findings to the whole group. Emphasize what changes have been made over time to improve the situation and invite students to suggest further changes that seem to be needed.

FIGURE 12–6   *Poetry about Time Periods*

POETIC HISTORY IN A HOUR

The following poems are from *A Book of Americans* by the Benets and from *View from the Air: Charles Lindbergh's Earth and Sky* by Reeve Lindberg.

Group 1: Reading poems related to 1400s: "Christopher Columbus," "Hernando De Soto," and "Miles Standish"

Group 2: Reading poems related to 1500s: "Indian"

Group 3: Reading poems related to 1600s: "Pilgrims and Puritans," "Peter Stuyvesant," "Southern Ships and Settlers," and "Captain Kidd"

Group 4: Reading poems related to 1700s: "Cotton Mather," "French Pioneers," "Oliver De Lancey," "George Washington," "John Paul Jones," "Abigail Adams," "John Adams," "Benjamin Franklin," "Benedict Arnold," "Thomas Jefferson," "Alexander Hamilton," "Aaron Burr," "Lewis and Clark," and "Daniel Boone"

Group 5: Reading poems related to 1800s: "Johnny Appleseed," "Dolly Madison," "James Monroe," "John Quincy Adams," "Andrew Jackson," "Zachary Taylor," "John James Audubon," "Nancy Hanks," and "Sam Houston"

Group 6: Reading poems related to 1900s: Selected verses by Reeve Lindbergh in *View from the Air: Charles Lindbergh's Earth and Sky* (Viking, 1993, all ages)

Activity #159: "Decision Making Across History"

With middle school and junior high school students, you will recognize the need to help your students focus on personal decision making during their time with you. To initiate this, initiate a discussion of "Decision Making" across periods of history. Collect books with settings in this century as well as other time periods that are suitable for a range of reading abilities with a focus on decision making. You might select *Number the Stars* (WorldWar II period) by Lois Lowry and *Sarah, Plain and Tall* (pioneer period) by Patricia MacLachlan, and ask the students to read for evidence of decision making. Encourage the students to tell about other stories they have read with a similar theme and discuss the universality of decision making.

Introduce a decision-making process with your students and ask them to apply the model to a decision a character made in a book they have read in the classroom collection. For example, a decision-making model can include (1) identifying facts, (2) indentifying issues, (3) identifying alternate solutions and the consequences of it, and (4) proposing alternatives. Ask students which steps the book character followed and what happened. Follow up by presenting primary source documents from different time periods—such as Patrick Henry's "Give Me Liberty or Give Me Death" speech or President Lincoln's Gettysburg Address—your students can discuss different and difficult economic, political, and social decisions that have been made by historical figures.

Know the Story of Our Country: We Go On

"It should go without saying, of course, that no matter what aid the teacher uses in locating the trade books to enhance the social studies program, nothing will replace the teacher's knowledge of what is in the books offered to the students," maintains Dewey Woods Chambers (1971). "The teacher will be effective, indeed, when s/he speaks of the books s/he offers from firsthand experience. Getting that firsthand experience, by reading books, will be an adventure any teacher will long remember."

Indeed, it is hoped that this book will help you in gaining additional firsthand experience with children's books related to history that lead to historical activities in your classroom and that the experience will be a rewarding one for you and your students. James E. O'Neill (1993), historian, referred to a rewarding experience such as this during an Annual National Archives Lecture in Washington, DC, when he said, "The legendary trunk in the attic exists and I would like people to feel the depth and color and adventure and tragedy and the stirring story of our culture—we don't know anything until we feel it," O'Neill emphasized, "Know the story of your country: We go on." Engage students in drawing posters to promote knowing the story of America. Display in appropriate places at school.

REFERENCES

Adams, J. M. (1993). "Christians See Evil Spirit in San Jose's Aztec God Sculpture." *The Sacramento* Bee, Oct. 10, p. A2

Adamson, L. G. (1981). *A Content Analysis of Values in Rosemary Sutcliff's Historical Fiction for Children*. Unpublished Ph.D. dissertation, University of Maryland.

Ammon, R., & Weigard, D. (1993). "A Look at Other Trade Book Topics and Genres." In M. O. Tunnell & R. Ammon (Eds.), *The Story of Ourselves* (pp. 93–113). Portsmouth, NH: Heinemann.

Anderson, B. S., & Zinsser, J. P. (1988). *A History of Their Own: Vols. 1 and 2*. New York: Harper & Row.

Anderson, T. (1993). "Peace Is Possible." *Parade Magazine* (August 22): 6, 7.

Ark, C. E. (1984). "Building a Famous Personality File." *School Library Journal* (May): 44.

Ayala, A. (1989). *K.E.E.P.H.R.A.* Unpublished paper that explains features to study in concept of culture. Sacramento, CA: California State University, Sacramento.

Banks, J. A. (1972). "Developing Racial Tolerance with Literature on the Black Inner-City." In Dorothy J. Skeel (Ed.), *The Challenge of Teaching Social Studies in the Elementary School: Readings* (pp. 207–213). Santa Monica CA: Goodyear.

Barfield, K. (1993). "Go from Drab to Dramatic with Vinegar Painting." *The Sacramento Bee*, January 2, p. C4.

Benet, R., & Benet, S. V. (1961). *A Book of Americans*. New York: Holt.

Bergdorf, A. B. (1966). *A Study of the Ability to Draw Inferences from Selections of Children's Literature*. Unpublished Ph.D. dissertation, Ball State University.

Bettinger, M. M. (1993). "Pomona Teachers Promote Diversity." California Teacher Association.

Beutler, S. (1988). "Using Writing to Learn about Astronomy." *The Reading Teacher, 41*, 4 (January): 412–417.

Blackway, M. E. (1986). *An Analysis of the Content to Determine the Relevance of Selected Grimms' Fairy Tales as Possible Agents for Conflict Resolution in Children*. Unpublished Ed.D. dissertation, Temple University.

Blos, J. W. (1985). "The Overstuffed Sentence and Other Means for Assessing Historical Fiction for Children." *School Library Journal, 32*, 3 (November): 38–39.

Bohning, G., & Radencich, M. (1989). "Information Action Books: A Curriculum Resource for Science and Social Studies." *Journal of Reading 32* (February): 434–439.

Bojorquez, J. (1993). "The Creative Mind." *The Sacramento Bee*, May 24, pp. B6–8.

Bolton, G. (1985). "Changes in Thinking about Drama in Education." *Theory Into Practice, 24*, 151–157.

Bradley Commission, The. (1988). *Report on the Bradley Commission on History in Schools: Building a History Curriculum: Guidelines for Teaching History in Schools*. Educational Excellence Network, 1112 Sixteenth Street N.W., Suite 500. Washington, DC 20036.

Bromley, K. D. (1991). *Webbing with Literature*. Boston: Allyn and Bacon.

Brown, M. W. (Ed.). (1988). *Homes in the Wilderness: A Pilgrim's Journal for Plymouth Plantation in 1620 by William Bradford et al*. New Hamden, CT: Linnet.

Bruner, K. E. (1988). "Stereotypes in Juvenile Historical Fiction." *School Library Journal, 35*, 1 (September): 124–125.

Bugeja, M. J. (1993). "Listen to Your Elders." *Writer's Digest* (December).

Burke, E. M. (1990). *Literature for the Young Child*. Boston Allyn and Bacon.

Caldwell-Wood, N. (1992). "Native American Images in Children's Books." *School Library Journal* (May): 47–48.

Camarata, C. (1991). "Making Connections: Introducing Multicultural Books." *School Library Journal, 37*, 9 (September): 190–192.

Carr, J. (1981). "What Do We Do about Bad Biographies?" *School Library Journal* (May): 19–20.

Carter, H. (1993). "Questioning Value of Flood-Control System Is Sadly Misinformed." *The Sacramento Bee/* Opinion. July 19, p. B15.

Cecil, N. L., & Roberts, P. L.(1992). *Developing Resiliency through Children's Literature: A Guide for Teachers and Librarians, K–8*. Jefferson, NC: MacFarland.

Chamberland, F. (1991). "Connecting Threads: The Quilt Project." *School Library Journal, 37*, 5 (May): 51.

Chambers, D. (1972). *Children's Literature in the Curriculum*. Chicago: Rand McNally.

Chambers, D., & Lowry, H. (1975). *The Language Arts: A Pragmatic Approach*. Dubuque, IA: William C. Brown.

Cianciolo, P. J. (1989). "No Small Challenge: Literature for the Transitional Readers." *Language Arts, 66,* 1 (January): 72-81.

Coe, M., et al (11986). *Atlas of Ancient America*. New York: Facts on File.

Cohen, C. L. (1985). "The Quest in Children's Literature." *School Library Journal, 31,* 10 (August): 28-29.

Collier, C. (1982). "Criteria for Historical Fiction." *School Library Journal* (August): 32-33.

Columbus, C., & Major, R. H. (1961). *Four Voyages to the New World*. Corinth Books.

Commanger, H. S. (1965, June). "Why History." *American Education*. Washington, DC: Office of Education.

Coody, B. (1983). *Using Literature with Young Children, (3rd ed.)*. Dubuque, IA: William C. Brown.

Crystal, J. (1972). "Role-Playing in a Troubled Class." In Dorothy J. Skeel (Ed.), *The Challenge of Teaching Social Studies in the Elementary School: Readings* (pp. 195-206). Pacific Palisades, CA: Goodyear.

Cullinan, B., Karrer, M., & Pillar, A. (1981). *Literature and the Child*. New York: Harcourt Brace Jovanovich.

Cummings, M. (1987). "Literature Based Reading." *Focus: A Potpourri of Practical Ideas, 13,* 2 (Winter): 23-27.

Dalkey, V. (1992). "Artful Deceit: Paintings of the 'Wild West' Reveal a Fraudulent Vision." *The Sacramento Bee*, January 12, pp. 3-4.

Davis, J. R. (1989). "Genealogy: Making Us a Part of History." *Teaching K-8* (October): 60-61.

de Filippo, K. B. (1984). "Little Girls and Picture Books: Problem and Solution." *Jump Over the Moon* (pp. 261-266). New York: Holt, Rinehart and Winston.

de Gerez, T. (1981). *My Song Is a Piece of Jade*. Ill. by W. Stark. Organization Editorial Novaro, S. A.: Little, Brown.

De La Habra, L. (1976). "The Shelters and the City: Four Ancient Societies." In Charles E. Stuart (Ed.), *Clues to America's Past*. Washington, DC: National Geographic Special Publications Department.

De la Vega, G. (1961). *The Incas*. New York: Orion Press

Diaz, B. (1963). *The Conquest of New Spain*. New York: Penguin Books.

Dobbin, M. (1993). "Political Scientists Say Clinton Lacks Focus, Ducks Risks." *The Sacramento Bee,* September 4, p. A9.

Dobrez, C. K. (1987). "Sharing and Preserving Family Stories." *School Library Journal, 33,* 6 (February): 40.

Downey, M. T., & Levstik, L. S. (1988). "Teaching and Learning History: The Research Base." *Social Education* (September): 336-342.

Downs, A. (1993). "Breathing Life into the Past: The Creation of History Units Using Trade Books." In M. Tunnel & R. Ammon (Eds.), *The Story of Ourselves* (pp. 137-145). Portsmouth, NH: Heinemann.

Drury, M. (1993). "Why She Wrote America's Favorite Song." *Reader's Digest* (July) 90-93.

DuBois, E. C., & Ruiz, V. (1990). *Unequal Sisters: A Multicultural Reader in* U.S. *Women's History* New York: Routledge, Chapman and Hall.

Dvorchak, R. (1991). "To Some Indians, Columbus Day is a Time to Mourn." Associated, *The Sacramento Bee*, October 7, p. A4.

Eagle, D. H., Jr. (1986). *The Earth Is Our Mother: A Guide to the Indians of California, Their Locales and Historic Sites*. San Francisco: Trees Company Press.

Egan, K. (1993). "Accumulating History." *History and Theory: Studies in the Philosophy of History* (pp. 237-255). Middletown, CT: Wesleyan University Press.

Ekhaml, L. (1991). "Practically Speaking: Peer Review: Student Choices." *School Library Journal, 37,* 9 (September): 196.

Fiore, C. D. (1987). "Bridging the Gap: Books for Transitional Readers." *School Library Journal, 33,* 11 (August): 39-40.

Fisher, A. B. (1957). *Stories California Indians Told*. Emeryville, CA: Parnassus Press.

Fisher, L. E. (1993). "Historical Nonfiction for Young Readers: An Artist's Perspective." In M. Tunnel & R. Ammon (Eds.), *The Story of Ourselves* (pp. 19-26). Portsmouth, NH: Heinemann.

Fredericks, A. D. (1991). *Social Studies through Children's Literature: An Integrated Approach*. Englewood, CO: Teacher's Idea Press/ Libraries Unlimited, Inc.

Gallagher, A. F. (1993). "Readers' Theater and Children's Literature." *CBC Features: The Children's Book Council, 46,* 1 (Winter/ Spring): 6-7.

Gardner, H. (1982). *In Defense of the Imagination*. Cambridge, MA: Harvard University Press.

Gerhart, L. (1978). "Book Dedications." *School Library Journal, 25,* 4 (December): 26–27.

Giddings, P. (1984). *When and Where I Enter: The Impact of Black Women on Race and Sex in America*. New York: Bantam.

Glazer, J., & Williams, III, G. (1979). *Introduction to Children's Literature*. New York: McGraw-Hill.

Godfrey, T. E. (1980). *Literature in the Elementary School: A Developmental Approach*. Unpublished Ph.D. dissertation, University of Nebraska-Lincoln. UMI No. 8017624.

Goller, G. N. (1976). "Mystery Writing for the Middle Grades." *Elementary English, 52,* 2 (February): 192–193.

Gordon, A. (1987). "In Pursuit of Reference Skills." *School Library Journal, 33,* 7 (March): 119.

Gregory, H. (1979). "Sing Me a Story." *School Library Journal* (September): 44–45.

Guy, R. (1985). "Innocence, Betrayal, and History." *School Library Journal, 32,* 3 (November): 33–34.

Haine, G. (1985). "In the Labyrinth of the Image: An Archetypal Approach to Drama in Education." *Theory Into Practice, 24*: 187–192.

Haining, P. (1979). *Moveable Books: An Illustrated History*. London: New English Library.

Haugaard, E. C. (1979). "Before I Was Born, History and the Child." *The Horn Book Magazine* (December): 700.

Haupt, C. M. (1984). *The Image of the American Indian Female in the Biographical Literature and Social Studies Textbooks of the Elementary Schools*. Unpublished Ed.D. dissertation, Rutgers University, State University of New Jersey-New Brunswick.

Hedges, N. S. (1968). *The Fable and the Fabulous: The Use of Traditional Forms in Children's Literature*. Ann Arbor, MI: University Microfilms, No. 68–18020.

Heizer, R. F., & Whippie, M. A. (1967). *The California Indians: A Source Book*. Los Angeles: University of California Press.

Heplar S. (1990). "Fooling with Folktales: Updates, Spin-Offs, and Roundups." *School Library Journal, 36,* 3 (March): 153–154.

Hepler, S. (1979). "A Visit to the Seventeenth Century: History as Language Experience." *Language Arts, 56,* 2 (February): 126–131.

Hiatt, F. (1993). "Russia's Oldest Love Letter Steals Archaeologist's Heart." *The Sacramento Bee*, November 27, p. A2.

Holternman, J. (1970). "Seven Blackfeet Stories." *Indian Historian, 3:* 39–43.

Hopkins, N. (1992). "Whether Good or Bad, Columbus's Impact Can't Be Ignored." *CTA Action* (October): 16–19.

Howe, L., & Howe, M. M. (1975). *Personalizing Education*. New York: Hart.

Huck, C., Hickman, J., & Hepler, S. (1987). *Children's Literature in the Elementary School* (4th ed.). New York: Holt, Rinehart and Winston.

Hurst, C. O. (1992). "Bewitching Books." *Teaching K–8* (November/December): 96–97.

Hurst, C. O., & Otis, R. (1992). "Whole Language and History." *Teaching K–8* (August/September): 86–87.

Hyde, A. A., & Bizar, M. (1989). *Thinking in Context: Teaching Cognitive Processes across the Elementary School Curriculum* (pp. 173–174). New York: Longman.

Jakes, J. (1990). *California Gold*. New York: Random House.

Jarolimek, J., & Parker, W. (1993). *Social Studies in Elementary Education* (9th ed.). New York: Macmillan.

Jenkinson, E. (1987). "Female Feats in Patricia Beatty's Historical Fiction." *Educational Horizons, 65,* 4 (Summer): 157–159.

Johnson, D. (1982). *Stratemeyer Pseudonyms and Series Books: An Annotated Checklist of Stratemeyer and Stratemeyer Syndicate Publications*. Westport, CT: Greenwood Press.

Jones, J. (1993). "Perform Your Poetry." *Writer's Digest* (June): 66.

Joyce, B. R. (1972). "Social Action for the Primary Schools." In D. J. Skeel (Ed.), *The Challenge of Teaching Social Studies in the Elementary School: Readings* (pp. 134–138). Pacific Palisades, CA: Goodyear.

Kalisa, B. G. (1990). "Africa in Picture Books: Portrait or Preconception." *School Library Journal, 36,* 2 (February): 36–37.

Kay, A. (1993). "Splendors of a Lost Metropolis Rise Again." *The Sacramento Bee,* June 20, p. 10.

Keeler, B. (1993). "50 Years Later, Memory of Anti-Nazi Youth Group Lives On." *The Sacramento Bee/Newsday,* February, 23, p. A2.

Kellough, R., & Roberts, P. L. (1993). *A Guide to Elementary School Teaching: Planning for Competence* (3rd ed.). New York: Macmillan.

Kelly, R. G. (Ed.). (1984). *Children's Periodicals of the United States*. Westport, CT: Greenwood Press.

Kirberg, M. (1992). "Student Archaeologists." *Learning, 92* (October): 15.

Kobrin, B. (1988). "How to Judge a Book by Its Cover: And Nine Other Clues." *School Library Journal* (October): 42–43.

Kuipers, B. J. (1991). *American Indian Reference Books for Children and Young Adults.* Englewood, CO: Libraries Unlimited.

Lambert, M. (1991). "Social Studies Texts Stir Fierce Debate." *The Sacramento Bee,* June 15, pp.1, 24.

Laughlin, M. K., & Kardaleff, P. P. (1991). *Literature-Based Social Studies: Children's Books & Activities to Enrich the K–5 Curriculum.* Phoenix, AZ: Oryx Press.

LaValley, M. (1982). "Bridging the Gap: Books for the Middle Grade Reluctant Reader." *School Library Journal* (April): 29–31.

Lewis, C. S. (1980). "On Three Ways of Writing for Children." In S. Egot (Ed.), *Only Connect* (2nd Ed., pp. 207–220). New York: Oxford University Press.

Lickteig, M. J. (1975). *Introduction to Children's Literature.* Columbus, OH: Charles E. Merrill.

Lindelof, B. (1993). "Harrowing Tale of Survival." *The Sacramento Bee,* June 21, pp. B1, 3.

Lindelof, B. (1993). "Sikhs' Feast, Charity Mark Founder's Birth." *The Sacramento Bee,* December 6, p. B3.

Lowry, L. (1990). "Newbery Medal Acceptance." *The Horn Book Magazine* (July/August): 412–421.

MacDonell, L., & McNabb, L. (1993). "A Gift of Joy: CRA's Books for the Homeless Project." *The California Reader, 27,* 2 (Fall): 40.

McCarthy, L. (1993). "Historical Trails Wagon Train Moving Along to Independence." *The Sunday Oregonian,* October 3, p. D4.

McCunn, R. L. (1988). "Chinese Americans: A Personal View." *School Library Journal, 35,* 9 (June/July): 50–55.

McEwan, B. (1989). "A New Approach to Classroom Management." *Teaching K–8* (October): 62–63.

McFarlane, M. "On to Oregon." *Odyssey* (Summer): 37–39.

Macon, J. (1993). "The Rough-Faced Girl." *The California Reader, 27,* 2 (Fall): 33.

Macon, J. (1993). "Teach Story Structure with Shirts and Shawls." *The California Reader, 26,* 3 (Spring): 24–25.

Makino, Y. (Comp.). (1985). *Japan Through Children's Literature: An Annotated Bibliography.* Westport, CT: Greenwood Press.

Mandell, P. L. (1992). "Native Americans." *School Library Journal* (May): 63–69.

Maness, M. (1976). "War Is Glorious; War Is Hell; War Is Absurd." *Language Arts, 53,* 5 (May): 560–563.

Mann, M. (1993). "Pyramid Workers Liked Their Beer." *The Union/Associated Press,* May 31, pp. Al, 5.

Manning, P. (1989). "History Outside the 900s: A Non-Dewey Approach." *School Library Journal, 35,* 9 (May): 47–48.

Manning, P. (1992). "The World of 1492: In Company with Columbus." *School Library Journal, 38,* 2 (February): 26–30.

Marchart, N. C. (1979). "Doing Oral History in the Elementary Grades." *Social Education, 43* (October): 479–480.

Max, A. (1993). "Topping Earth's Highest Mountain." *The Sacramento Bee/Associated Press,* May 24, p. A4.

Maxwell, L. (1993). "The Significance of Letters in Young Adult Historical Fiction." *SIGNAL* (Journal of International Reading Association's Special Interest Group-A Network on Adolescent Literature), *27,* 3 (Spring/Summer): 17–19.

Miles, R. (1989). *Women's History of the World.* New York: Harper and Row.

Miller, S. (1993). "Writing to Authors." *School Library Journal, 39,* 6 (June): 8.

Millhofer, D. J. (1993). "The American Frontier—Tall Tales." *Voyages: Teaching History Through Literature, 3,* 2 (Spring): 3.

Misheff, S. (1991). "The Jewish Experience in America." *The Dragon Lode, 9,* 2 (Spring): 3.

Moir, H. (1978). "Profile: James and Christopher Collier: More Than Just a Good Read." *Language Arts, 55,* 3 (March): 373–378.

Moore, A. W. (1985). "A Question of Accuracy: Errors in Children's Biographies." *School Library Journal, 31,* 6 (February): 34–35.

Moore, K. (1992a). "The Book Bonanza." *Voyages: Teaching History Through Literature IRA SIG, 2,* 1 (Fall 1992): 2.

Moore, K. (1992b). "Teaching Idea: Primary: A Snapshot of Time." *Voyages: Teaching History through Literature IRA SIG, 2,* 2 (Spring): 5.

Moore, K. (1993a) "Joan Lowery Nixon: Journeys of the Past." *Voyages: Teaching History Through Literature IRA SIG, 3,* 2 (Spring): 5.

Moore, K. (1993b). "Literature Companions: History from Many Voices." *Voyages: Teaching History Through Literature, 4,* 1 (Fall 1993): 3.

Morgan, N., & Saxton, J. (1988). "Enriching Language through Drama." *Language Arts, 65,* 1 (January): 34–40.

Morrissey, J. (1991). "Pilgrim's Primer." *The Sacramento Bee,* November 28, p. 1.

Mueller, M. E. (1991). "History and History Makers: Give YAs the Whole Picture." *School Library Journal, 37,* 11 (November): 55–56.

Murray, M. (1993). "Little Green Lie." *Reader's Digest* (July): 100–104.

Naidoo, B. (1987). "The Story Behind *Journey to Jo'Burg.*" *School Library Journal, 33,* 8 (May): 43.

National Commission on Social Studies in the Schools. (1989). *Charting a Course: Social Studies for the* 21st Century. Washington, DC: NCSS.

National Commission on Social Studies in the Schools. (1992). *History Standards Task Force.* Washington, DC: NCSS.

Nelson, P. A. (1988). "Drama, Doorway to the Past." *Language Arts, 65,* 1 (January): 20–25.

Nessel, D. D. (1985). "Storytelling in the Reading Program." *The Reading Teacher, 38,* 4 (January): 378–381.

Nicholas, J. (1993). "The Final Miles West." *The Sacramento Bee,* January 3, 1993 pp. 1, 3.

O'Neill, J. E. (1993). "Know the Story of Your Country." Presentation at the Annual National Archives Lecture, Washington, DC July 5.

O'Steen, K. (1987). *Caldecotts: An Avenue to Critical Thinking and Creative Expression.* Huntington Beach, CA: O'Steen.

Painter, H. W. (1966). "Marcia Brown: A Study in Versatility." *Elementary English, 43:* 855.

Parikh, N., & Schneider, M. (1988). "Book Buddies: Bringing Stories to Hospitalized Children." *School Library Journal, 35,* 4 (December): 35–37.

Peters, D. (1992). *The Incas: A Magical Epic about a Lost World.* New York: Random House.

Peters, D. (1986). *The Luck of Huemac: A Novel about the Aztecs.* New York: Random House.

Piehl, K. (1987). "Babes in Toyland." *Children's Literature Association Quarterly, 12,* 2: 79–83.

Pillar, A. M. (1980). *Dimensions of the Development of Moral Judgment as Reflected in Children's Responses to Fables.* Unpublished Ph.D. dissertation, New York University.

Polese, C. (1991). "War Through Children's Eyes." *School Library Journal, 37,* 4 (April): 43–44.

Polkingham, A. (1983). "Brown Bag Book Exchange." *School Library Journal, 30,* 1 (September): 50.

Poma, H. (1978). *Letter to a King.* London: George Allen & Unwin.

Ponte, L. (1993). "The Trail That Won the West." *Reader's Digest* (August): 100–105.

Poole, G., & Poole, S. (1986). *Using Notable Children's Literature and Questioning Techniques to Enhance Comprehension.* Paper presented at the annual meeting of the Colorado Language Arts Society/National Council of Teachers of English Regional Conference, Colorado Springs, CO. ED 273 936.

Ramsay, D. (1992). "Putting History in Perspective." *Learning, 92* (October): 77–79.

Ravitch, D. (1985). "The Precarious State of History." *American Education, 9,* 4 (Spring): 11–17.

Reasoner, C. F. (1975). *When Children read.* New York: Dell/Yearling Books.

Reed, J. G. (1981). *Sixth Graders' Need for, Use, and Acquisition of Background Knowledge in Comprehending Fables.* Unpublished Ed.D. dissertation, Temple University.

Rinehart, J. (1980). "Heritage & Concept Boxes." *School Library Journal* (March): 108.

Roberts, P. L. (1976). *The Female Image in the Caldecott Medal Books.* Monograph N2 Laboratory of Educational Research, University of the Pacific, Stockton, CA. ERIC ED 181467.

Roberts, P. L. (1976). "Getting the Message Via Content Analysis." *Resources in Education,* October.

Roberts, P. L. (1976, November) *Have a Star-Spangled Bicentennial with Children's Literature.* Sacramento Public Library, Sacramento, CA.

Roberts, P. L. (1977, January). "Sugar and Spice and Almost Always Nice: A Study of the Caldecotts." *Resources in Education.* ED 127556.

Roberts, P. L. (1988). *Alphabet Books as a Key to Language Patterns.* Hamden, CT: Library Professional Publications.

Roberts, P. L. (1989). *Counting Books Are More Than Numbers.* Hamden, CT: Library Professional Publications.

Roberts, P. L. (1991). "Let's Take Off: Revisiting People and Places with Books about Flight." *The Dragon Lode, 9,* 2 (Spring): 1–2.

Roberts, P. L. (1992). *A Green Dinosaur Day: A Guide to Developing Thematic Units with Children's Literature, 1–6.* Boston: Allyn and Bacon.

Roberts, P. L. (1992). "History Through Story Songs in Picture Books." *Voyages: Teaching History Through Literature, 3,* 3 (Fall): 3.

Roberts, P. L., & Cecil, N. (1993). *Developing Multicultural Awareness Through Children's Liter-*

ature: *A Guide for Teachers and Librarians, Grades K–8*. Jefferson, NC: MacFarland.

Roberts, P. L., Cecil, N., & Alexander, S. (1993). *Gender Positive! A Teachers and Librarians' Guide, K–8*. Jefferson, NC: MacFarland.

Rossabi, M. (1988). *Khublai Khan: His Life and Times*. Berkeley/Los Angeles: University of California Press.

Rovenger, J. (1987). "Picture Books for Older Children." *School Library Journal, 33*, 8 (May): 38–39.

Rovenger, J. (1988). "Children's Literature as a Moral Compass." *School Library Journal, 34*, 11 (August): 45–51.

Rubin, N. (1991). *Isabella of Castile*. New York: St. Martin's Press.

Russell, D. (1991). *Literature for Children: A Short Introduction*. New York: Longman.

The Sacramento Bee. (1991a). "Noted Author-Called Ex-Klan Leader." Associated Press, October 5, p. Al4.

The Sacramento Bee. (1992a). "Opinion: Responding to Gang Violence." January 4, p. B6.

The Sacramento Bee. (1992b). "Origin of Humans a Group Project?" Associated Press, June 4, p. A23.

Sales, K. (1990). *The Conquest of Paradise: Christopher Columbus and the Columbian Legacy*. New York: A. A. Knopf.

San Jose, C. (1988). "Story Drama in the Content Areas." *Language Arts, 65*, 1 (January): 26–33.

Schiissel, L. (1989). *Women's Diaries of the Westward Journey: 1840–1870*. New York: Random House.

Schon, I. (1978). *A Bicultural Heritage: Themes for the Exploration of Mexican and Mexican-American Cultures in Books for Children and Adolescents*. Metuchen, NJ: Scarecrow.

Schon, I. (1990). "Recent Good and Bad Books about Hispanics." *The Reading Teacher, 34*, 1 (September): 76–77.

Searle, B. P. (1984). "Add Some Facts to Your Fiction." *School Library Journal* (August): 35.

Sebesta, S. L., & Iverson, W. J. (1975). *Literature for Thursday's Child*. Palo Alto, CA: Science Research Associates, Inc.

Seidenberg, R. N. (1985). *Strategies of Fourth-Grade Students in Recalling and Comprehending Fables*. Unpublished Ph.D. dissertation, University of South Florida.

Seif, E. (1977). *Teaching Significant Social Studies in the Elementary School*. Chicago: Rand McNally.

Sherman, L. (1986). "Have a Story Lunch." *School Library Journal, 33*, 2 (October): 120–121.

Shirts, R. G. (1972). "Simulations, Games, and Related Activities for Elementary Classrooms." In D. J. Skeel (Ed.), *The Challenge of Teaching Social Studies in the Elementary School: Readings*. Pacific Palisades, CA: Goodyear.

Slapin, B., & Seale, D. (1992). *Through Indian Eyes: The Native Experience in Books for Children*. Billings, MT: New Society Pub.

Smith, J. A. (1993). "Laurence Yep: Dragonwings in the Classroom." *Voyages: Teaching History Through Literature, 3*, 2 (Spring): 6.

Smith, J. A. (1992). "Literature Study Groups: Combining History and Literary Response." *Voyages: Teaching History through Literature SIG, 2* (Spring): 4–5.

Sorin, T. (1993). *"One More River." The Web, 26*, 3 (Spring/Summer): 13–14.

Soustelle, J. (1961). *The Daily Life of the Aztecs*. London: Weidenfeld & Nicholson.

Spender, D. (1988). *Women of Ideas and What Men Have Done to Them*. New York: Pandora Press.

Sperling, J. (1993). "Dear Brother." *The Web, 26*, 3 (Spring/Summer): 2–3.

Stark, L. S. (1986). "Understanding Learning Disabilities Through Fiction." *School Library Journal, 32*, 5 (January): 31.

Stewig, J. W. (1988). *Children and Literature*. Boston: Houghton Mifflin.

Stott, J. C. (1984). "Profile: Paul Goble." *Language Arts, 61*, 8 (December): 867–873.

Stotter, R. (1993). "Storytelling as a Cooperative Learning Experience." *The California Reader, 27*, 2 (Fall): 2–6.

Stuart, G. C. (1976). *Clues to America's Past*. Washington, DC: National Geographic, Special Publications Division.

Stuart, G. E.(1993). "New Light on the Olmec." *National Geographic* (November): 88–115.

Sutherland, Z., & Arbuthnot, M. H. (1986). *Children and Books* (7th ed.). Glenville, IL: Scott, Foresman.

Szulc, T. (1993). "The Greatest Danger We Face." *Parade* (July 25): 4–5.

Terry, W. (1992). "Kids Are Begging for Something Different." *Parade* (January 12): 16–17.

Thuente, M. H. (1985). "Beyond Historical Fiction: Speare's The Witch of Blackbird Pond." *English Journal, 74*, 5 (October): 50–55.

Tiedt, 1. M. (1979). *Exploring Books with Children*. Boston: Houghton Mifflin.

Touscany, M., & McDermott, T. C. (1993). "Geography Through Literature: Strategies for Successful Traveling." *The California Reader, 26* (Summer): 30–31.

Trease, G. (1972). "The Historical Novelist at Work." *Children's Literature in Education* (March): 12.

Tunnell, G., & Ammon, J. (Eds.). (1991). "Teaching the Holocaust through Trade Books." In *The Story of Ourselves* (pp. 115–134). Portsmouth, NH: Heinemann.

Van Kirk, E. (1993). "Imagining the Past Through Historical Novels." *School Library Journal, 39,* 8 (August): 50–51.

Vandergrift, K. E., & Hannigan, J. A. (l993). "Reading Images: Videos in the Library and Classroom." *School Library Journal 39,* 1 (January): 20–25.

Vugrenes, D. E. (1981). "North American Indian Myths and Legends for Classroom Use," *Journal of Reading, 24,* 6 (March): 494–496.

The Web (1993). "African Americans," *27,* 2 (Winter): 18–21. College of Education, The Ohio State University.

Whitehead, R. J. (1984). *A Guide to Selecting Books for Children.* Metuchen, NJ: Scarecrow Press.

Wilford, J. N. (1991). "What Doomed the Mayas." *The Sacramento Bee,* December 9, p. 1.

Wilson, P. J. (1985). *Children's Classics: A Reading Preference Study of Fifth and Sixth Graders.* Unpublished Ed.D. dissertation, University of Houston.

Wolfson, E. (1988). *From Abenaki to Zuni: A Dictionary of Native American Tribes.* New York: Walker.

Wooster, J. (1993). "Approaches for Using Children's Literature to Teach Social Studies." In M. O. Tunnel & R. Ammon (Eds.), *The Story of Ourselves* (pp. 105–113). Portsmouth, NH: Heinemann.

Zarnowski, M. (1990). *Learning about Biographies: A Reading and Writing Approach.* National Council for the Social Studies and National Council for Teachers of English, joint publication.

Zarnowski, M. (1988). "Learning about Fictionalized Biographies: A Reading and Writing Approach." *The Reading Teacher, 42,* 2 (November): 136–142.

Zvi Dor-Ner (1991). *Columbus and the Age of Discovery.* New York: William Morrow.

Zwick, L. Y. (1989). "Recordings in Spanish for Children." *School Library Journal, 35,* 6 (February 1989): 23–25.

RESOURCES

AIT/Agency for Instructional Television, Box A, Bloomington, IN 47402. *Landmarks of Westward Expansion: First Peoples* (AIT, 1987, grades 4–6) shows that Native People of the Pacific Northwest had different lifestyles after crossing the land bridge from Asia to North America but similar beliefs about the value and connectedness of living things.

Barr Films, 12801 Schabarum Ave., Box 7878, Irwindale, CA 91706. *Indians of the Southeast* (1991, grades 3–6) presents Cherokee activities, customs, and tribal organization. *Queen Victoria and the Indians* (1985, grades 3–6) is an account of Ojibwa Indians who danced at the opening of the Indian Gallery (London, 1840) and who had an audience with Queen Victoria. *Letter from an Apache* (Barr Films, 1985, grades 4–6) is an adaptation of a letter written by an Apache, Wassajah, who became American's first Native American physician. *My Country: A Navajo Boy's Story* (1989, grades 4–6) shows life on the Navajo Reservation.

Bullfrog Films, Oley, PA 19547. *Voices of the Land* (Bullfrog Films, 1991, advanced grades 6 and up) discusses why certain places are held sacred by Native People. *The Taos Pueblo* (1986, grades 2–6) portrays traditional activities at the 1,000-year-old pueblo in Taos, New Mexico.

Catalog of Western History, Jefferson National Expansion Historical Association 11, North Front St., Saint Louis, MO 63102. For free catalog copy, call 1-800-537-7962.

Chip Taylor Communications, 15 Spollett Dr., Derry, NH 03038. *Missions of California: Mission Santa Barbara*, 1989, video, grades 4–8. Founded by the Franciscans in 1786, Mission Santa Barbara has a history that includes its reconstruction in 1815 and its display of Native American crafts.

Creative Teaching Press, P.O. Box 6017, Cypress, CA 90630–0017. Offers bulletin board borders with shapes titled "Red, White and Blue," "Covered Wagons," "Patriotic," "Native American," "Stars and Stripes," and "Let's Celebrate." Has blank "Write Your Own Headlines" strips to personalize history topics for the bulletin boards. Has social studies charts showing "Ancient Civilizations," "Native Americans," "Explorers," "Colonial America," "Westward Movement," "Black Americans," "Celebrating Diversity," and "Democracy." Write to request a current catalog. All grades.

Direct Cinema Ltd., Box 69799, Los Angeles, CA 90069. *Contrary Warriors: A Film of the Crow Tribe* (1986, advanced grade 6 and up) presents tribal history.

EBEC/Encyclopedia Britannica Educational Corp., 31 0 S. Michigan Ave., Chicago, IL 60604. (Ute Pass Historical Society, Ohio/EBEC, *Bear Dance* 1988.) Portrays the experience of one Indian boy at a cultural practice of the Ute Indians of Colorado, the Bear Dance. Grades 4–6.

Encounter Video, 2580 N.W.Upshur, Portland, OR 97210. *Kids Explore Alaska* (1990, grades 3–5) shows pen pal correspondence, a way for children to learn about the culture and history of Alaska, the Gold Rush Days, and the life of Native People.

Explorers, 3225 West 17th Ave., Eugene, OR 97402. Simulation game.

Films for the Humanities, *Ramona: A Story of Passion and Protest*, 1988 video cassette, adult Ramona, based on a novel by Helen Hunt Jackson, is now a legend based on an event for California. Gives social background about the cause of the indigenous natives that this novel championed.

Films for the Humanities & Sciences, Box 2053, Princeton NJ 08543. *American's Indian Heritage: Rediscovering Columbus* (1991, advanced grade 6 and up) reviews history of ancient Native People who lived in the area of Columbus, Ohio.

Finley-Holiday Film Corp., Box 619, Whittier, CA 90601. *Monument Valley: Navajo Homeland* (1991, grades 3–6) shows tribal lands, customs, and crafts. *Ancient Indian Cultures of Northern Arizona* (1985, grades 3–6) portrays ancient civilizations the Sinugua and Anasazi developed and shows national monuments of Montezuma Castle, Wupatki, Tuzigoot, Walnut Canyon, and Sunset Crater. *Mesa Verde* (Finley-Holiday Film Corp., 1989, 3–6) portrays ancient and early history of Mesa Verde, Colorado, and its cliff dwellings, ancient pottery, and exhibits of other artifacts.

Hearth Song, P.O. Box B, Sebastopol, CA 95473–0601. Senet is an ancient game modeled after ancient Egyptian games found in archeological ruins.

Magazine Market Place, Inc., Peoria, IL 61644. Inquire about complimentary and reduced fee copies of magazines for a class display related to historical subjects and time periods: *Archae-*

ology, Wild Bird, and *Natural History* (all time periods); *Quilting* (1600s–1700s) *Civil War* (1860s); *Wild West* (1800s); *The Information Please Almanac, American Artist,* and *The Artist's Digest* (1990s).

Montana Council for Indian Education, 3311 1/2 4th Avenue North, Billings, MT 59101. Has extensive list of books about Native People, which includes Kathleen Meyer's *Tul-tok-A-Na*, the legend of El Capitan; Olga Cossi's *Fire Mate,* the struggle of a modern California Indian girl; and Allan Shields's *The Tragedy of Tenaya,* a true account of Tenaya, the leader of the Indians in Yosemite Valley.

New Day Films, 121 W. 27th St., New York, NY 10001. *Of Land and Life: People of the Klamath,* (1988, advanced grade 6 and up) presents Karuk Indians vs. the U.S. Forest Service over the protection of ceremonial lands. *Ghost Dance* (1991, advanced grade 6 and up) commemorates the 1890 Wounded Knee Massacre with work of Lakota artists. *Preserving a Way of Life: People of the Klamath* (1989, advanced grade 6 and up) shows how tribal culture is passed from the elderly to the young. *The Right to be Mohawk* (1990, advanced grade 6 and up) presents conversations with contemporary Mohawk leaders about building their nation.

New Dimension Media, 85803 Lorane Highway, Eugene, OR 97405. *The Drum* (1987, grade 4 and up) portrays the importance for cultural/ethnic groups to affirm their heritages.

PBS Video, 1320 Braddock Place, Alexandria, VA 22314. *Moyers/Oren Lyons the Faithkeeper* (1991, advanced grade 6 and up) offers stories of the Onondaga.

Questar Video, Box 11345, Chicago, IL 60611. *I Will Fight No More* (1990, advanced grade 6 and up) shows the leadership of Chief Joseph during the fighting retreat of the Nez Perce covering 1,700 miles in over three months.

Readings for the Christopher Columbus Quincentenary, Kindergarten Through Grade Twelve: An Annotated List. Sacramento, California Department of Education, 1992.

Swan Books P. O. Box 2498, Fair Oaks, CA 95628. Offers Shakespeare for Young People series that includes A *Midsummer Night's Dream, Romeo and Juliet,* and others along with stage directions and production notes. Grades 5–8.

Troll Associates, 100 Corporate Dr., Mahwah, NJ 07430. *Great Native American Heroes* series. Grades 4–6.

Wings for Learning/Sunburst, 1600 Green Hills Rd., Box 660002, Scotts Valley, CA 95067. *Solve It! American History Mysteries, 1492–1865,* Apple II computer software, grade 4 and up. Mysteries and problems in scenes based on historical events.

Wireless Productions, Minnesota Public Radio, P.O. Box 64422, St. Paul, MN 551640422. "The Story of Flight Wall Chart," videos of Laurel and Hardy films, tapes of radio shows such as "The Whistler," "Suspense," "The Shadow," and "Fibber McGee and Molly."

Yellow Moon Press, Box 1316, Cambridge, MA 02238. Has Iktomi tales and other Native American stories on an audio cassette, *Wopila: A Giveaway, Lakota Stories.* Grade 3 and up.

Information Web

Make a transparency and use the overhead projector to project on the chalkboard.

_____   _____   _____

_____   _____

_____

_____   _____

_____   _____   _____

Traditional Folktales

Research statement to prove or disprove: Six groups of folktales come from all countries and their people: cumulative tales, talking animal tales, noodle tales, "Why" tales, realistic fanciful, and fairy tales.

Group 1: Cumulative Tales

Group Statement: In cumulative tales from different cultures, there is increasing repetition of details building up to a quick ending or climax.

Asian American: *African American:*

Hispanic American: *Original Native American:*

European American: *Other:*

Group 2: Talking Animal Tales

Group Statement: In talking animal tales from different cultures, animals act and talk like human beings.

Asian American: *African American:*

Hispanic American: *Original Native American:*

European American: *Other:*

Group 3: "Why" Tales

Group Statement: "Why" tales come from different culture groups and explain natural situations such as why the sea has salt.

Asian American: *African American:*

Hispanic American: *Original Native American:*

European American: *Other:*

Group 4: Noodlehead Stories

Group Statement: Noodlehead stories from different cultural groups follow the pattern of a foolish character following the right advice at the wrong time.

Asian American:

African American:

Hispanic American:

Original Native American:

European American:

Other:

Group 5: Realistic Fanciful Fiction

Group Statement: With realistic settings, tales of magic are found in various culture groups.

Asian American:

African American:

Hispanic American:

Original Native American:

European American:

Other:

Group 6: Fairy Tales

Group Statement: With various settings, fairy tales are found in various culture groups.

Asian American:

African American:

Hispanic American:

Original Native American:

European American:

Other:

Folk Literature from Different Cultures

African Heritage

Grafalconi, A. *The Village of Round and Square Houses*. Little, Brown, 1986. Origin of the custom of men living in square houses and women and children in round houses. Grade 4 and up.

Asian Heritage

Heyer, M. *The Weaving of a Dream: A Chinese Folktale*. Viking, 1986. Fairies steal a poor widow's brocade woven with her dreams, and her three sons attempt to recover it. Grades 4–5.

Roland, D. *More of Grandfather's Stories from Cambodia*. Open My World Pub., 1984. Tales from Vietnam, the Philippines, and other cultures. Grade 6 and up.

European Heritage

Asbjornsen, C., and Moe, J., collectors. *East o' the Sun and West o' the Moon*. Dover, 1970 reprint. "The Three Billy Goats Gruff" and other stories gathered in the early 1840s. Grade 4 and up.

Bierhorst, J., trans. *The Glass Slipper: Charles Perralt's Tales of Times Past*. Four Winds, 1981. Includes "Red Riding Hood," "Puss in Boots," and others. Grade 4 and up.

Gag, W., reteller. *Tales from Grimm*. Coward, 1981. Collection of read-aloud tales. Grade 4.

Grimm Brothers. *The Juniper Tree and Other Tales from* Grimm. Farrar, Straus, 1973. Ill. by M. Sandak. Reminds readers that adults were the first audience for the stories. Grade 5 and up.

Mayer, M., ill. *Favorite Tales from Grimm*. Four Winds, 1982. Includes stories such as "Cinderella," "Rapunzel," and others. Grades 4–5.

Rockwell, A. *The Three Sillies and Ten Other Stories to Read Aloud*. Harper, 1986. Noodlehead stories. Grade 4 and up.

Singer, I. B. "The Devil's Trick." In *Zlateh the Goat and Other Stories*. Harper & Row, 1966. On the first night of Hannukah, David looks for his lost parents and the devil whips up a storm. Grade 5 and up.

Latino/Hispanic Heritage

Alexander, E. *Llama and the Great Flood: A Folktale of Peru*. Crowell, 1989. Tale from the Andes about a llama who leads people to safety. Grade 4.

Belpre, Pura. *The Dance of the Animals: A Puerto Rican Folk Tale*. Warne, 1972.

Hueur, M. *El Zapato y el Pez*. Mexico City: Trillas, 1983. A Spanish language version of the shoe and the fish. Grade 4.

Pitre, F. *Juan Bobo and the Pig*. Lodestar, 1993. Similar to a fable with a moral, this tale is about Juan's silly behavior and what happens when he dresses up the family pig and takes him to church. Grade 4.

Roland, D. *More of Grandfather's Stories from the Philippines*. San Diego: Open My World Pub., 1985. Folk tales from different ethnic groups. Grade 4.

Original Native American Heritage

Bierhorst, J. *The Naked Bear: Folktales of the Iroquois.* Ill. by D. Zimmer. Morrow, 1987. Explains ways the tales were collected and offers traditional characters. Grade 4 and up.

Other Heritage

Walker, B. reteller. A *Treasury of Turkish Folktales.* Linnet Books, 1988. Tales from Europe for story-telling. Grades 4–6.

Others Selected by Students:

Multicultural Legends and Myths

African Heritage

Maddern, E. *The Fire Children: A West African Creation Tale.* Ill. by F. Lessac. Dial, 1993. Released by the sky god, Nyame, with a sneeze, Aso Yaa and Kwakuy Ananse, two spirit people, went to Earth, where they made clay figures of themselves. When Nyame came to check on them, they hid the figures from him by putting them in the fire, where they turned dark brown. When Nyame breathed life into the figures, they were all the colors of the people of the world. Grade 4.

Asian Heritage

McAlpine, H. *Japanese Tales and Legends.* Oxford, 1989. Collection of standard tales. Grade 6 and up.

Saunders, T. *Dragons, Gods and Spirits from Chinese Mythology.* Schocken, 1983. Collection of myths from traditional versions. Grade 6 and up.

Vuong, L. D. *Six Legends of Vietnam.* Ill. by Vo-Dinh Mai. HarperCollins, 1993. Six legends about events in the sky and sky fairies who confront humans. Author's notes tell of the legends' origins and explain the folklore of Vietnam. Pronunciation guide of Vietnamese names is included. Grades 4–7.

European Heritage

Bullfinch, T. *Myths of Greece and Rome.* Penguin, 1982. Retellings of familiar stories. Grades 4–6.

Colum, P. *The Children of Odin: The Book of Northern Myths.* Macmillan, 1984. Over 20 tales of northern Europe. Grades 4–6.

Harris, G. *Gods and Heroes from Viking Mythology.* Schocken, 1982. Origin stories about Odin, Thor, Balder, and others. Grade 6 and up.

Hawthorne, N. *Tanglewood Tales.* Ohio State University Press, 1981. Author's adaptations of ancient myths. Grade 6 and up.

Low, A. *The Macmillan Book of Greek Gods and Heroes.* Macmillan, 1985. Over 30 myths of struggles of gods and humans. Grade 6 and up.

Price, M. E. *A Child's Books of Myths and Enchantment Tales.* Checkerboard, 1989. Familiar myths of Greece. Grade 6 and up.

Latino/Hispanic Heritage

Alexander, E. *Llama and the Great Flood: A Folktale of Peru.* Crowell, 1989. Tale from the Andes about a llama who leads the people to safety. Grades 4–5.

Beals, C. *Stories Told by the Aztecs: Before the Spaniards Came.* Abelard, 1970. Myths about the Plumed Serpent, Toltec leaders, and the Aztec war god, Mexitli. Grade 4 and up.

Bierhorst, J. *Black Rainbow: Legends of the Incas and Myths of Ancient Peru.* Farrar, Strauss & Giroux, 1976. Traditional tales. Grades 4–6.

Bierhorst, J. *The Hungry Woman: Myths and Legends of the Aztecs.* Morrow, 1984. Origin of legends and myths of times before the Aztecs. Grade 6 and up.

Bierhorst, J. *The Mythology of South America.* Morrow, 1988. Useful reference containing South American tales. Grade 6 and up.

Mediterranean Heritage

Al-Saleh, K. *Fables Cities, Princess and Jinn from Arabic Myths and Legends*. Schocken, 1985. Tales for storytelling from Arabian and Persian cultures. Grade 4 and up.

Original Native American Heritage

Baylor, B. *And It Is Still That Way: Legends Told by Arizona Indian Children*. Scribner's, 1976. Collection of authentic retellings. Grades 4–6.

Erdoes, R. & A. Ortiz. *American Indian Myths and Legends*. Scribner's, 1976. Collection of myths from various tribes. Grades 4–6.

Van Laan, N. *Buffalo Dance: A Blackfoot Legend*. Little, Brown, 1993. A story of the interdependence of humans and animals. Grade 4.

Others Selected by Students:

Multicultural
"How and Why" Tales

HOW ANIMALS GOT THEIR CHARACTERISTICS

Africa

Aardema, Verna. *Why Mosquitoes Buzz in People's Ears.* Dial, 1975. Accumulating African folktale. Grades 4–6.

Bryan A. "How the Animals Got Their Tails" in *Beat the Story Drum, Pum-Pum.* Atheneum, 1980. The creator Raluvhimba realizes his mistake in creating skin-biting flies and gives animals their tails so they can swish the pests away. Grades 4–5.

Knutson, B. *Why the Crab Has No Head.* Carolrhoda, 1987. A Zaire tale about how the Creator was offended by Crab's pride and why the embarrassed Crab now walks sideways. Grades 4–5.

Asia

Hong, L. T., reteller. *How the Ox Star Fell From Heaven.* Albert Whitman, 1991. The ox, in disfavor, is sent to earth to be a beast of burden. All grades.

Australia

Maralngura, N., et al. *Tales from the Spirit Time.* Indiana University Press, 1976. A revised edition of several "Why" tales about animals collected from Aborigine student teachers. Grades 4–5.

Brazil

Flor, A. A. *Feathers Like a Rainbow: An Amazon Indian Tale,* Harper, 1989. This is a tale from the Yanomami people, an ancient society (15,000 B.C.) of the Stone Age, who lived in Brazil's Amazon jungle. Set in the Amazon rain forest, the tale explains how birds got their colors. Grade 4 and up.

Mexico

Kurtycz, M., & Kobeh, A. G. *Tigers and Opossums.* Little, Brown, 1984. Tales from Mexico that explain ways animals received their characteristics and includes why the hummingbird is brightly dressed, how the opossum got his tail, and the way the tiger got his stripes. Grade 4 and up.

North America

Baylor, B. *Moonsong.* Ill. R. Himler. Scribner's, 1982. Tale from the Pima Indians of how Coyote was born of the moon. All grades.

Conolly, J. E. *Why the Possum's Tail Is Bare and other North American Indian Nature Tales.* Stemmer House, 1985. Presents more than 10 tales with morals related to ancient tribal laws from different tribes. Grades 4–6.

Goble, P. *The Gift of the Sacred Dog.* Bradbury, 1980. Explains how the horse was given to the Sioux People. Grades 4–6.

Goble, P. *The Lost Children.* Ill. by author. Bradbury, 1993. A Blackfoot tale about six orphaned brothers scorned by others who go to the Above World to become the Pleiades. Grades 4–5.

Taylor, H. P. *Coyote Places the Star*. Ill. by author. Bradbury, 1993. This is a Wasco Native American legend about how Coyote moved the stars around and formed the shapes of his animal friends. We see them today as the designs of the constellations. Grade 4.

Toye, W. *The Loon's Necklace*. Ill. E. Cleaver. Oxford University Press, 1977. Tells how the loon received his markings because of his kindness to an elderly blind man. Grade 4 and up.

WHAT CAUSED NATURAL EVENTS

Africa

Elkin, B. *Why the Sun Was Late*. Parents, 1966. African myth about the self-delusion of a fly who thinks his small weight upsets the ecology of the forest and when the sun fails to rise, the birds appeal to the Great spirit. Grades 4–5.

Hawaii

Hill, W. M. *Tales of Maui*. Dodd, Mead, 1964. Nature tales. Grades 4–5.

North America

Baylor, B. *A God on Every Mountain Top: Stories of Southwest Indian Mountains*. Scribner's, 1981. Tales about the sacred mountains from the southwest Indian people. Grades 4–5.

Bierhorst, J. *The Woman Who Fell from the Sky: The Iroquois Story of Creation*. Morrow, 1993. This is a Native American story of Sky Woman who created the earth, stars, and sun while her twin sons made the animal and plant life and created snow, monsters, and river water. Grades 4–8.

Dixon, A. *How Raven Brought Light to People*. Ill. by J. Watts. McElderry, 1992. Trickster Raven tricks a powerful Tinglit Indian leader and releases the sun, moon, and stars. Escaping through a smoke-hole in the lodge, Raven was covered with soot and has remained black forever. Grades K–4.

Mayo, G. W. *Earthmaker's Tales: North American Indian Stories about Earth Happenings*. Walker, 1989. Stories about the natural events such as daylight, earthquakes, and thunder are explained. Grade 4 and up.

Mayo, G. W. *More Earthmaker's Tales: North American Indian Stories about Earth Happenings*. Walker, 1989. Stories about the natural events such as eclipse, fog, and volcanoes are explained. Grade 4 and up.

HOW THE SEASONS BEGAN

Greece

Hodges, M. *Persephone and the Springtime*. Little, Brown, 1973. Greek story explaining the change of seasons. Grade 5 and up.

Italy

McDermott, G. *Daughter of Earth: A Roman Myth*. Delacorte, 1984. The illustrations for this Demeter-Persephone story resemble the ancient art work of Romans. Grade 5 and up.

continued

North America

Leland, C. G. "How Glooskap Found the Summer." *The Algonquin Legends of New England*. Houghton Mifflin, 1984. Glooskap saves his people from Winter and persuades Summer to stay for part of the year. Grade 4 and up.

WHAT CAUSED THE SKIES

Africa

Dayrell, E. *Why the Sun and the Moon Live in the Sky*. Ill. by B. Lent. Houghton Mifflin, 1968. A nature myth about Water visiting the house of the Sun and the Moon. Grades 4–5.

Asia

Lin, A. *The Milky Way and other Chinese Folk Tales*. Harcourt Brace Jovanovich, 1961. These are "Why" tales about the patterns of stars and other origin stories. Grades 4–6.

Greece

Green, R. L. *A Book of Myths*. Ill. by J. Kiddell-Monroe. Dutton, 1965. Stories of how a sunflower turns into the sun and the beginnings of the constellations of Bellerophon, Pegasus, and Pleiadades. Grade 5 and up.

North America

Bruchac, J. *The First Strawberries: A Cherokee Story*. Dial, 1993. A woman who was scolded by her husband leaves in anger. When her husband is saddened, the sun helps him by causing strawberries to grow in the woman's path to slow her down so the husband can catch up and apologize. Grades 4–6.

Goble, P. *The Lost Children*. Ill. by author. Bradbury, 1993. This is a sacred Blackfoot myth that tells the origin of the Pleiades and gives contemporary meaning through a final illustration showing modern cars and telephone poles. All grades.

Mayo, G. W. *Star Tales*. Walker, 1989. Stories about the stars are explained. Includes background information on the sources and a glossary. Grade 5 and up.

Monroe, J. G., & Williamson, R. A. *They Dance in the Sky: Native American Star Myths*. Houghton Mifflin, 1987. Tales from different Native people. Grade 5 and up.

Oughton, J. *How the Stars Fell from the Sky: A Navajo Legend*. Houghton Mifflin, 1992. Coyote, helping First Woman place the stars into the pattern of laws for the people, grows impatient and just tosses the remaining stars into the sky, which rearranges the pattern. Grade 5 and up.

Shetterly, S. H. *Raven's Light: A Myth from the People of the Northwest*. Atheneum, 1992. Traditional stories of the tribes as used as the basis of this creation myth. Grades 4–5.

Others Selected by Students:

Heroes and Heroines

	Country	Hero and Heroine
Partnership #1	**Area now North America**	**Nanabush (Ojiobway)**

Coatsworth, E., & Coatsworth, D. *The Adventures of Nanabush: Ojibway Indian Stories*. Atheneum, 1980. Elders of Ojibway people tell tales of the hero Nanabush. Grades 4–8.

Partnership #2	**China**	**Monkey, trickster-hero**

Yep, L. *Dragon Cauldron*. HarperCollins, 1991. Thorn, a human boy, sacrifices himself to reforge the dragon cauldron and becomes its soul and a source of enormous power. Grade 6 and up.

Yep, L. *Dragon of the Lost Sea*. HarperCollins, 1992. Thorn, a human boy, becomes the constant compaions of Shimmer, the dragon princess and her friends. Grade 6 and up.

Yep, L. *Dragon War*. HarperCollins, 1992. Shimmer and her friends join her kin as they fight for their lives against the Boneless King, Butcher, who has declared war on dragonkind. Monkey, the trickster-hero of Chinese legend, is the narrator who tells of the battles, escapes and shape changes. Grade 6 and up.

Partnership #3	**Greece**	**Odysseus**

Sutcliff, R. *Black Ships Before Troy: The Story of the Iliad*. Ill. by A. Lee Delacorte, 1992. This is the story of the Trojan War that ended with Helen's safe return to Menelaus. Grade 4 and up.

Partnership #4	**Greece**	**Heroes and Gods**

D'Aulaire, I., & D'Aulaire, E. P. *D'Aulaires Book of Greek Myths*. Doubleday, 1980. Myths about Greek major goddesses and gods beginning with Gaea, Mother Earth, the Titans, and Zeus and his family, to the minor gods (Eros and others) and the mortal descendants of Zeus—Hercules, Theseus, etc. Grade 5 and up.

Fisher, L. E. *Theseus and the Minotaur*. Holiday, 1988. The tale of the strong hero of Athens, Theseus, who, with his bare hands, slew the monster who devoured humans. Grades 4–6.

Hutton, W. *Theseus and the Minotaur*. Macmillan, 1989. Theseus, mortal descendant of Zeus, takes the place of a victim sent to the minotaur. Grades 4–6.

Richardson, I. M. *Demeter and Persephone, The Seasons of Time*. Troll, 1983. Greek myth explains the reason for the seasons. Grades 4–6.

Richardson, I. M. *Prometheus and the Story of Fire*. Troll, 1982. Myth explains how Prometheus, a minor Greek god, gave mortals an ember from the sacred hearth on Olympus and received the punishment of being chained to the top of the Caucasus Mountains. Mortals were punished by Pandora and her jar of miseries—greed, vanity, slander, envy, and other evils. Grades 4–6.

Yolen, J. *Wings*. Ill. Dennis Nolan. Harcourt Brace Jovanovich, 1991. Recounts Daedalus's exile from Greece and his imprisonment by Minos for treason. To escape, Daedalus and his son, Icarus, make large wings of feathers and wax. A Greek chorus in the text is represented by a commentary in italics. Grades 4–5.

Partnership #5	**Peru**	**Acuri**

Dewey, A. *The Thunder God's Son: A Peruvian Folktale*. Ill. author. Greenwillow, 1981. The son of the thunder god is sent down to earth to learn about the people and their ways. Grades 4–6.

Partnership #6	**Japan**	**Yuriwaka**

Haugaard, E., & Haugaard, M., retellers. *The Story of Yuriwaka: A Japanese Odyssey*. Translated from Japanese by retellers. Ill. Birgitta Saflund. Roberts Rhinehart, 1991. Jesuits took Homer's tales to Japan in the 16th century and the storytellers retold them with Yuriwaka as the hero Odyssesus. Grades 4–5.

continued

Partnership #7   Italy   **Hercules and Other Heroes and Heroines**

Richardson, I. M. *The Adventures of Hercules.* Troll, 1983. A hero (Greek name is Heracles) and mortal descendant of Zeus performs 10 tasks. Grades 4–6.

Partnership #8   **England**   **Beowulf**

Crossley-Holland, K. *Beowulf.* III. Charles Keeping. Oxford, 1982. Struggles against evil monster, Grendel, and the dragon, Firedrake. Grades 5–6.

Partnership #9   **Babylon**   **Gilgamesh**

Zeman, L. *Gilgamesh the King.* Tundra, 1993. Portrays the rivalry between Enkidu, a man from the wilderness, and Gilgamesh, their combat, and finally, their friendship. Grades 4–6.

Partnership #10   **Mali in Africa**   **Sundiata, Hero-King**

Bertol, R. *Sundiata. The Epic of the Lion King.* 1970. The king-hero who established the early empire of Mali in Africa. Grades 4–6.

Partnership #11   **Switzerland**   **William Tell**

Bawden, N. *William Tell.* III. Lothrop, Lee & Shepard, 1981. The Swiss patriot Tell inspires his people to fight for freedom in 14th century. Grade 4 and up.

Early, M. *William Tell.* III. Abrams, 1991. Events include more than the shooting of the apple and describes Tell's fight for freedom and conflict with Gessler who wants to imprison him. Grade 4 and up.

Partnership #12   **England**   **Saint George**

Hodges, M. *Saint George and the Dragon.* III. Trina Schart Hyman. Little Brown, 1984. A legend from Edmund Spenser's *The Faerie Queene.* Grade 4 and up.

Partnership #13   **England**   **Robin Hood**

Hastings, S. *Sir Gawain y la abominable dama. Sir Gawain and the Loathly Lady.* Translated from English by Clara Ardenay. III. by Juan Wijingaard. Madrid: Altea, 1991. Illustrated with paintings with details about clothing of the time period. Grade 4 and up.

Hodges, M. *The Kitchen Knight.* Holiday House, 1990. A retelling of a tale of King Arthur and his knights. Grade 4 and up.

McKinley, R. *The Outlaws of Sherwood.* Greenwillow, 1988. Introduces Alan-a-Dale and other outlaws. Grade 4 and up.

Partnership #14   **England**   **King Arthur**

Hastings, S. *Sir Gawain and the Loathly Lady.* Lothrop, Lee & Shepard, 1981. This Arthurian legend is about Sir Gawain, who offers himself in marriage to the Loathy Lady. Grade 5 and up.

O'Neal, M. *King Arthur.* Greenhaven Press, 1992. Discusses the reality of King Arthur being a factual figure. Grades 5–6.

Riordan, J. *Tales of King Arthur.* III. Victor G. Ambrus. Rand McNally, 1982. A retelling of classic tale of Arthur. Grade 5 and up.

Sutcliff, R. *The Sword and the Circle: King Arthur and the Knights of the Round Table.* Dutton, 1981. Thirteen Arthurian legends beginning before Arthur becomes king. Grade 6 and up.

Sutcliff, R. *The Light Beyond the Forest.* Dutton, 1981. A quest for the Holy Grail by Lancelot, Galahad, Percival, and other knights. Grade 6 and up.

Conflicts Faced by Early People in Folktales

CONFLICT AND BOOK

Autonomy

The Jade Stone (Holiday, 1992) by C. Yacowitz tells of a humble stone carver who keeps his autonomy by carving only what he hears—three carp—in the piece of jade given him by the Great Emperor of All China who really wanted a "dragon of wind and fire." Grades 4–6.

Two of Everything (Albert Whitman, 1993) by L. Toy Hong is a Chinese folktale about Mr. Haktak who finds the magic secret of an unearthed brass pot—it duplicates everything placed inside—hairpins, purses, gold coins. All goes well until Mrs. Haktak falls headfirst into the pot and loses her autonomy in the household. Grade 4.

Nine-In-One, Grr! Grr! (Children's Book Press, 1993) by Blia Xiong is the story of Shao, the great god, who promises Tiger nine cubs in a year. Bird keeps her autonomy with a trick that prevents the earth from being inhabited by too many tigers in this Hmong tale from Laos. Grades 4–8.

Maturity

The Girl Who Loved Caterpillars (Philomel, 1992) by J. Merrill is a Japanese story that originated in the twelfth century. The pretty daughter of an inspector in the Emperor's court studies the nature of things and loves caterpillars. When a young nobleman is attracted to her, he immaturely concludes he is not "good enough" for her. The author explains the abrupt story ending and says that the rest of the story has been lost. Grades 4–8.

Screen of Frogs (Orchard, 1993) by S. Hamanaka is the story of Koji, a wastrel, who inherits his family's wealth and immaturely spends it on a life of luxury. When he decides to sell a lake and mountain, he is visited in a dream by a frog who begs Koji not to sell its home. Koji repents and becomes a fine farmer of the land. Grades 4–6.

Rivalry

Salt (Hyperion, 1992) by J. Langtron is a Russian tale of a fool who discovers salt, becomes rich, and triumphs over his jealous brothers. Grade 4.

The Twenty-Five Mixtec Cats (Tambourine, 1993) by M. Gollub is a tale about a butcher who is placed under an evil spell by a rival, an evil healer, but is saved by many loyal and useful cats so peace can return to the Mexican village. Grades 4–6.

Self-Esteem

The Fourth Question (Holiday House, 1991), retold by R. C. Wang, tells of Yee-Lee who asks the questions of three strangers rather than his own when he meets a wise man. However, Yee-Lee finds happiness in helping others. Grades 4–6.

Separation, Loss

Love Flute (Bradbury, 1992) by P. Goble is the story of a boy's love for a girl, but the boy is unable to speak of his love and leaves the people's camp. When he receives a flute from the Elk Men that makes the sounds of the birds and animals, he is able to tell the maiden of his love for her through music. Grades 4–6.

Motifs in Folk Literature from Different Cultures

The letters in the word *motifs* can identify examples of motifs (patterns as the smallest parts of a folktale that can exist meaningfully and independently) that are found in tales.

Example: *M* stands for magical places or magical (enchanted) states of being

China

The Rainbow People (Harper & Row, 1989, grades 5–6) by L. Yep (magical mountain)

Germany

Snow White and the Seven Dwarfs: A Tale from the Brothers Grimm (Farrar, Straus & Giroux, 1972) by Randall Jarrell (enchanted sleep)

Example: *O* stands for objects of power or magic

Arabia

Aladdin and the Wonderful Lamp (Viking, 1981, grades 4–5) by A. Lang (geni in lamp grants wishes)
Chen Ping and His Magic Axe (Dodd, Mead, 1987, grade 4) by Demi (magic axe)

Germany

The Twelve Dancing Princesses (Morrow, 1989, grades 4–6) by Grimm Brothers and retold by M. Mayers (garment causes invisibility)

Japan

Kenji and the Magic Geese (Simon & Schuster, 1992, grades 4–5) by R. Johnson (picture of five flying geese)

Example: *T* stands for transformations

China

Legend of the Milky Way (Holt, 1982, grades 4–6) by J. Lee (earthly husband and heavely wife changed to stars)

France

Beauty and the Beast (Clarion, 1989, grades 4–6) by J. Brett (prince to beast)

Italy

The Crab Prince (Holt, 1991, grades 4–6) by C. Manson (portrays power of Rosella's love to turn an enchanted giant crab into his former self, Prince Florian)

America

The Girl Who Loved Wild Horses (Bradbury, 1978, grades 4–6) by P. Goble (girl, transformed, goes to live with them)

Buffalo Woman (Macmillan, 1974, grades 4–6) by P. Goble (hunter marries female buffalo in form of beautiful woman)

Russia

The Frog Princess (Crowell, 1984, grades 4–6) by E. Isele (Vasilisa the Wise is in an enchanted form)

Example: *T* also stands for tricksters

America

Wiley and the Hairy Man (Macmillan, 1976, grade 4 and up) by M. Bang (Wiley and his mother play tricks on the Hairy Man who lives in the swamp)

France

Balarin's Goat (Crown, 1972, grades 4–6) by H. Berson (a wife tricks her husband and gets more attention)

Example: *I* stands for identities (creatures with super characteristics)

Arabia

Juma and the Magic Jinn (Lothrop, Lee & Shepard, 1986, grades 4–6) by J. Anderson (jinn)

Africa

Nomi and the Magic Fish (Doubleday, 1972, grades 4–5) by P. Mbane (fish)

India

Once a Mouse (Scribners, 1961, all grades) by M. Brown (mouse transformed into cat, dog, and tiger)

Mexico

The Flame of the Aztecs (Harper & Row, 1987, grades 4–6) by D. N. Lattimore (nine demons)

Peru

The Thunder God's Son: A Peruvivian Folktale (Greenwillow, 1981, grades 4–6) by A. Dewey (son of the thunder god is sent down to earth)

Russia

The Devils who Learned to Be Good (Little, Brown, 1987, grades 4–5) by M. McCurdy (band of devils in Tsar's palace)

continued

Example: *F* stands for a force (power, wishes)

India

Rum Pum Pum: A Folk Tale from India (Macmillan, 1978, grades 4–6) by M. Duff (talents of animals help Blackbird)

North America

The Rough-Faced Girl (Putnam, 1992, grade 6 and up) by R. Martin (sees the Invisible Being)

Poland

The Woodcutter's Duck (Macmillan, 1973, grades 4–6) retold by K. Turska (overcomes obstacles)

Russia

The Fool of the World and the Flying Ship (Farrar, 1968, grades 4–6) by A. Ransome (overcomes obstacles)

The Little Hump-Backed Horse (Farrar, Straus & Giroux, 1980, grades 4–5) retold by M. Hodges (a horse has power to fly)

The Moon-Brothers: A Slavic Tale (Morrow, 1983) by T. P. Whitney (brothers have powers over the seasons)

Example: *S* stands for symbols as a pattern

Africa

The Third Gift (Little, Brown, 1974, grades 4–6) by J. Carew (gifts of beauty, work, and imagination)

Germany

The Seven Ravens (Morrow, 1981, grade 4) by Grimm Brothers, translated by E. Crawford (birds)

Japan

The Five Sparrows: A Japanese Folktale (Atheneum, 1982, grades 4–5) by P. M. Newton (birds)

Russia

Ana and the Seven Swans (Morrow, 1984, grade 4) by M. Silverman (birds)

Others Selected by Students:

Intergenerational Relationships

Ackerman, K. *Song and Dance Man*. Knopf, 1988. The grandchildren persuade Grandpa to go to the attic, get out his tap-dancing shoes, his top-hat and cane, and give them his old-fashioned vaudeville song and dance routine. Grades 4–6.

Brooks, B. *Everywhere*. Harper & Row, 1990. News that his grandfather has suffered a heart attack is bad news for a 10-year-old boy but Grandfather recovers. Grades 4–6.

Conrad, P. *My Daniel*. Harper & Row, 1989. Eighty-year-old Julia Creath Summerwaite shares memories of her brothers work with her grandchildren when she flies to New York to visit them. Grades 4–6.

Fox, P. *Western Wind*. Orchard, 1993. When her new baby brother arrives and 11-year-old Elizabeth Benedict is sent to spend a month with her eccentric artistic grandmother, she is angry at her parents. She matures, however, and grows in wisdom about her relationships with others. Grades 5–8.

Gleeson, L. *Eleanor, Elizabeth*. Holiday, 1990. Eleanor finds the diary, written in 1895 by her grandmother, Elizabeth, that tells how Elizabeth came to understand and love the bush country in Western Australia. Grades 4–6.

Hamilton, V. *Junius Over Far*. Harper & Row, 1985. Fourteen-year-old Junius goes looking for his grandfather on an island in the Carribean. Grades 4–6.

Hoyt-Goldsmith, D. *Totem Pole*. Holiday House, 1990. In the Pacific Northwest, a Native American woodcarver and his son carve a 40-foot totem pole, a tradition to record memories of their tribe. Grades 4–6.

Johnson, A. *Toning the Sweep*. Orchard, 1993. When Grandmother leaves her desert home, Emily, an African American teenager, uses a video and records her grandmother's friends and documents her home for future memories. In doing so, she learns more about her heritage. Grades 6–8.

Martin, B., & Archambault, J. *Knots on a Counting Rope*. Holt, Rinehart and Winston, 1987. Boy-Strength-of-Blue Horses, a blind boy, asks his grandfather to tell him again the story of the night he was born. The boy teaches his horse to run the trails and to race. Grades 4–6.

Morrow, L. K. *Dancing on the Table*. Holiday House, 1990. Jenny doesn't want her grandmother to get married and move but copes with the fact that their life together has changed. Grades 4–6.

Others Selected by Students:

Historical Time Travelers

Pre–19,000 B.C.: Stone Age Nomads

Bosse, Malcom. *Cave Beyond Time*. Crowell, 1980. In America's southwest, a contemporary teenager, Ben finds himself in another time period three different times. Grades 5–8.

19,000 B.C.: Ancient Egypt

Stolz, M. *Cat in the Mirror*. Dell, 1978. A girl living in ancient Egypt becomes aware of another girl's existence in New York City 3,000 years later. Grade 6 and up.

500: A Bard in Early Wales

Bond, N. *A String in the Harp*. Atheneum, 1976. An American boy, 12-year-old Peter, finds a harp key of Taliesin that pulls him back to the 500s. Grades 6–8.

1100: People in Early France

Velde, V. V. *A Well-Timed Enchantment*. Crown, 1990. Deanna and Oliver, a cat, are pulled into an old well and go back in time to learn of the problems of living in Medieval France. Grade 7 and up.

1200: King Arthur's Court

Clemens, Samuel [Twain, Mark]. *A Connecticut Yankee in King Arthur's Court*. Dodd, Mead, 1960. A modern character is transferred into the past. Grade 6 and up.

1400: Time of Richard the Third in England

Rabinowitz, A. *Knight on Horseback*. Macmillan, 1987. Touring England, Eddy Newby finds a small carving of a knight on horseback that begins his adventures with the ghost of Richard the Third (1452–1485). Grades 4–6.

1600: America's Seventeenth Century

Boston, L. *The Children of Green Knowe*. Harcourt Brace Jovanovich, 1989. A small boy, nicknamed Tolly, begins to see his ancestors. Additional books in this series (all Harcourt Brace Jovanovich) where the descendants meet their ancestors are *The Treasure at Green Knowe* (1958), *The River at Green Knowe* (1959), *A Stranger at Green Knowe* (1961), and *An Enemy at Green Knowe* (1964). Grade 7 and up.

Norton, A. *Lavender Green Magic*. Ill. by J. Gwyn. Crowell, 1974. Three African American children travel back in time to colonial days to discover that good is stronger than evil. Grade 6 and up.

1600: England's Seventeenth Century

Bellairs, J. *The Venegence on the Witch-Finder*. Dial, 1993. Jonathan Barnavelt and his newphew, Lewis, release Malachiah Pruitt's evil ghost. Grades 4–7.

1700 America's Revolutionary War

McKean, T. *The Secret of the Willows*. Simon & Schuster, 1991. This is a one-sided time travel story that presents the idea that the Whigs' point of view was "good" and the Torys' view was "bad." Grade 5 and up.

Wooddruff, E. *George Washington's Socks*. Scholastic, 1992. Three children travel back in time to 1776 and see the good and bad sides of the war. Grade 5 and up.

1800: America's Nineteenth Century

Ringgold, F. *Aunt Harriet's Underground Railroad in the Sky*. Crown, 1992. Cassie and Be Be Lightfoot take a fanciful flight with Aunt Harriet on the railroad in the sky that retraces her route to freedom every 100 years. Grade 4.

1800:

Conrad, P. *Stonewords*. HarperCollins, 1990. In the present, Zoe discovers she can travel back and forth in time through a back staircase. Grade 7 and up.

Estem, A. G. *Letters from Philippa*. Bantam, 1991. In present-day Connecticut, Sarah believes that Aunt Philippa is trying to communicate with the present to clear her name. Grade 7 and up.

Griffin, P. R. *Switching Well*. McElderry, 1993. In 1991, Amber and Ada, in 1890, become time-traveling newcomers to new and unfamiliar societies. Grades 5–8.

Hurmence, B. *A Girl Called Boy*. Houghton Mifflin, 1992. A modern girl travels back in time to 1853 and lives through the ghastly experience of being a slave. Grade 6 and up.

Lunn, J. *The Root Cellar*. Scribner, 1983. In 1861, Rose discovers an old root cellar that takes her back to the world of over 100 years ago where she meets new friends—Susan and Will. Grades 4–6.

Williams, R. L. *The Silver Tree*. HarperCollins, 1992. In the present, Micki discovers she can travel back in time to 1891 through a dollhouse and she meets a new friend, Sarah. Grade 5 and up.

Wiseman, D. *Thimbles*. Houghton Mifflin, 1982. A young girl travels back in time with two thimbles she finds in her grandmothers trunk and uses one of the thimbles to finish a cap of liberty for a protest march demanding the right to vote. Grade 4 and up.

1800: England's Nineteenth Century

Walsh, J. P. *A Chance Child*. Avon, 1980. A contemporary boy, Creep, follows a water canal back to the days of England's Industrial Revolution. Grade 7 and up.

Wise, D. *Jeremy Visick*. Houghton Mifflin, 1981. Twelve-year-old Matthew goes back in time to find an escape route from the mine. Grade 6 and up.

1873: Australia's Past

Park, R. *Playing Beatie Bow*. Atheneum, 1982. Abigail follows a little girl, Beatie Bow, back to the year 1873 and returns a more tolerant and mature person. Grade 6 and up.

continued

1938: Europe's Holocaust in World War II

Yolen, J. *The Devil's Arithmetic.* Viking/Kestrel, 1988. Hannah, becomes the villager, Chaya, whose name means "Life." Through Chaya's life, she experiences the Holocaust at a concentration camp. Grade 7 and up.

Others Selected by Students:

Ancient Egypt

Architecture

Croshier, J. *Ancient Egypt*. Viking, 1993. Acetate overlays show exterior and interior views of an Egyptian temple, tomb, palace, and home. Grades 5–8.

Macaulay, D. *Pyramid*. Houghton Mifflin, 1975. Includes the step-by-step process of building an Egyptian pyramid and includes detailed drawings of workers and their tools. Grade 4 and up.

Unstead, R. J. *See Inside an Egyptian Town*. Warwick, 1978. Shows buildings in an Egyptian town around 1375. B.C. Grade 6 and up.

Game of Senet

Senet (Hearth Song, 1992). This is a game modeled after ancient Egyptian games found in archeological ruins.

Gods in Ancient Egyptian Myths

Ions, V. *Egyptian Mythology*. Bedrick, 1983. A collection of Egyptian myths. Grade 6 and up.

McDermott, G. *The Voyage of Osiris: A Myth of Ancient Egypt*. Windmill, 1977. A retelling of a myth that is over 5,000 years old. Grade 5 and up.

Government

Hart, G. *Exploring the Past: Ancient Egypt*. Harcourt Brace Jovanovich, 1989. Describes aspects of public life. Grade 6 and up.

Jewelry

Nesbit, E. *The Story of the Amulet*. Dell, 1987. A combination of historical fiction and fantasy as a magical amulet takes several youngsters back in time to ancient Egypt. Grade 5 and up.

Mummies

Lauber, P. *Tales Mummies Tell*. Harper, 1985. Includes information about ways the study of mummies can reveal information about an ancient civilization. Grade 5 and up.

Putnam, J. *Mummy*. Ill. by P. Hayman. Knopf, 1993. Discusses Egyptian burial customs as well as other preserved people such as the lava-covered citizens of Pompeii and other people preserved by bog, ice, and sand. Includes diagrams, photographs, and index. Grades 4–8.

Reeves, N. *Into the Mummy's Tomb*. Scholastic, 1992. Portrays expeditions of Lord Carnarvon and Howard Carter in the 1920s. Grades 4–7.

Netherworld of Egypt

Lattimore, Deborah Nourse. *The Winged Cat: A Tale of Ancient Egypt*. Harper & Row, 1990. In a story of honesty and deception, Merit and her cat are betrayed by an unscrupulous high priest. Includes translations of heiroglyphics so readers can decode messages. Grades 2–6.

continued

Pharaohs

Carter, D. *His Majesty, Queen Hatshepsut*. Lippincott, 1987. Portrays life of Hatshepsut, a queen in ancient Egypt. Grade 5 and up.

Harris, G. *Gods and Pharaohs from Egyptian Mythology*. Shocken Press, 1983. Discusses aspects of culture, government, and religion of Egypt. Grade 6 and up.

Reeves, N. *Into the Mummy's Tomb: The Real-Life Discovery of Tutankhamun's Treasures*. Scholastic, 1992. Reviews mysteries about Tut's reign and his untimely death. Grades 4–6.

Rosetta Stone

Giblin, J. C. *The Riddle of the Rosetta Stone: Key to Ancient Egypt*. Crowell, 1991. Recounts the discovery and deciphering of the stone and ways it increased our knowlege of Egyptian civilization. Grades 4–6.

Scientific Achievements

Woods, G. *Science in Ancient Egypt*. Watts, 1988. Discusses achievements of people of ancient Egypt. Grade 5 and up.

Stone Carver

Stolz, M. *Zekmet, the Stone Carver: A Tale of Ancient Egypt*. Ill. by D. N. Lattimore. Harcourt Brace Jovanovich, 1988. Egyptian King Kharfe orders a monument and the Vizier, Ho-tep, meets with Zekmet, a skilled stone carver, whose ideas result in the Great Sphinx. Grades 4–6.

Writing

Hackwell, W. J. *Signs, Letters, Words: Archaeology Discovers Writing*. Scribner, 1987. Portrays the development of writing as a natural outgrowth of change in the societies of early humans. Grade 6 and up.

Other Selected by Students:

Journey-and-Return Stories

My notes for a "Journey-and-Return" pattern in a story:

1. Name of story:

2. Author:

3. Publisher:

4. Date:

5. The character(s) are:

6. The heroines/heroes (helpers as parents, animals, supernaturals) are:

7. The hinderers (opponents such as nature, spirits, and monsters) are:

continued

8. My story web is:

What character found   How character changed   What character learned

The Main Character

How character proved   The character's return   How character defeated
herself/himself   an adversary

9. Other comments I want to make:

Problems of Characters, Then and Now

Choices for Inquiry and Projects

1. Select two books where the character journeys and returns on a quest of some kind. The character will go on a journey to find something (or to change something, learn something, prove herself or himself, or defeat an adversary) and then return.

2. Select a story with a setting in a time period of history and another with a setting in modern times.

3. For each story, write down the thoughts you want to discuss after reading about the quest of a character. In a quest, which is a journey-and-return story, a character will struggle with a needed understanding in order to deal with a problem. As the character struggles with the problem, the character gains an inner strength and the needed understanding. This understanding brings a sense of peace (or truth) that ends the quest.

4. Use the chart to help you record your thoughts about what you read. Plan to discuss your written notes with others in a group.

Problems of Characters	*Then*	*Now*
With Family		
Problem:		
Struggle:		
Realization:		
Resolution:		
With Peers		
Problem:		
Struggle:		
Realization:		
Resolution:		
With Communities		
Problem:		
Struggle:		
Realization:		
Resolution:		

Stories about
Health Care

Ancient Pompeii

Yarbro, C. Q. *Locadio's Apprentice*. Harper, 1984. In the last days of Pompeii, physician Locadio Priscus accepts a young boy, Enecus Cano, as his apprentice. Fiction. Grade 6 and up.

Barrett, N. *Timelines/Medicine: Doctors, Demons & Drugs*. Franklin Watts, 1992. Overview with glossary and index. Nonfiction. Grades 5–8.

Ancient Rome

Sabuda, R. *Saint Valentine*. Atheneum, 1993. In ancient Rome, Valentine is a physician who heals with herbs and powders. Biography. Grades 4–6.

Seventeenth-Century England

Burton, H. *Beyond the Weir Bridge*. Ill. V. A. Ambrus. Crowell, 1970. Richard and Richenda, whose father had been killed in 1644 in Cromwell's service, join the Quakers. Richard becomes a doctor and returns to plague-ridden London. Fiction. Grade 6 and up.

Yount, L. *William Harvey: Discoverer of How Blood Circulates*. Enslow, 1994. Depicts the events in Harvey's (1578–1657) life story related to the early theories of blood circulation. Includes quotes, medical diagram, and portrait reproductions. Biography. Grades 4–8.

Seventeenth-Century America

Schaeffer, E. *Dandelion, Pokeweed. and Goosefoot: How the Early Settlers Used Plants for Food, Medicine and in the Home*. Addison-Wesley, 1972. Discusses ways settlers use plants for nutrition, cures, and cleaning products. Nonfiction. Grade 4 and up.

Smith, C. *The Arts and Sciences: A Sourcebook on Colonial America*. Millbrook, 1991. Facts about medicine and science in the colonies. Nonfiction. Grade 6 and up.

Terkel, S. N. *Colonial American Medicine*. Franklin Watts, 1993. Gives overview with research tools that include illustrations, maps, sources, bibliograpy, glossary, and index. Nonfiction. Grade 5 and up.

Eighteenth-Century America

Fleischman, P. *Path of the Pale Horse*. Harper & Row, 1983. In 1793, a young apprentice doctor, Lep, helps take care of the sick during a Yellow Fever epidemic in Philadelphia that killed 10 percent of the people. Fiction. Advanced grade 6 and up.

Nineteenth-Century America

Bredeson, C. A. *Jonas Salk: Discoverer of the Polio Vaccine*. Enslow, 1993. Emphasizes Salk's discovery of the polio vaccine as well as his research since 1950. Grades 5–9.

Brown, M. M. *Susette La Flesche: Advocate for Native Ameican Rights*. Children's, 1992. Portrays the life of the first Native American woman physician (1854–1917). Biography. Grades 4–6.

Clapp, P. *Dr. Elizabeth: The Story of the First Woman Doctor*. Lothrop, 1974. Life of the first female physician (1821–1910). Biography. Grades 5–7.

Crofford, E. *Frontier Surgeons: A Story about the Mayo Brothers*. Ill. by Karen Ritz. Carolrhoda, 1989. Good introduction with anecdotes about the Mayo brothers. Dual biography. Grades 4–5.

Drotar, D. L. *The Fire Curse and Other True Medical Mysteries*. Walker, 1994. Documented medical mysteries are explored and theories are presented to explain each happening. Grades 4–5.

Ferris, J. *Native American Doctor: The Story of Susan LaFlesche Picotte*. Carolrhoda, 1991. Primary sources of letters, family papers, photographs from government archives, and interviews with descendants are included. Biography. Grades 6–8.

Lee, B. *Charles Eastman: The Story of an American Indian*. Dillon, 1979. Portrays Eastman's poverty and ability to overcome prejudice to become a physician. Biography. Grades 4–6.

Sherrow, V. *Jonas Salk*. Facts on File, 1993. Reviews life and career of Salk and discusses his development of the polio vaccine. Biography. Grades 6–8.

Twentieth-Century Australia

Crofford, E. *Healing Warrior: A Story about Sister Elizabeth Kenny*. Ill. by S. Michaels. Carolrhoda, 1989. Portrays adventures in the Australian outback with Kenny and reviews her medical sucesses. Biography. Grades 3–5.

Twentieth-Century England

Kaye, J. *The Life of Alexander Fleming*. 21st Century Books, 1993. Describes Fleming's life (1881–1955) and years as a student in St. Mary's Hospital Medical School in London and as a bacteriologist at the University of London. Biography. Grades 5–7.

Values of People in Early India and Other Cultures in Different Time Periods

Research Group #1: Here are books about the trait of *unselfishness* valued by many cultures in different time periods.

African Heritage: Aardema, V. *Bringing the Rain to Kapiti Plain: A Nandi Tale.* Ill. by B. Vidal. Dial, 1981. Cumulative tale from Kenya portrays a man's unselfishness and his contribution to his people. Folk literature. Grades 4–6.

Asian Heritage: Ishii, M. *The Tongue-Cut Sparrow.* Trans. Katherine Paterson. Ill. by S. Akaba. Dutton, 1987. Different rewards are given to a selfish greedy wife and a kind husband. Folk literature. Grades 4–5.

European Heritage: Schlee, A. *Ask No Questions.* Holt, Rinehart and Winston, 1982. In London in the 1800s, Laura, a young girl, feeds hungry children. Fiction. Grade 6 and up.

Latino/Hispanic Heritage O'Dell, Scott. *The King's Fifth.* Houghton Mifflin, 1966. A young unselfish man travels with Coronado's army as the soldiers search for gold. Fiction. Grade 6 and up.

Research Group #2: Here are books about the trait of *compassion* valued by many cultures in different time periods.

African Heritage: Hamilton. V. The *Magical Adventures of Pretty Pearl.* Harper & Row, 1983. An unearthly being, a goddess-child, transforms into a human and helps poor black people. Fiction. Grade 6 and up.

Asian Heritage: Fleischman, P. *Path of the Pale Horse.* Harper & Row, 1983. In Philadelphia in the late 1700s, a doctor and a 14-year-old treat Yellow Fever. Fiction. Grade 6 and up.

European Heritage: Lowry, L. *Number the Stars.* Houghton Mifflin, 1989. The Danes try to save the Jewish people in Copenhagen in 1943. Fictionalized biography. Grade 6 and up.

Latino/Hispanic Heritage: Aiken, J. *Bridle the Wind.* Delacorte, 1985. In the 1820s, a young boy rescues another from hanging and they escape to Spain. Fiction. Grade 6 and up.

Original Native American Heritage: Speare, E. G. *The Sign of the Beaver.* Houghton Mifflin, 1983. An Indian friend teaches survival skills to a young boy living in a frontier cabin. Fiction. Grade 6 and up.

Research Group 3: Here are books about the trait of *nonviolence* valued by many cultures in different time periods.

Asian Heritage: Hodges, M., reteller. *The Golden Deer.* Ill. by D. San Souci. Scribner's, 1992. This story is from the *Jataka Tales* and reflects its Buddhist origins as the King of Benares grows weary of his daily hunting, recognizes the beauty of the golden deer (the transformed Buddha), and realizes he should protect all living creatures of the land, air, and sea. Folk literature. Grade 5 and up.

European Heritage: McCurdy, M. *The Devils Who Learned to Be Good.* Little, Brown, 1987. An old soldier promises the Tsar that he will spend one night in the palace and rid it of devils with his magical deck of cards. Folk literature. Grades 4–5.

Davis, M. G. *The Truce of the Wolf: A Legend of St. Francis of Assisi.* In *Anthology of Children's Literature* by Edna Johnson et al. Houghton Mifflin, 1979. Assisi makes peace between a hungry wolf and fearful villagers. Folk literature. All grades.

Latino/Hispanic Heritage: Bierhorst, J. *Spirit Child: A Story of the Nativity.* Morrow, 1984. An Aztec story with pre-Columbian illustrations. Grade 4 and up.

Original Native American Heritage: Jassem, K. *Sacajawea, Wilderness Guide.* Troll Assoc., 1979. Portrays life of the Shoshone woman who guided the Lewis and Clark Expedition. Biography. Grade 6 and up.

Others Selected by Students:

Life in the First Century

Early America

El Hombre Prehistorico. Mexico: Los Grandes Libros, 1985. The Spanish text portrays life of humans in early times. Grade 6 and up.

Early Britain and Scotland

Sutcliff, R. *Song for a Dark Queen*. Crowell, 1978. Queen of the Iceni leads a tribal revolt against the Romans in A.D. 62. Grade 7 and up.

Hunter, M. *The Stronghold*. Harper, 1974. To protect his people from invading Romans, Coll plans strongholds of stone ("brochs") that can be seen today in northern Scotland. Grades 5–6.

Early Europe

Conolly, P. *Pompeii*. Oxford University Press, 1990. This is the story of the city destroyed by Vesusvius. Grade 4 and up.

Goor, R., & Goor, N. *Pompeii: Exploring a Roman Ghost Town*. Ill. R. & Nancy Goor. Crowell, 1986. A concise overview of the social, political, cultural, and religious life in the ancient Roman city of Pompeii. Grade 4 and up.

Macaulay, D. *City: A Story of Roman Planning and Construction*. Houghton, 1983. Ways the Romans planned and build their cities. Grade 6 and up.

Rutland, J. *See Inside a Roman Town*. Warwick, 1986. Shows different views of a Roman town and includes homes, businesses and shops, baths, theater, and temple. Grade 6 and up.

Bisel, S. *The Secrets of Vesuvisus*. Scholastic, 1990. Anthropologist Bisel discusses two time periods: the moment of the volcano's eruption and the present-day workings of the anthropologist. Grades 5–8.

What People Value

Individuals Use Their Knowledge to Help Their People

Early History: Osborne, Chester. *The Memory String*. New York: Atheneum, 1984. Grades 6–7.

1400s: McLanathan, Richard. *Leonardo da Vinci*. Ill. Abrams, 1990. Grades 5–12.

1600s: Sewall, Marcia. *People of the Breaking Day*. Ill. author. Atheneum, 1990. Grades 4–5.

1700s: Quackenbush, Robert. *Benjamin Franklin and His Friends*. Pippin Press, 1991. Grade 4.

1800s: Douty, E. *Charlotte Forten: Free Black Teacher*. Garrard, 1971. Grades 4–6.

1900s: Freedman, Russell. *The Wright Brothers: How They Invented the Airplane*. Ill. Holiday House, 1991. Grades 4–8.

Other books about using knowledge to help people:

_____

Title   Author

My Thoughts: _____

_____

Title   Author

My Thoughts: _____

People Suffer Under Dominance and Fear Aggression

Early Times: Walsh, Jill (Gillian) Paton. *Children of the Fox*. Ill. by Robin Eaton. Farrar, 1978. Grades 5–6.

Searcy, M. Z. *Ikwa of the Mound-Builder Indians*. Pelican, 1989. Grade 5 and up.

1400s: Columbus, Christopher. *The Log of Christopher Columbus*. Translated by Robert H. Fuson. A Common Reader, 1987.

1600s: Knight, James E. *Blue Feather's Vision: The Dawn of Colonial America*. Troll Associates, 1982. Grades 4–6.

1700s: Forbes, Esther. *Johnny Tremain*. Ill. by Lynd Ward. Boston: Houghton Mifflin, 1943. Grade 7 and up.

1800s: Holland, Cecilia. *The Bear Flag*. Boston: Houghton, 1990. Grade 6 and up.

1900s: Armstrong, William. *Sounder*. Ill. James Barkley. Harper, 1969. Grade 6 and up.

continued

Other books about people suffering and fearing aggression:

_____
Title   Author

My Thoughts: _____

_____

_____
Title   Author

My Thoughts: _____

People Are Recognized for Their Contributions

Early Times: Dyer, T. A. *A Way of His Own.* Boston: Houghton Mifflin, 1981. Grade 6 and up.

Sutcliff, R. *Frontier Wolf.* Dutton, 1981. Grade 6 and up.

1400s: Caxton, William. *Aesop's Fables.* Westminster, England. 1484. Grades 4–5.

1600s: Holler, A. *Pocahontas: Powhatan Peacemaker.* Chelsea, 1993. Grade 6 and up.

1700s: Rinaldi, Ann. *A Ride into Morning: The Story of Tempe Wick.* Gulliver, Harcourt Brace Jovanovich, 1991. Grade 7 and up.

1900s: Collier, James Lincoln. *Louis Armstrong.* Macmillan, 1987. Grade 6 and up.

Other books about people being recognized for their contributions:

_____
Title   Author

My Thoughts: _____

_____

_____
Title   Author

My Thoughts: _____

People Desire Independence

Early times: Coolidge, Olivia. *Men of Athens.* Ill. by M. Johnson. Houghton Mifflin, 1962. Grade 6 and up.

1200s: Carrick, D. *Harald and the Giant Knight.* Clarion, 1982. Grades 4–5.

1400s: Fradin, Dennis. *Hiawatha: Messenger of Peace.* Margaret K. McElderry, 1992. Grades 4–6.

1600s: Clapp, Patricia. *Constance: A Story of Early Plymouth*. Lothrop, 1968. Grade 6 and up.

1700s: Stevens, Bryna. *Deborah Sampson Goes to War*. Ill. Florence Hill. Carolrhoda, 1984. Grade 6 and up.

1800s: Paterson, Katherine. *Lyddie*. Lodestar, 1991. Grade 6 and up.

1900s: Sherman, Eileen B. *Independence Avenue*. Jewish Publication Society, 1992. Grade 6—8.

Other books about people wanting their independence:

_____

Title   Author

My Thoughts: _____

_____

Title   Author

My Thoughts: _____

People Demonstrate Generosity

Early History: Schweitzer, Byrd Baylor. *One Small Blue Bead*. Ill. by Symeon Shimin. New York: Macmillan, 1965. Grade 4.

1600s: Ziner, Feenie. *Squanto*. Ill. Linnet, 1988. Grade 4.

1700s: Lindbergh, Reeve. *Johnny Appleseed*. Ill. by Kathy Jacobsen. Joy Street/Little, Brown, 1990. Grades 4—5.

1900s: Sebestyen, Ouida. *Words by Heart*. Atlantic/Little, Brown, 1979. Grade 6 and up.

Other books about people demonstrating generosity:

_____

Title   Author

My Thoughts: _____

_____

Title   Author

My Thoughts: _____

Cinderella: Tales from Different Cultures

Africa

Fairman, T. "Omutugwa." In *Bury My Bones but Keep My Words: African Tales for Retelling*. Ill. by M. Asare. Holt, 1992. Grades 4–7.

Arabia

Lewis, N., reteller. *Stories from the Arabian Nights*. Ill. by A. Pieck. Henry Holts, 1987. Grade 5 and up
Caribbean and West Africa
San Souci, R. D. *Sukey and the Mermaid*. Ill. by B. Pinkney. Four Winds, 1992. Grade 4 and up.

China

Louis, Ai-Lang. *Yeh Shen: A Cinderella Story from China*. Ill. by E. Young. New York: Philomel, 1982.

Czechoslovakia

Philip, N. "The Twelve Months." In *Fairy Tales of Eastern Europe*. Clarion, 1992. Grades 4–5.

England

Stell, F. A. *Tattercoats*. Ill. by D. Goode. Bradbury, 1978. Grade 4 and up.

Germany

Grimm, The Brothers. *Iron John*. Adapted by E. A. Kimmel. Ill. by T. S. Hyman. Holiday, 1994. Grades 4–5.

Ireland

Nimmo, J. *The Starlight Cloak*. Dial, 1993. Grade 4.

Italy

Delamare, D. *Cinderella*. Green Tiger Press, 1993. Grades 4–6.

Philippines

De La Paz, Myrna. *Abadeha: The Philippine Cinderella*. Pacific Queen Pub., n.d. Grade 4.

Russia

Afanasyev, A. *Vasilisa the Beautiful*. Trans. by T. P. Whitney. Ill. by N. Hogrogian. Macmillan, 1970. Grades 4–5.
Mayer, Marianna, reteller. *Baba Yaga and Vasilisa the Brave*. Ill. by K. Y. Craft. Morrow, 1994. Grade 4.
Winthrop, E., adapter. *Vasilissa the Beautiful: A Russian Folktale*. Ill. by A. Koshkin. HarperCollins, 1990. Grades 4–5.

United States

Cole, Babette. *Prince Cinders*. New York: Putnam, 1988. Male Cinderella. Grade 4 and up.

Davenport Films. *Ashpet: An American Cinderella* (Box 527, Delaplane, VA 22025). Grade 5 and up.

de Wit, D., ed. "Little Burnt Face." In *The Talking Stone: An Anthology of Native American Tales and Legends*. Ill. by D. Crews. Greenwillow, 1979. Grades 4–6.

Haviland, V., ed. "The Indian Cinderella" In *North American legends*. Ill. by A. Strugnell. Collins, 1979. Grades 4–6.

Hooks, W. H. *Moss Gown*. Ill. by D. Carrick. Clarion, 1987. Grade 4 and up.

Martin, R. *The Rough-Faced Girl*. Ill. by D. Shannon. Putnam, 1992. Grade 4 and up.

Murphy, S. R. *Silver Woven in My Hair*. Aladdin, 1992. Grades 4–6.

San Souci, R. D. *The Talking Eggs*. Ill. by author. Dial Books, 1989. Grades 4–5.

Wegman W. *Cinderella*. Ill. by author. Hyperion, 1993. Grades 4–6.

Vietnam

Clark, A. N. *In the Land of Small Dragon* Ill. by T. Chen. Viking, 1979. Compare with *The Brocaded Slipper*. Grade 4 and up.

Vuong, L. D. *The Brocaded Slipper and Other Vietnamese Tales*. Ill. by Vo-Dinh Mai. Addison-Wesley, 1982. Grades 4–6.

Garland, S. *Song of the Buffalo Boy*. Harcourt Brace Jovanovich, 1992. Contemporary version of the Cinderella pattern. Grade 7 and up.

Others Located by Students:

Book Selection Committee

- If you enjoy reading books, you can be a member of the Book Selection Committee.
- You can read as many books as you like and select the best books to add to a reading list to give to other students in another classroom.
- When you have read a book that you would suggest to others, write information about the book below and then place the page in a class book, *The Best Books We've Read*.

-- cut --

_____

Author

_____

Title

_____

Illustrator

_____

City Where Published and Publisher

_____

Publishing Date

Remarks about the Book:

The Maya, Aztec, and Inca

Beck, B. *The Aztecs.* Watts, 1983. Portrays achievements of the Aztec people and has directions for making simulations of Aztec artifacts. Nonfiction. Grade 7 and up.

Berler, B. *The Conquest of Mexico: A Modern Rendering of William H. Prescott's History.* Corona Pub., 1988. Retells episodes of the conquest by Cortes that includes his meetings with Navarez, the Native people's rebellion, Montezuma's death, and other events. Nonfiction. Grade 7 and up.

de Verona, F., ed. *Hernando de Soto, Explorer, 1500–1542.* Spanish translation G. Contreras, n.d. De Soto explored the American southeast and central America for gold and discovered the Mississippi River. Biography. Grade 6 and up.

Gerson, S., & Goldsmit, S. *La Civilization Maya (The Mayan Civlilization).* Ill. B. Lopez. Mexico City: Trillas, 1988. A chronicler, a mythical character, takes children on a journey to these cultures to explain the customs and way of life. Nonfiction. Grade 6 and up.

Gerson, S., & Goldsmit, S. *Las Culturas Prehispanicas: Olmecas, Zapotecos, Mixtecos, Teotihaucanos, Toltecas (Prehispanic Cultures).* Ill. B. Lopez. Mexico City: Trillas, 1987. A mythical narrator gives details about the early civilizations of Mexican tribes from the third to ninth centuries and explains customs, calendars, and ways of life. Nonfiction. Grades 4–6.

Hicks, P. *The Aztecs.* Thomson Learning, 1993. Has basic information along with photographs of artifacts and ancient buildings. Pronunciation guide included. Nonfiction. Grades 4–6.

James, S. *The Aztecs.* Viking, 1992. Clear acetate pages are sequenced throughout the book and can be lifted to show the inner workings of illustrated Aztec structures. Nonfiction. Grades 4–6.

McKissack, P. *Aztec Indians.* Children's Press, 1985. Describes the Aztec people and their customs, history, language, and religion. Nonfiction. Grade 7 and up.

Marrin, A. *Inca and Spaniard: Pizarro and the Conquest of Peru.* Atheneum, 1989. Some of the text comes from the accounts of Guaman Pomo, an Indian who served the Spaniards as a minor official. Nonfiction. Grade 7 and up.

Meltzer, M. *Gold: The True Story of Why People Search for It, Mine It, Trade It, Steal It, Mint It, Hoard It, Shape It, Wear It, Fight and Kill for It.* HarperCollins, 1993. Recounts history of gold and what people do because of it. Nonfiction. Grade 4 and up.

Meyer, C., & Gallenkamp, C. *The Mystery of the Ancient Maya.* Atheneum, 1985. Presents the ancient Maya cities of this period recently discovered in the jungles of Central America. Nonfiction. Grade 7 and up.

Castles

Book	Feature
Aliki. *A Medieval Feast*. Harper & Row, 1983.	Feast for a king
Brouchard, P. *Castles of the Middle Ages*. Silver Burdett, 1980.	Art appreciation
Caselli, G. *A Medieval Monk*. Bedrick, 1986.	Monastary community training
Corbin, C. *Knights*. Watts, 1989.	
Clark, R. *Castles*. Bookwright, 1986.	Castle construction
Cunningham, J. *The Treasure Is the Rose*. Pantheon, 1973.	Woman defends a castle
De Angeli, M. *The Door in the Wall*. Doubleday, 1949.	Historical fiction
Funcken, L. *The Age of Chivalry*. Prentice Hall, 1983	Daily life, period poetry
Gee, R. *Castle Times*. EDC Pub., 1982.	Background knowledge
Hastings, S. *Sir Gawain and the Loathly Lady*. Mulberry, 1987.	Arthurian legend
Holme, B. *Medieval Pageant*. Thames & Hudson, 1987.	Pageantry
Lewis, N. *Proud Knight, Fair Lady*. Viking, 1989.	Tales of minstrels
Macaulay, D. *Castle*. Houghton Mifflin, 1977.	Castle construction
MacDonald, F., ed. *The Middle Ages*. Silver Burdett, 1984.	Art appreciation
Miguel, P. *The Days of Knights and Castles*. Silver Burdett, 1985.	Castle facts
Morgan, G. *Life in a Medieval Village*. Lerner, 1982.	Life in English village in 1200s
Oakes, C. *The Middle Ages*. Harcourt Brace Jovanovich, 1989.	Background; daily life
Platt, R. *Castle*. Dorling Kinderley, 1994.	Life in fourteenth century
Ruis, M. *A Journey through History: The Middle Ages*. Barron's, 1988.	Background knowledge
San Souci, R. D. *Young Guinevere*. Doubleday, 1992.	Life of Guinevere
Smith, B. *Castles*. Wayland, 1988.	Ghost stories

Others Located by Students:

Artists and Their Art

1400: Leonardo da Vinci in Italy

Noble, I. *Leonardo da Vinci: The Universal Genius.* Norton, 1965. Depicts the life of the painter. Biography. Grades 5–8.

1500: Hieronymus Bosch in The Netherlands

Willard, N. *Pish, Posh, Said Hieronymus* III. by L. & D. Dillon. Harcourt Brace Jovanovich, 1991. Bosch's (1450–1516) housekeeper leaves and is followed by winged fish and other fantastic creatures who want her attention. She returns resigned to a life with Bosch's creatures (based on Bosch's painting, *Heaven and Hell*, now in the Vienna Academy.) Fiction. Grade 4 and up.

1600: Life of de Pareja, a Black Slave, in Spain

De Trevino, E. B. *I, Juan de Pareja.* Farrar, Straus & Giroux, 1965. Early in the seventeenth century, Juan de Pareja is born the son of a black slave and a Spaniard. At age 12, Juan becomes the property of the painter, Don Diego Rodrequez de Silva y Velasquez of Madrid, later the court painter to King Philip IV. Juan teaches himself to paint, and Velasquez gives Juan his freedom and makes him his studio assistant. Historical fiction. Grades 5–8.

1600: N. C. Wyeth's Pilgrims in North America

San Souci, R. *N. C. Wyeth's Pilgrims.* Chronicle Books, 1990. Wyeth's 14-panel mural of the pilgrims in their early years is reproduced with a text that tells of the first Thanksgiving. Nonfiction. Grade 4 and up.

1606: Life of Rembrandt in the Netherlands

Raboff, E. *Rembrandt.* Harper & Row, 1987. Depicts life of Rembrandt (1606–1669), who becomes a famous Dutch painter from the Netherlands. Biography. Grade 7 and up.

1738: Benjamin West in America and England

Henry, M., & Dennis, W. *Benjamin West and His Cat Grimalkin.* III. by W. Dennis. Bobbs, 1947. Life of one of America's first artists (1738–1820) who was widely recognized in England for his historical paintings of figures wearing regular clothing, not long classical gowns or robes. Biography. Grades 4–6.

1796: George Catlin in America's West

Sufrin, M. *George Catlin: Painter of the Indian West.* Atheneum, 1991. From Catlin's (1795–1872) own journals and letters, the text describes the life of early nineteenth-century Plains Indians. Biography. Grades 5–9.

1800s:

Brenner, B. *On the Frontier with Mr. Audubon.* Coward, 1977. A fictionalized account of Audubon's "assistant's journal" of the trip in 1820. Based on the journal of John James Audubon. Biographical fiction. Grades 4–5.

continued

1811: George Caleb Bingham in America

Woodridge, R. *That's the Way, Joshuway.* Independence Press, 1965. In Missouri, Josh is helped by George Caleb Bingham (1811–1879), an artist who he meets while working in his uncle's harness shop. Fiction. Grade 5 and up.

1833: Explorers and Artists in America's Missouri River Valley

Freedman, R. *An Indian Winter.* Ill. by K. Bodmer. Holiday House, 1992. Maximilian, a German prince, and Karl Bodmer, a Swiss artist, travel by river to area now North Dakota. They both record the journey through the Missouri River Valley. Fiction. Grades 4–6.

1834: Degas in France

Skira-Venturi, R. *A Weekend with Degas.* Rizzoli, 1992. Portrays techniques and experiments of Hilaire Germain Edgar Degas (1834–1917), who became a French painter whose work affected modern painting. Biography. Grades 5–9.

1836: Winslow Homer

Beneduce, A. K. *A Weekend with Winslow Homer.* Rizzoli, 1993. This is a fictionalized autobiography (written in first-person) that explains Homer's involvement in his sketches and his wood engravings. Grades 5–8.

1840: Museums in France

Bjork, C. *Linnea in Monet's Garden.* Ill. by L. Anderon. Trans. J. Sandin. Stockholm: Raben and Sjogen/ Farrar, Straus & Giroux, 1987. Linnea and Mr. Bloom visit Monet's home and garden in Giverny and see his work in museums. Fiction. Grade 4 and up.

1850: A Young American Girl Loses Her Paint Box

Ackernman, K. *Araminta's Paint Box.* Ill. by Betsy Lewin. Atheneum, 1990. On a wagon train, Araminta loses her paint box when their wagon breaks a wheel and all is tossed out. Fiction. Grade 4.

1853: Van Gogh in The Netherlands

Dobrin, A. *I Am a Stranger on the Earth: The Story of Vincent Van Gogh.* Warner, 1975. An account of the famous Dutch painter with reproductions of his art works. Biography. Grade 5 and up.

1856: Whistler in London

Merrill, L., & Ridley, S. *The Princess and the Peacocks.* Ill. by T. Dixon. Hyperion, 1992. A princess in a painting tells how James Abbott McNeill Whislter created the Peacock Room with his painting "The Princess from the Land of Porcelain" as the centerpiece. Grades 4–6.

1881: Picasso in Spain

Raboff, E. *Picasso.* Harper & Row, 1987. This reissue tells about Pablo Picasso (1881–1973), a famous Spanish painter, and interprets certain full-page reproductions. Biography. Grades 6–8.

1886: Rivera in Mexico

Braun, B. *A Weekend with Diego Rivera*. Rizzoli, 1994. This biography portrays the major art works of Rivera, information on producing murals and his political views and relationships with the Communist party. Grades 5–8.

Raintree Series. *Diego Rivera, Artist 1886–1957*. Raintree Pub., 1988. Portrays life of Rivera, (1886–1967), a famous Mexican artist known for his murals and fresco paintings of Mexican life and history. Biography. Grades 4–6.

1887: Chagall in France

Greenfield, H. *Marc Chagall*. Follett, 1967. Depicts the life of Marc Chagall (1887–1985), who becomes a famous French artist. Biography. Grades 6–8.

1900: Mary Cassatt, an American in Paris

Wilson, E. *American Painter in Paris: A Life of Mary Cassatt*. Farrar, 1971. This focuses on Cassatt's life (1845–1926) in Paris with reproductions of her art works, paintings, pastels, and prints. Biography. Grade 5 and up.

1900s: O'Keeffe and Ringgold, American Artists

Turner, R. M. *Georgia O'Keeffe*. Little, 1991. Portrays the life of an American artist known for vivid colors and shapes in her paintings. Biography. Grade 5 and up.

Venezia. Mike. *Georgia O'Keeffe*. Ill. by the author. New York: Children's, 1993. Portrays O'Keeffe's childhood and adult life. Grades 1–2.

1900s: Faith Ringgold

Turner, R. M. *Faith Ringgold*. Little, 1993. Portrays an inspiring African American artist who remains true to her heritage. Includes diagrams and photographs of her paintings. Biography. Grades 5–8.

1989: Wang Yani in China

Zhensun, Z., & Low, A. *A Young Painter*. Scholastic, 1991. Depicts the talent of Wang Yani from age 4 to 16 and discusses her remarkable use of space with monkeys, birds, mountains, and trees. Biography. Grade 5 and up.

1993: Native American Artists of North America

Moore, R. *Native Artists of North America*. Ill. by C. Brigman. John Muir Pub., 1993. Profiles young native American artists from different regions of America. Nonfiction. Grades 5–8.

Others Selected by Students:

Inventors, Inventions, and Discoveries

1400s

Fisher, L. E. *Gutenberg*. Macmillan, 1993. Grades 4–5.

Yue, C., & Yue, D. *Christopher Columbus: How He Did It*. Houghton Mifflin, 1992. Grades 4–6.
1500s–1600s
Rosen, S. *Galileo and the Magic Numbers*. Ill. M. Stein. Little, Brown, 1958. Grades 5–6.

1700s

Fritz, J. *What's the Big Idea, Ben Franklin?* Ill. by M. Tomes. Coward, 1976. Grades 4–6.

Judson, C. I. *Boat Builder: The Story of Robert Fulton*. Ill. by A. Sperry. Scribner's, 1940. Grades 4–6.

Meltzer, M. *Benjamin Franklin: The New American*. Watts, 1988. Grades 5–6.

1800–1900s

Aliki. *A Weed Is a Flower: The Life of George Washington Carver*. Ill. by author. Prentice, 1965. Grade 4.

Dank, M. *Albert Einstein*. Watts, 1983. Grades 5–7.

Freedman, R. *The Wright Brothers: How They Invented the Airplane*. Holiday, 1991. Grades 4–8.

Haskins, J. *Outward Dreams: Black Inventors and Their Inventions*, Bantam, 1992. Grade 4 and up.

Landau, E. *Robert Fulton*. Watts, 1991. Grades 4–6.

Reef, C. *Albert Einstein, Scientist of the 20th Century* Ill. by L. & D. Dillon. Macmillan, 1991. Grades 4–6.

St. George, J. *Dear Dr. Bell...Your Friend, Helen Keller*. Putnam, 1992. Grade 6 and up.

Swanson. D. *David Bushnell and His Turtle: The Story of America's First Submarine*. Athenum, 1991. Grade 6 and up.

Towle, W. *The Real McCoy, The Life of an American Inventor*, Ill. by W. Clay. Scholastic, 1993. Grade 4.

Vare, E. A., & Ptacek, G. *Women Inventors and Their Discoveries*. Oliver Press, 1993. Grades 4–7.

Veglahn, N. *The Mysterious Rays: Marie Curie's World*. Ill. by V. Juhasz. Coward, 1977. Grades 4–5.

Others Selected by Students:

Christopher Columbus

1492 and Later

Anderson, J. *Christopher Columbus: From Vision to Voyage.* Ill. by G. Ancona. Dial, 1991. Biography. Grades 4–5.

Conrad, P. *Pedro's Journal.* Ill. by P. Koeppen. Caroline House, 1991. Fiction. Grades 4–5.

Cuautli, H. C. *Cristobal Colon y Su Gran Travsia (Christopher Columbus and His Great Voyage.* Mexico: Fernandez Editores/ New Braunfels, TX: T. R. Books, 1991. Biography. Grades 4–5.

Dolan, S. J. *Christopher Columbus: The Intrepid Mariner.* Fawcett Columbine, 1990. Biography. Grade 7 and up.

Fritz, J. *Where Do You Think You Are Going, Christopher Columbus?* Ill. by M. Tomes. G. P. Putnam's, 1980. Biography. Grades 4–6.

Levinson, N. S. *Christopher Columbus: Voyage to the Unknown.* Lodestar, 1991. Biography. Grades 4–5.

Litowinsky, O. *The High Voyage—A Novel.* Viking, 1977. Fiction. Grade 5 and up.

Los Casos, B. *The Log of Christopher Columbus' First Voyage to America in the Year 1492.* Repr. 1938/84. Linnet Press, 1989. Nonfiction. Grade 4 and up.

Martin, S. *I Sailed with Columbus.* Ill. by T. La Padula. Overlook, 1991. Fiction. Grades 6–9.

Meltzer, M. *Columbus and the World Around Him.* Watts, 1990. Nonfiction. Grade 4 and up.

Pelta, K. *Discovering Christopher Columbus: How History Is Invented.* Lerner, 1991. Nonfiction. Grade 6 and up.

Roop, P., & Roop, C. *I, Columbus: My Journal.* Walker, 1991. Nonfiction. Grades 4–5.

Schlein, M. *I Sailed with Columbus.* Ill. by T. Newsom. HarperCollins, 1991. Fiction. Grades 4–6.

Others Selected by Students:

Civilization: Explore a Concept

Feature	Maya	Aztec	Inca	Time Period
Architecture				
Family pattern				
Work done				
Schooling				
Government				
Jewelery				
Recreation				
Religion				
Authority				
Health care				
Other				

Historical Periods in
If You Lived Series

1600s

McGovern, A. *If You Sailed on the Mayflower in 1620*. Ill. by A. DeVito. Scholastic, 1991. Questions reflect the problems and concerns of the early Pilgrims on the ship and during the first year in the colony. Fiction. Grade 4 and up.

McGovern, A. *If You Lived in Colonial Times*. Scholastic, 1969. Includes a question-answer approach that helps students review the people's lives in the colonial time period. Grades 4–5.

1700s

Gross, R. B. *If You Grew Up with George Washington*. Scholastic, 1985. Includes a question-answer format about the historical times during which President Washington lived. Grades 4–5.

Levine, E. *If You Were There When They Signed the Constitution*. Ill. by R. Rosenblum. Scholastic, 1987. Includes a question-answer format about the delegates to the Constitutional Convention, the compromises they made, and how the document can be changed. Grade 5 and up.

1800s

Levine, E. *If Your Name Was Changed At Ellis Island*. Ill. by W. Parmenter. Scholastic, 1993. Questions reflect problems and concerns faced day-by-day by the immigrants who entered America through Ellis Island. Grades 4–5.

Levine, E. *If You Traveled West in a Covered Wagon*. Scholastic, 1986. Questions reflect day-by-day problems and concerns faced by travelers in wagon trains. Fiction. Grade 4 and up.

McGovern, A. *If You Lived with the Sioux Indians*. Scholastic, 1972. Portrays activities of the Sioux people living in Dakota Territory prior to the 1850s. Grade 4 and up.

Moore, K. *If You Lived in the North/South During the Civil War*. Ill. by Anni Matsick. Scholastic, 1994. Provides facts about the two sides in America's Battle Between the States. Grade 5 and up.

1900s

Levine, E. *If You Lived at the Time of the Great San Francisco Earthquake*. Scholastic, 1987. Provides facts about the disastrous quake, the damage it caused, and some heroic acts. Grade 4 and up.

Levine, E. *If You Lived at the Time of Martin Luther King*. Scholastic, 1990. Focuses on King's involvement in the struggles of the civil rights movement. Grade 4 and up.

What Are the Lists Describing?

What are the lists describing? City names? Bodies of water?

Group A
Cahuilla
Chumash
Gabrielino
Karok
Klamath
Maidu

Group B
Cadoo
Catawba
Cherokee
Chickasaw
Chitamacha
Choctaw

Group C
Kickapoo
Maliseet
MicMac
Mohawk
Oneida

Group D
Kiowa
Mandan
Omaha
Osage
Oto

Group E
Kwakiutl
Nootka
Quinault
Tingit
Tsimshian

Notes:

What Were the Patterns of Settlement of People on Lands Inhabited by Native Americans?

With a Partner:

1. Inquire into the fate of some of the Indian tribes in the Americas and investigate the patterns of settlement of immigrants from different European countries in the United States.
2. To do this, find information in books about:
   a. Who were the immigrants?
   b. Where did the immigrants originate?
   c. Why did the immigrants come?
   d. Where did the immigrants go? Why there?
3. You can find books that discuss different parts of the country and investigate the diverse groups of immigrants who settled in different locations.
4. You may write an original story after you study the history of Native People of their regions.
5. The names of Native tribes that follow represent many other tribes who lived in the different geographical regions. (All tribal names may not be found in the list.)

Patterns of Immigrant Settlement Affecting Native People

United States Region	Some Major Groups Affected	Immigrants
Northwest	Bella Coola, Chinook, Haida, others	
Plains	Apache, Blackfoot, Cheyenne, Crow, Lakota, Comanche, Kiowa, Omaha, Pawnee, Teton, others	
Southwest	Apache, Hopi, Navajo, Papago, Zuni, others	
Southeast	Cherokee, Choctaw, Natchez, Seminole, others	
Northeast	Abenaki, Chippewa (Ojibwa), Mohawk, Mic-Mac, Seneca, Shawnee, Wampanoag, Winnebago, Onondaga, others	
Hawaiian	Native Hawaiians, others	

Notes:

Those Who Risked
Their Lives for Others

1580 B.C.: Early Egypt

McGraw, E. J. *Mara, Daughter of the Nile.* Coward, 1953. During the rule of Hatshepsut, Mara, a slave, tries to escape and is bought by a man who offers her luxury if she will spy for the queen. Fiction. Grade 7 and up.

800 B.C.: Early Greece

Gates, D. *A Fair Wind for Troy.* Ill. by C. Mikolaycak. Penguin, 1984. Recounts myth that begins when Paris, falls in love with Helen, the wife of Menelaus, the King of Sparta, and and takes her by force to Troy. Folk literature. Grade 6 and up.

A.D. 110: Early Briton

Haugaard, E. C. *A Slave's Tale.* Ill. by L. & D. Dillion. Hoghton Mifflin, 1963. In this sequel to *Hakon of Rogen's Saga*, Hakon leaves aboard ship to take Rark, a former slave, back to his Briton homeland. Fiction. Grades 5–6.

A.D. 400: Early Israel

Haugaard, E. C. *The Rider and His Horse.* Houghton Mifflin, 1968. In the time of the Roman conquest of Jerusalem, a young man, David Ben Joseph, makes a heroic contribution to his people. Fiction. Grade 6 and up.

1745: Early Scotland

Hendry, F. *Quest for a Kelpie.* Holiday House, 1988. In Nairn, Scotland, Jeannie is caught in the conflict between the Scots loyal to Prince Charlie, and the king's armies. Fiction. Grade 5 and up.

1776: Revolutionary America

Berleth, R. *Samuel's Choice.* Ill. by J. Watling. Whitman, 1990. In the 1776 Battle of Long Island, a 14-year-old slave makes an important contribution. Includes author's historical note. Fiction. Grades 4–7.

Haley, Gail E. *Jack Jouett's Ride.* Ill. by author. Viking, 1973. Jouett warns Virginia's legislators that the British troops were marching in their direction. Fiction. Grades 4–5.

Stevens, B. *Deborah Sampson Goes to War.* Ill. by F. Hill. Carolrhoda, 1984 Describes her early life and her later experiences as a soldier in America's revolution. Biography. Grades 4–6.

1850: Southern United States

Haskins, Jim. *Get On Board: The Story of the Underground Railroad.* Scholastic, 1993. Depicts the history of the Underground Railroad, the network of blacks and white who helped slaves maked their way to freedom in the United States, and portrays the conductors and the stationmasters, such as Harriet Tubman, Frederick Douglass, Henry "Box" Brown, and others. Includes photographs, index, and bibliography. Nonfiction. Grades 5–8.

Rappaport, D. *Escape from Slavery: Five Journeys to Freedom.* Ill. by C. Lilly. HarperCollins, 1991. Describes true stories of slaves who acquire their freedom with the help of both blacks and whites. Bibliography. Nonfiction. Grade 8 and up.

1881: Iowa

Wettener, M. K. *Kate Shelley and the Midnight Express.* Ill. by K. Ritz. Carolthoda, 1990. In 1881, a 15-year-old girl overcomes her own fears and warns the railroad of a train bridge that is washed out in a flood. Fiction. Grades 4–5.

1810: Mexico

Lampman, E. *The Tilted Sombrero.* Ill. by R. Cruz. Doubleday, 1966. In 1810, at the beginning of Mexico's War of Independence, Father Hidalgo y Costilla, leads the first Indian revolt against Spain. Fiction. Grade 5 and up.

1900: Texas

Nelson, T. *Devil Storm.* A Richard Jackson Book. Orchard Books/ Franklin Watts, 1987. On a sparsely populated peninsula, 13-year-old Walter Carroll and his little sister Alice meet Old Tom the Tramp who is rumored to be the offspring of the pirate Jean Lafitte. Fiction. Grades 5–6.

1939: Poland

Bernhelm, M. *Father of the Orphans: The Story of Janusz Korczak.* Dutton, 1989. When the Nazis in Poland close Dr. Korczak's orphanages in 1939, he goes with the children to the Warsaw ghetto and then to the concentration camp at Treblinka. Biography. Advanced grade 7 and up.

1939: Germany

Neimark, A. E. *One Man's Valor: Leo Baeck and the Holocaust.* Lodestar, 1986. After Hitler's rise to power in 1939, Leo Baeck, the chief rabbi of Berlin, helped many Jews, especially children, to escape from Germany. Bibliography and index included. Biography. Grade 8 and up.

1940: France

Morpurgo, M. *Waiting for Anya.* Viking, 1991. In southern France in 1940, Jo discovers that the elderly Widow Horcada is sheltering Benjamin, her Jewish son-in-law, and is smuggling Jewish children over the border. Fiction. Grades 5–8.

1943: Denmark

Matas, C. *Lisa's War.* Scribner's, 1987. In 1943, Lisa and her Brother, Stefan, Jewish teenagers with the organized Resistance movement, fight against Jews being sent to camps. Nonfiction. Grade 6 and up.

continued

1943: Hungary

Atkinson, L. *In Kindling Flame: the Story of Hannah Senesh. 1921–1944.* Beech Tree Books, 1992. As a teenager, Hannah Szenes leaves the anti-Semitism of Hungary in 1939 for a new life in Palestine but returns to Nazi-occupied Yugoslavia to save the lives of Jews. Biography. Grade 7 and up.

Schur, M. *Hannah Szenes: A Song of Light.* Jewish Publication Society, 1991. This is an inspirational version of a young women's bravery. Biography. Grade 6 and up.

1944: Hungary

Linnea, S. *Raoul Wallenberg: The Man Who Stopped Death.* Jewish Publication Society, 1993. Portrays the life of Wallenberg, who led efforts in 1944 to save Hungarian Jews from Nazi extermination. Biography. Grade 6 and up.

1950: Vietnam

Myers, W. D. *A Place Called Heartbreak: A Story of Vietnam.* Ill. by F. Porter. Steck-Vaughn, 1993. This is a nonfiction account of Col. Fred V. Cherry, U.S.A.F. (now retired), who was the first black pilot to become a prisoner of war in North Vietnam. Author's notes about the interviews with Col. Cherry. Nonfiction. Grades 5–8.

Others Suggested by Students:

America's Tall Tale Characters

Roles

Baseball Player: *Fleet-Footed Florence* (Doubleday, 1981) by Marilyn Sachs has two sports rivals who marry and live happily ever after in a nonsexist baseball story infused with tall tale humor.

Cowboy: *Bowleg Bill: Seagoing Cowpuncher* (Prentice, 1957) by Harold W. Felton is tall-tale nonsense about a cowboy who solves his problems in a unique manner; *Pecos Bill* (Whitman, 1937) by James C. Bowman shows Pecos Bill as the tall-tale hero of the Wild West; *Pecos Bill* (Mulberry Books, 1992) by Steven Kellogg tells how Bill invented cattle drives, lassos, and rodeos. *The Legend of Lightning Larry* (Scribner's, 1993, grades 4–5) by Alan Shepard includes such characters as Crooked Curt, Devilish Dick, Dismal Dan, Evil-Eye McNeevil, and Moldy Mike.

Farmer: *Johnny Appleseed* (Morrow, 1988) by Steven Kellogg is a biographical retelling of this pioneer's contribution now considered a folk legend.

Keelboat Worker: *Mike Fink* (Little, 1957) by James C. Bowman is a story of the legendary boatman and his adventures; *Mike Fink: A Tall Tale Retold* (Morrow, 1992) by Steven Kellogg tells the story of the King of the Keelboatmen who floated cargo downriver to New Orleans and his adventures of facing former king Jack Carpenter in a wrestling match and H. P. Blathersby and his powerful steamboat.

Lumber Worker: *Ol' Paul, the Mighty Logger* (Holiday, 1949) by Glen Rounds with earthy zeal and zest; *Paul Bunyan* (Morrow, 1984) by Steven Kellogg offers specific details in doublepage spreads; *Paul Bunyan* (Harcourt, 1941) by Esther Shepard is a substantive edition of these tales.

Railroad Worker: *John Henry: An American Legend* (Pantheon, 1965) by Ezra Jack Keats retells this familiar tale.

Sailor: *Tall Tales of Stormalong: Sailor of the Seven Seas* (Prentice-Hall, 1968) by Harold W. Felton; *John Tabors Ride* (Atlantic, 1966) by Blair Lent is a tall tale based on a New England legend about a shipwrecked sailor with exaggeration, fantastic situations, and salty marine terms; *John Tabor's Ride* (Knopf, 1989) by Edward C. Day is an account from a 1846 book of whaling adventures kept as a seaman's journal, about a Tabors self-told story to a young seaman. *Tall Tales of Stormalong: Sailor of the Seven Seas* (Prentice-Hall, 1968) by H. W. Felton is a collection of exaggerations of a sailor's life aboard ship and his adventures.

Sign Painter: *Mr. Yowder and the Train Robbers* (Holiday, 1981) by Glen Rounds is about the self-proclaimed "World's Bestest and Fastest Sign Painter" and his run-in with robbers and rattlers. *The Legend of Slappy Hooper* (Scribner's, 1993, grades 4–7) by A. Shepard is about a sign painter so good that his pictures come to life.

Steel Worker: "Joe Magarac" is found in *Heroes in American Folklore* (Messner, 1962) by Irwin Shapiro, along with stories about Casey Jones, John Henry, Steamboat Bill, and others.

Selected Story Songs

Always Room for One More (Holt, 1965) by Sorche Nic Leodhaus

Bring a Torch, Jeanette Isabella (Playspace, 1963) by Pam Adams

Casey Jones: The Story of a Brave Engineer (Children's Press, 1968) by Glen Rounds

The Farmer in the Dell (Little, Brown, 1978) by Diane Zuromskis

The Fox Went Out on a Chilly Night (Doubleday, 1961) by Peter Spier

Freedom Songs (Orchard, 1990) by Yvette Moore

Froggy Went A-Courtin' (Stewart, Tabori, & Chang, 1992) by Kevin O'Malley

Go Tell Aunt Rhody (Macmillan, 1974) by Aliki

Go Tell Aunt Rhody (Lippincott, 1973) by Peter Spier

I Know an Old Lady (Rand McNally, 1961) by Rose Bonne & Alan Mills

The Man on the Flying Trapeze (Lippincott, 1975) by Robert Quackenbush

Oh, A-Hunting We Will Go (Atheneum, 1974) by John Langstaff

Old MacDonald Had a Farm (Lippincott, 1972) by Robert Quackenbush

One Wide River to Cross (Prentice-Hall, 1966) by Barbara and Ed Emberley

Over in the Meadow: An Old Nursery Counting Rhyme (Prentice-Hall, 1986) by Paul Galdone

She'll Be Comin' Round the Mountain (Lippincott, 1973) by Robert Quackenbush

Songs of the Wild West (Metropolitan Museum of Art/Simon & Schuster, 1991) by Alan Exelrod

There's a Hole in the Bucket (Harper & Row, 1990) by Nadine Barnard Westcott

This Old Man (Grosset & Dunlap, 1974) by Pam Adams

The Zebra Riding Cowboy: A Folk Song from The Old West (Holiday, 1988) by Brett Harvey

Others Selected by Students:

Role of Women and Girls

Akers, C. *Abigail Adams: An American Woman*. Scott, Foresman, 1980. Portrays life of Adams and the politics and social milieu of the times. Biography. Grade 5 and up.

Brady, E. W. *Toliver's Secret*. Crown, 1988. Ten-year-old Ellen carries secret messages to couriers waiting behind British lines. Fiction. Grades 4–6.

Clapp, P. *I'm Deborah Sampson: A Soldier in the War of the Revolution*. Lothrop, 1977. Told by Deborah Sampson Garnett (1760–1827) herself, this retells her childhood, war experiences, marriage, and family life. Biography. Grade 5 and up.

Dalgliesh, A. *The Courage of Sarah Noble*. Ill. by L. Weisgard. Scribner's, 1954. Sarah remembers her mother's words, "Keep up your courage, Sarah Noble" as she stays alone with a Native American family while her father returns for the rest of the family. Based on a true episode in 1707. Fiction. Grade 4.

Evans, E. *Weathering the Storm: Women of the Revolution*. Scribner, 1975. Includes journal entries of women who describe life in their homes during the Revolution. Nonfiction. Grade 6 and up.

Green, R. *Women in American Indian Society*. Ill. Chelsea House, 1992. Discusses Native American women from the pre-explorers' contact to the present when over 10 percent of the tribes have women leaders. Includes bibliography, glossary, and index. Nonfiction, Grade 7 and up.

Marsh, J. *Martha Washington*. Watts, 1992. Describes Martha's childhood, first marriage, remarriage to Washington, her life at Mount Vernon, and her role as first lady. Grades 4–6.

Moore, R. *The Bread Sister of Sinking Creek*. Lippincott, 1990. Fourteen-year-old Maggie Callahan arrives in Pennsylvania to become a hired girl for the McGrew family. Fiction. Grades 5–8.

Peterson, H. S. *Abigail Adams: Dear Partner*. Garrard, 1967. Includes excerpts from primary sources, Adams's own writings. Biography. Grade 5 and up.

Stevenson, A. *Molly Pitcher: Young Patriot*. Macmillan, 1986. Portrays Pitcher and her heroism and courage during America's Revolution. Biography. Grade 5 and up.

Others Suggested by Students:

Women's Rights

Individuals

Connell, K. *They Shall Be Heard: Susan B. Anthony & Elizabeth Cady Stanton.* Ill. by B. Kiwak. Steck-Vaughn, 1993. Reviews the women's experiences and includes quotes from primary sources. Grades 4–8.

Cooper, I. *Susan B. Anthony.* Watts, 1984. Biography. Grade 6 and up.

Jacobs, W. J. *Mother, Aunt Susan and Me.* Coward, 1979. A point of view from Stanton's 16-year-old daughter, Harriet, who sees the efforts of her mother and her aunt, Susan B. Anthony, to win equal rights for women. Grade 6 and up.

Kendall, M. E. *Elizabeth Cady Stanton.* Highland, 1988. Biography of founder of American women's rights movement. Grade 6 and up.

Groups

Evans, E. *Weathering the Storm: Women of the Revolution.* Scribner, 1975. Includes journal entries of women during the Revolution. Grade 5 and up.

Levinson, N. S. *The First women Who Spoke Out.* National Women's History Project. Dillon, 1982. Traces the women's rights movement. Grade 6 and up.

Oneal, Z. *A Long Way to Go.* Viking, 1990. Depicts the women's suffrage movements during World War I. Grades 4–6.

Saxby, M. *The Great Deeds of Heroic Women.* Peter Bedrick, 1992. Accomplishments of 15 women from Joan of Arc, Scheherazade, and others. Grade 6 and up.

Smith, B. C. *Women Win the Vote.* Silver Burdett, 1989. Reviews major figures and events in women's rights. Advanced grade 6 and up.

Stein, C. *The Story of the Nineteenth Amendment.* Children's Press, 1982. Recounts this development in women's rights. Grade 7 and up.

Sullivan, G. *The Day the Women got the Vote: A Photo History of the Women's Rights Movement.* Scholastic, 1994. Records the women's movement from Seneca Falls to contemporary times and includes the history of the Nineteenth Amendment, suffragists, the struggle for equal rights, and the defeat of the ERA. Grades 4–8.

Vare, E. A., & Placek, G. *Women Inventors & Their Discoveries.* Oliver Press, 1993. Provides information about women who were not always given credit for their inventions. Madam C. J. Walker, Betty Graham, Grace Hopper, Ruth Handler, and others are included. Grades 4–7.

Warren, R. *A Pictoral History of Women in America.* Crown, 1975. Portrays the role of females in America's history. Grade 7 and up.

Zane, P., & Zane, J. *American Women: Four Centuries of Progress.* The Proof Press, 1989. Biographical sketches of over 20 women in history. Grade 7 and up.

Others Located by Students:

How the West Was Fun

1700s: Davy Crockett

Quackenbush, R. *Quit Pulling My Leg, Davy Crockett.* Prentice-Hall, 1987. Portrays life of Crockett as a
frontiersman and separates facts from fanciful stories. Biography. Grade 4 and up.

1800s: Artemis Bonner

Myers, W. D. The *Righteous Revenge of Artemis Bonner.* HarperCollins, 1992. As an African American
in the wild west in 1880, Artemis Bonner teams up with his friend, Frolic, to avenge a murder
against the Evil Catfish Grimes and his friend, Lucy Featherdip. Grade 5 and up.

1880s: Stagecoach Driver on America's Western Frontier

Kimmel, E. A. *Charlie Drives the Stage.* Ill. by G. Rounds. Holiday House, 1989. In 1887, Charlie Drummond is the only stagecoach driver who has "a ghost of a chance of getting through" to take Senator Roscoe McCorkle to the train so the senator can arrive in Washington for an important
meeting with the president. Humorous view. Fiction. Grades 4–5.

1800s: An Elephant Chase

Cross, G. *The Great American Elephant Chase.* Holiday House, 1993. In 1881, a con man's daughter is
helped by an orphan boy as they travel from Pennsylvania to Nebraska and try to keep her elephant away from a thief. Grades 4–6.

1800s: Theodore Roosevelt

Quackenbush, R. *Don't You Dare Shoot That Bear!* Simon & Schuster, 1984. Humorous introduction to
the personality of Theodore Roosevelt (1858–1919). Grade 4.

1800s: Cowboys in America's West

Shepard, A. *The Legend of Lightning Larry.* Scribner's, 1993. Crooked Curt, Devilish Dick, Dismal Dan,
Evil-Eye McNeevil, and Moldy Mike meet their match with Lightning Larry. Grades 4–5.

Informational Books and Biographies to Pair Together

Birth of Our Nation

Biography: Meltzer's *George Washington and the Birth of Our Nation* (Watts 1986, grade 4 up).

Information: Marrin's *Struggle for a Continent: The French and Indian Wars* (Atheneum, 1987, grade 4 and up); Marrin's *The War for Independence* (Atheneum, 1988, grade 4 and up).

People of Early African States

Biography: Wisniewski's *Sundiate: Lion King of Mali* (Clarion, 1992, grade 4 and up).

Information: McEvedy's *Atlas of African History* (Penguin, 1980, grade 7 and up).

Battle at the Alamo

Biography: Fritz, J. *Make Way for Sam Houston* (Putnam, 1986, grade 7 and up).

Information: Richards, N. *The Story of the Alamo* (Children's Press, 1970, grade 4 and up).

Slavery in America

Biography: Scott's *John Brown of Harper's Ferry* (Facts on File, 1988, grade 5 and up); Meltzer's *Thomas Jefferson: The Revolutionary Aristocrat* (Watts, 1991, grade 5 and up).

Information: Faber's *The Birth of a Nation* (Scribner's, 1989, grade 5 and up).

Civil Rights

Biography: Aldred's *Thurgood Marshall* (Chelsea House, 1990, grade 6 and up); Bernard's *Journey Toward Freedom: The Story of Sojourner Truth* (Feminist Press, 1990, grade 6 and up).

Information: Levine's *Freedom's Children: Young Civil Rights Activists Tell Their Own Stories* (Putnam, 1993, grade 7 and up); Meltzer's *All Times, All Peoples: A world History of Slavery* (Harper, 1980, grade 6 and up): McKissack's *The Civil Rights Movement in America: From 1865 to the Present* (Childrens Press, 1991, grades 5–8); Walter's *Mississippi Challenge* (Bradbury Press, 1992, grade 7 and up).

Others Paired by Students:

America's Westward Expansion

African Americans

Blassingame, W. *Jim Beckwourth: Black Trapper and Indian Chief* (Garrard, 1973)

Felton, H. *Jim Beckwourth: Negro Mountain Man* (Dodd, 1966)

Katz, W. L. *Black People Who Made The Old West* (Crowell, 1977)

Pelz, R. *Black Heroes of the Wild West* (Open Yesterday and Today Hand Pub., 1990)

Asian Americans

Crofford, E. *Born in the Year of Courage* (Carolrhoda, 1992)

Wong, D., & Collier, I. *Chinese Americans, Past and Present* (Association of Chinese Teachers/ California State Department of Education, 1977)

Yep, L. *Mountain Light* (Harper, 1985)

Frontier Life and Travel

Dutton, D. *Missions of California (Ballantine, 1972)

Hill, W. E. *The Oregon Trail* (Caxton Printers, 1989)

Wagner, S. R. *The Daughters of Dakota* (Daughters of Dakota/Robinson Museum, 1990)

Life Along Waterways

Fichter, G. S. *First Steamboat Down the Mississippi* (Pelican, 1989)

Native Americans and Their Leaders

Cwiklik, R. *Tecumseh: Shawnee Rebel* (Chelsea, 1993)

Freedman, R. *Indian Chiefs* (Holiday, 1987)

Gilber, B. *God Gave Us This Country: Tekamthi and the First American Civil War* (Anchor Books, 1989)

Trafzeer, C. *California's Indians and the Gold Rush* (Sierra Oaks, 1989)

Other Mountain Men, Trail Blazers, and Scouts

McCall, E. *Message from the Mountains* (Walker, 1985)

Mexican and Spanish Pioneers

Anderson, J. *Spanish Pioneers of the Southwest* (Lodestar, 1989)

Pinchot, J. *Mexicans in America* (Lerner, 1979)

Other Books Suggested by Students:

Mitakuye Oyasin:
We Are All Related

Stories That Show the Idea That We Are All Related

1. *The Friendly Wolf* (Bradbury, 1974), a story about the best characteristics of wolves, shows how Native Americans understand the language of animals and try to learn their wisdom. Wandering about from a berry-picking expedition, two small children become lost in the hills and are protected by a wolf who leads them back to the tribe.

2. In *The Girl Who Loved Wild Horses* (Bradbury, 1978), a girl feels close to the horses *and* is eventually transformed into one, becoming the wife to the leader of a wild herd. In *Buffalo Woman* (Bradbury, 1984), a buffalo turns herself into a woman and marries a young man and says, "You have always had good feelings for our people. They know you are a good and kind man. I will be your wife. My people wish for the love we have for each other will be an example for both our peoples to follow."

3. In *The Gift of the Sacred Dog* (Bradbury, 1980), the Native Americans hope they can acquire some of the powers of the horse and a boy climbs a mountain to seek a vision that will help his starving people. On the mountain top, "The clouds parted. Someone came riding toward the boy on the back of a beautiful animal. There was thunder in its nostrils and lighting in its legs; its eyes shone like stars and hair on its neck and tail trailed like clouds."

4. In *Star Boy* (Bradbury, 1982), a boy journeys to the sun and brings back the secrets of the Sun Dance Lodge, which becomes the sacred edifice of great annual festivals for the people. Just as the scar-faced boy was renewed through his journey to the sun, so too were the people physically and spiritually renewed by observing their rituals.

Others Selected by Students:

Newcomers

1600s:

Anderson, J., Ancona, G. *Pioneer Settlers of New France*. Ill. by G. Ancona. Lodestar, 1990.

Haugaard, E. D. *The Untold Tale*. Ill. by L. & D. Dillon. Houghton Mifflin, 1971.

Meltzer, M. *The Black Americans: A History in Their Own Words 1619–1983*. Crowell, 1984.

Monjo, F. N. *The House on Stink Alley: A Story about the Pilgrims in Holland*. Ill. by R. Quckenbush. Holt, 1977.

1700s:

Collier, J. L., & Collier, C. *Jump Ship to Freedom*. Dell, 1987.

1800s:

Fisher, L. E. *Ellis Island*, Holiday House, 1986.

Fisher, L. E. *A Russian Farewell*. Four Winds, 1980.

Fisher, L. E. *Letters from Italy*. Four Winds, 1977.

Levine, E. *...If Your Name Was Changed at Ellis Island*. Ill. by W. Parmenter. Scholastic, 1993.

Winter, J. *Klara's New World*. Knopf, 1992.

Wisler, G. C. *Jericho's Journey*. Lodestar, 1993.

1900s

Bartone, E. *Peppe the Lamplighter*. Ill. by T. Lewin. Lothrop, Lee & Shepard, 1993

Halliburton, W. J. *The West Indian-American Experience*. Millbrook, 1994.

Hoobler, D., & Hoobler, T. *The Italian American Family Album*. Oxford, 1994.

Kidd, D. *Onion Tears*. Ill. by L. Montgomery. Orchard, 1991.

Lord, B. B. *In the Year of the Boar and Jackie Robinson*. Harper & Row, 1984.

Others Suggested by Students:

Children in
Twentieth-Century Conflicts

Prior to World War I

Kherdian, David. *The Road from Home*. Greenwillow, 1979. Portrays a girl's survival of the Armenian genocide in the years before World War I. Suffering of the innocent. Grade 6 and up.

Rosen, B. *Andi's War*. Dutton, 1989. A family is torn apart and tries to survive during the Greek Civil War. Suffering of the innocent. Grade 6 and up.

World War I

Rostkowski, M. L. *After the Dancing Days*. Harper, 1986. In a veterans' hospital in Kansas, Annie, 13 years old, becomes a friend of a young veteran, a burn patient, who has been severely injured. Emotions of returning service people. Grade 5 and up.

World War II Effects in the United States

Levoy, M. *Alan and Naomi*. Harper & Row, 1977. Alan, an American boy, helps Naomi, a young Jewish refugee, back to health as she suffers from the trauma of seeing her father killed by the Germans. Separation. Grade 5 and up.

Hahn, M. D. *Stepping on the Cracks*. Clarion, 1991. Margaret misses her brother fighting overseas, and when she finds out that Gordy's brother is a deserter hiding in the woods, she helps him. Separation. Grade 6 and up.

Murray, M. *The Crystal Nights*. Seabury, 1973. After suffering the terror of the "Crystal Nights" in Germany, Jewish refugees flee to live with relatives in America. Separation. Grade 5 and up.

Uchida, Yoshiko. *Journey to Topaz*. Celestial Arts, 1984. A story of the experiences of 11-year-old Yuki Sakane and her family who become victims of a change in America's values and Executive Order 9066 when they are sent to a Japanese internment camp in Topaz, Utah, during World War II. Change in values. Grade 5 and up.

Hamanaka, Sheila. *The Journey*, Orchard, 1990. Shows four generations of the author's family life in America with an emphasis on their values and the impact of World War II. Change in values. Grade 6 and up.

Mazer, H. *The Last Mission*. Delacorte, 1979. A young Jewish-American soldier finds his idealistic values changed when he becomes a German prisoner. Change in values. Grade 7 and up.

World War II in England

Baldwin, N. *Carrie's War*. Lippincott, 1973. Sent to a Welsh mining town to escape the bombing of London, Carrie develops deep feelings over the evacuation. Suffering of the innocent. Grade 5 and up.

Garrigue, S. *All the Children Were Sent Away*. Bradbury, 1976. This is the author's autobiography of her own experiences during the war. Suffering of the innocent. Grade 5 and up.

Hannam, C. *A Boy in That Situation*. Harper & Row, 1978. This is the authors autobiographical account of his war days as a young boy, somewhat spoiled, who faced injustice and prejudice. Suffering of the innocent. Grades 7–8.

Orgel, D. *A Certain Magic*. Dial, 1976. A young Jewish refugee flees Europe and the war regions and lives with an English family. Suffering of the innocent. Grade 5 and up.

Streatfield, N. *When the Sirens Wailed*. Random House, 1976. Three children are evacuated to England's countryside to escape the bombing of London. Suffering of the innocent. Grade 5 and up.

World War II in Europe

France: Bishop, C. H. *Twenty and Ten*. Viking, 1964. In a boarding school in France, refuge is given to 10 Jewish children. Separation. Grades 4–5.

Tunis, J. R. *His Enemy, His Friend*. Morrow, 1967. A young French boy is helped by a German soldier. Grade 5 and up.

Tunis, J. R. *Silence Over Dunkerque*. Morrow, 1962. A British soldier is befriended by a young French girl. Change in values. Grade 5 and up.

Germany: Koehn, I. *Mischling, Second Degree: My Childhood in Nazi Germany*. Greenwillow, 1977. This is the authors autobiographical account of her separation from her family in the hope that German officials would not find out that she had a Jewish grandparent. Suffering of the innocent. Grades 7–8.

Van Stockum, H. *The Borrowed House*. Farrar, Straus & Giroux, 1973. A young girl realizes her family is now living in a house taken from a Jewish family. Suffering of the innocent. Grade 5 and up.

Norway: Sommerfelt, A. *Miriam*. Criterion, 1963. When Norway is occupied by the Germans, a young girl goes into hiding with her family. Separation. Grade 5 and up.

Poland: Zemian, J. *The Cigarette Sellers of Three Crosses Square*. Lerner, 1976. Based on the true story of Jewish "street" children who survived in Nazi-occupied Warsaw. Suffering of the innocent. Grade 5 and up.

World War II in Asia

Bauer, Marion Dane. *Rain of Fire*. Clarion, 1983. Matthew takes no pride in defeating the Japanese after World War II. Emotions of returning service people. Grade 6 and up.

DeJong, Meindert. *The House of Sixty Fathers*, Harper, 1956. Tells of the fear, hunger, and loneliness suffered by Tien Pao when his family flees before the Japanese invasion. Suffering of the innocent. Grade 6 and up.

Morimoto, Junko. *My Hiroshima*. Viking, 1987. Portrays witness's story about the reality of destruction from the first atomic bomb. Suffering of the innocent. Grade 6 and up.

Vietnam War Action

Ashabranner, B. *Always to Remember: The Story of the Vietnam Veterans Memorial*. Ill. by J. Ashabranner. Dodd, Mead/Putnam's, 1988. Portrays the drive for a memorial led by a Vietnam veteran, Jan C. Scruggs, and its design by Maya Ying Lin. Emotions of returning service people. Grade 4 and up.

Bunting, Eve. *The Wall*. Clarion, 1990. A small boy finds his grandfather's name on the Vietnam Memorial Wall. Suffering of the innocent. Grade 4.

Myers, Walter Dean. *Fallen Angels*, Scholastic, 1988. In 1967, a 19-year-old African American, Richie Perry, ships out for his military action and finds himself changed through the horrors of war. Separation. Grade 6 and up.

Nelson, T. *And One for All*. Orchard, 1989. When the Vietnam war action ensues, Geraldine's older brother enlists but his best friend becomes a war protester. Suffering of the innocent. Grade 4 and up.

continued

Paterson, K. *Park's Quest*. Dutton/Lodestar, 1988. Park travels to Vietnam to uncover reasons why his mother has never told him more about his father's death while fighting in Vietnam. Suffering of the innocent. Grade 6 and up.

Wolitzer, M. *Caribou*. Greenwillow, 1984. In 1970, Becca's older brother flees to Canada to avoid the Vietnam draft and she faces conflicts with her feelings and beliefs. Suffering of the innocent. Grades 7–8.

Gulf War

Bratman, F. *War in the Persian Gulf*, Millbrook, 1991. Describes the history of conflict in the region importance of oil in international politics, the rise of Saddam Hussein, the use of sanctions, the fear of war, and the war itself. Grade 6 and up.

Giff, P. *The War Began at Supper: Letters to Miss* Loria. Ill. by B. Lewin. Dell, 1991. When the Gulf War begins in January in 1991, five children—Alice, Jessica, Karl, Michael, and Sara–write to their former student teacher, Miss Loria. In their letters, they tell how each one is affected by the war and how they cope with what is going on. Grades 4–6.

Others Selected by Students:

America's Culturally Diverse Families

1839

Sterne, E. G. *The Slave Ship*. Scholastic, 1983. On June 30, 1893, a young slave cuts his chains and tries to free the others who are held aboard the ship. Abducted from their homes in West Africa, the Africans find themselves in the middle of the ocean and a great distance from home. Grade 6 and up.

1847

Branson, K. *Streets of Gold*. Putnam, 1981. In 1847, 14-year-old Maureen O'Connor and her family voyage from Ireland to America to escape the potato famine. Grade 6 and up.

1849

Fisher, L. *Across the Sea from Galway*. Four Winds, 1975. To escape the continuing famine in Ireland, two children are sent by their parents to Boston. Grade 6 and up.

1861

Beatty, P. *Wait for Me. Watch for Me, Eula Bea*. Morrow, 1976. In Texas in 1861, two children survive a Comanche raid. Grade 6 and up.

1872

Talbot, C . An *Orphan for Nebraska*. Atheneum, 1979. In 1872, 11-year-old Kevin O'Rourke immigrates to New York and confronts what happens in the city's streets, with western migration, the Children's Aid Society, and life on America's frontier. Grade 6 and up.

1890

Hamilton, V. *The Bells of Christmas*. Harcourt Brace Jovanovich, 1989. In the midwest in 1980, an African American family celebrates the holiday. Grade 6 and up.

1892

Freedman, R. *Immigrant Kids*. Dutton, 1980. Over 100 years ago, children of poor European immigrants to America are shown in photographs as they live in immigration ships, and go to school, work, and play. Grade 6 and up.

1900

Bales, C. A. *Tales of the Elders: A Memory Book of Men and Women Who Came to America as Immigrants, 1900–1930*. Follett, 1977. Records 12 interviews with people who came to America at the turn of the century. Includes their memories of why they came, ways they traveled, the family and friends they left, and ways they changed their lives. Grade 6 and up.

Lenski, L. *Strawberry Girl*. Lippincott, 1945. Ten-year-old Birdie Boyer meets 12-year-old Shoestring Slater and sees the conflict that develops between the Slater family, who let their cattle range free, and the Boyer family, who farm in Florida. Grades 4–6.

continued

Sachs, M. *Call Me Ruth*. Doubleday, 1982. In the early 1900s, Faigel and her daughter, Rika (Ruth), journey from Russia to the United States to join her husband. Grade 6 and up.

1929

Kherdian, D. *A Song for Uncle Harry*. Philomel, 1989. During the Great Depression in the midwest, an Armenian American family shows affection and keeps their strong ties with one another. Grade 6 and up.

1938

Levitin, S. *Journey to America*. Macmillan, 1986. Portrays a story of newcomers to the United States. Grade 6 and up.

1947

Adler, D. *Jackie Robinson: He Was the First*. Holiday House, 1989. Portrays the great athlete's hardships, tradegies, and triumphs. Grade 5 and up.

1950–90

Bawden, N. *Humbug*. Clarion, 1992. Ma Potter, Angelica's grandmother, tells 9-year-old Cora to say "Humbug" to help her through the days she has to live at Angelica's house while her parents are away and her own grandmother is in the hospital. Grades 4–6.

Irwin, H. *The Original Freddie Ackerman*. Mulberry, 1992. Twelve-year-old Freddie feels alienated from his family when he goes to spend the summer with his two great-aunts who are eccentric and off-beat. Grades 4–6.

Myers, A. *Red-Dirt Jessie*. Walker, 1992. Twelve-year-old Jessie overcomes her sadness when her younger sister dies and sees her father sink into a major depression, making him unreachable. Grades 4–6.

Polikoff, B. D. *Life's a Funny Proposition, Horatio*. Holt, Rinehart and Winston, 1992. Horatio Tuckerman's father dies of cancer and he and his mother move to Wisconsin to be near other members of their family. There, they adjust when his paternal grandfather and his dog move in with them. Grades 4–7.

Others Selected by Students:

Poetry to Review
Historical Periods

Dinosaur Days

Dinosaurs (Harcourt, 1987) by Lee Bennett Hopkins has 18 reading choices about the intellectual giants of the times.

Prehistoric Times

"Orion" in *One at a Time* (Little, Brown, 1980, all ages) by David McCord is a "giant in stellar space" who walks steadfast and alone.

Aesop's Fables (Morrow, 1988) by Tom Paxton is a poetic version of the brief tales.

Early Times

Beneath the Rainbow: A Collection of Children's Stories and Poems from Kenya (Jacaranda Designs, 1994) edited by Bridget A. C. King and Kioi wa Mbugua is based on Gikuyu lore and the theme of nature.

"Eskimo Chant" in *The New Wind Has Wings: Poems from Canada* (Oxford University Press, 1984, all ages) by Mary Alice Downie and Barbara Robertson is a collection of poetic words.

Moon Song (Scribners, 1982) by Byrd Baylor is a retelling of a Pima Indian legend about how Coyote was born.

Moonsong Lullaby (Lothrop, 1981) by Jamake Highwater has poetic words from ancient stories of Native People.

Hiawatha (Putnam, 1988) and (Dutton, 1983) and *Hiawatha's Childhood* (Farrar, 1984) by Henry Wadsworth Longfellow focus on the peacemaker's boyhood.

Shadow (Scribners, 1982) by Blaise Cendrars is a description of shadows and how they act during the day and in night's darkness.

In the Trail of the Wind: American Indian poems and Ritual Orations (Farrar, 1987) by John Bierhorst presents thoughts of Native Americans from a time before white settlers arrived. Grade 5 and up.

Middle Ages Period

"Robin Hood and Alan a Dale" in *The Golden Treasury of Poetry* (Golden/Western, 1959, grades 1–6) by Louis Untermeyer.

The Pied Piper of Hamelin (Warne, 1988, reissued) by Robert Browning.

Sir Cedric (Farrar, 1984) by Roy Garrard recounts heroic deeds.

Fly with the Wind, Flow with the Water (Scribner's, 1979) and *Haiku: The Mood of Earth* (Scribner's, 1971) both by Ann Atwood are collections of Haiku thoughts about actions in nature.

Exploration Period

"Columbus" in *America Forever New* (Crowell, 1968, grade 4 and up) by Sara and John E. Brewton describes feelings of a Native Person who first saw the ships of Columbus sail near the shore.

"Immortal Morn" by Hezekiah Butterworth, "Columbian Ode" by Paul Laurence Dunbar, and "Columbus" by Joaquin Miller all in *Poems for Red Letter Days* (Macrae Smith, 1951, grade 4 up) compiled by Elizabeth Sechrist.

continued

Where the Buffalo Roam (Ideals, 1992, grade 2–5) by J. Geis.

Colonial Period

The Gift Outright: America to Her Poets (Greenwillow, 1977, grade 4 and up) edited by Helen Plotz has verses describing life in the United States.

Revolutionary War

A Book of Americans (Holt, Rinehart and Winston, reissue, 1988, grades 1–6) by Rosemary and Stephen Vincent Benet.

Beat the Drum: Independence Day Has Come (Harcourt, 1976, grades 2–4) by Lee Bennett Hopkins.

Pre-Civil War

Whirlwind Is a Ghost Dancing (Dutton, 1974, grade 4 and up) and *Our Fathers Had Powerful Songs* (Dutton, 1974, grade 4 and up) both by Natalia Belting.

Songs of the Chippewa (Farrar, Straus & Giroux, 1974, grade 4 and up) and *A Cry from the Earth: Music of the North American Indians* (Scholastic, 1979, grade 4 and up) by John Bierhorst, both collections of music of America's Native People.

The Sacred Path: Spells, Prayers and Power Songs of the American Indians (Morrow, 1983) by John Bierhorst.

Gunga Din (Harcourt, 1987) by Rudyard Kipling retells events in India in the Nineteenth century.

Dancing Teepees (Holiday House, 1989) by V. Sneve. Don't miss the quote by Black Elk, who says that the life of a person "is a circle from childhood to childhood," a circle that is protected by Wakan-Tanka, the power of the world, and brings good wakan as long as it is unbroken.

America's Civil War

Singing Soldiers: A History of the Civil War in Song (Grosset & Dunlap, 1969) by Paul Glass has poetic lyrics of songs from the time period.

Post-Civil War

The Voyage of the Ludgate Hill: Travels with Robert Louis Stevenson (Harcourt, 1987) retold by Nancy Willard, relates Stevenson's adventures on a cargo ship.

Wait Whitman (Creative Education, 1994) edited by Nancy Loewen is a combination of poetry, history, and photographs with "Civil War" and other poetry selections from Whitman's *Leaves of Grass*.

Newcomers

Doctor Knickerbocker and Other Rhymes (Ticknor & Fields, 1993, grades 2–6) by David Booth has rhymes grouped by topics under categories of "Echoes from Long Ago: A Century of Schoolyard Rhymes," "Mamma Said It and I Say It, Too: Schoolyard Rhymes Said Yesterday and Still Heard Today," and "Out Loud Right Now."

If I Had a Paka: Poems in Eleven Languages (Greenwillow, 1982) by Charlotte Pornerantz.

Bronzeville Boys and Girls (Harper & Row, 1956) by Gwendolyn Brooks explores the feelings of children.

Southern Sharecroppers

Something Permanent (Harcourt, 1994, grades 8 and up) by Cynthia Rylant offers over 20 brief poems that are related to the photographs of poor southern sharecroppers taken by Walker Evans and James Agee in the 1930s. Their photographic essay of the sharecropers in the South was first published as *Let Us Now Praise Famous Men*.

Civil Rights Movement

Let Freedom Ring: A Ballad of Martin Luther King, Jr. (Holiday House, 1992, grade 4) by Mya Cohn Livingston includes quotes from Dr. King's speeches and sermons, and the retrain, "From every mountain, let freedom ring" recalls his famous "I Have a Dream" speech on the steps of the Lincoln Memorial in 1963.

Gulf War

"Fantasia" in *Finding a Poem* (Atheneum, 1970, grade 4 and up) by Eve Merriam, where a child asks, "What was war?"

Culturally and Linguistically Diverse Families

All the Colors of the Earth (Morrow, 1994, grades 4–5) by Sheila Hamanaka is a description of children's skin tones and hair in poetic words (e.g., hair can be the color of the "browns of bears"). Expresses appreciation and love for the children, saying love comes in such colors as "cinnamon, walnut, and wheat."

And the Green Grass Grew All Around (HarperCollins, 1992, grade 4 and up) collected by Alvin Schwartz is a collection of children's folk poetry including "On Top of Spaghetti," and "Mine Eyes Have Seen the Glory (of the Closing of the School)."

At the Crack of the Bat: Baseball Poems (Hyperion, 1992, grade 4 and up) compiled by Lillian Morrison offers "The New Kid" where a girl saves the game for a little league team and other poems about the sport.

Cool Salsa: Bilingual Poems on Growing up Latino in the United States (Holt, 1994, grade 7 and up) edited by Lori M. Carlson. Enriches perceptions of understanding the desire to belong, feeling frustrations of not being able to speak English, and suffering from violent acts in the local neighborhood as well as in the larger community.

Neighborhood Odes (Harcourt, 1992, grade 4 and up) by Gary Soto has poems related to a Chicano neighborhood and weddings, fireworks, grandparents, and the library.

Talking Like the Rain: A First Book of Poems (Little, 1992, grade 4) selected by Dorothy and X. J. Kennedy features poets and their work over time periods—Stevenson, Milne, Lear, Ciardi, Livingston, and Yolen.

Who Shrank My Grandmother's House: Poems of Discovery (HarperCollins, 1992, grades 4–5) collected by Barbara Juster Esbensen are written in the first person and narrated by various ethnic voices.

Other Sources Suggested by Students:

Index of Children's Books, Authors, and Illustrators

Subject Index